HISTORIC PHOTOS OF
MILWAUKEE

Text and Captions by
Elizabeth A. Chasco

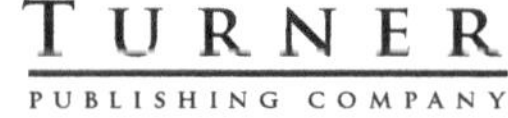
TURNER
PUBLISHING COMPANY

This photograph shows an alley in Milwaukee that connected Park Hill Avenue with Mount Vernon Avenue. It was taken in 1925 from the Interurban streetcar line, which offered people a way to move around the city more easily.

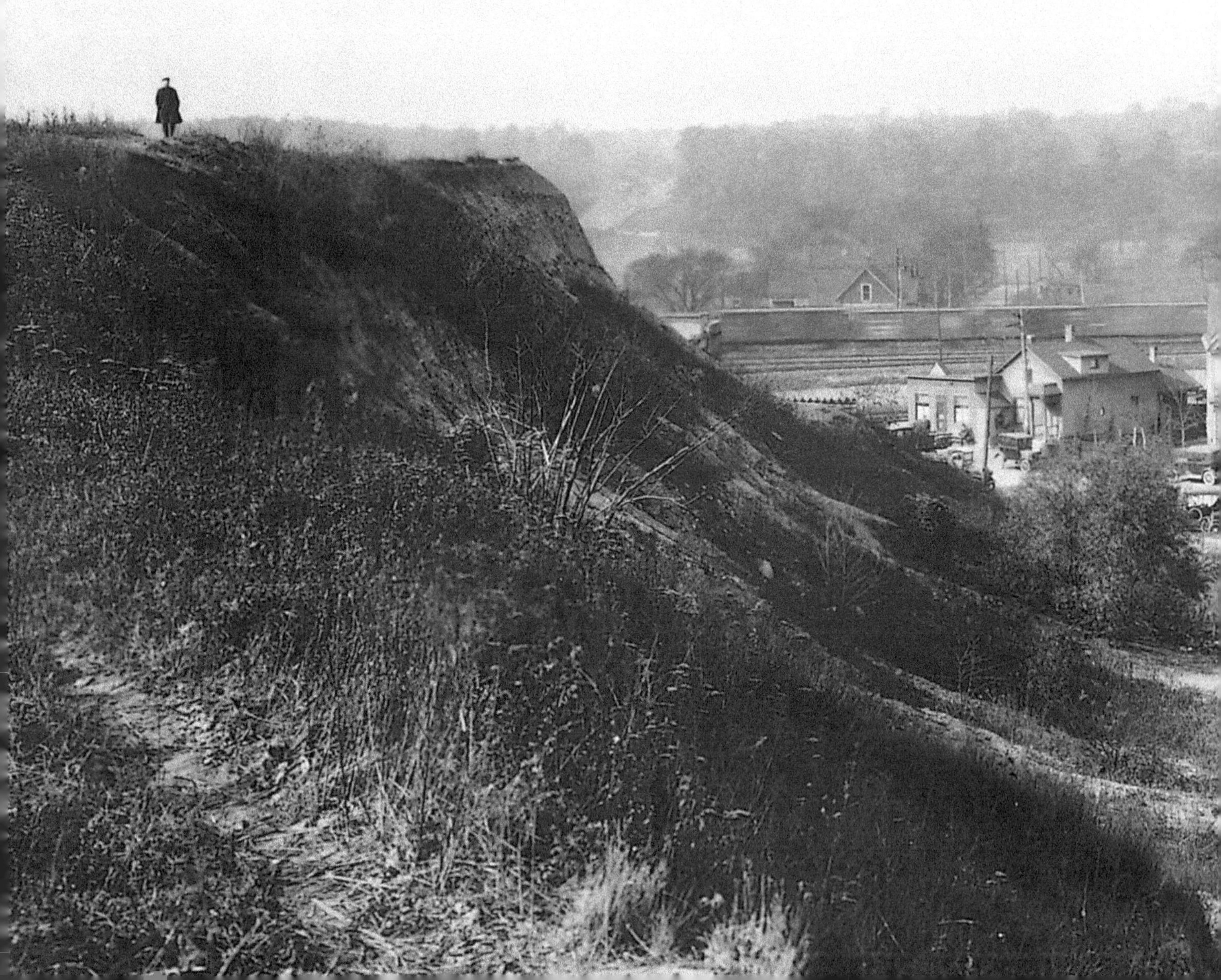

HISTORIC PHOTOS OF
MILWAUKEE

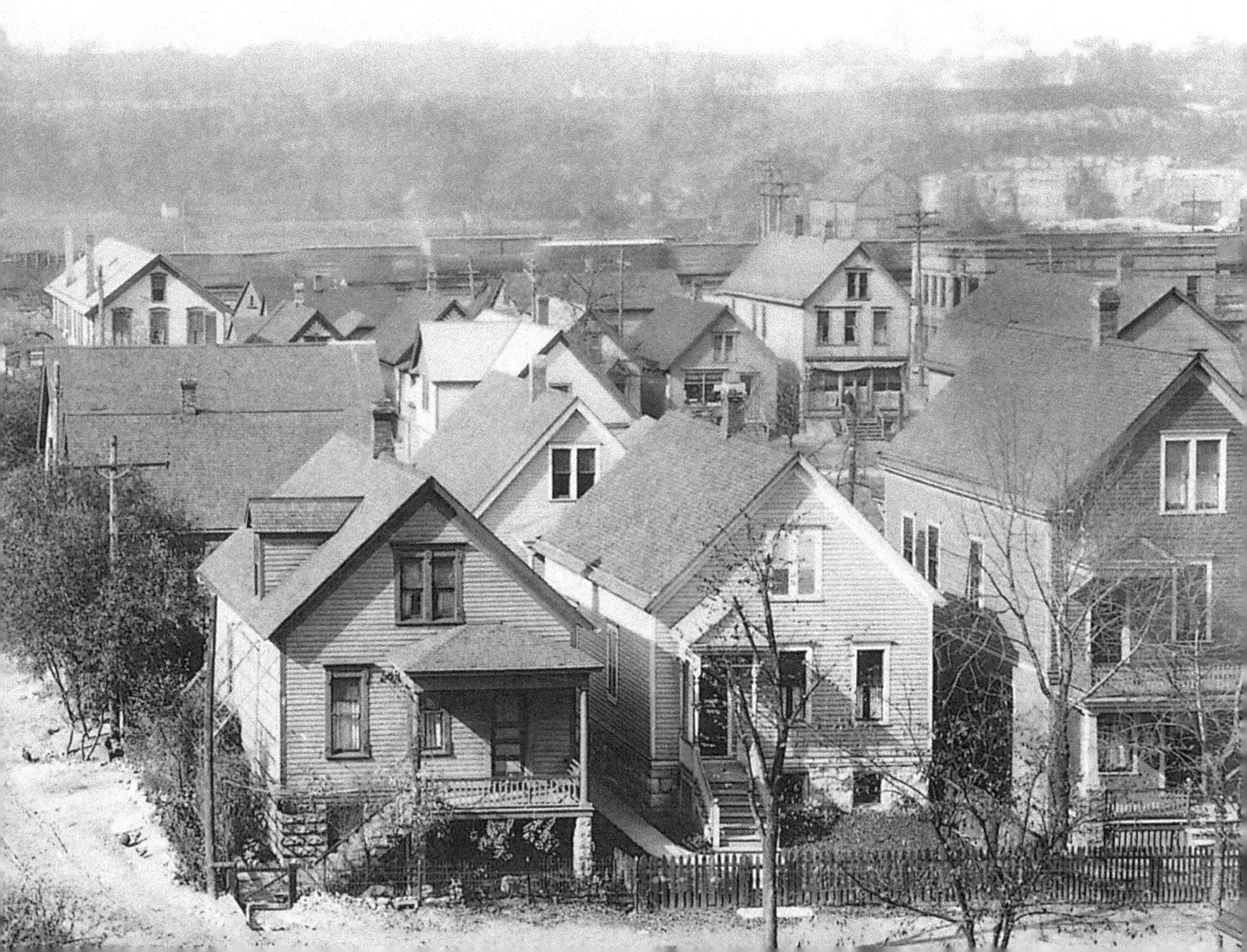

Turner Publishing Company
www.turnerpublishing.com

Historic Photos of Milwaukee

Library of Congress Control Number: 2007923669

ISBN-10: 1-59652-337-9
ISBN-13: 978-1-59652-337-1

Printed in the United States of America

ISBN 978-1-68336-951-6 (hc)

Contents

Astronaut Jim Lovell is seen here accepting cheese from the governor, Warren Knowles. Although Lovell was not born in Milwaukee, he did attend the University of Wisconsin at Milwaukee before transferring to the U.S. Military Academy. Lovell flew in space on four different missions, his last being the ill-fated Apollo 13.

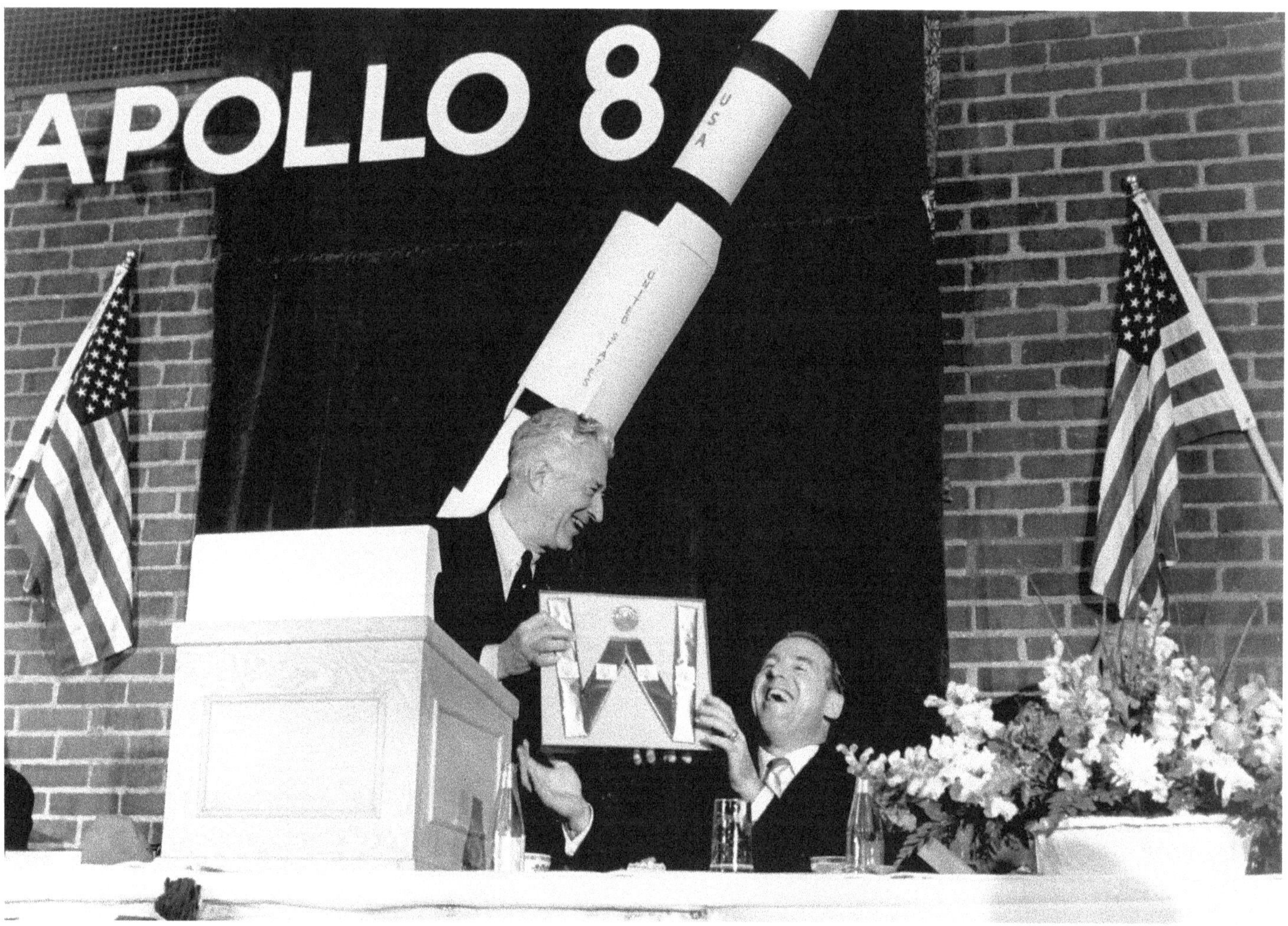

Acknowledgments

This volume, *Historic Photos of Milwaukee,* is the result of the cooperation and efforts of many individuals, organizations, and corporations. It is with great thanks that we acknowledge the valuable contribution of the following for their generous support:

Wisconsin Historical Society
The Milwaukee Public Library—Historic Photo Collection

We would also like to thank Elizabeth A. Chasco, our writer, for valuable contributions and assistance in making this work possible.

Preface

Milwaukee has thousands of historic photographs that reside in archives, both locally and nationally. This book began with the observation that, while those photographs are of great interest to many, they are not easily accessible. During a time when Milwaukee is looking ahead and evaluating its future course, many people are asking, How do we treat the past? These decisions affect every aspect of the city—architecture, public spaces, commerce, infrastructure—and these, in turn, affect the way that people live their lives. This book seeks to provide easy access to a valuable, objective look into the history of Milwaukee.

The power of photographs is that they are less subjective than words in their treatment of history. Although the photographer can make decisions regarding subject matter and how to capture and present it, photographs do not provide the breadth of interpretation that text does. For this reason, they offer an original, untainted perspective that allows the viewer to interpret and observe.

This project represents countless hours of review and research. The researchers and writer have reviewed thousands of photographs in numerous archives. We greatly appreciate the generous assistance of the individuals and organizations listed in the acknowledgments of this work, without whom this project could not have been completed.

The goal in publishing this work is to provide broader access to this set of extraordinary photographs that seek to inspire, provide perspective, and evoke insight that might assist people who are responsible for determining Milwaukee's future. In addition, the book seeks to preserve the past with adequate respect and reverence.

With the exception of touching up imperfections caused by the damage of time and cropping where necessary, no other changes have been made. The focus and clarity of many images is limited to the technology and the ability of the photographer at the time they were taken.

The work is divided into eras. Beginning with some of the earliest known photographs of Milwaukee, the first section records photographs through the end of the nineteenth century. The second section spans the beginning of the twentieth century to World War I. Section Three moves into the era between the wars. The last section covers the World War II era to recent times.

In each of these sections we have made an effort to capture various aspects of life through our selection of photographs. People, commerce, transportation, infrastructure, religious institutions, and educational institutions have been included to provide a broad perspective.

We encourage readers to reflect as they go walking in Milwaukee, strolling through the city, its parks, and its neighborhoods. It is the publisher's hope that in utilizing this work, longtime residents will learn something new and that new residents will gain a perspective on where Milwaukee has been, so that each can contribute to its future.

Todd Bottorff, Publisher

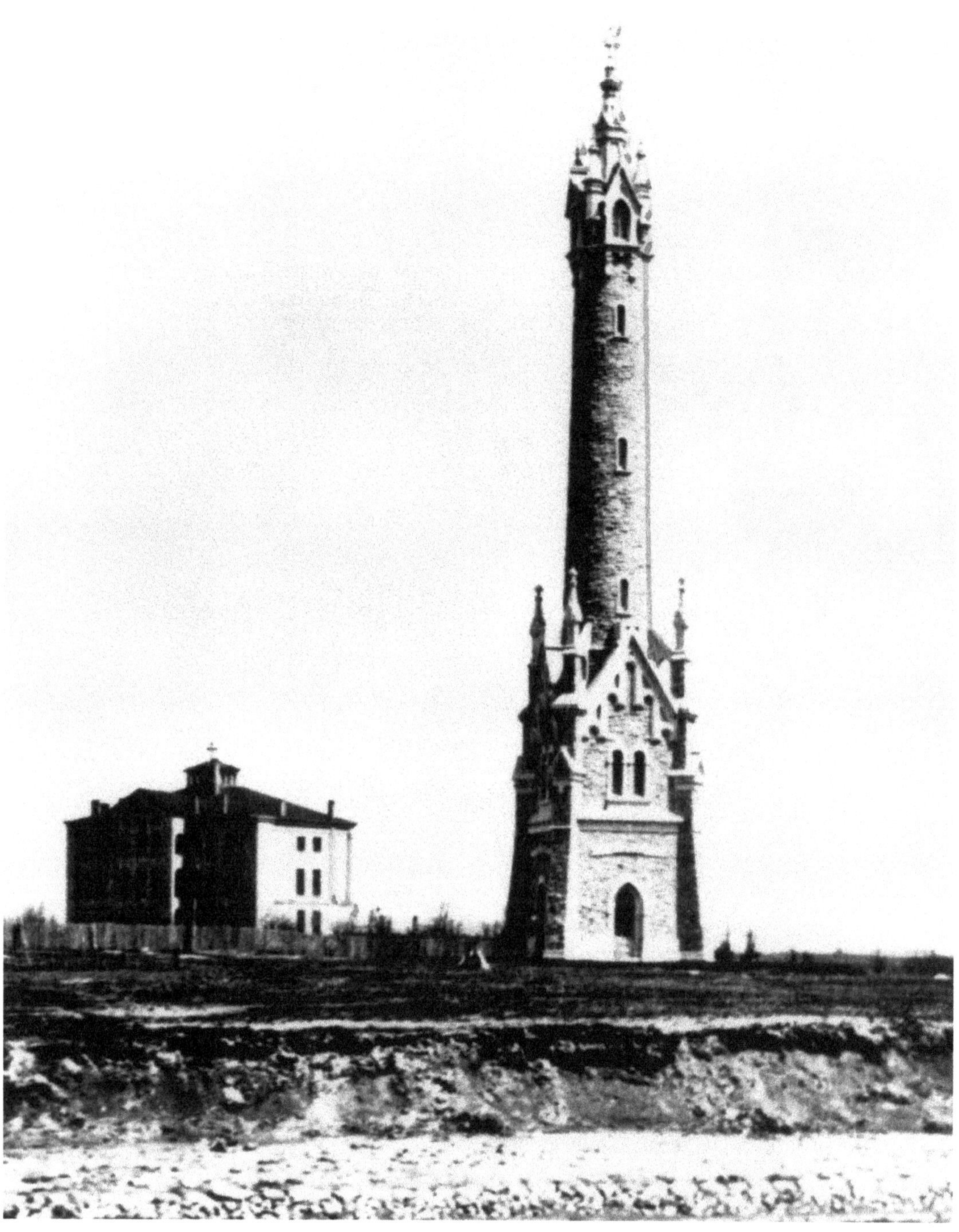

The Milwaukee water tower was built in 1874. One of the most recognizable structures in Milwaukee, it was added to the National Register of Historic Places in 1973. It originally served as a standpipe to aerate the water pumped to it from the station at the bottom of the hill. The water was then pumped to the city's reservoir. The original St. Mary's hospital can be seen in the background.

The Immigrant City

(1860s–1899)

Milwaukee's three "founding fathers," Solomon Juneau, Byron Kilbourn, and George Walker, had similar plans when they came to the Wisconsin territory. They were going to take advantage of the area's location on Lake Michigan. They all chose to start their own towns, all of which, in the end, grew into unique and distinct neighborhoods within metropolitan Milwaukee.

In the mid nineteenth century, and increasingly after the three towns incorporated to become the city of Milwaukee in 1846, with Solomon Juneau serving as the first mayor, immigrants, particularly Germans, started to arrive and make a huge cultural impact. They started a multitude of businesses including breweries, bakeries, and butcher shops. At one time, Milwaukee was considered the most "foreign" of cities in the United States. By no means were Germans the only immigrants to Milwaukee. Poles, Dutch, and Irish immigrants, to name just a few, joined the growing city and left their mark, creating neighborhoods as culturally diverse as the original three towns from which the city emerged.

Along with Milwaukee businesses, agriculture helped the economy to prosper. Milwaukee was one of the leading producers of wheat and on occasion was known as the "breadbasket of the Midwest." The railroad system also was instrumental in helping the economy to grow. Alexander Mitchell, a railroad magnate as well as a banker, took the Milwaukee rails and turned them into a profitable business, which generated the wealth he used to build his extravagant house, still standing on Wisconsin Avenue downtown.

As the turn of the century neared, Milwaukee started to switch from farming to developing industry and building manufacturing plants. With that switch came a new kind of business owner in the city. The "captains of industry" would turn Milwaukee into one of the largest cities in the nation.

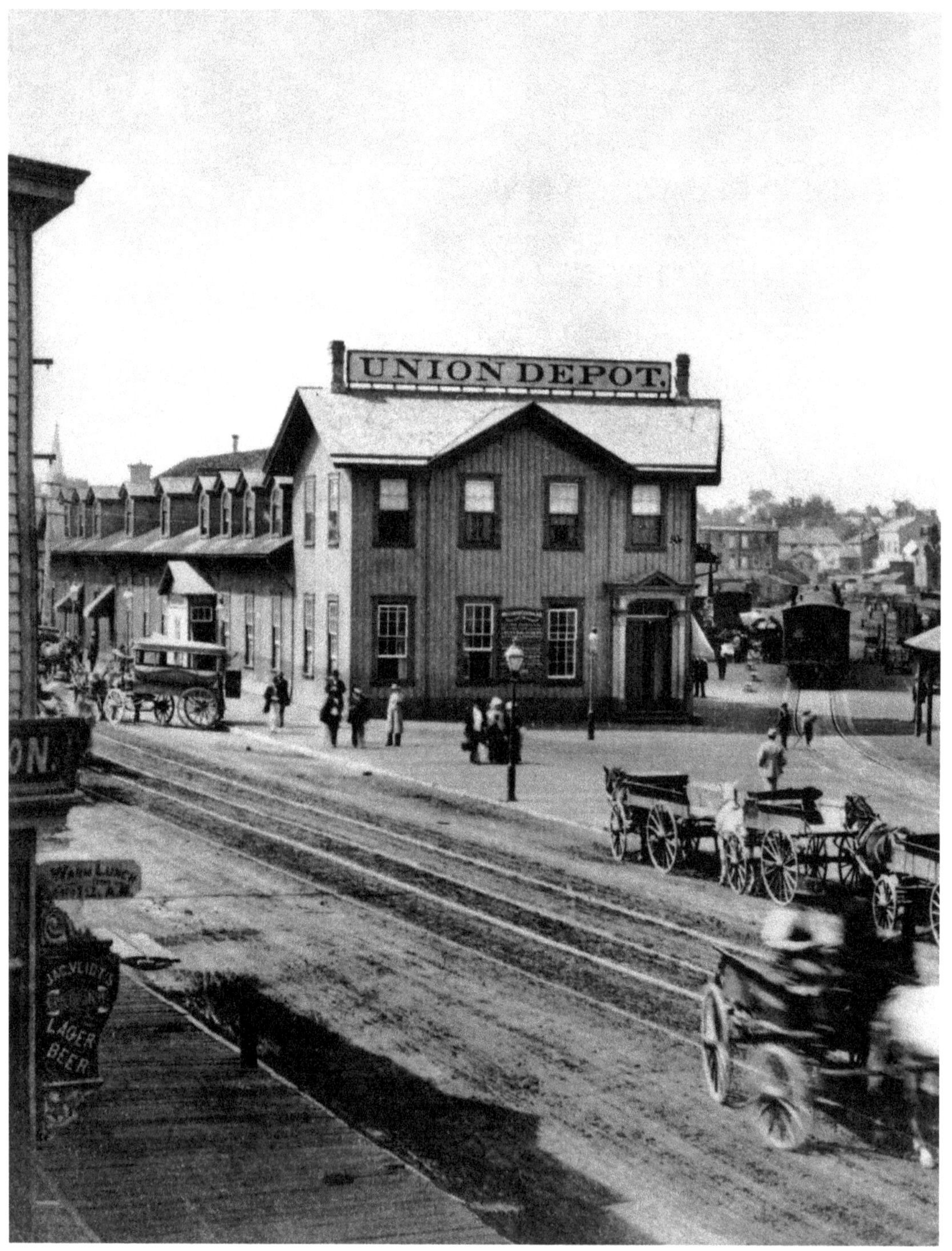

The Union Depot, built in 1866, was the main stop for trains entering Milwaukee. It was located on Reed Street (later 2nd Street), which served as one of the main shopping centers for Milwaukeeans in the 1860s and 1870s. Toward the late nineteenth century, two new stations were built, one in 1886 on Michigan Avenue and another in 1889 near the lakefront.

Chapman's and Co., established in 1853, was one of the largest dry goods houses of its time. The store in this photograph was built in 1873 at the corner of Milwaukee Street and E. Wisconsin Ave. In October 1884, fire burned this store to the ground. The proprietor, T. A. Chapman, rebuilt a bigger, more luxurious store in just five and a half months on the same site.

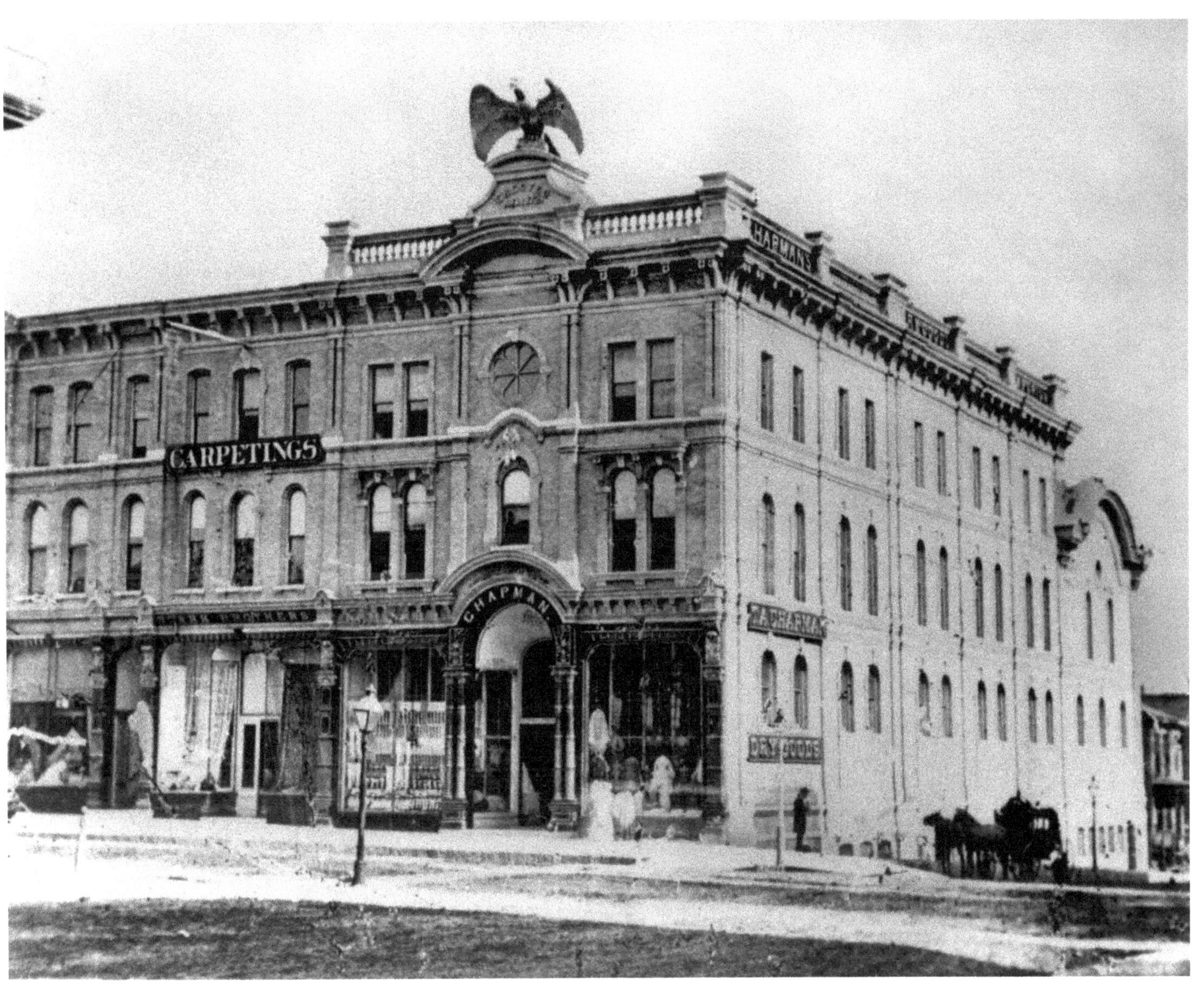

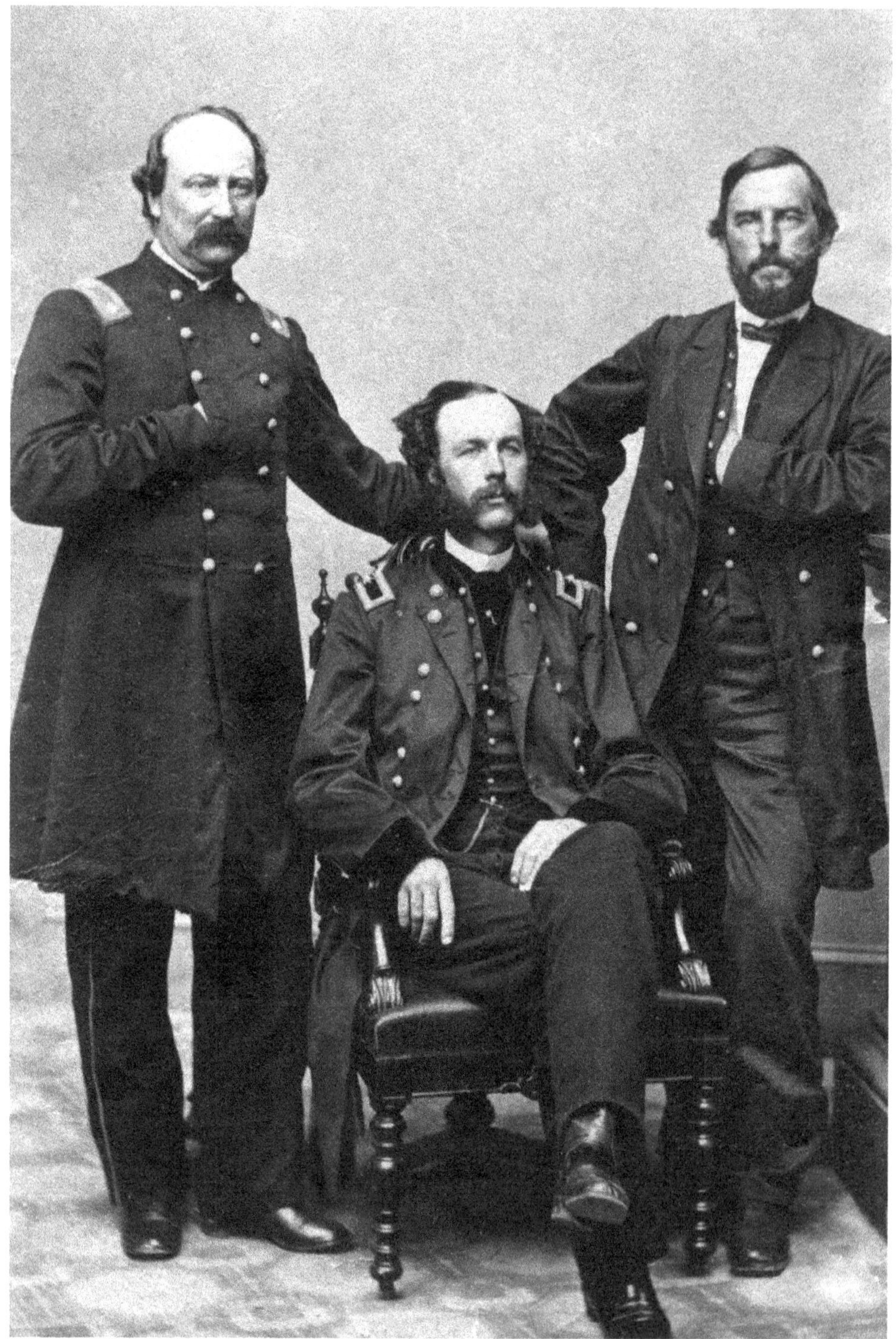

Civil War Lt. Colonel George B. Bingham, left, General John C. Starkweather, center, and General Rufus J. King, right, all served in the Iron Brigade, one of the most well-known military units of the Civil War. Men from Milwaukee and all around Wisconsin served in this brigade. A high school bearing the name of General Rufus J. King now stands at 1801 West Olive Street.

Photographed in 1870, buildings as tall as four stories line Wisconsin Avenue, which was still a dirt road at the time. Wisconsin Avenue was and still is one of the main streets in downtown Milwaukee.

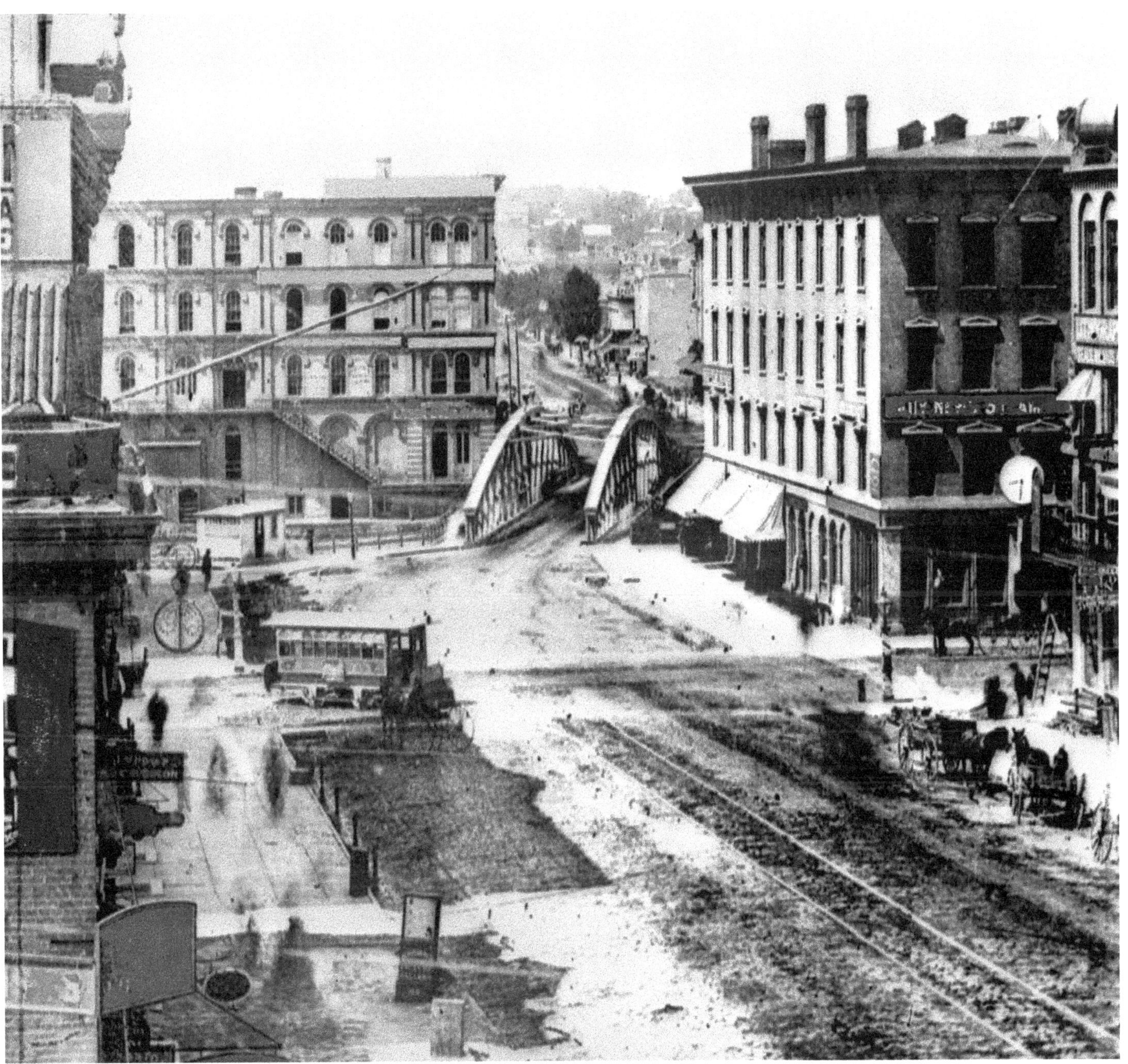

Once offering a large, open view of the bluffs and Lake Michigan, the area along the lakefront is now covered with foliage, buildings, and public parks. Railroad tracks visible near the edge of the lake are also a thing of the past. The shoreline was moved farther out into the lake to accommodate the growing city.

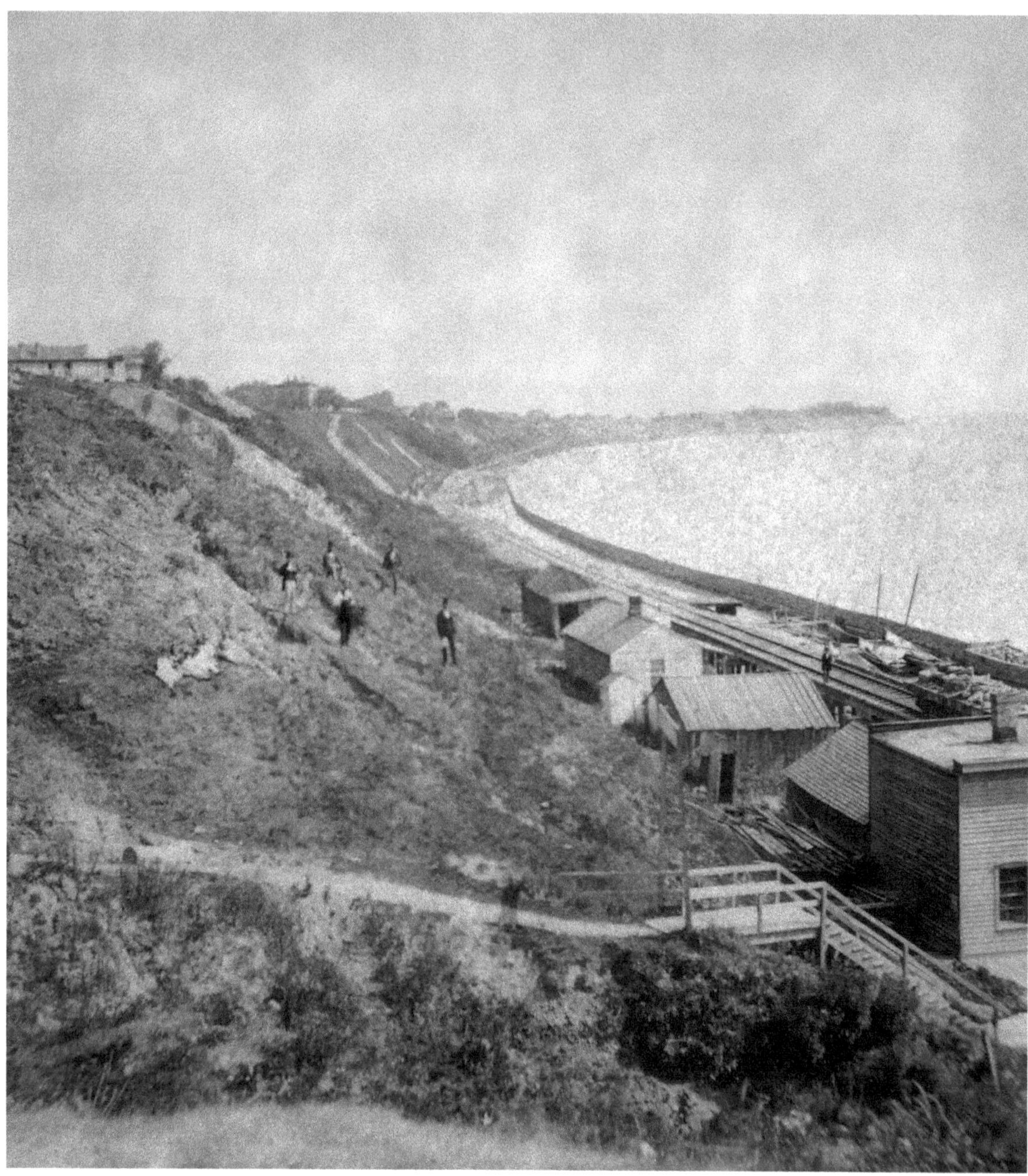

The Chamber of Commerce, on the corner of Broadway and Michigan streets, was built in 1879. It was home to Western Union telegrams as well as a place for trading commodities such as grain. The building still stands at its original location and was added to the National Register of Historic Places in 1973 under the name of the Mackie Building.

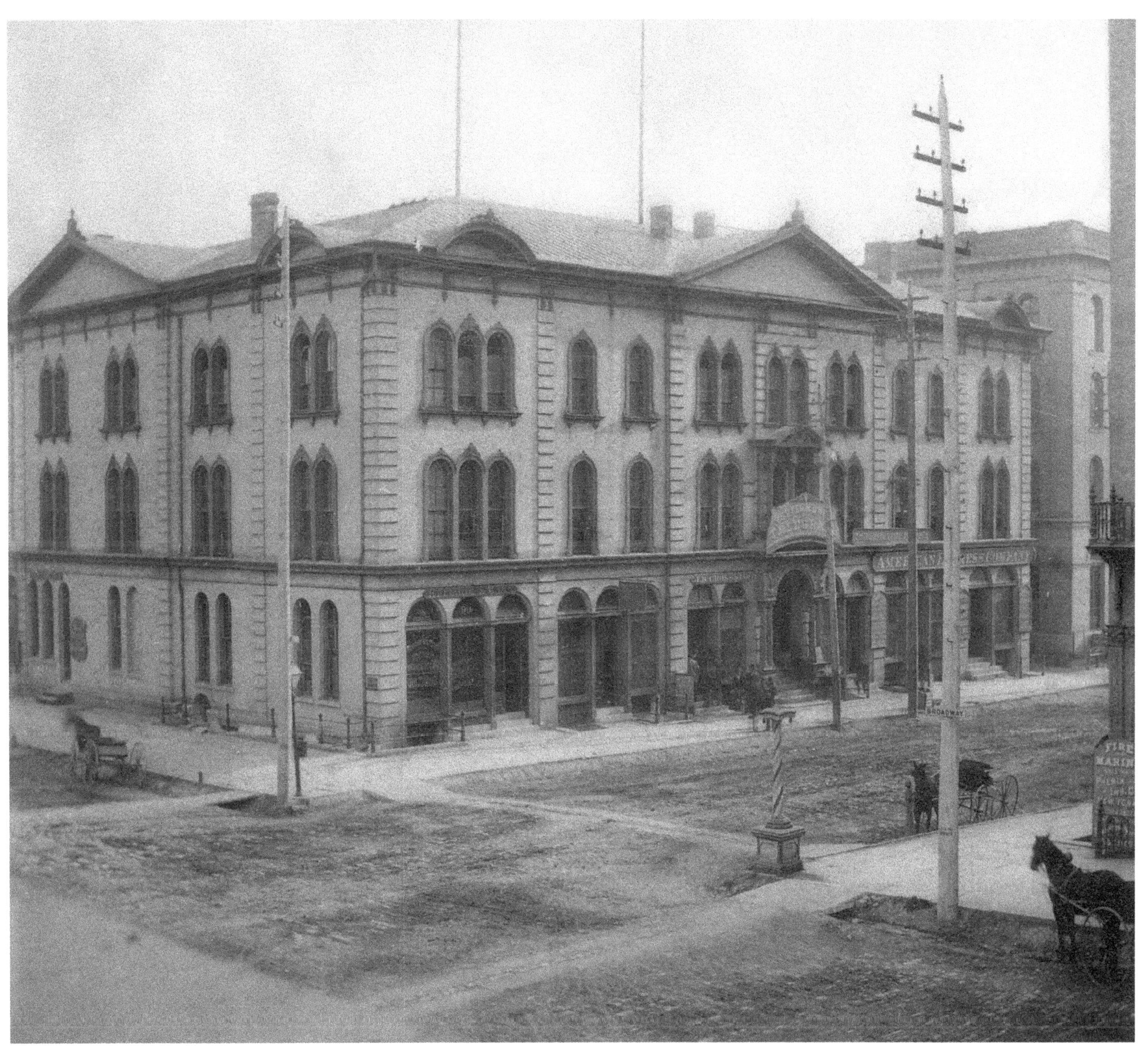

A sailing ship enters port on the Milwaukee River. Milwaukee was a large distributor of grain, particularly wheat, and for a while was known as the breadbasket of the Midwest.

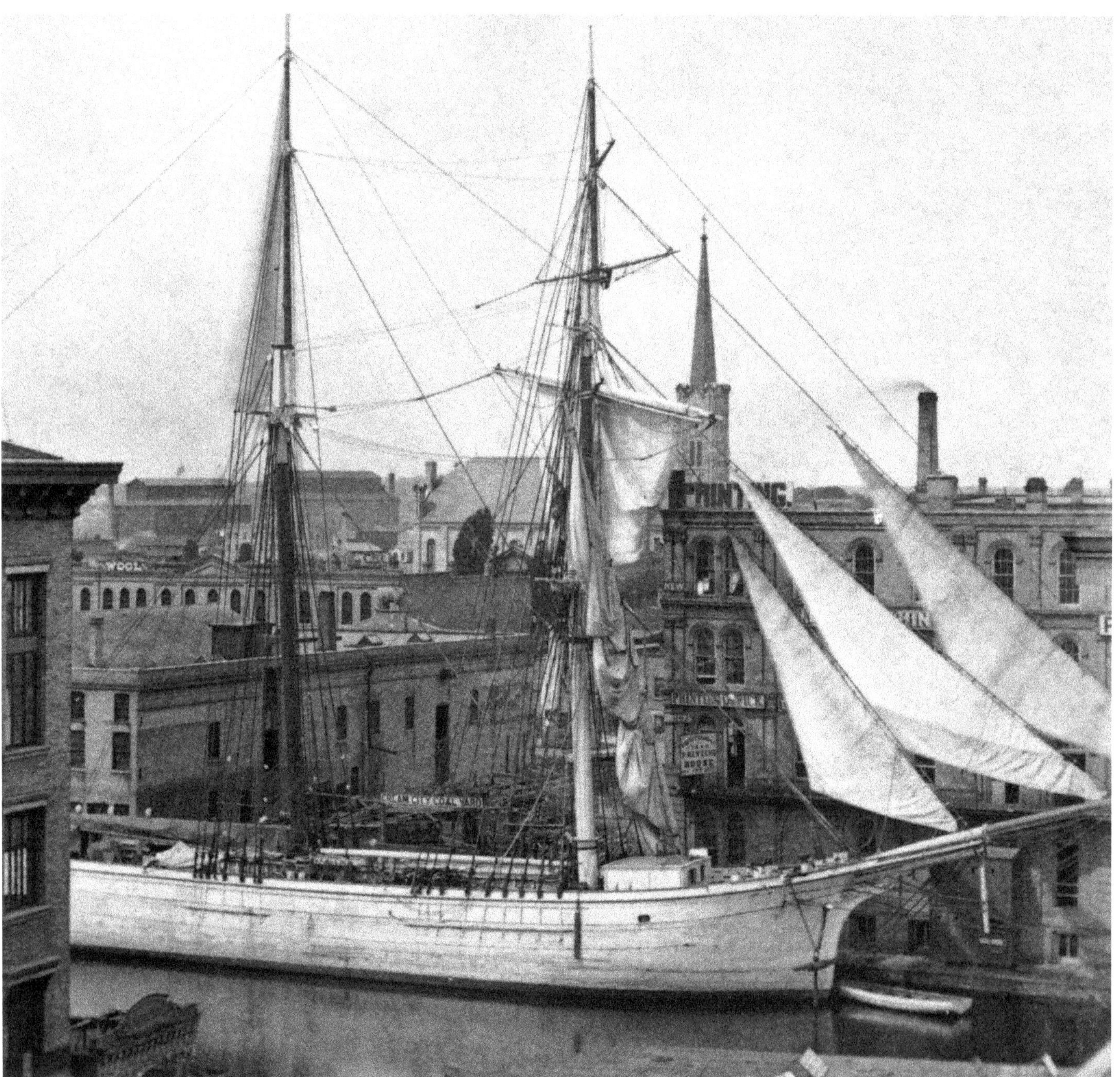

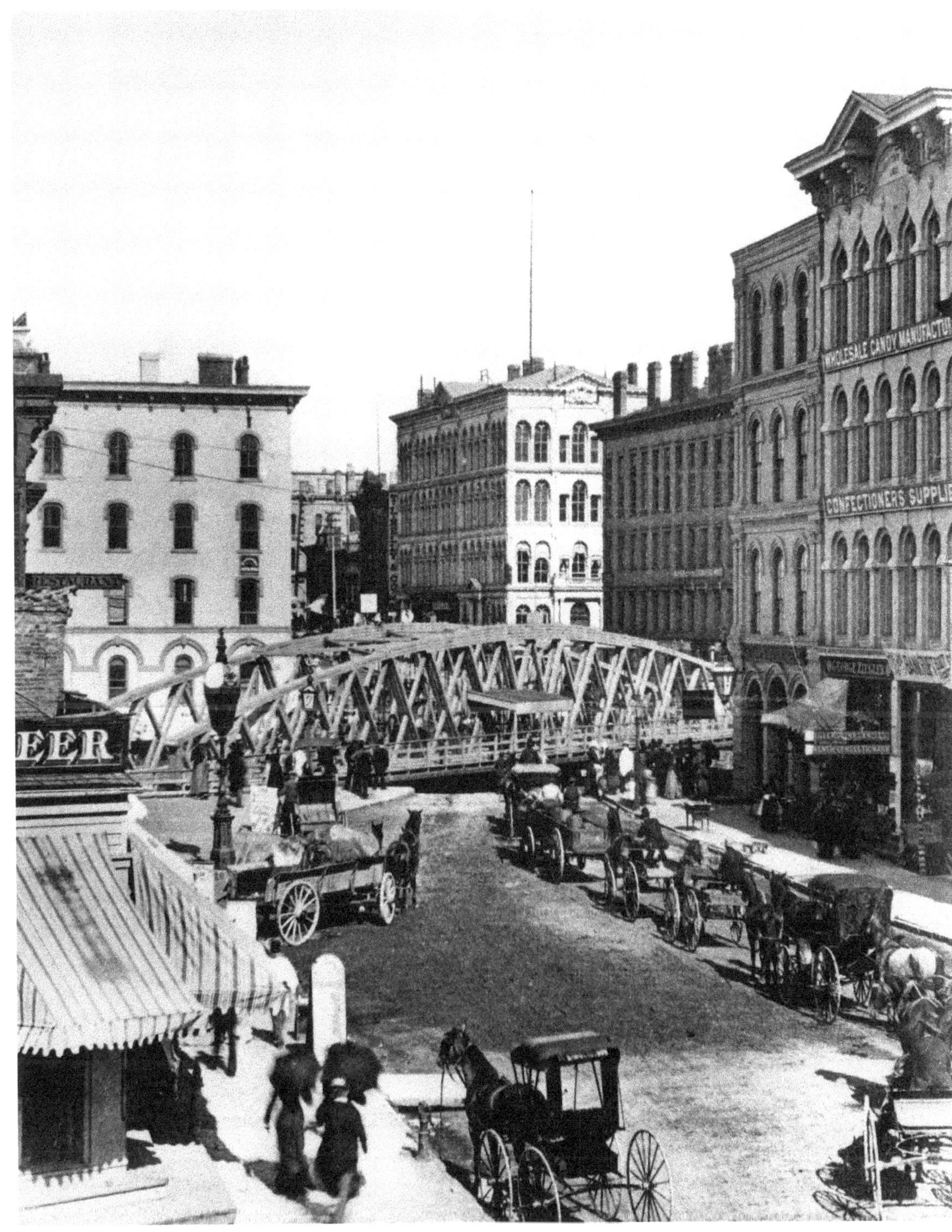

Traffic jams were an everyday occurrence at the swinging bridge on Grand Avenue. The bridge, moved by two operators using a hand crank, would swing around to permit the passage of a boat on the river. Horses and carriages can be seen lined up in front of the Ziegler confectionery, now the Grand Avenue Mall.

The Republican House, or Rebulikaner Haus as it was often referred to, served as a luxury hotel, a meeting place for politicians, and a restaurant for locals and out-of-town visitors. Located on N. 3rd and W. Kilbourn, it was a favorite meeting spot for Civil War veterans and was an excellent place for watching parades. The building was also the birthplace of professional baseball's American League. It was leveled in 1961 to make room for the Journal Company's expansion.

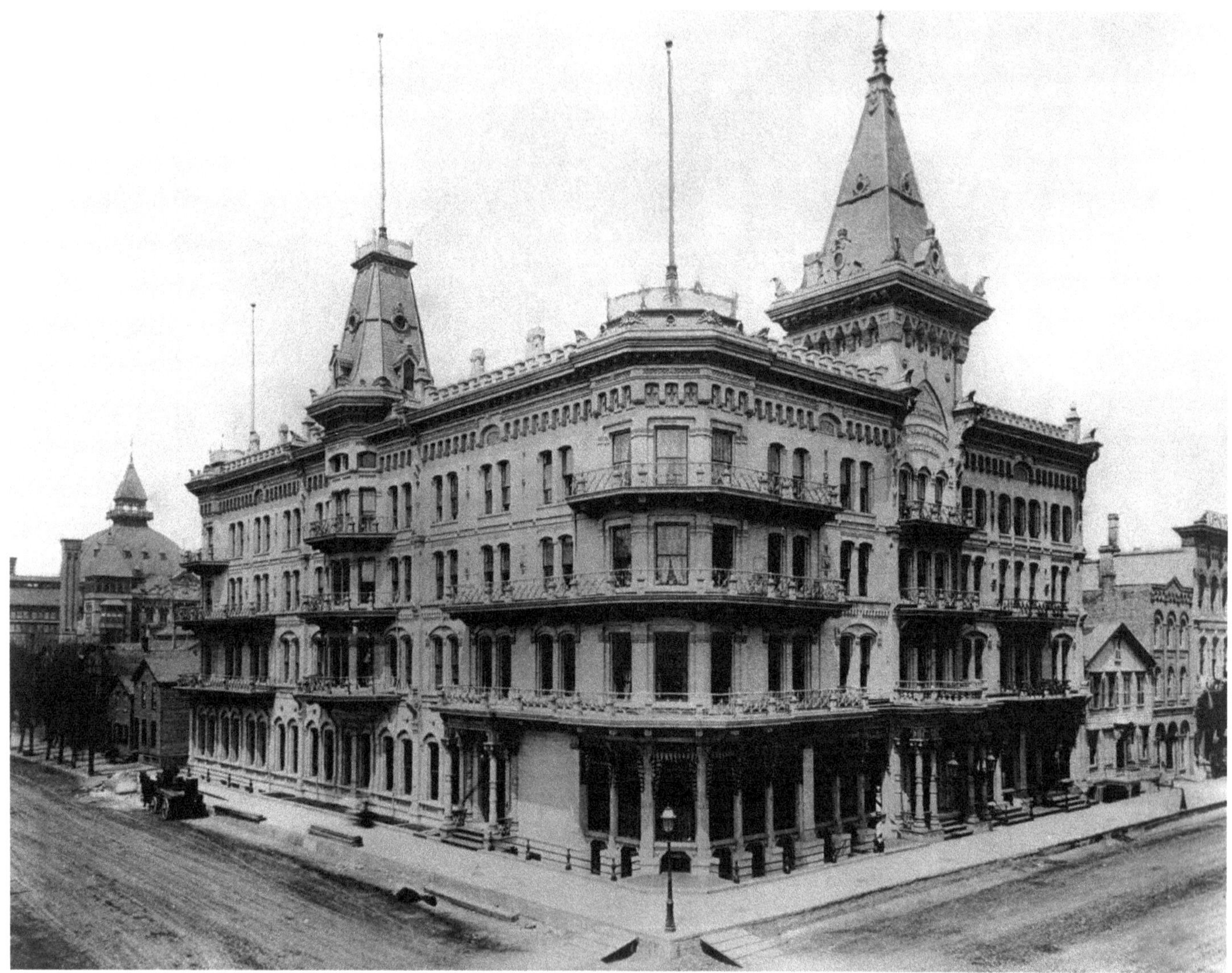

The German Market made its home here in the early 1870s, serving as a commercial center for Milwaukee's large German population. It also served as a social gathering place for German housewives who came here to shop and for friends and immigrants. Main Milwaukee businesses such as Baumgarten-Krueger florist gained loyal customers during their stay in the German Market.

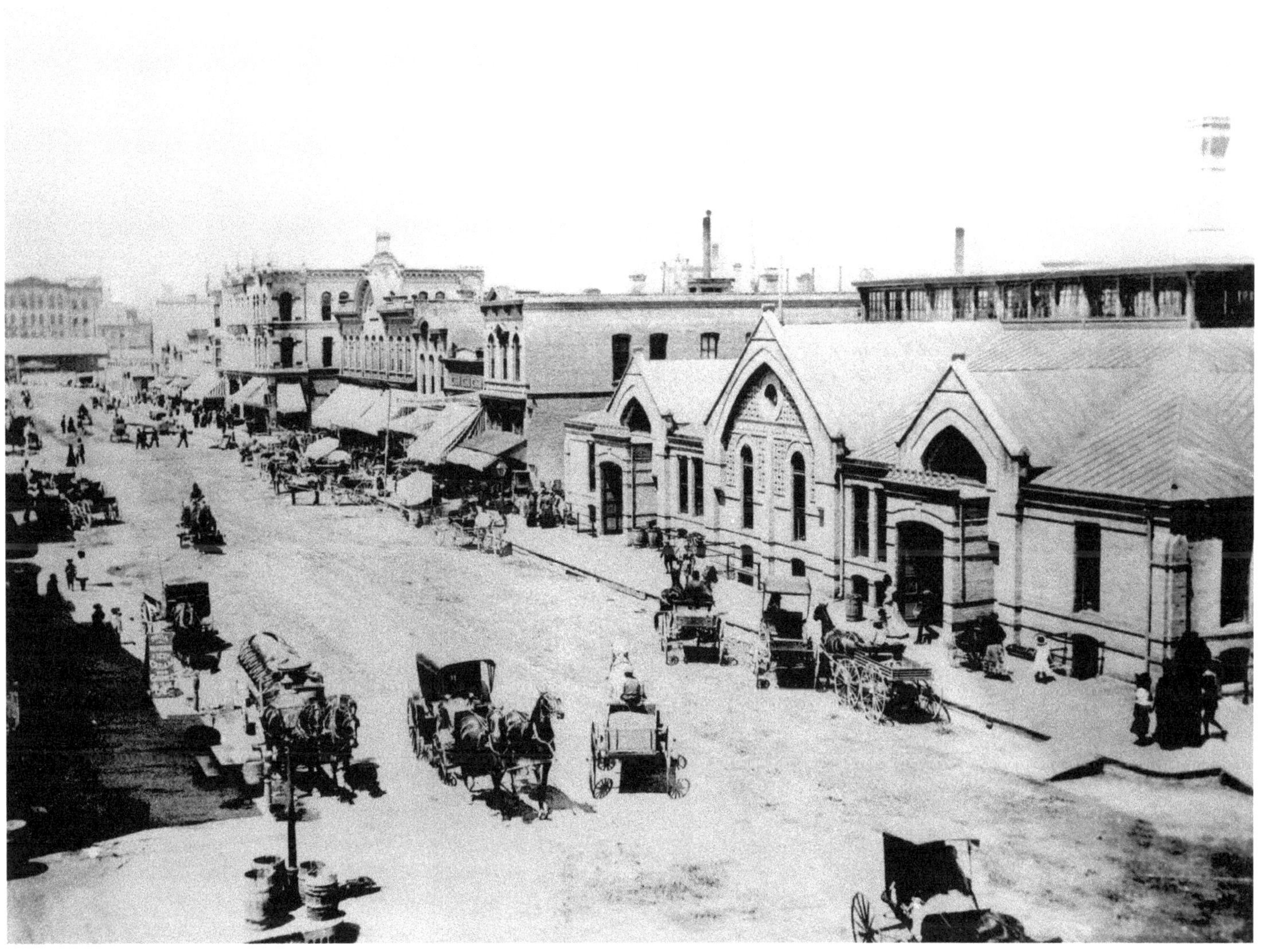

This building served as Marquette University's first home. It was not always called Marquette. St. Aloysius and St. Gall's were also names for the school before Marquette became the permanent moniker. Because the building was on the top of a hill, the name "Hilltoppers" stuck and has served Marquette University high school for many years.

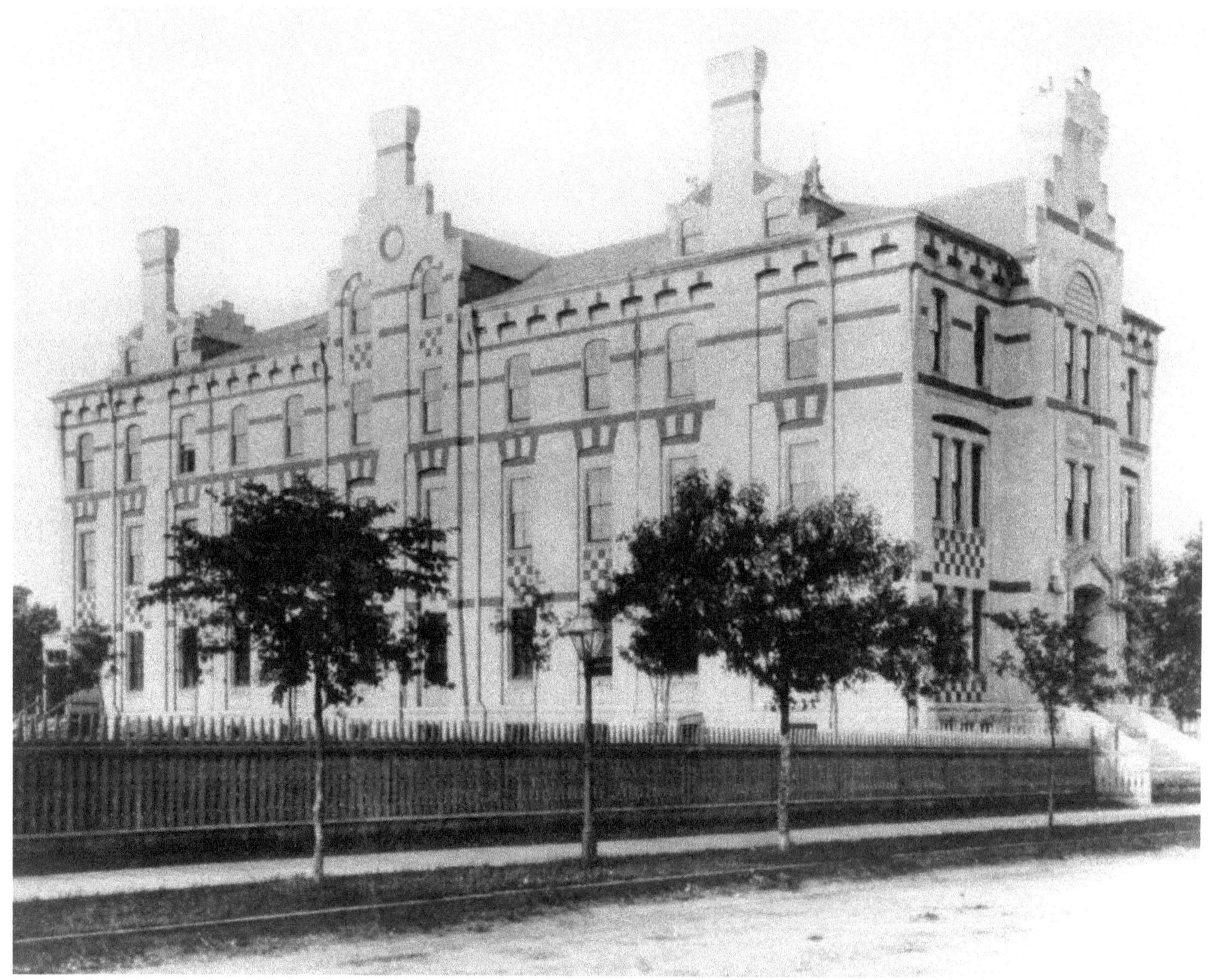

Heinrich Lieber's winery stood on Janesville Plank Road, now Forest Home Avenue. Open year-round, Lieber did business even in the worst Wisconsin weather with people who appreciated his wines made of grapes, currants, and elderberries. No longer a winery, the building is today a private residence.

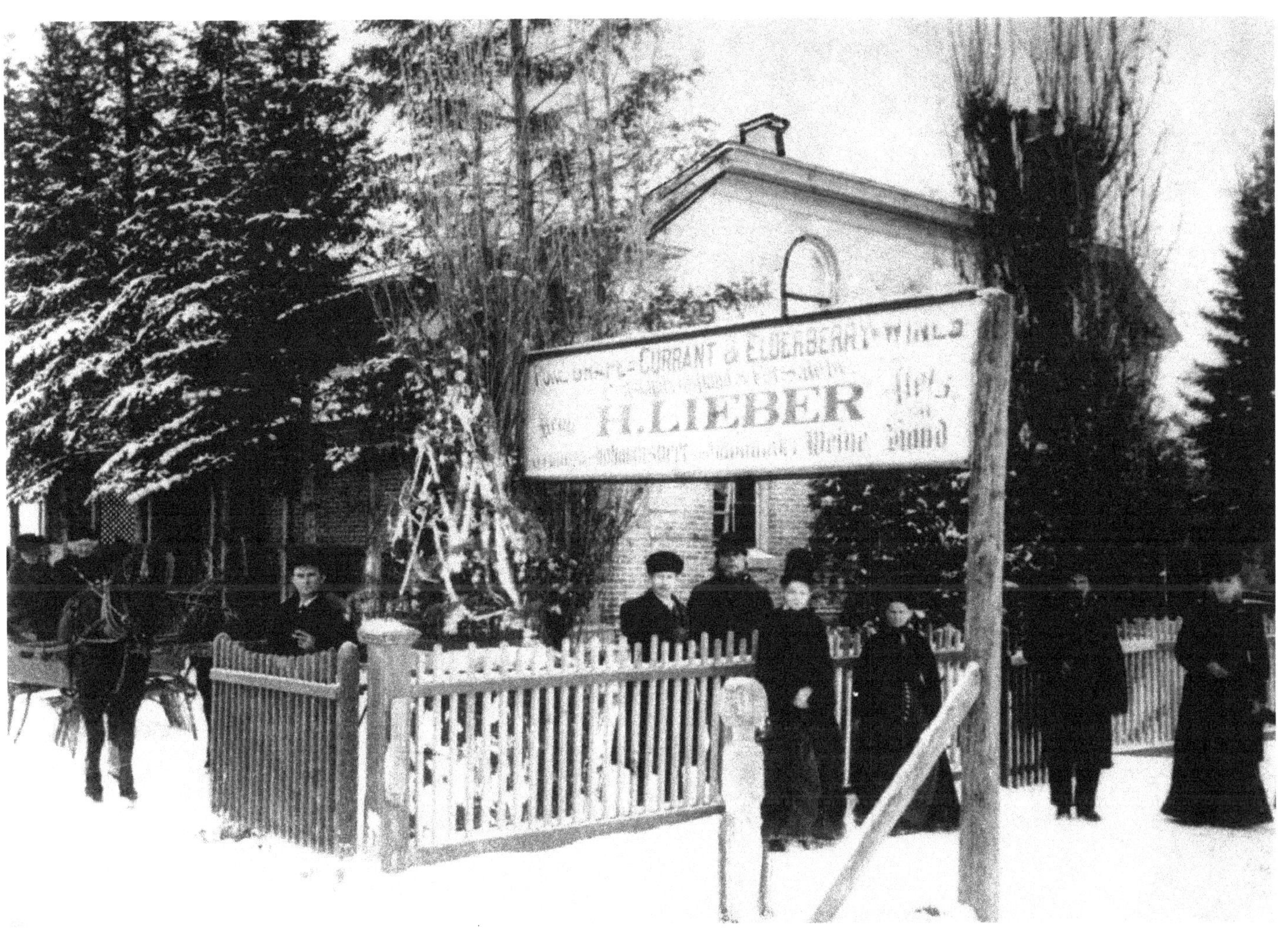

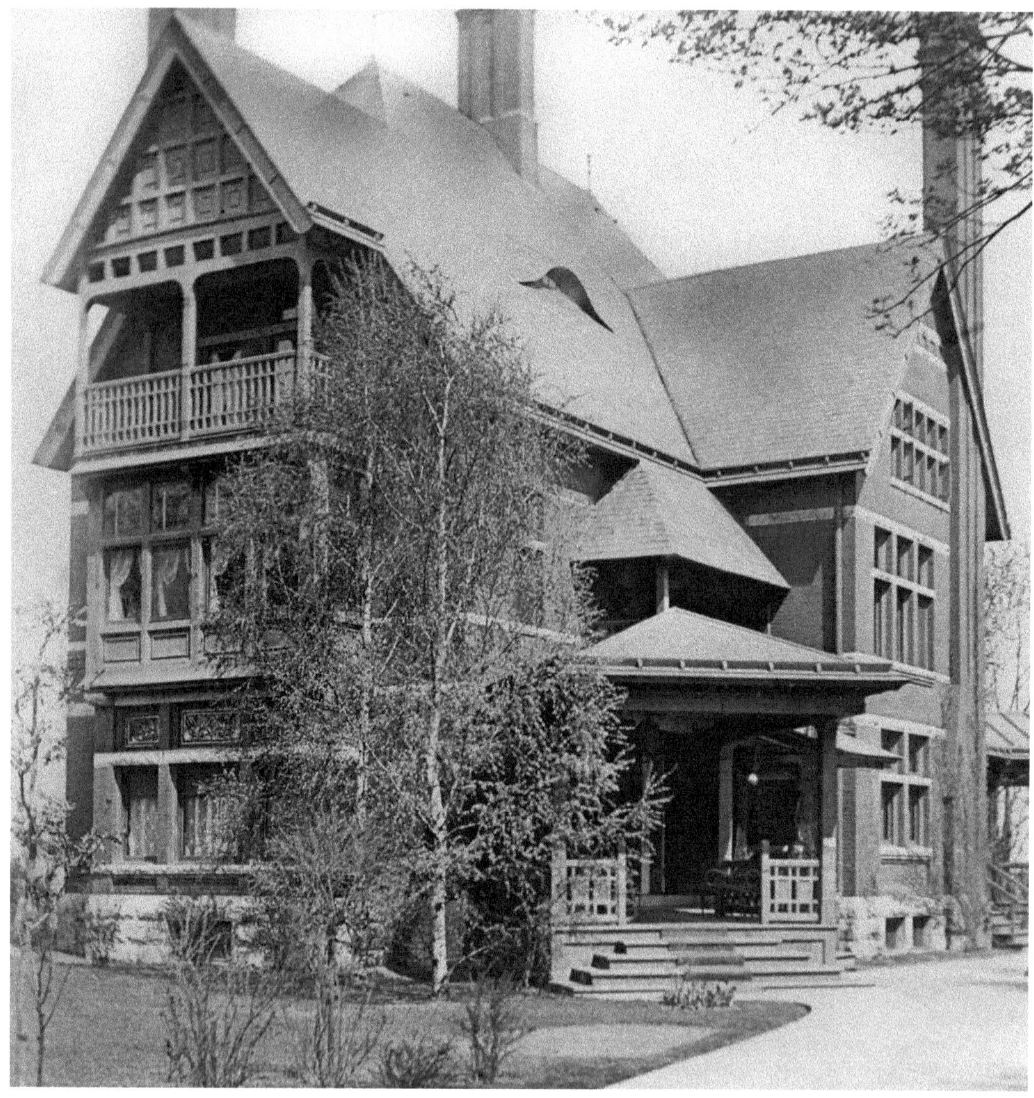

This house once belonged to Frederick Finney, a well-known civil engineer, who came to Wisconsin at the age of 25. He played an important part in the construction of the Union Pacific Road as well as the transcontinental railway, later returning to Wisconsin to manage the Wisconsin Central Railroad. The house is an excellent example of the mansions that the Milwaukee "captains of industry" built during this time.

In 1883, women work diligently to connect phone calls at Milwaukee's only telephone exchange, located on Broadway across the street from Wisconsin Bell, its owner.

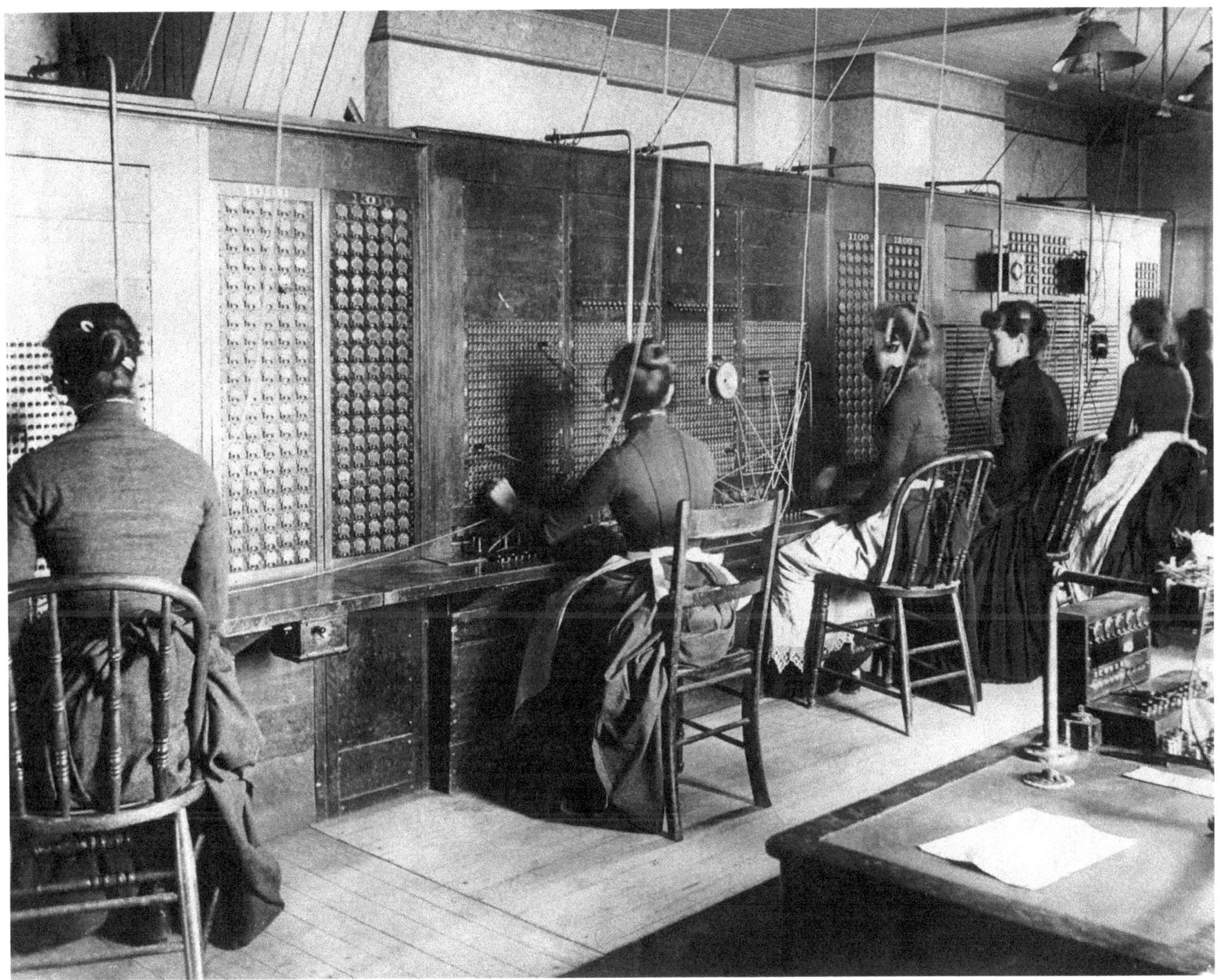

This hotel was designed by John Francis Rague and built in 1849 for John Layton and his son Frederick, of later fame for the Layton Art Gallery. It was located on Forest Home Avenue and served as a hotel until 1885 under Victor Schuette. It is now a privately owned apartment building.

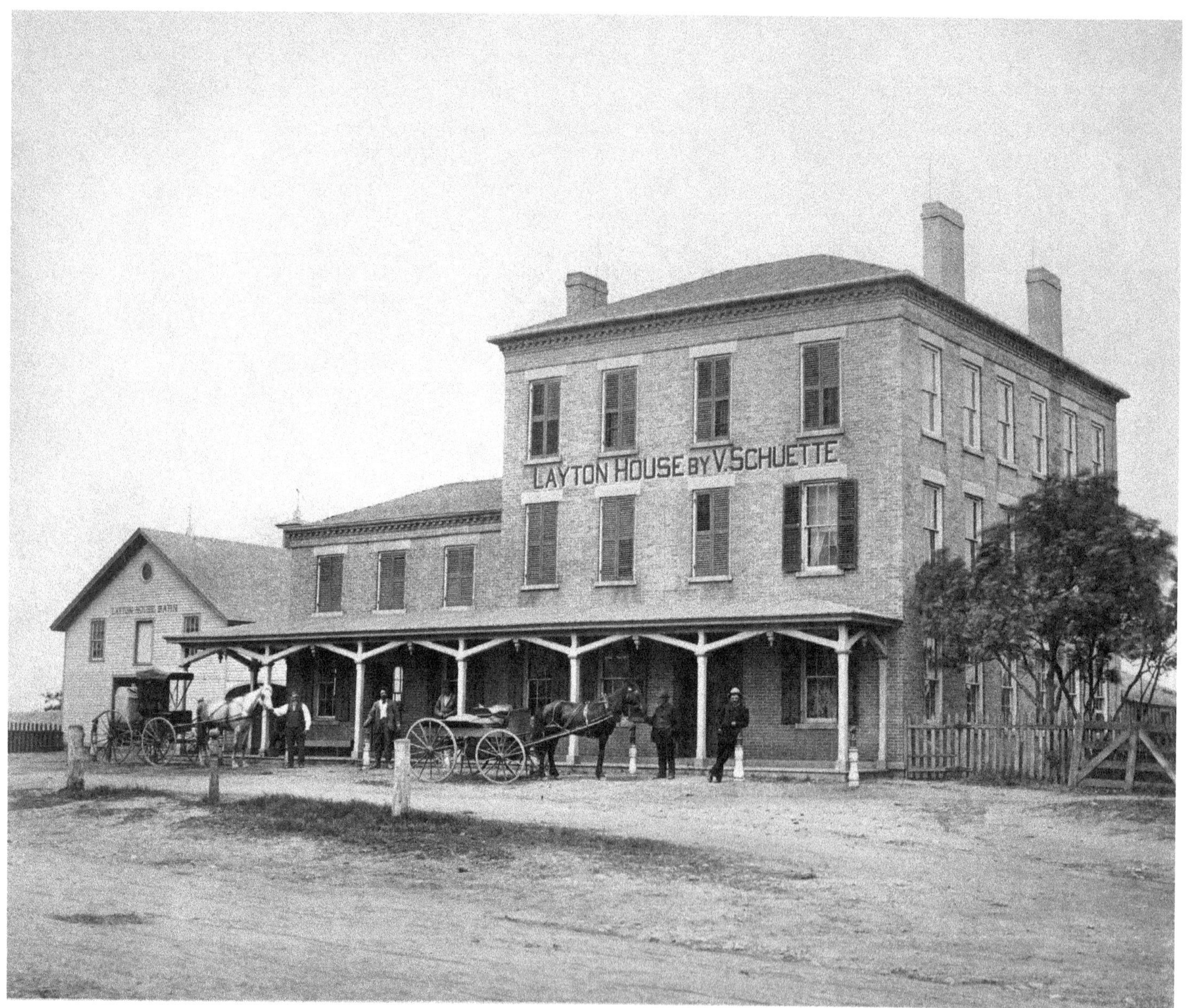

Offering to buy, sell, and exchange books, Carl Caspar's bookstore overflowed with literature. Located at 35 Oneida (later 35 E. Wells) with a second location at E. Water Street, the business lasted until 1903. Books from Caspar's bookstore can still be found in many of Milwaukee's historical literature collections.

Panorama artists from Milwaukee are shown standing on scaffolding with a painting of the Battle of Chattanooga in the background. The artists spent countless hours re-creating historical scenes on canvas for the public to enjoy.

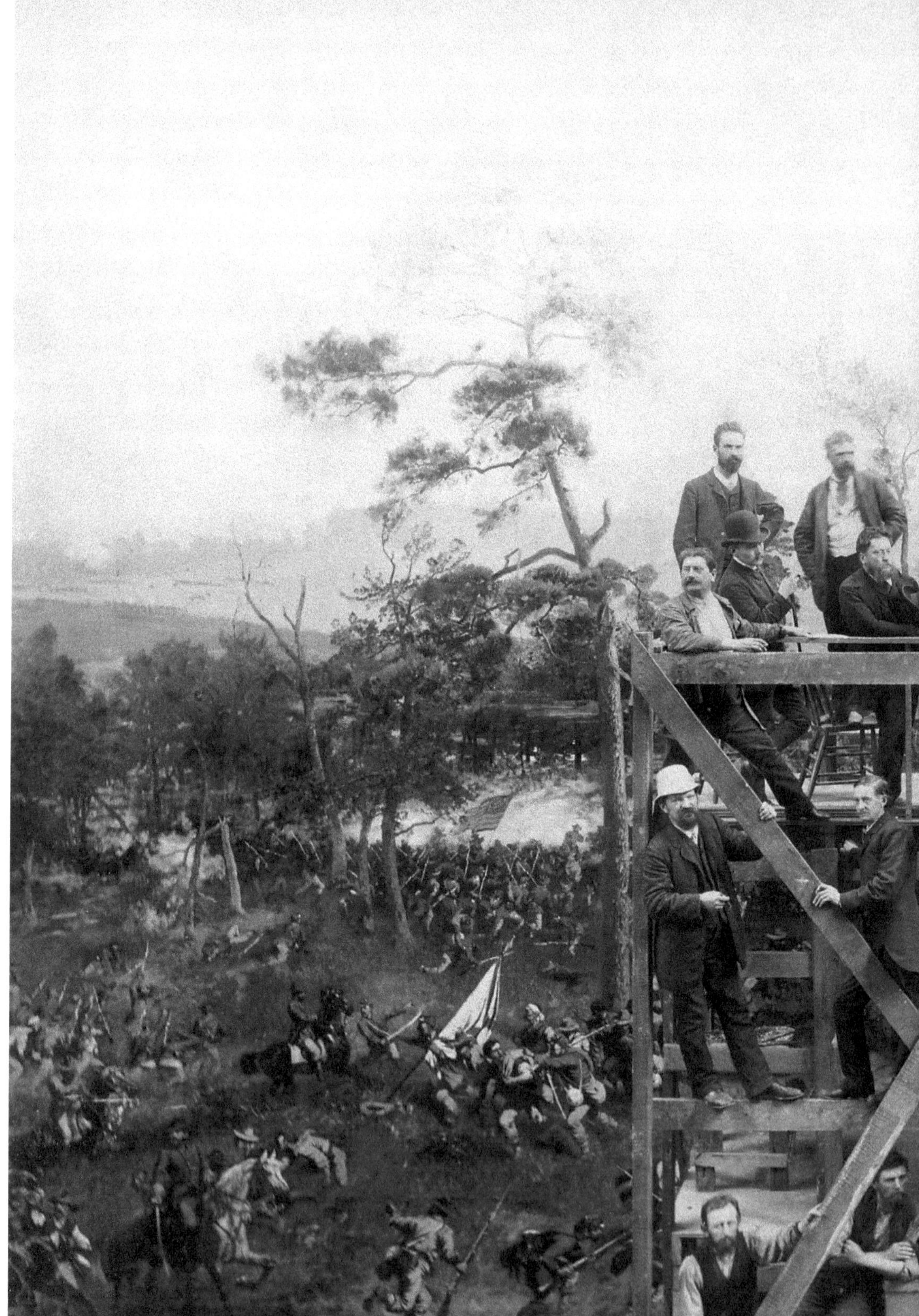

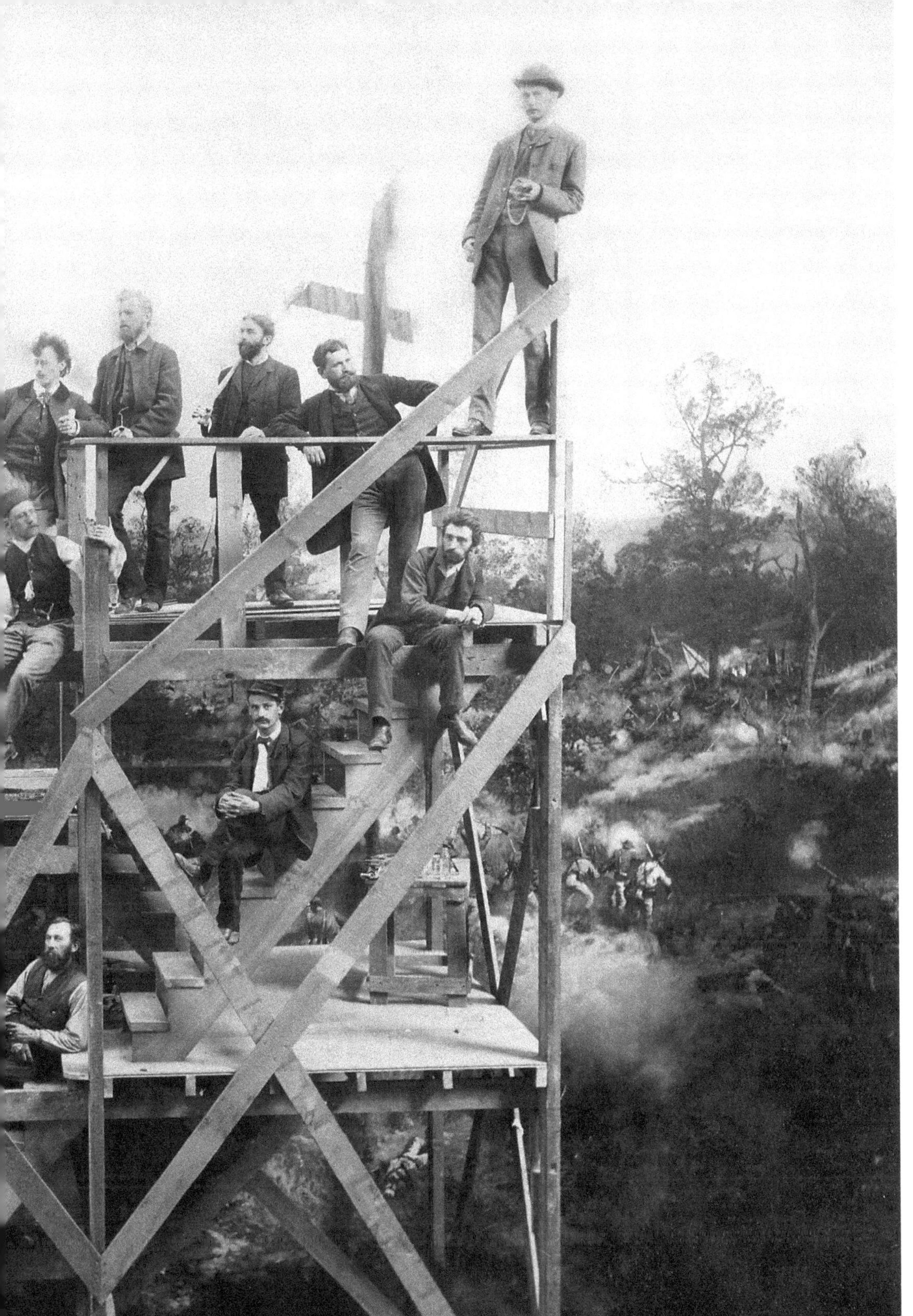

Located at 4th and Sycamore streets in the mid 1880s, this private hospital boasted a Turkish bath and comfortable lodging. It also touted a medical treatment for diseases such as diabetes and consumption that traditional medicine could not offer, referring to itself as a "curative institution."

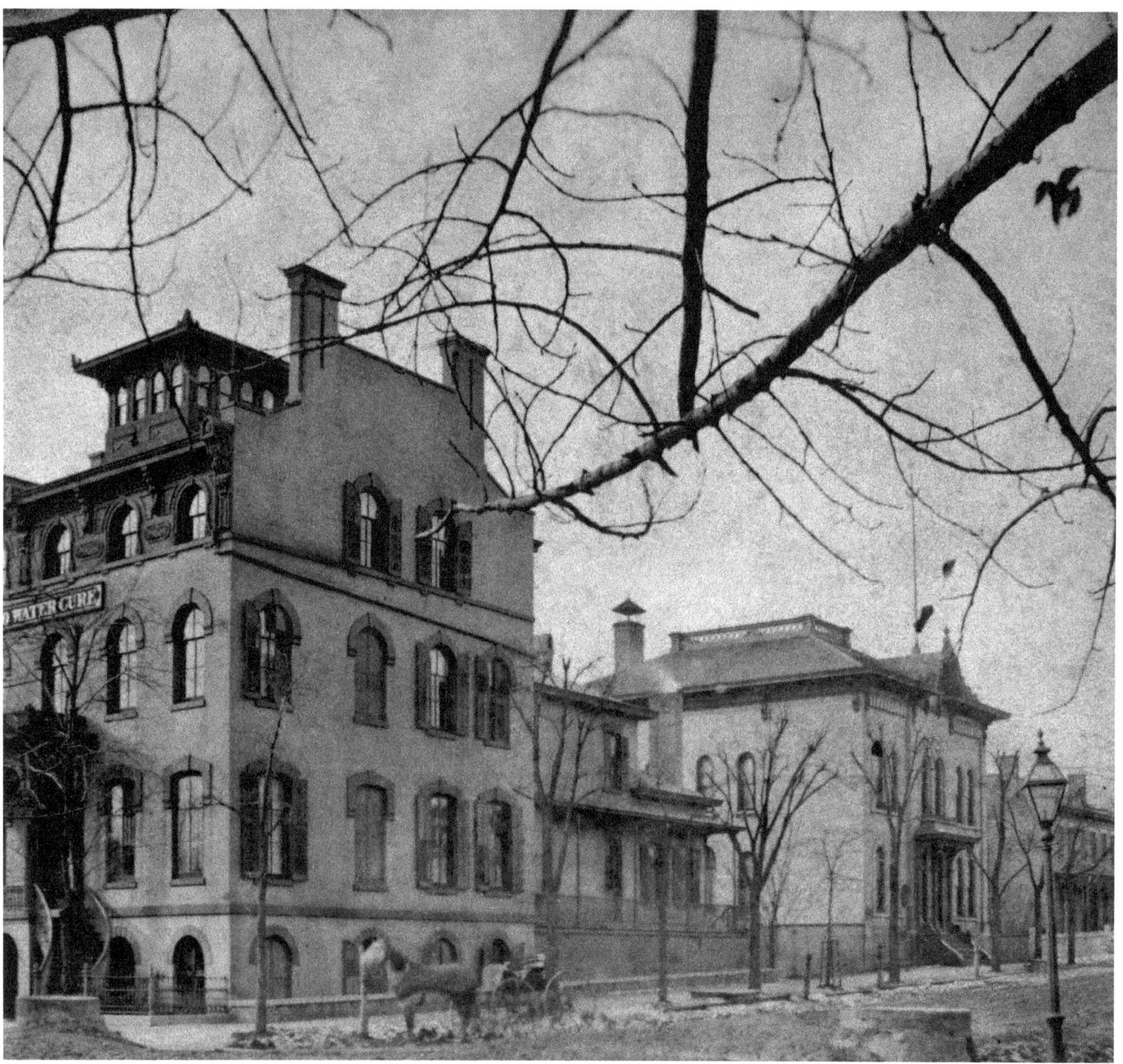

Firemen pose with a steam fire engine at the National Soldier's Home, later known as the Clement J. Zablocki Veterans Administration Medical Center. Altogether, between 1869 and 1979, 125 buildings have stood on the grounds0, some demolished by Milwaukee County.

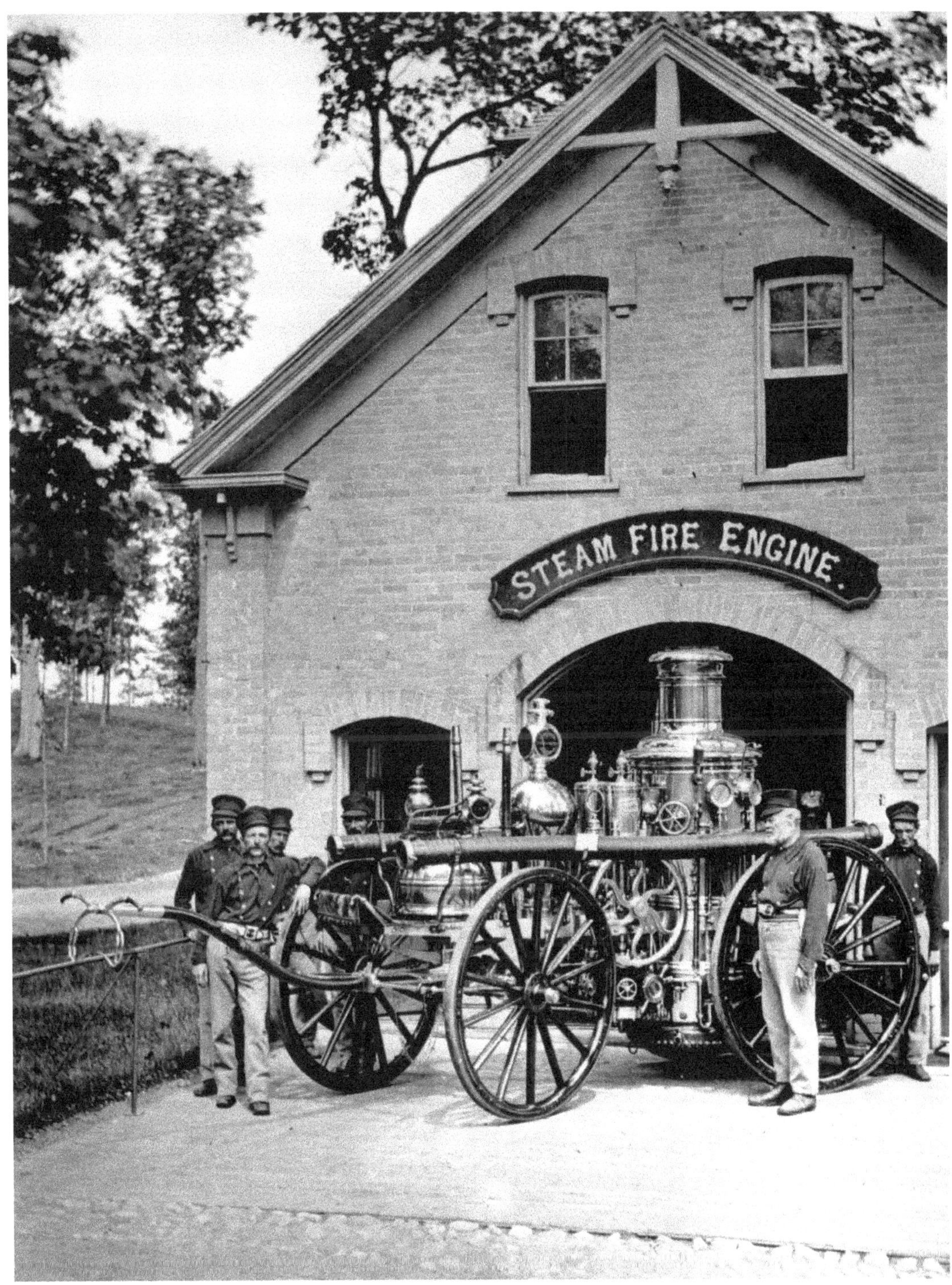

Workers for Edward P. Allis Reliance Works went on strike fighting for an eight-hour workday. This strike is part of what is often referred to as the Bay View Massacre. The state militia can be seen protecting the business from the strikers. Allis Reliance Works was a large manufacturer of engines, mills, and other machinery.

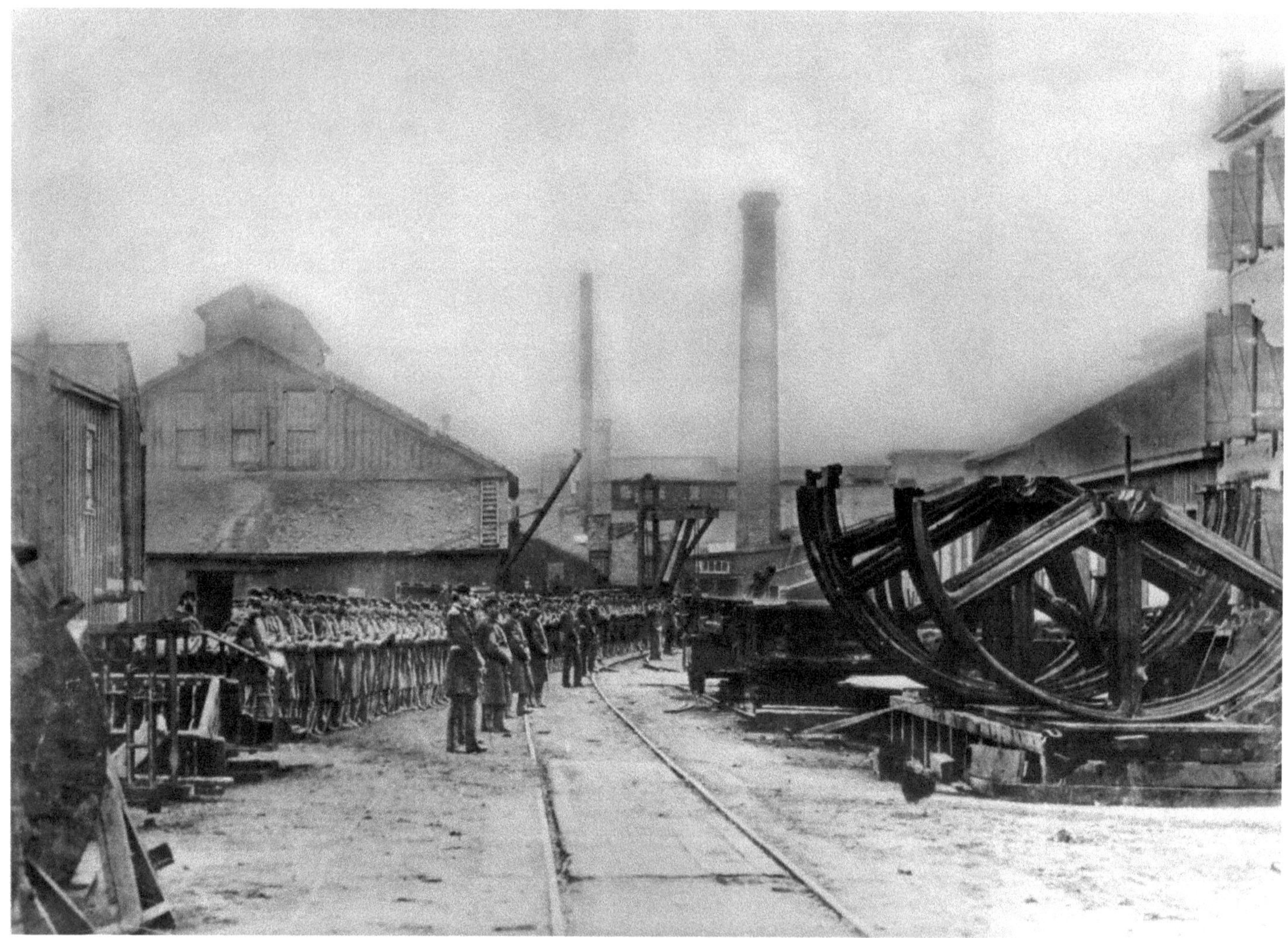

A Civil War cannon stands on the grounds of the Milwaukee Soldier's Home. The home was built in 1867 to care for veterans of wars gone by. The buildings are now a part of the Veterans Administration in Milwaukee.

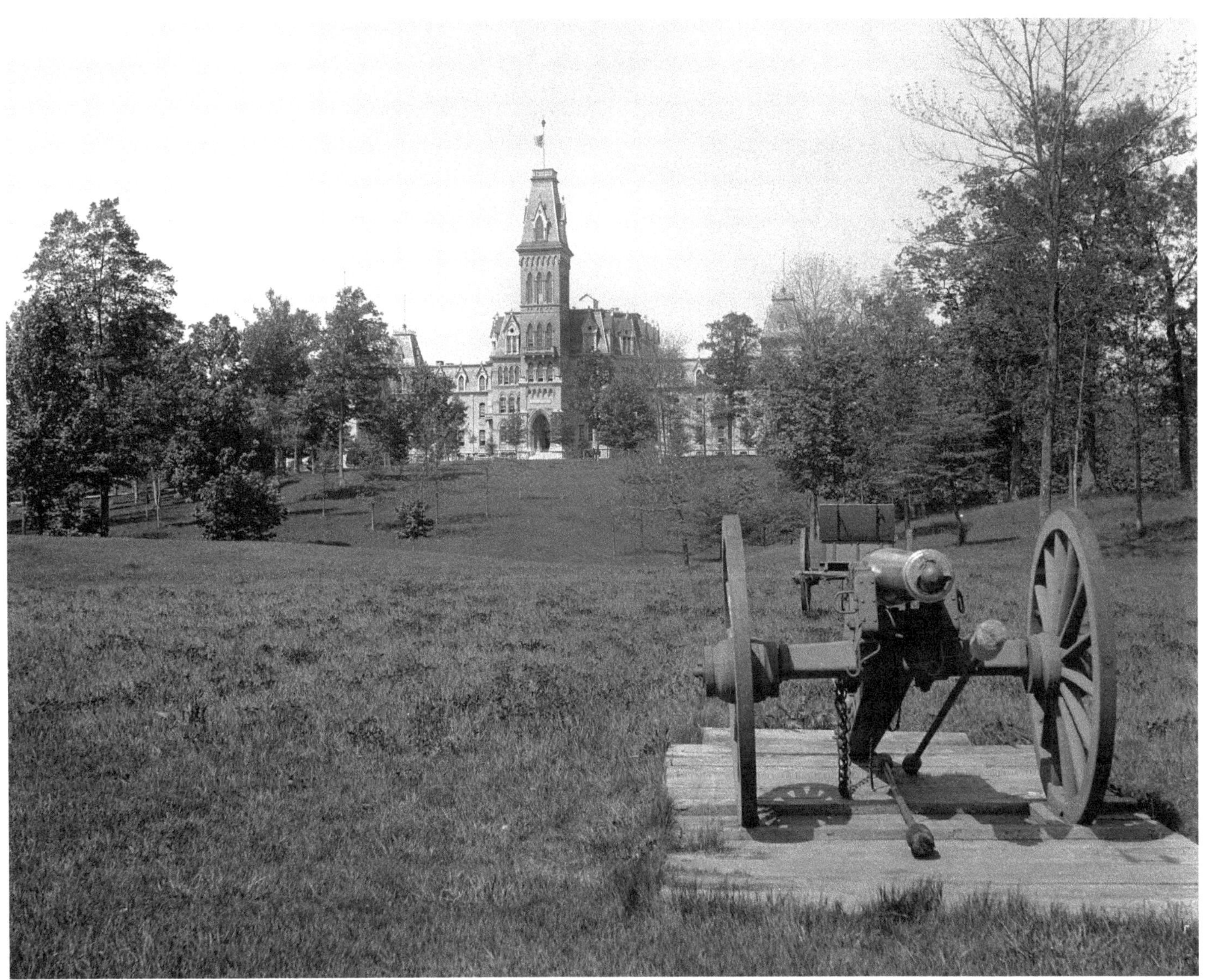

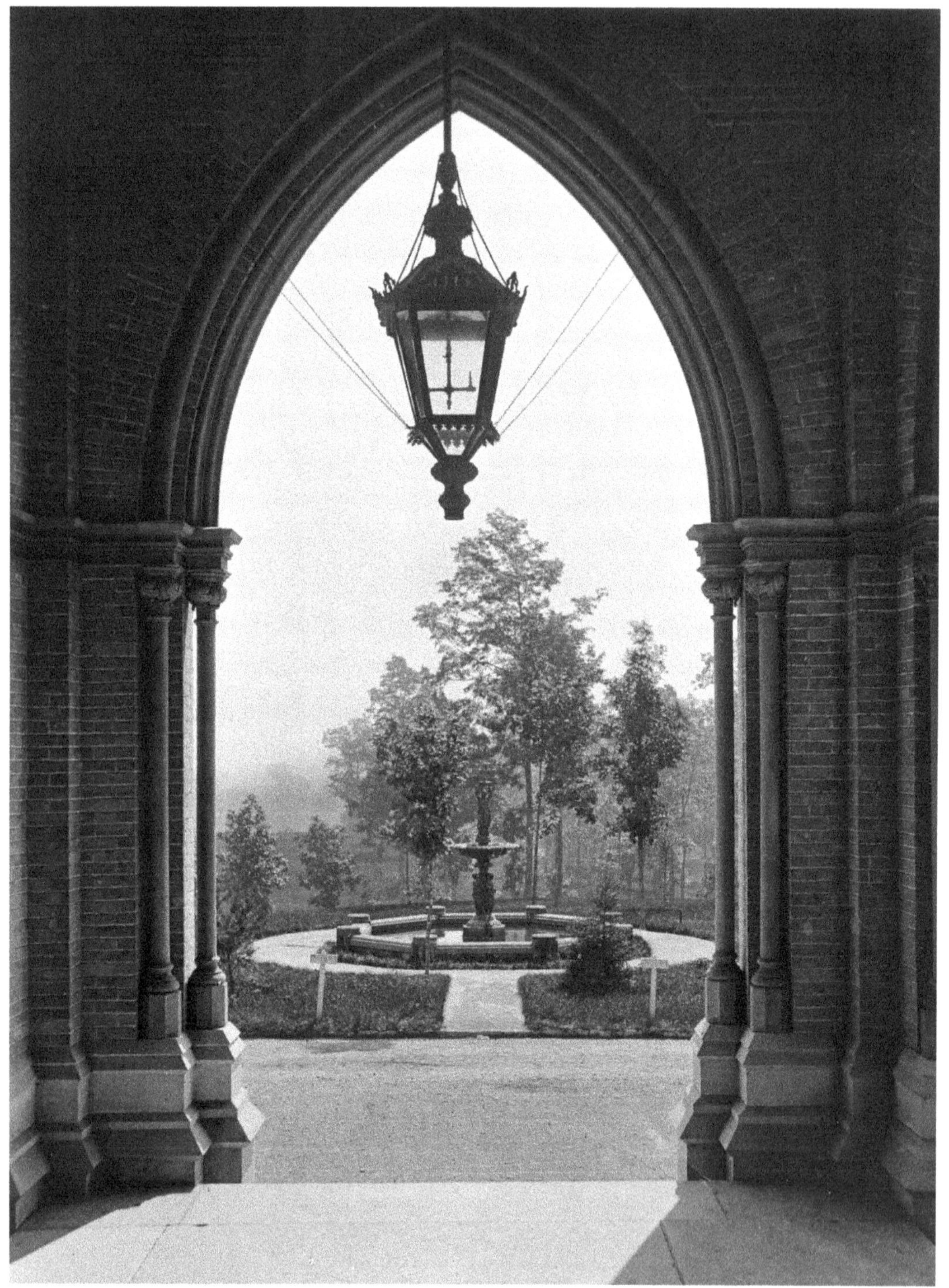

This photograph, taken in 1887, offers a view out the entrance of the National Soldier's Home in Milwaukee, obscuring the city that is rising up around the home's picturesque landscape.

Photographed in the studio of the American Panorama Company in 1887, these painters are taking a break from their latest project, the crucifixion of Christ in Jerusalem. The scaffolding they use can be seen in the background, surrounded by paintings and photographs of unknown persons.

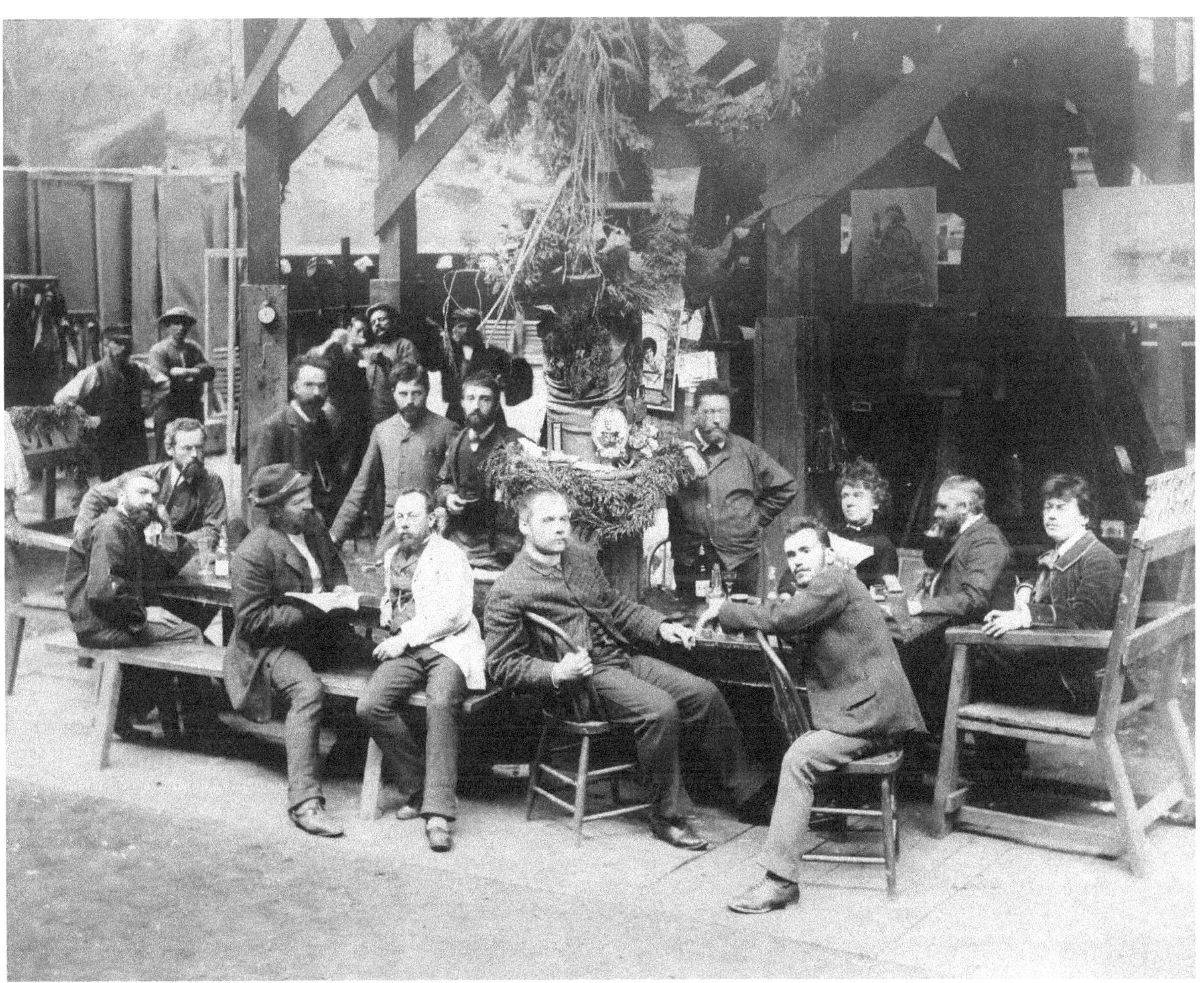

The Mitchell Building, built in 1878 for Alexander Mitchell, one of Milwaukee's captains of industry, which included banking, railroad, and lumber. It housed the offices of the Chicago, Milwaukee and St. Paul Railroad Company seen here. It still stands on the corner of Michigan Street and North Water Street.

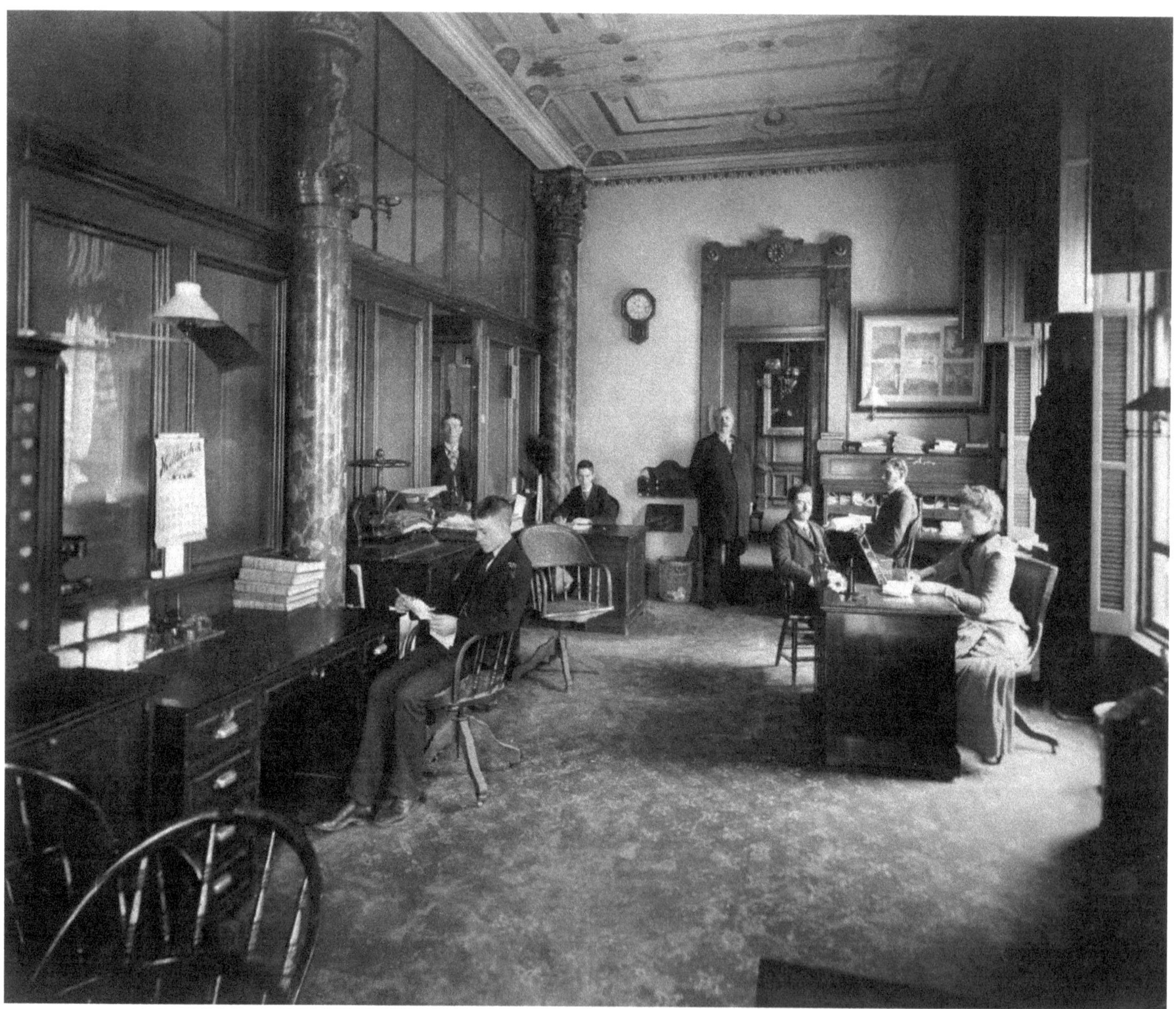

This market was also referred to as "Der Gruner market" for the abundance of vegetables and plants sold there, although meat, dairy, and the daily gossip were also available. This market was similar to today's farmers markets that pop up all over the city, particularly in the summer months.

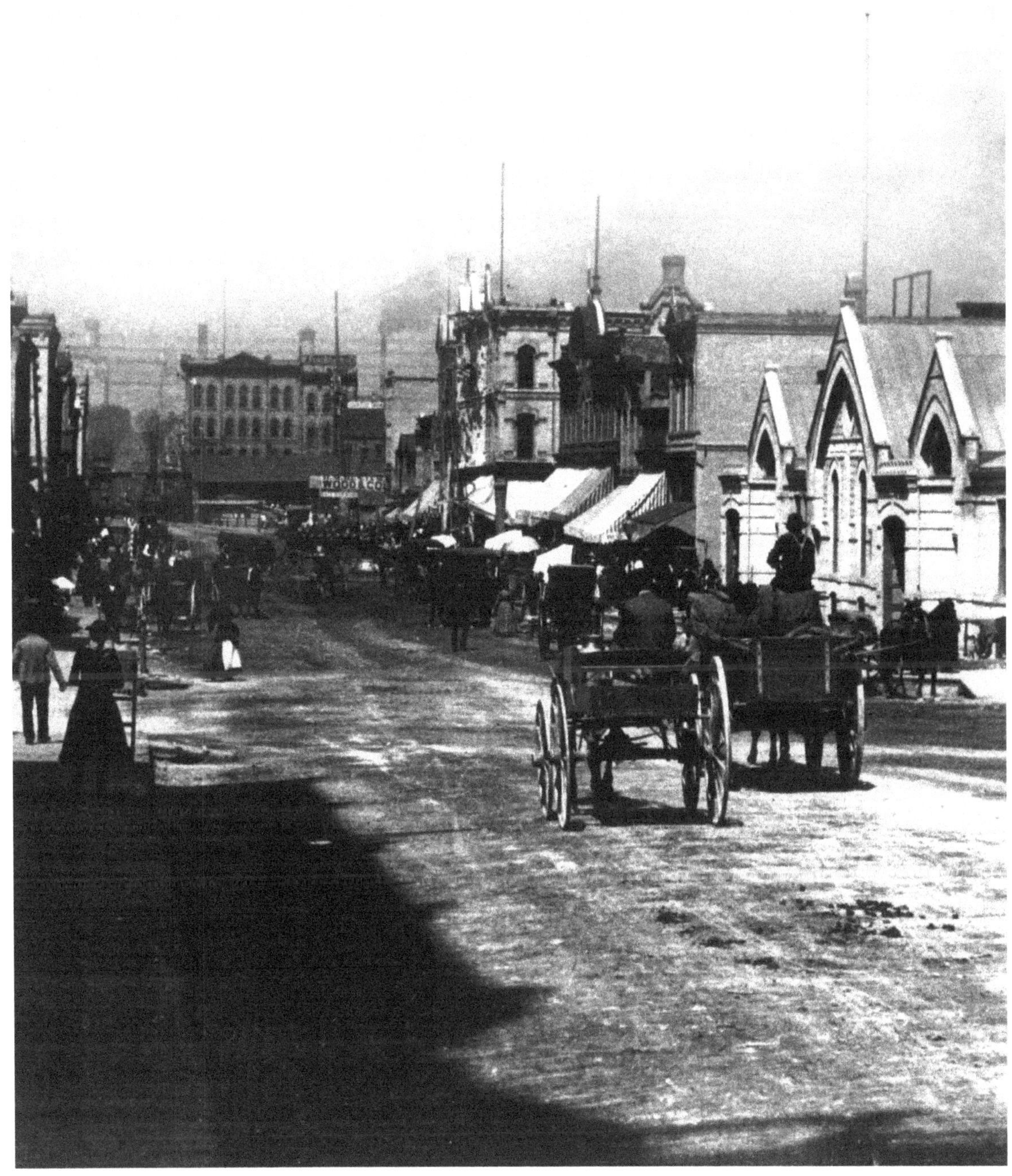

Civil War veterans and their families enjoy the Iron Brigade reunion in 1887, sitting for a photograph in front of the Armory building.

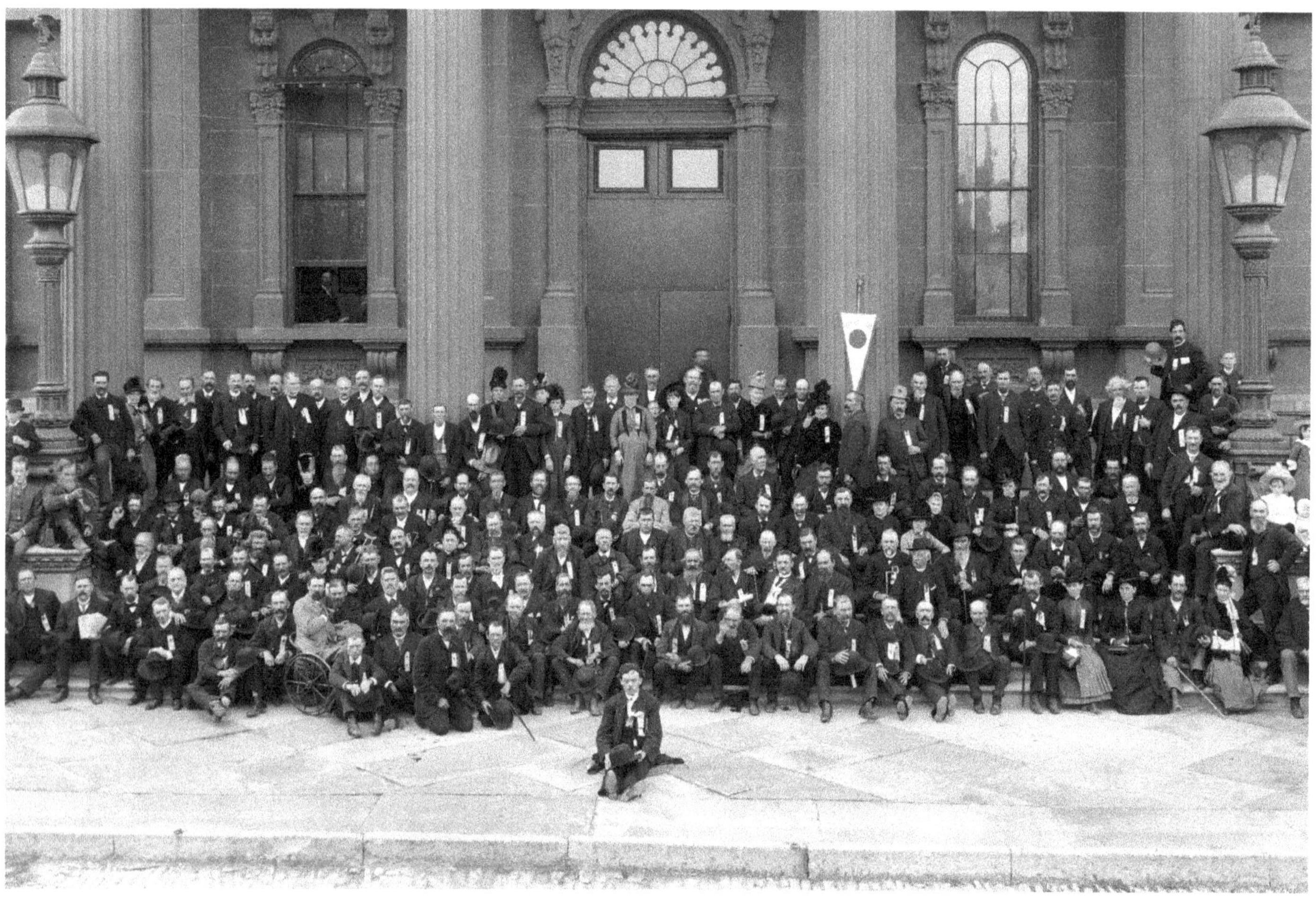

The Davidson Theatre was one of the premier entertainment spots in Milwaukee, touting names such as Al Jolson and Boris Karloff on its playbills. Fire broke out in the theater in 1894. No one was inside at the time, but members of the Lilliputian Opera Company were rescued from the adjacent Davidson Hotel. The theater was rebuilt and later became an office building. It was leveled in 1963.

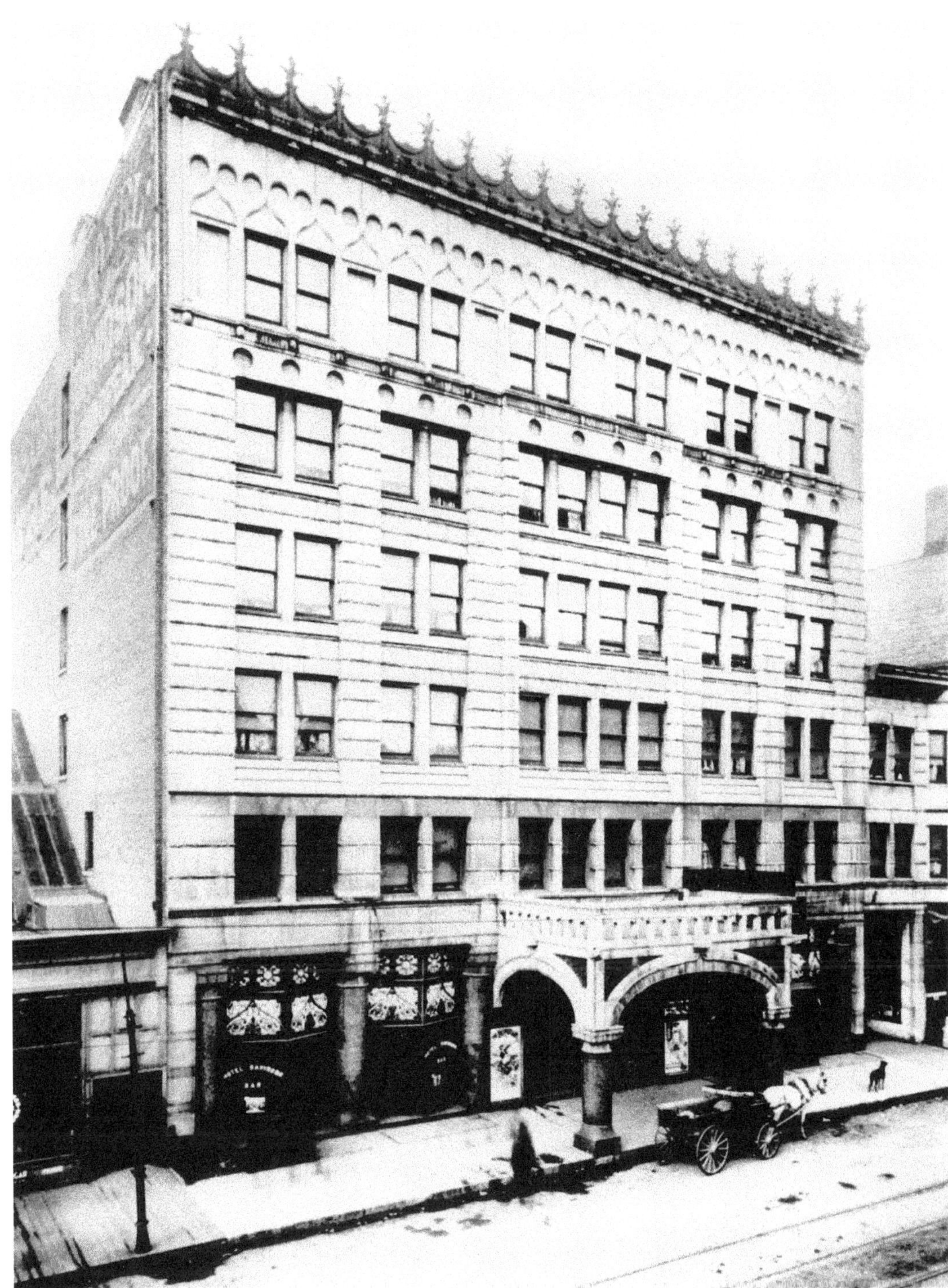

Ellen Lemke and her escort, Will Brown, enjoy a carriage ride with her sister Rose and her escort. Ellen's father, Albert, was a pharmacist who delivered medicine to places all over Wisconsin and Illinois.

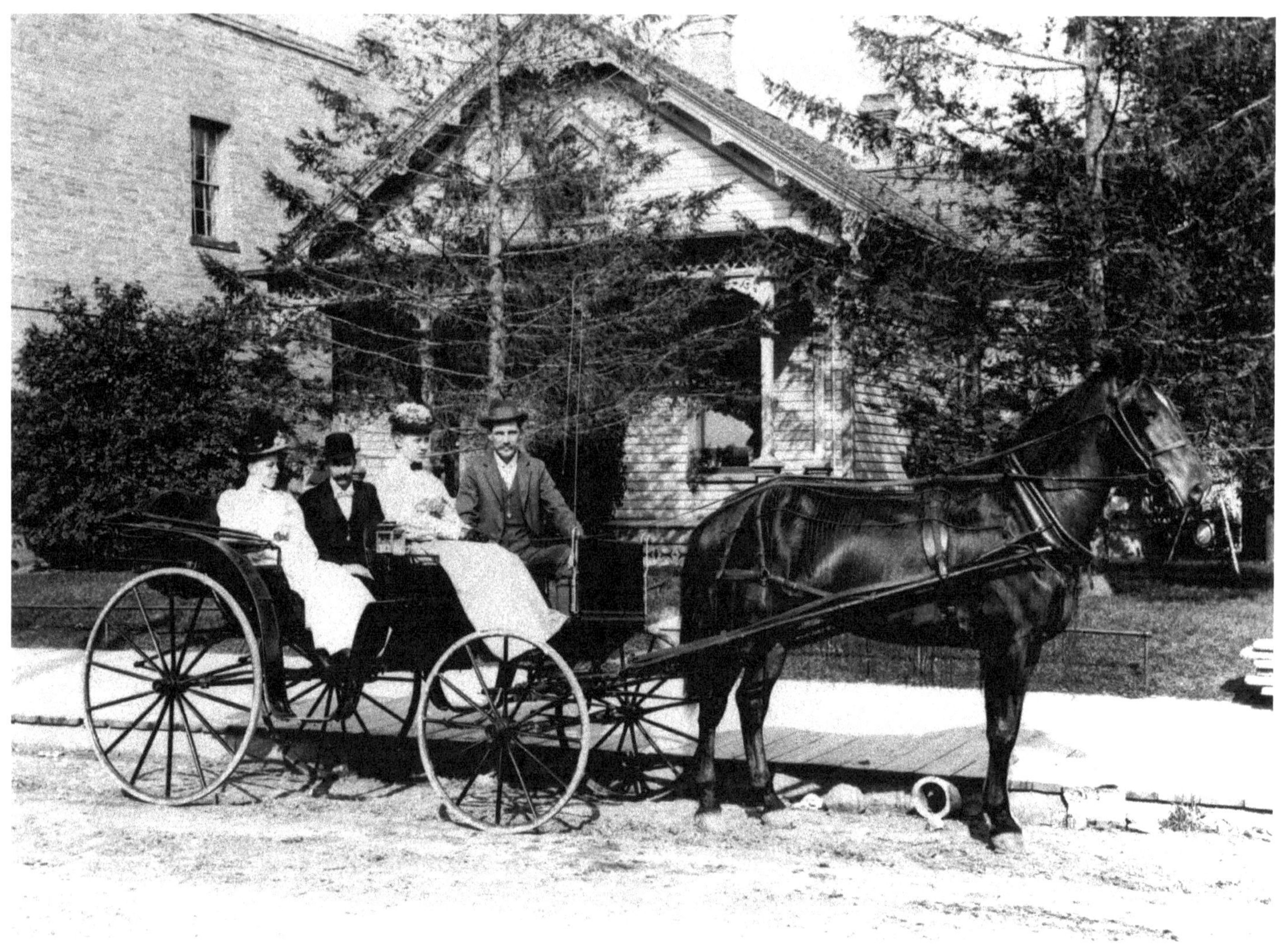

Jones Island was once a bustling community of Polish and German immigrants who made their living by fishing Lake Michigan. In the late 1890s Milwaukeeans started to venture to Jones Island looking for a break from the hustle and bustle of city life, visiting places like this tavern. Eventually the island was taken over by the City of Milwaukee for use as a location for a sewage plant and incinerator, forcing the inhabitants of the island to leave.

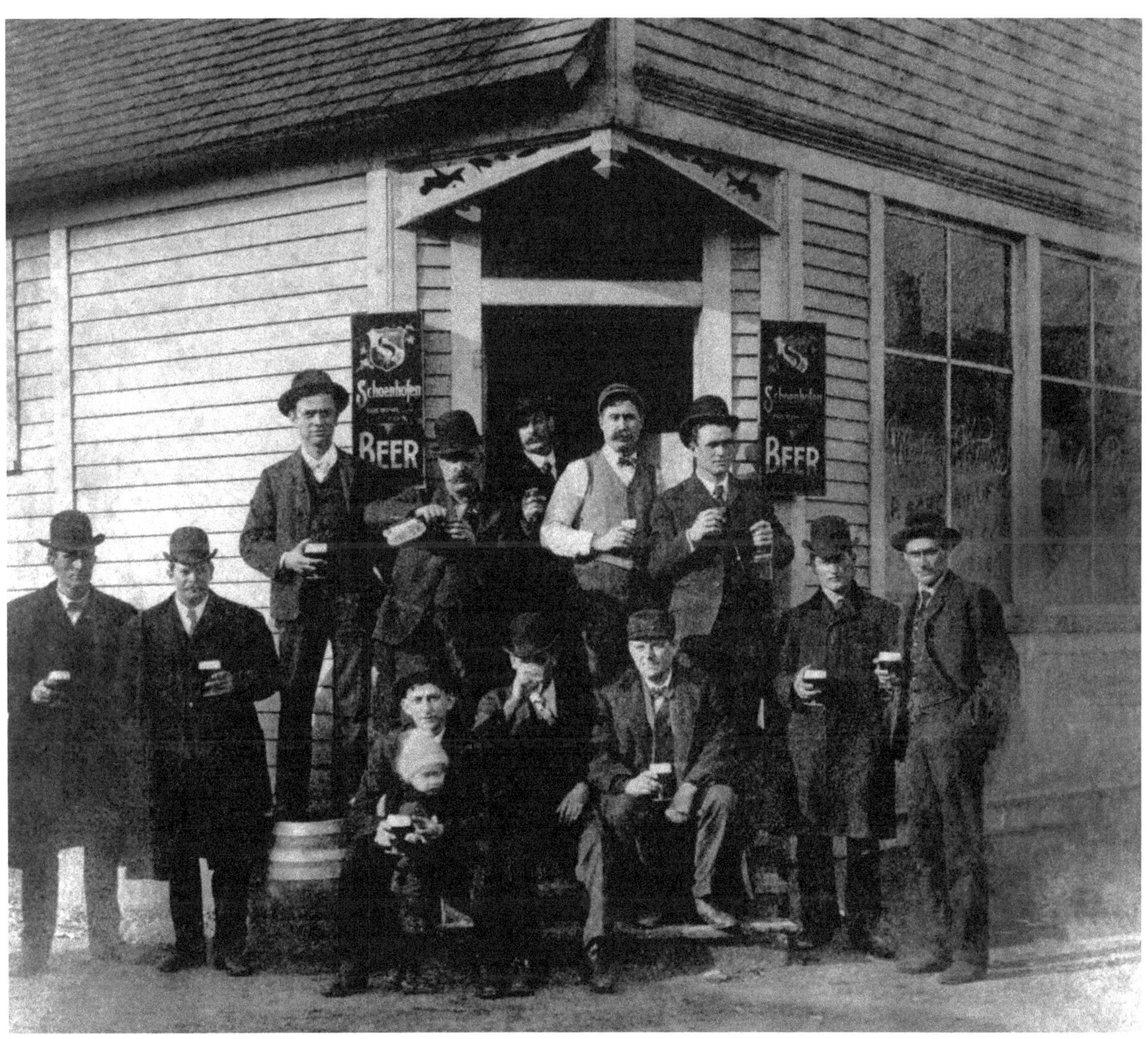

Once located at 5th and Poplar (now McKinley), this market was peopled by a lively community of German immigrants, who ventured to the square to purchase hay for their horses and chat with their neighbors about the goings on in their community. With the advent of the automobile the need for hay slowly dwindled, as did the need for the haymarket.

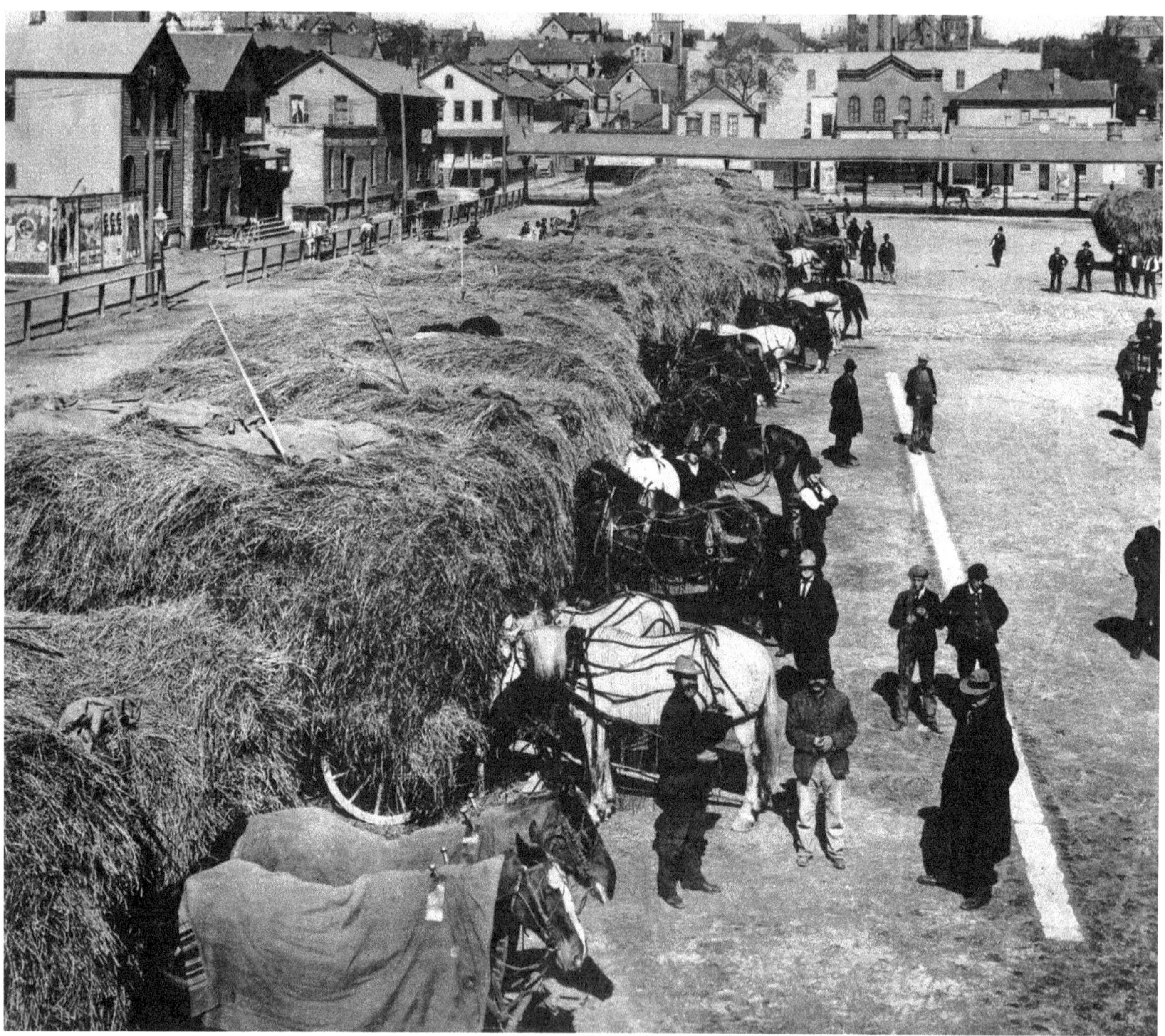

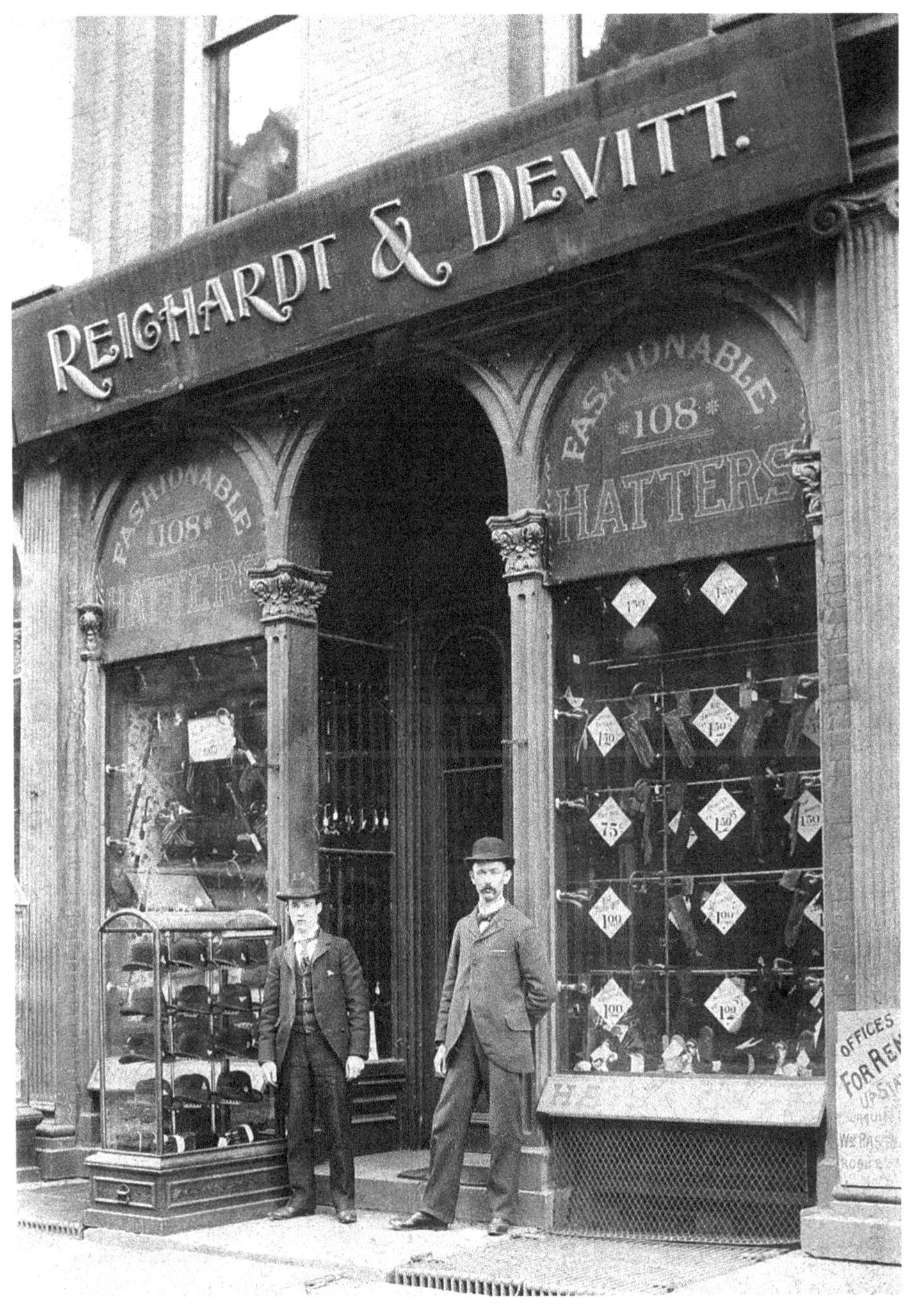

Located at 108 Grand Avenue (later Wisconsin Avenue), Reichardt and Devitt offered a wide variety of hats, as well as gloves and umbrellas, showcasing the fashion trends of the 1880s.

Commission Row served as Milwaukee's wholesale market. Whereas the German markets on Division offered goods from local farmers directly, the merchants on Commission Row sold their goods indirectly to the local grocers in each unique neighborhood.

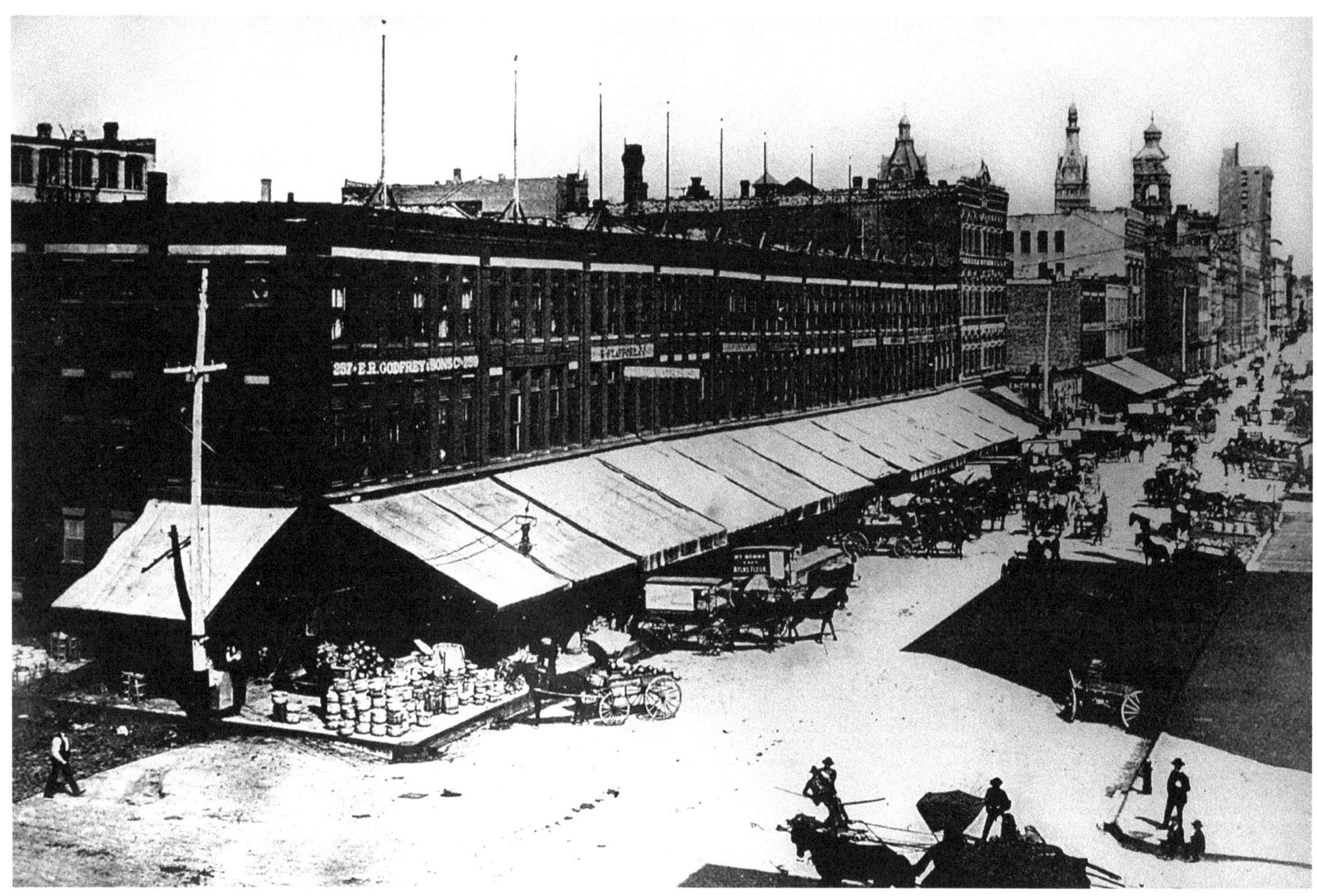

Schlitz Park was one of Milwaukee's foremost beer gardens. It was used as a place of relaxation, offering concerts, open air, and a spectacular view of downtown. It was also reminiscent of the German beer gardens many Milwaukee immigrants had left behind.

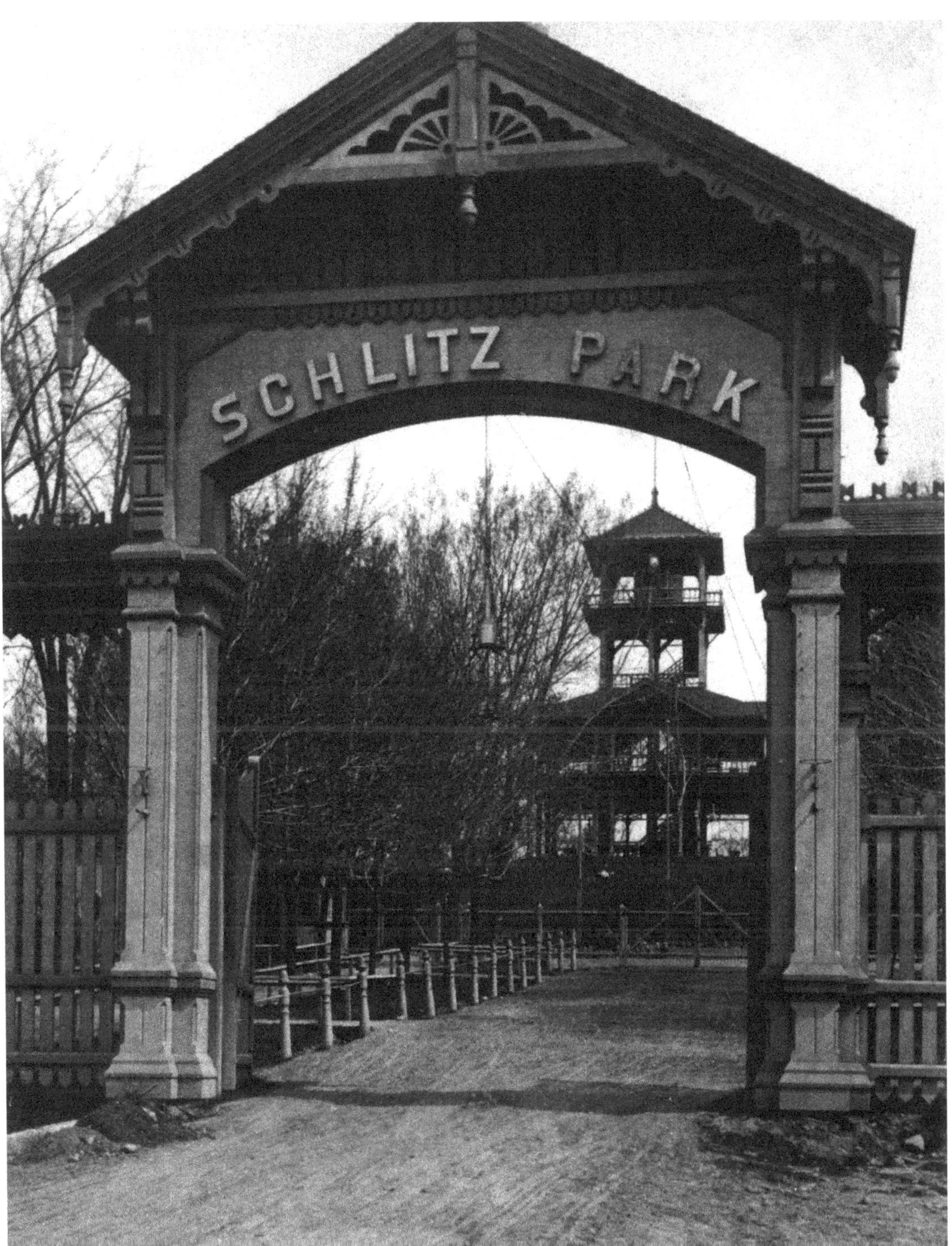

This mansion was built by John Plankinton for his daughter Elizabeth and her fiancé as a wedding gift. Sadly the wedding never took place and Elizabeth lost interest in the house, devoting her time to the development of the arts in Milwaukee. The mansion housed the Knights of Columbus for many years until it was razed in 1980 after a long struggle to preserve it.

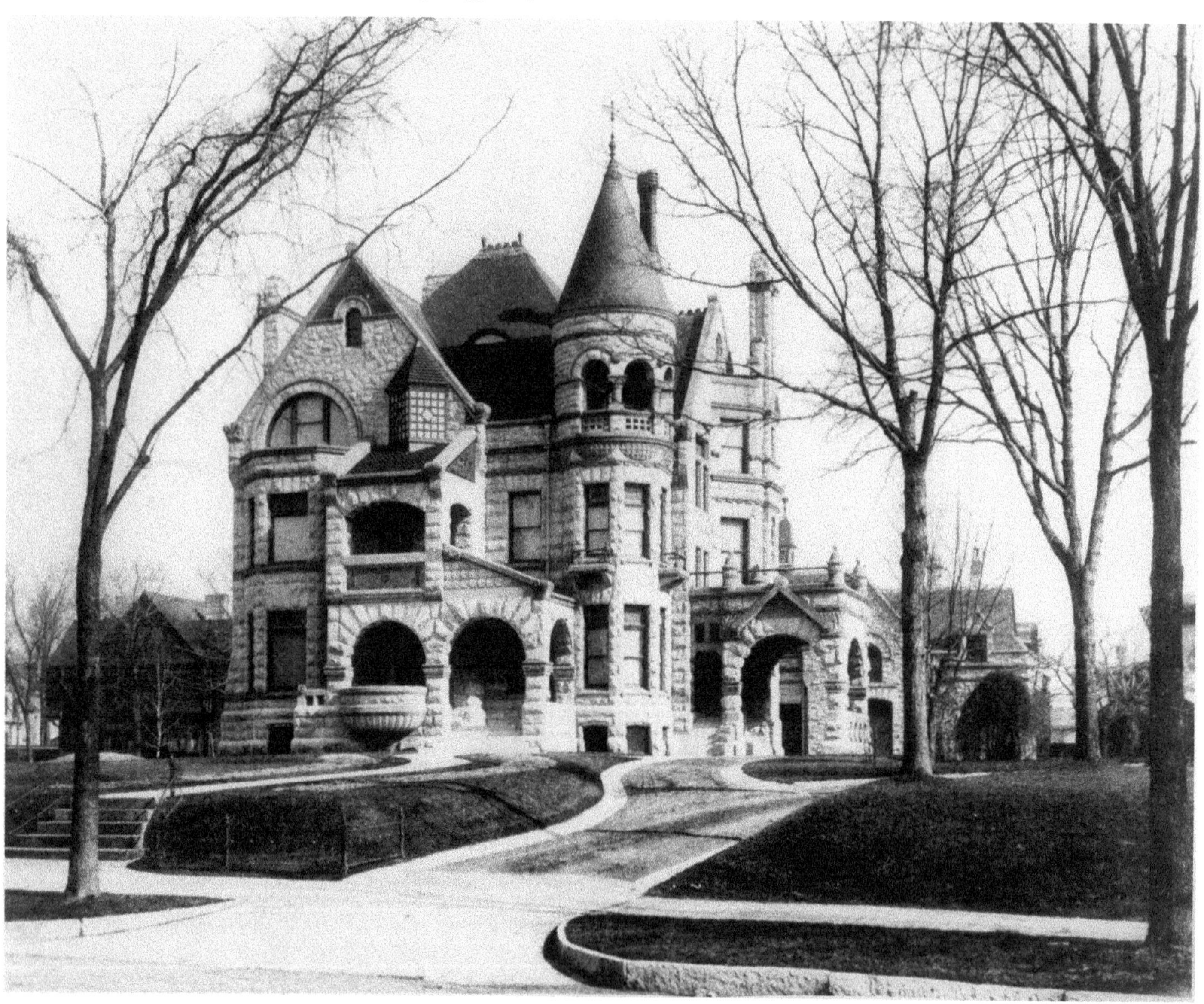

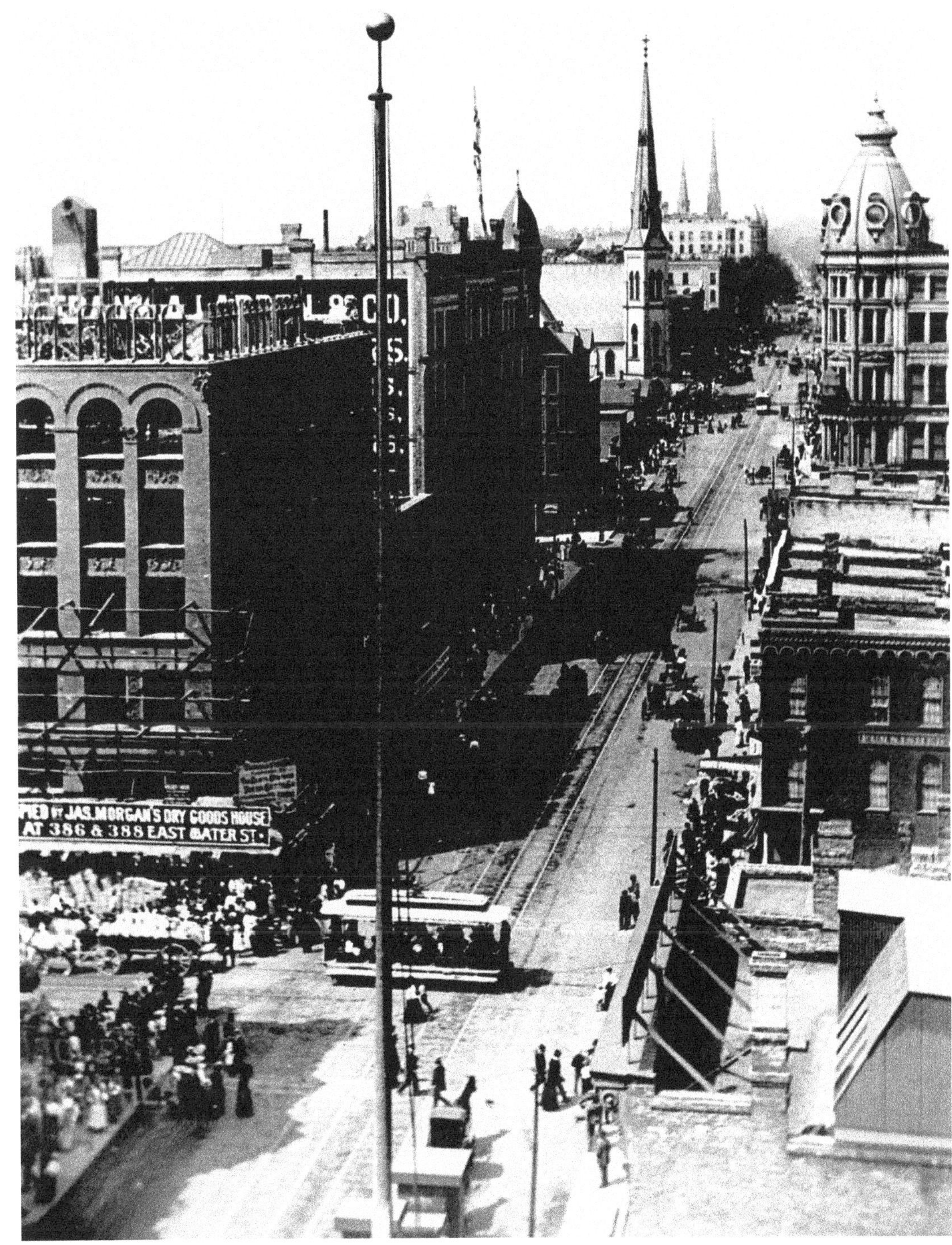

The last wagon in Barnum's circus parade can be seen in the lower left corner of this image. Approximately 100,000 people watched the parade pass through downtown. The Great Circus Parade, a re-creation of the one seen here in 1892, was hosted in Milwaukee from 1985–2004.

J. M. Allcott and his employees can be seen standing in front of his establishment at 90 Wisconsin Street in 1890. The local pharmacist was a person of great importance in each community. Along with medicine, Allcott sold candy, aerated cream, and soda water.

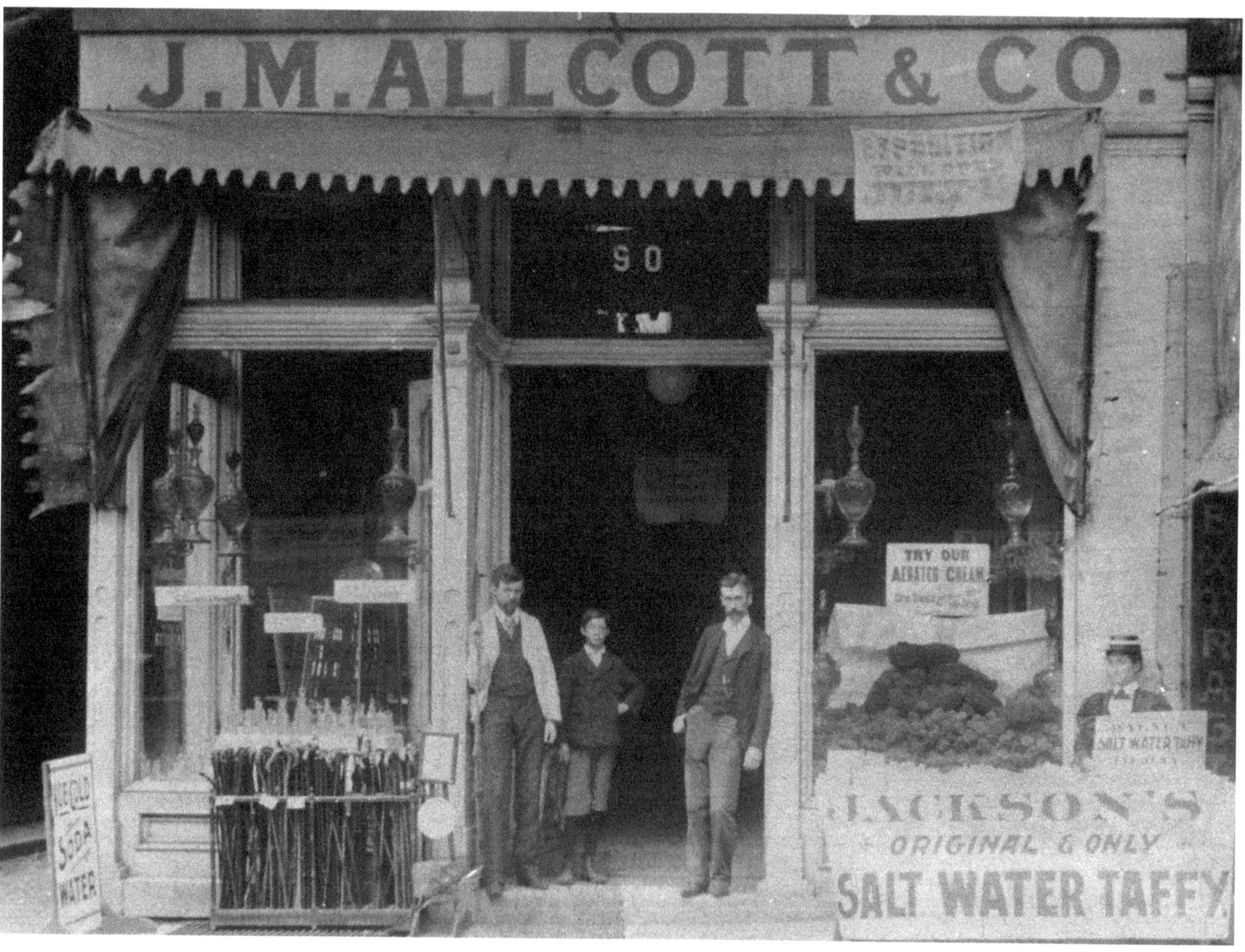

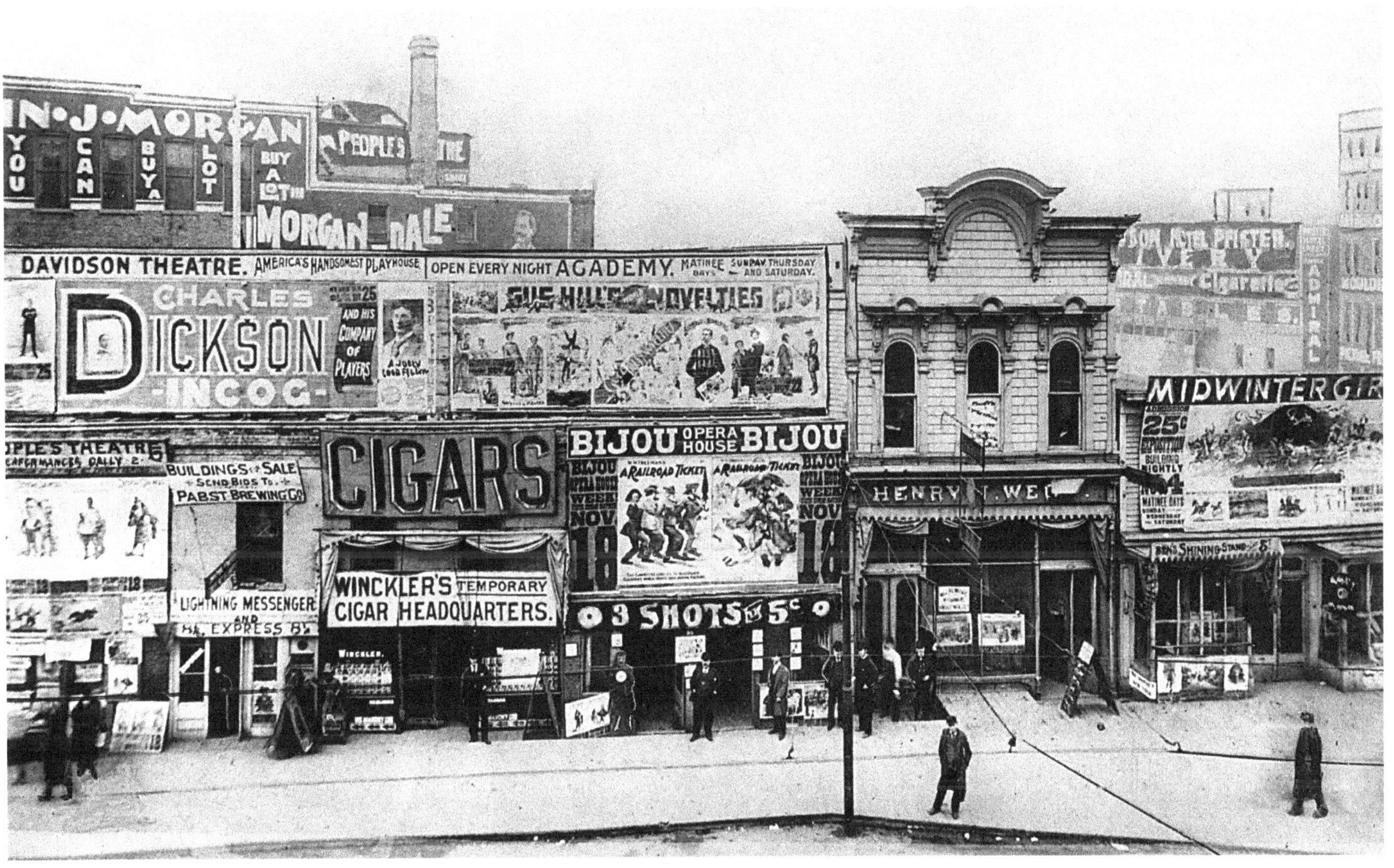

Grand Avenue looked quite different in 1892. Billboards advertising local theater acts abound, attempting to attract visitors to the shows. Ads for a local cigar shop, bar, and shoe shining spot can also be seen. The Riverside Theatre now stands in this location.

Stenographers for the law firm of Winkler, Flanders, Smith, Bottum, and Vilas pose for a photograph. Many people in 1890s Milwaukee worked in offices like this one. The business, still in Milwaukee under a different name, is located at 100 East Wisconsin Avenue.

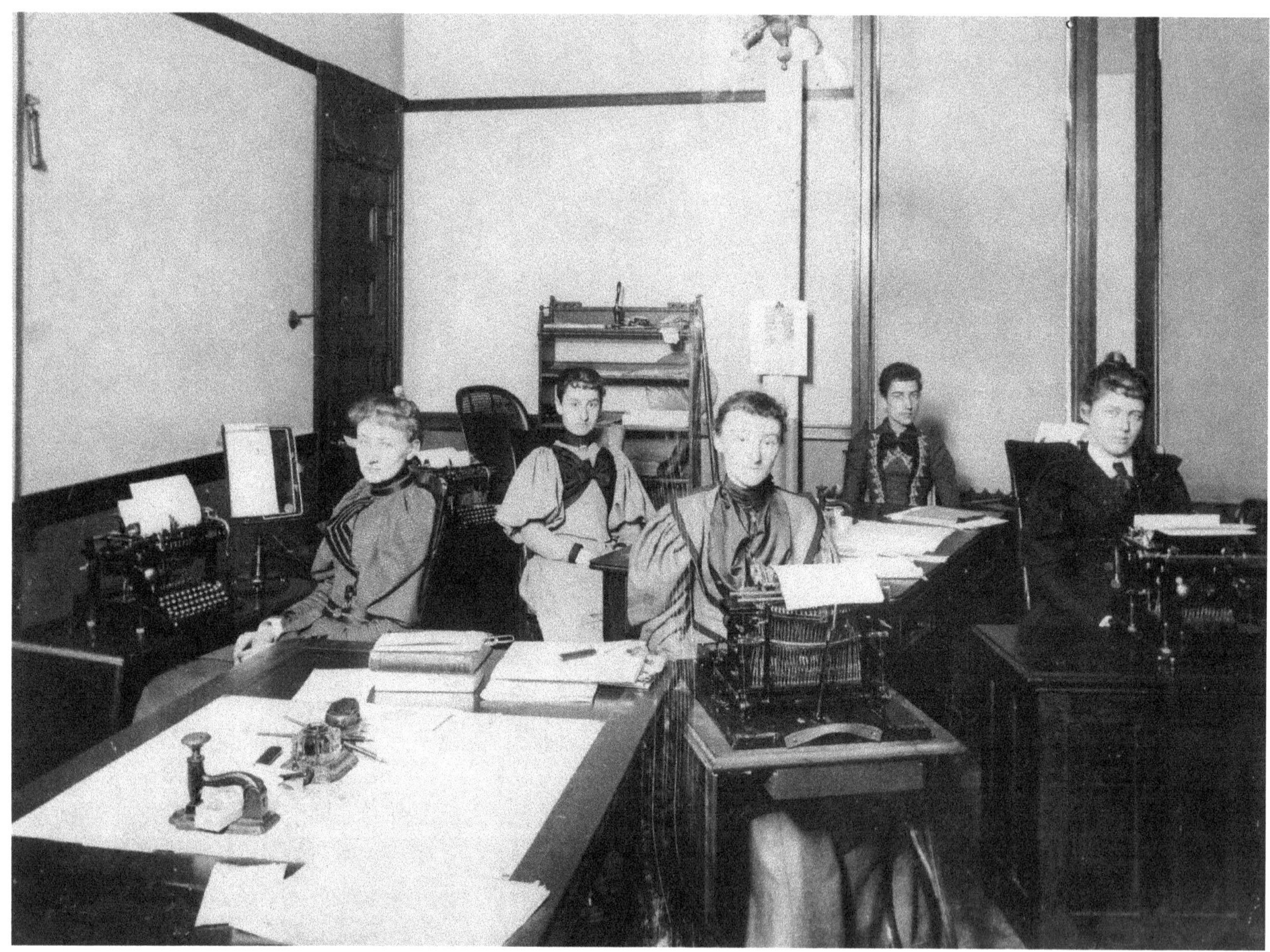

Johnston emergency hospital was first organized in 1888. After years of finding temporary locations, a building was constructed by John Johnston costing $40,000. It quickly became a reputable hospital and remained in use until 1931, when a new, more modern hospital was built on Milwaukee's south side. The building was located at what is now 4th and Michigan.

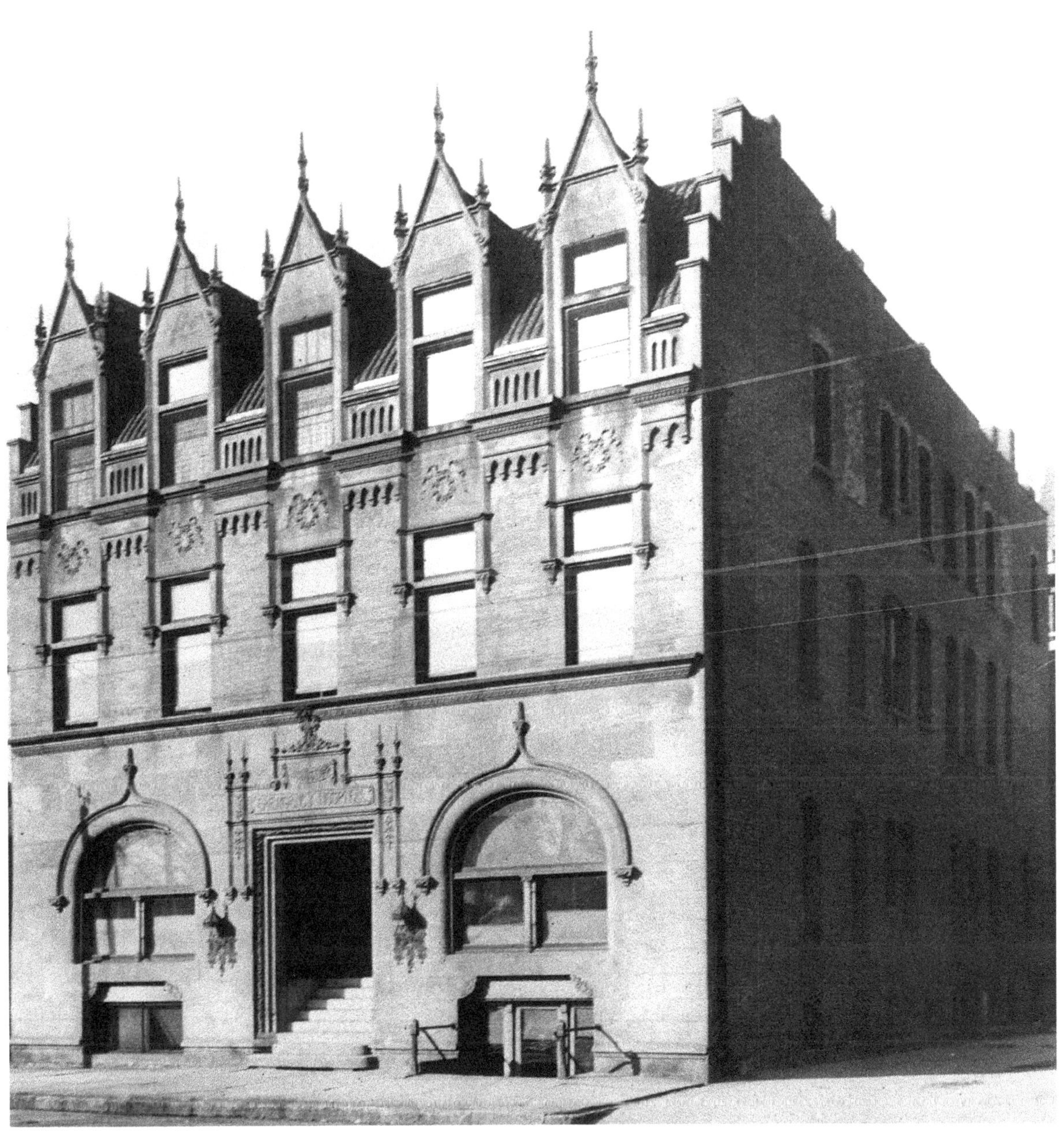

The *Waukesha Scoot,* more formally known as engine #212 for the Chicago, Milwaukee, St. Paul Railway, idles in front of Milwaukee's Union Depot in 1894. At this time, Waukesha was a small suburb of the growing city. Railroad transportation was essential to these outlying areas to support the farming communities that existed at that time.

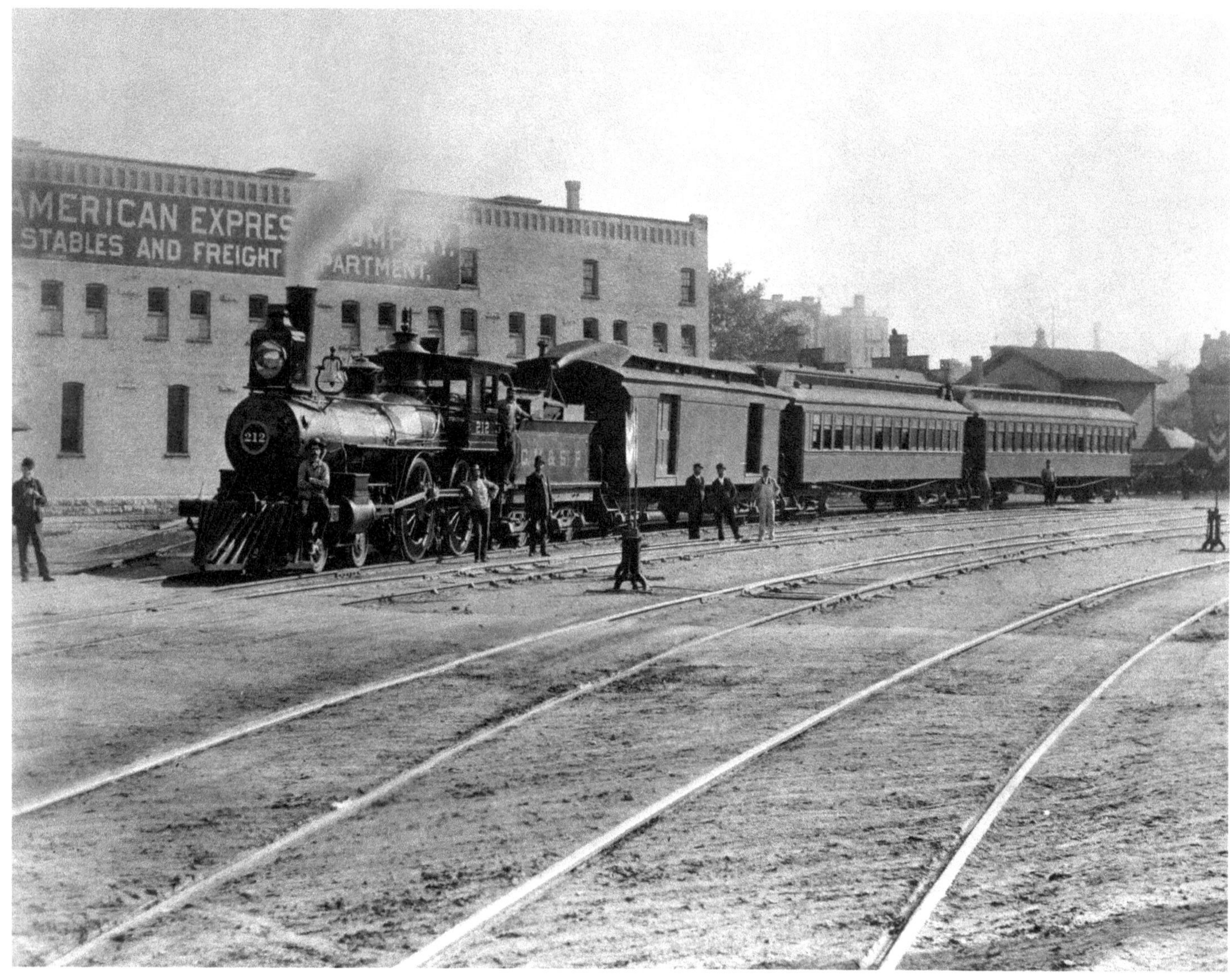

Cyrus McCormick, the inventor of the reaper, started McCormick Harvesting Company in 1847. Its continuing success was due at least in part to the large amounts of grain transported through the city. After McCormick's death in 1884, his son took over the business, merging in 1902 with four other companies to become the International Harvester Co.

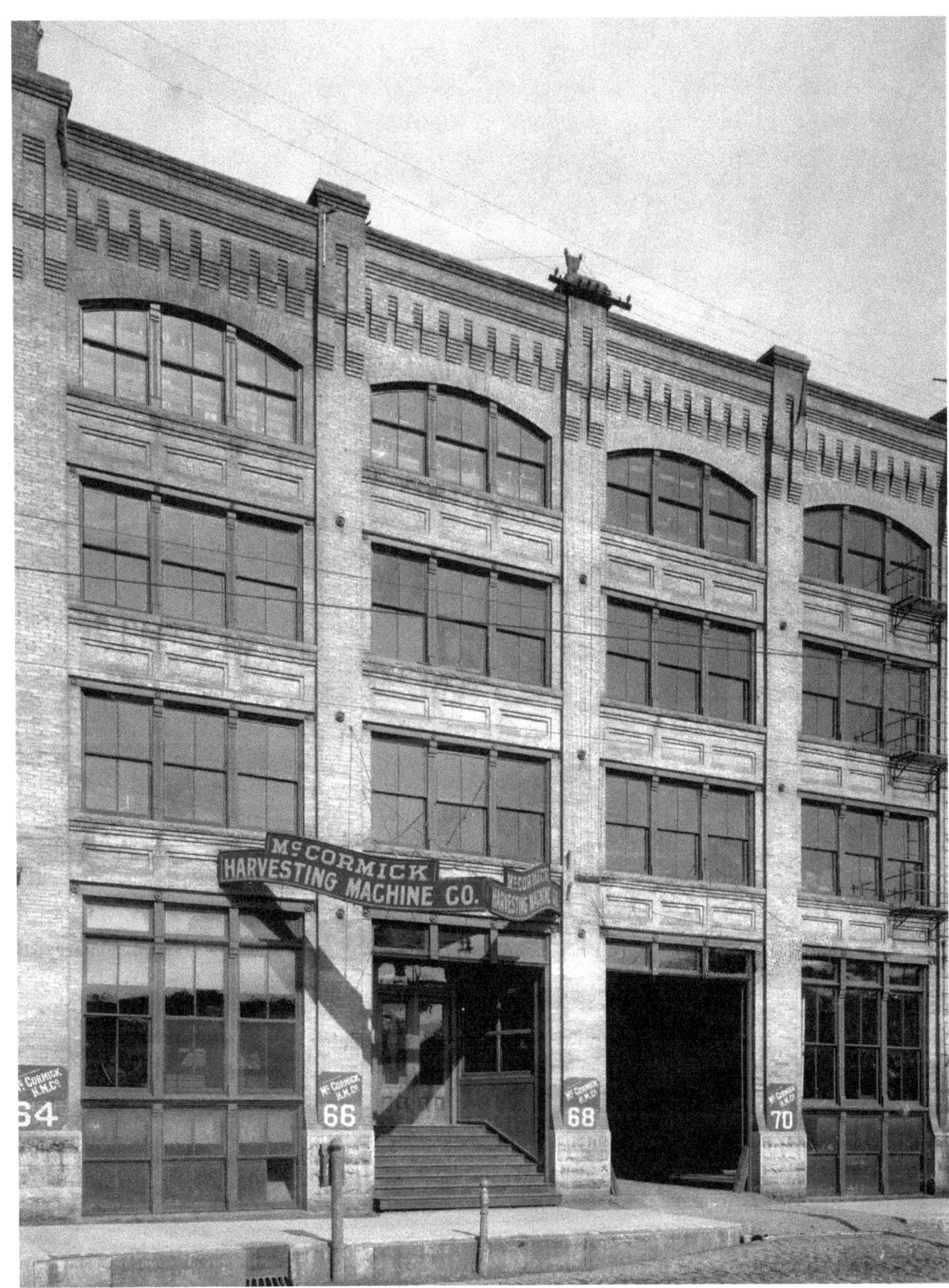

In 1896 creating medicine was not an easy task. These young men are using pharmaceutical equipment to create Dr. Brown's Cough Balsam. The knowledgeable pharmacist could concoct a medication for almost any illness. Remedies such as ipecac, morphine, and ethyl ether and chloroform were popular.

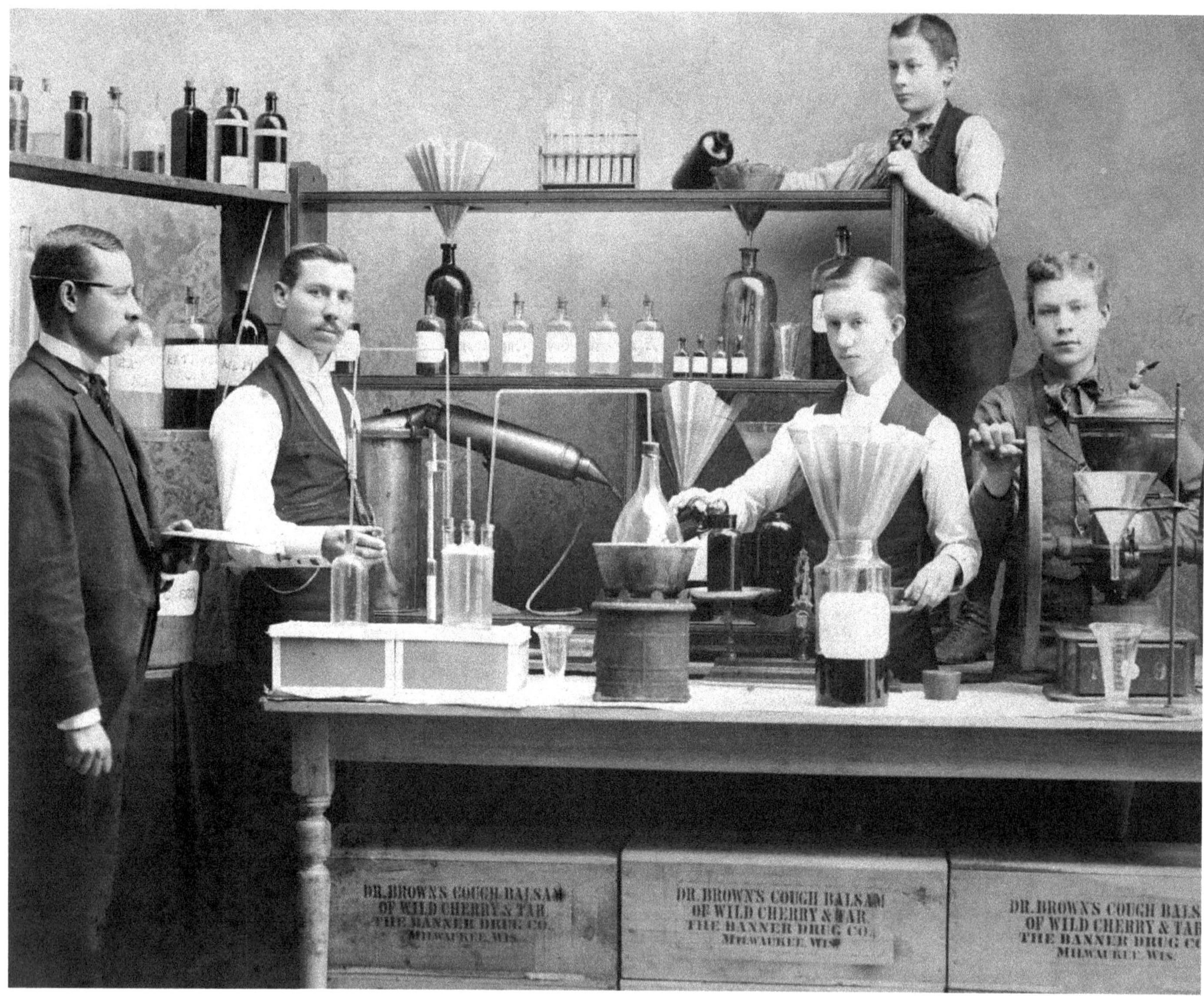

Ice skaters enjoy the Milwaukee River in 1897. Cold Wisconsin winters often froze the river to thicknesses safe for skating. At that time skaters had the run of the frozen river; today this is no longer true.

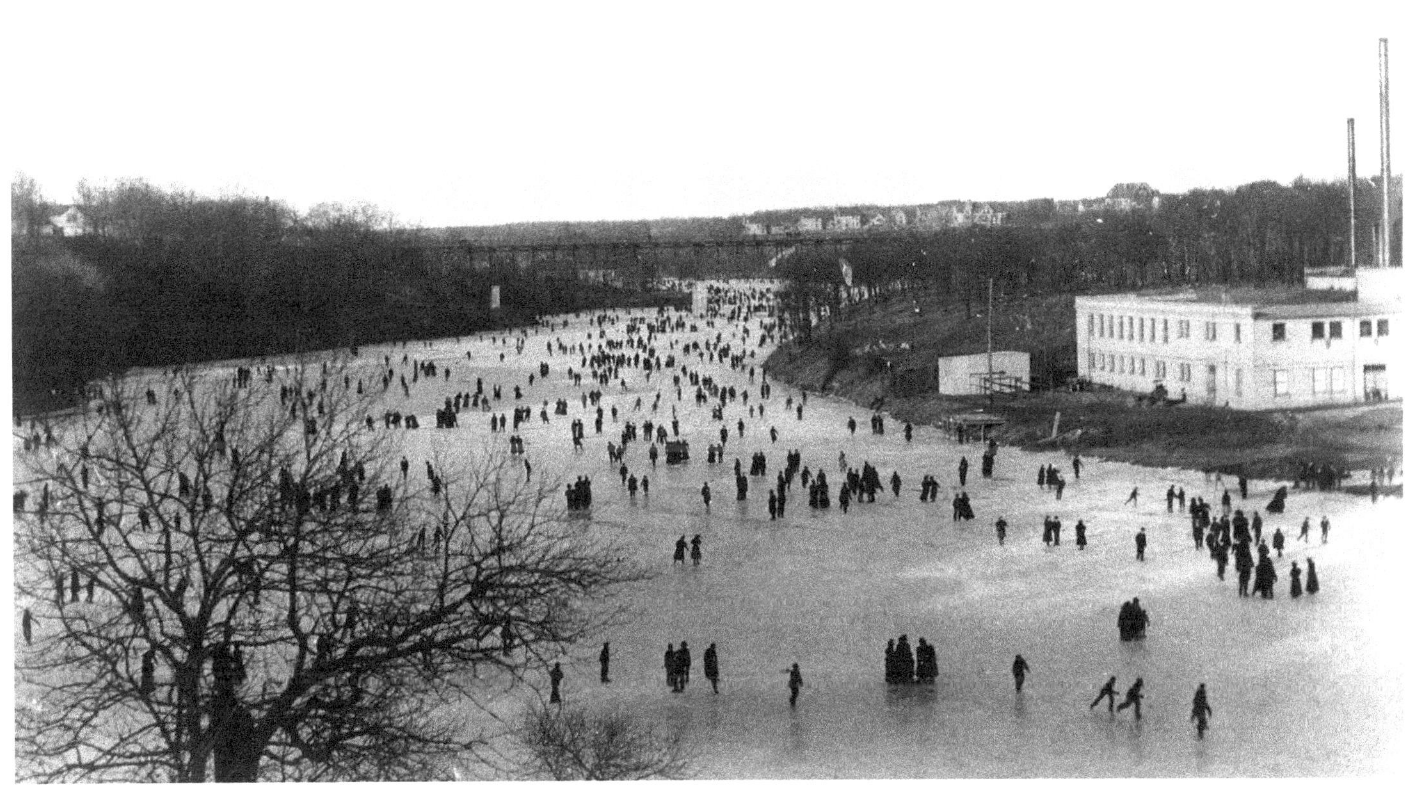

Richard Laacke was once in the business of sign hanging. In 1897, at a mere 18 years of age, he went into business for himself. It was not until 1948 that the R. Laacke Co. joined with the Joy Brothers Co. to form what is known as Laacke and Joys, a popular outdoor sporting goods shop located at 1433 N. Water Street.

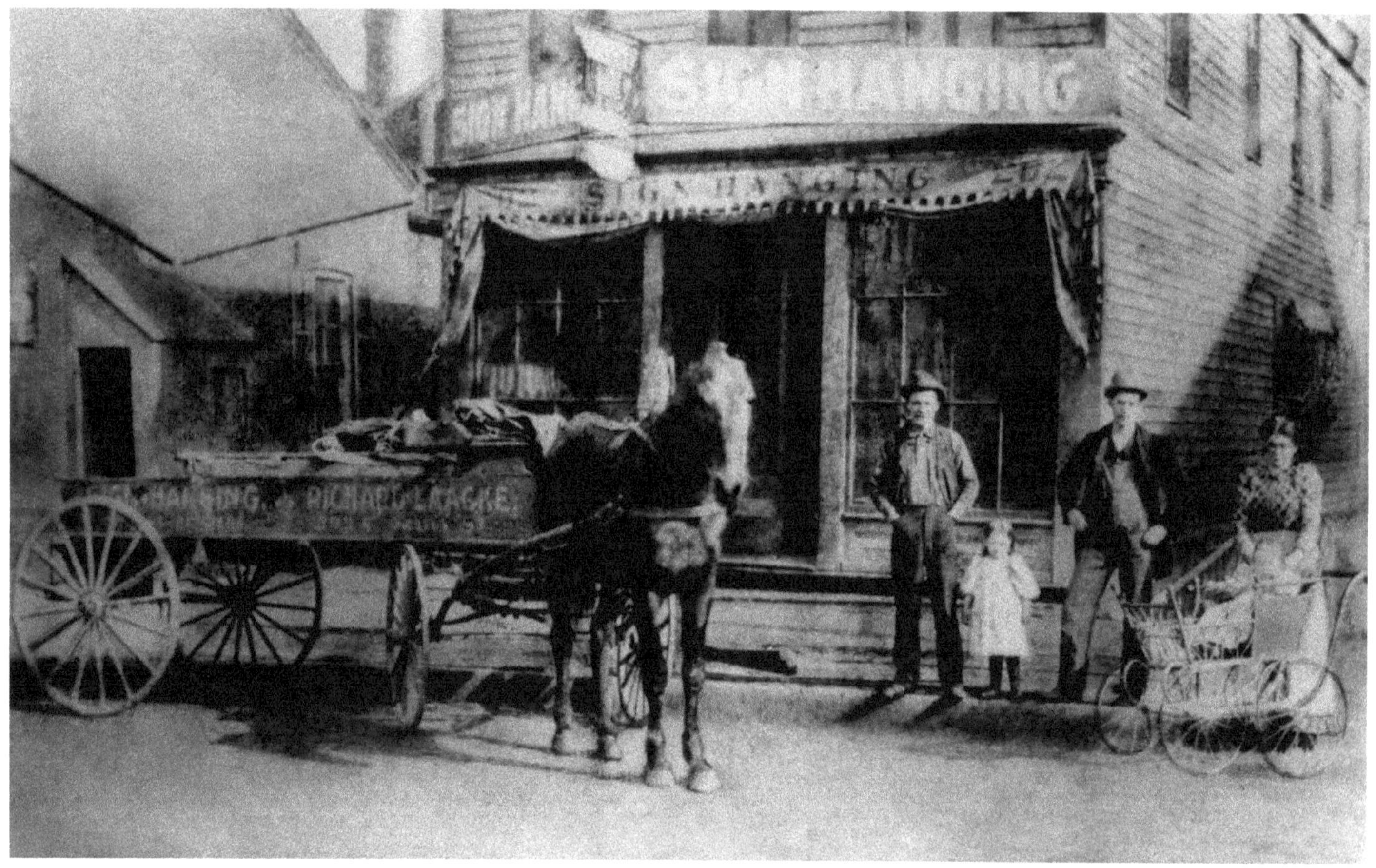

An annual street fair held around the turn of the century, the Jahrmarkt drew people of all ages. It offered something for everyone, including shops, food, drink, and rides. It was located at what is now 5th and National Avenue.

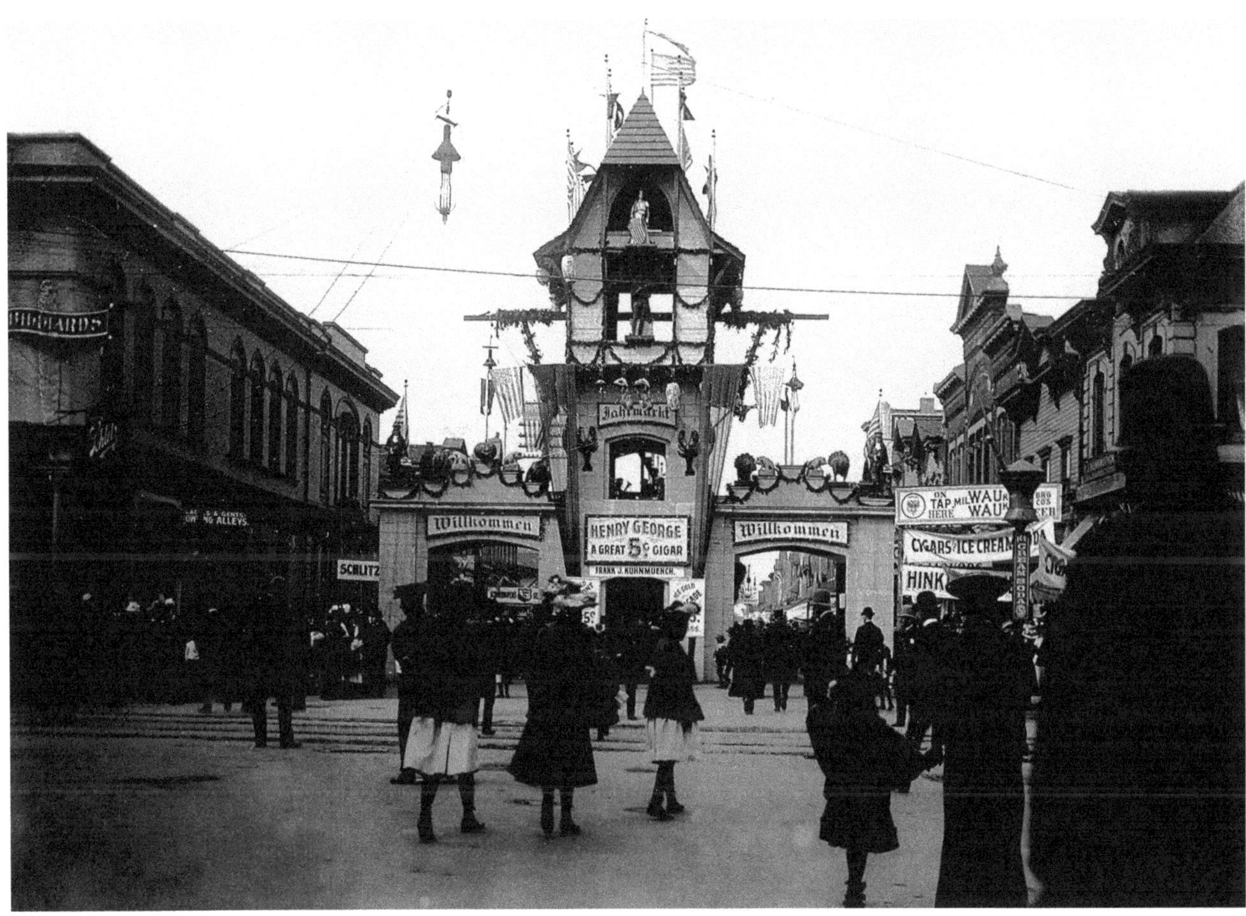

This steam fire engine from the Milwaukee Fire Company #2, drawn by horses, was a common sight at the turn of the century. Unfortunately the burning building would often be closer to rubble by the time the engine arrived.

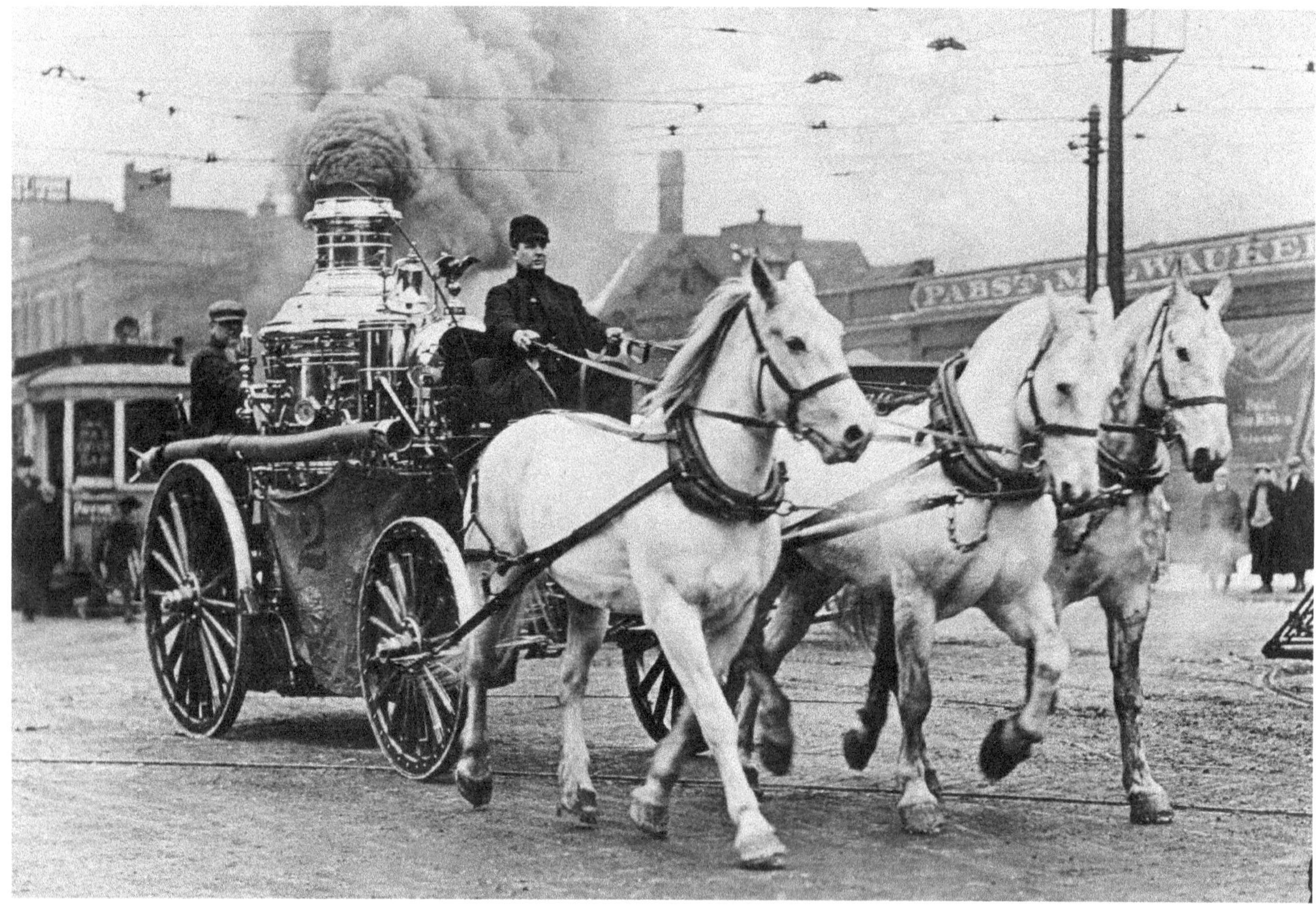

Captains of Industry

(1900–1917)

At the turn of the century, the paving of Milwaukee's muddy streets was still a dream, but businesses like Pfister and Vogel, Pabst Brewing, and E. P. Allis Works flourished. Industry and manufacturing were now at the heart of the city's economy. With industry come labor disputes, and Milwaukee was no exception. From the Bay View Tragedy in 1886, in which seven people died, to strikes by streetcar employees, the workers of Milwaukee intended to be heard. They fought for the eight-hour workday and fair wages. The labor disputes would continue—labor unions were plentiful and very active and they were not afraid to strike.

The administration of Mayor David Rose, noted for corruption, gave way to reform in the guise of Emil Seidel, elected in 1910 as the nation's first socialist mayor of a leading United States city. Mayor Seidel established the city parks system, the public works department, and the fire and police commissions, and closed the brothels that the Rose administration had permitted to operate. Seidel also employed, for a time, the poet Carl Sandburg. In 1912, he would run with Eugene Debs on the Socialist ticket in a bid for the White House. With Seidel and likeminded successors at the helm of city government, and given the continuing influence of organized labor, Milwaukee would become famous as the hub of the socialist movement.

On the national front, Teddy Roosevelt escaped an attempt at assassination during his campaign visit in 1912. The bullet, slowed by items in the former president's shirt pocket, including a speech, stopped short of delivering a lethal wound. The former president, determined to press on, gave his speech the same evening in blood-stained vest.

City Hall, when completed in 1895, had become the third-tallest structure in the nation, rising handsomely over the city. In 2007 the landmark structure is slated for renovation.

Harley-Davidson, founded in 1903, was begun in 1901 in the Davidson garage. A total of three motorcycles were built the first year. By 1917, interest in the vehicle had grown considerably. As the nation entered World War I, Harley-Davidson was asked to build vehicles for the war effort, completing 20,000 of the machines by war's end.

Standing outside their place of employment, these nurses are probably members of the Red Cross Association of Wisconsin, an organization that later became the Milwaukee Chapter of the Red Cross. Nursing standards around the turn of the century required nurses to be mentally strong, soft-spoken, well-mannered, and accustomed to all manner of cantankerous patients.

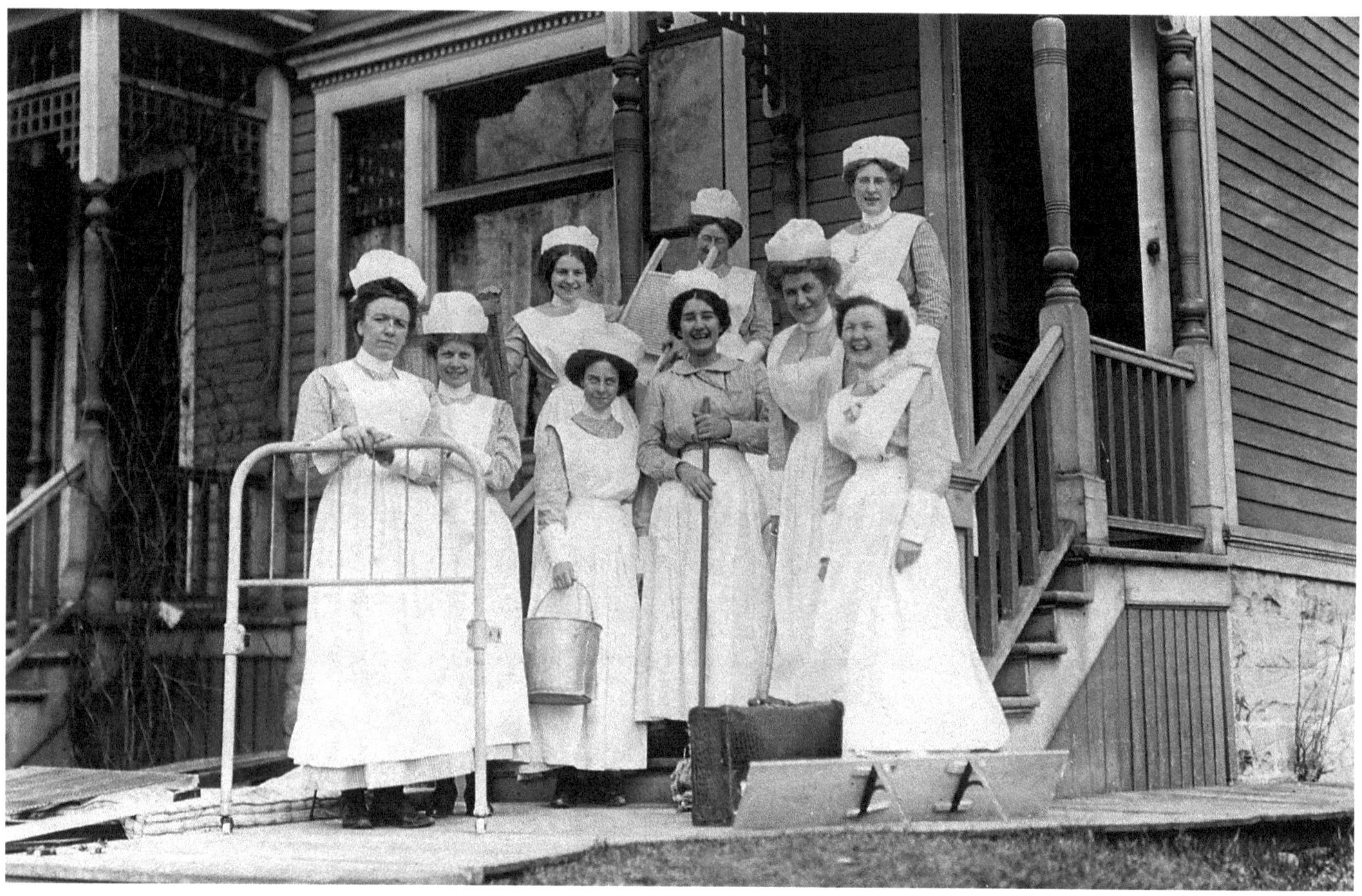

The turn of the century brought many things to Milwaukee, paved streets not among them. The muddy intersection of Wisconsin and Milwaukee streets was hardly navigable by horse-drawn carts, still less by pedestrians, in the early 1900s.

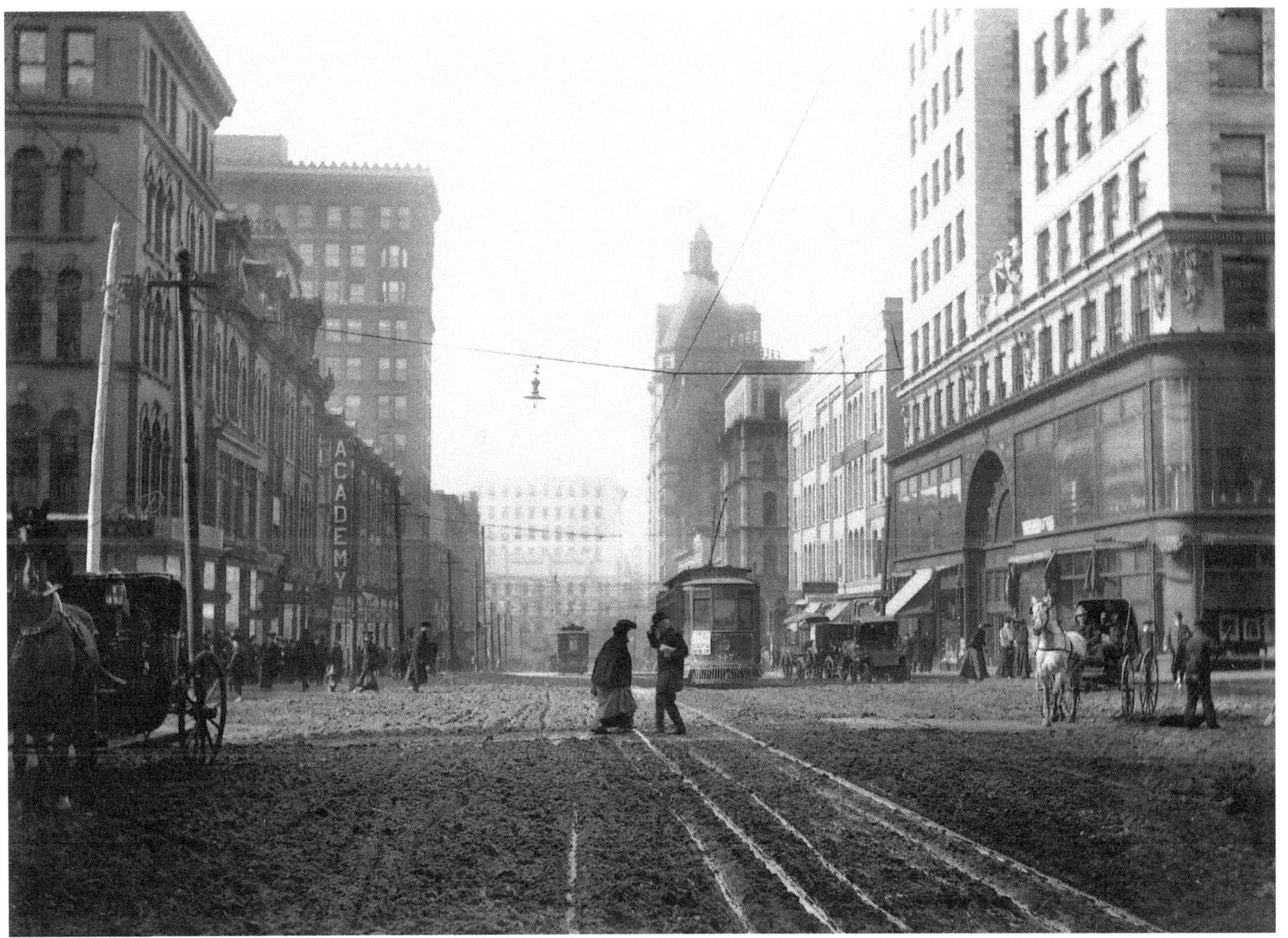

These three buildings owned by Gerber and Son undertakers and embalmers and A. J. Best Livery and Stable were once located on what is now Juneau Avenue. Best would care for the horses that brought hearses to Gerber and Son funeral homes. Gerber would later move his business out to Wauwatosa and merge with another funeral home, Schmidt and Bartelt, where it resides today, although "Gerber" has been dropped from the company name.

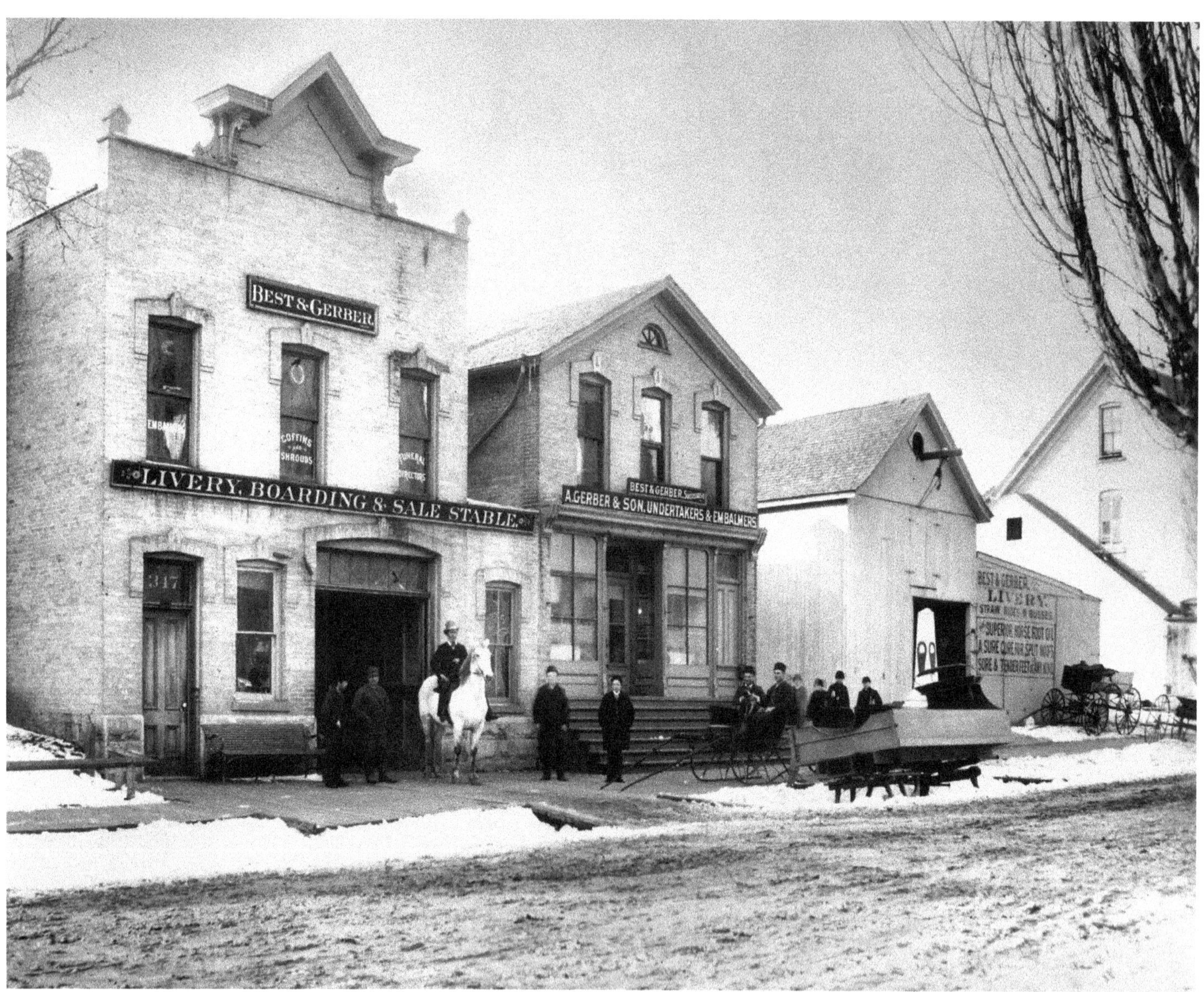

Men and children spend the day fishing on the breakwater at the turn of the century.
The North Point Water Tower can be seen in the far right background.

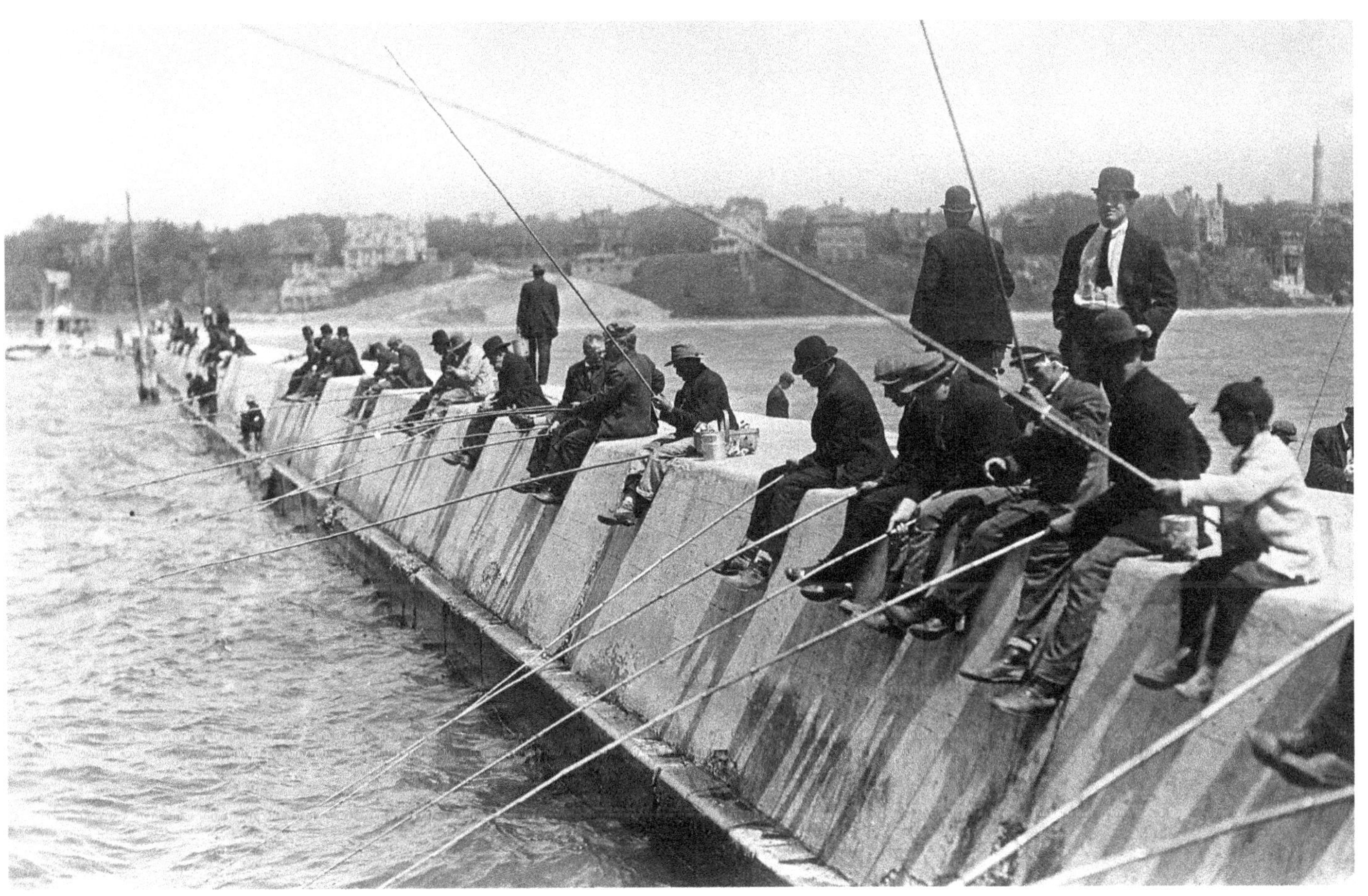

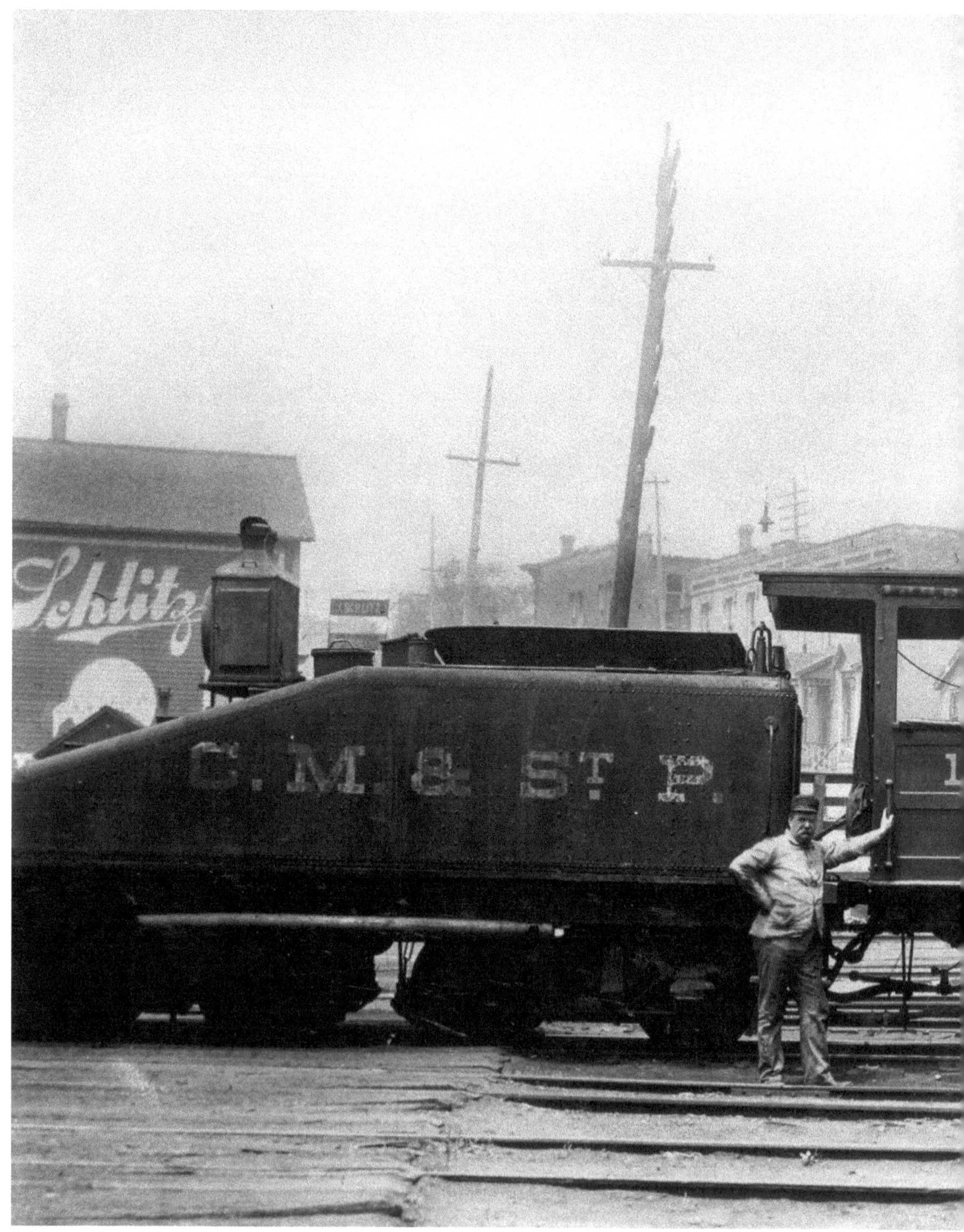
Schlitz
C.M.& ST P.

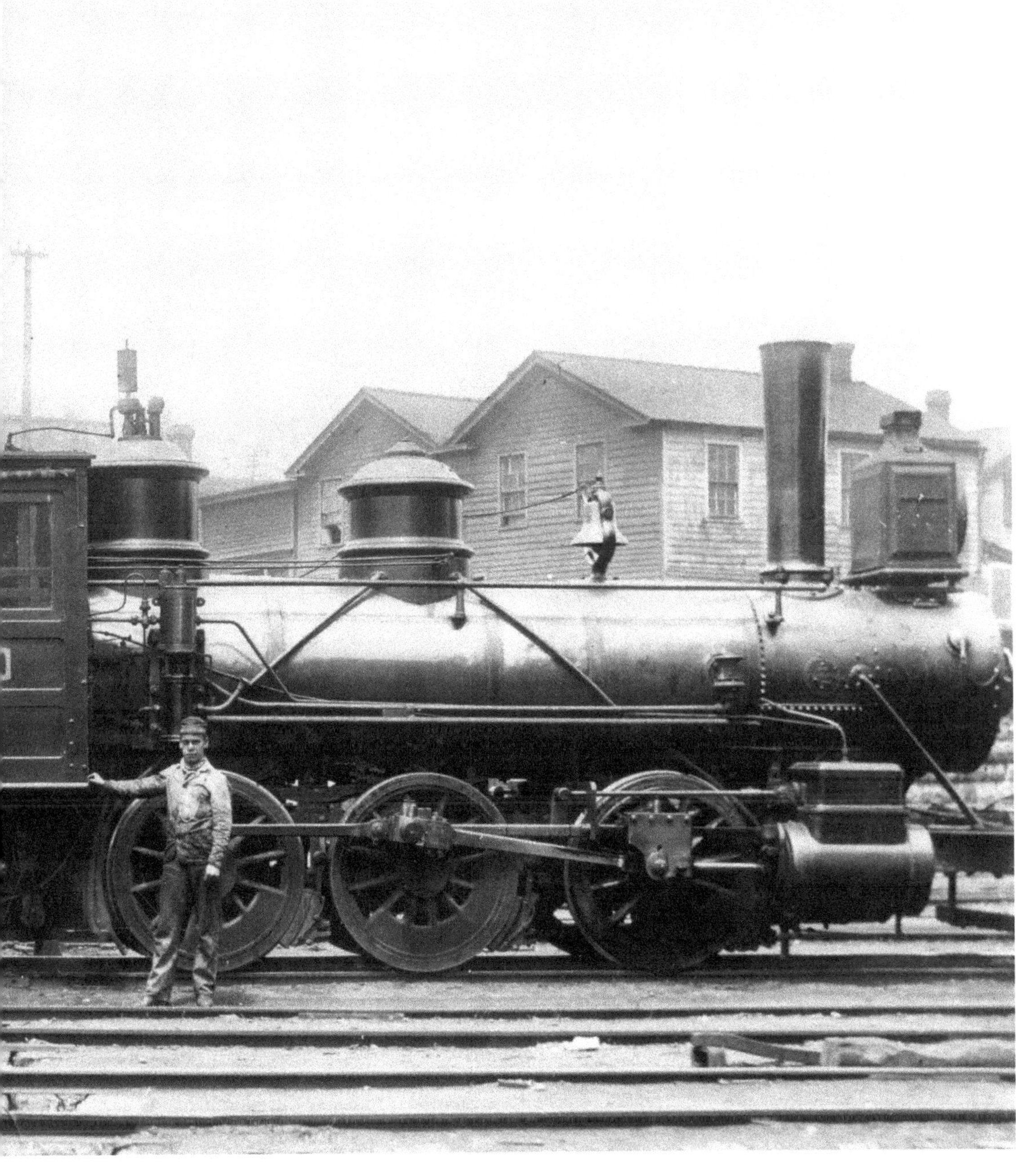

This Chicago Milwaukee & St. Paul engine was number 1100 until it was scrapped in 1917. The Milwaukee Road, as it was called, was one of the primary railroads in the Midwest, with more than 10,000 miles of track by 1919.

These girls appreciate the late afternoon sunshine as they jump rope on a Milwaukee street. Their clothes are fairly typical of those worn by children near the turn of the century.

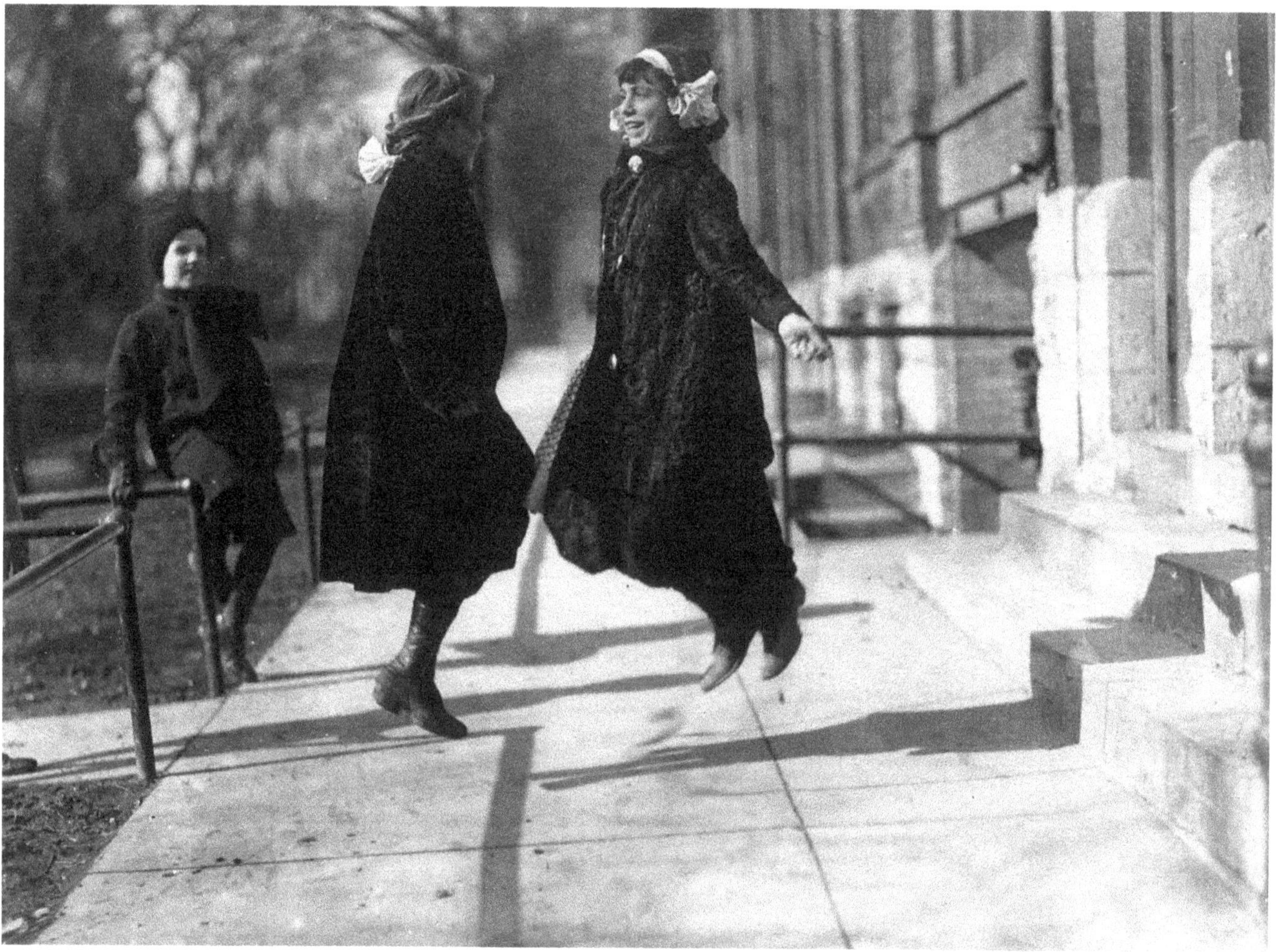

The Otto Ganhs bakery and confectionery was located at 1248 W. Center in 1902. Watching the staff pose somewhat awkwardly for this photograph, passersby were treated to the smell of bread, cake, and cookies wafting out the door. Each of Milwaukee's neighborhoods had a bakery similar to that of Otto Ganhs within blocks of residents' homes.

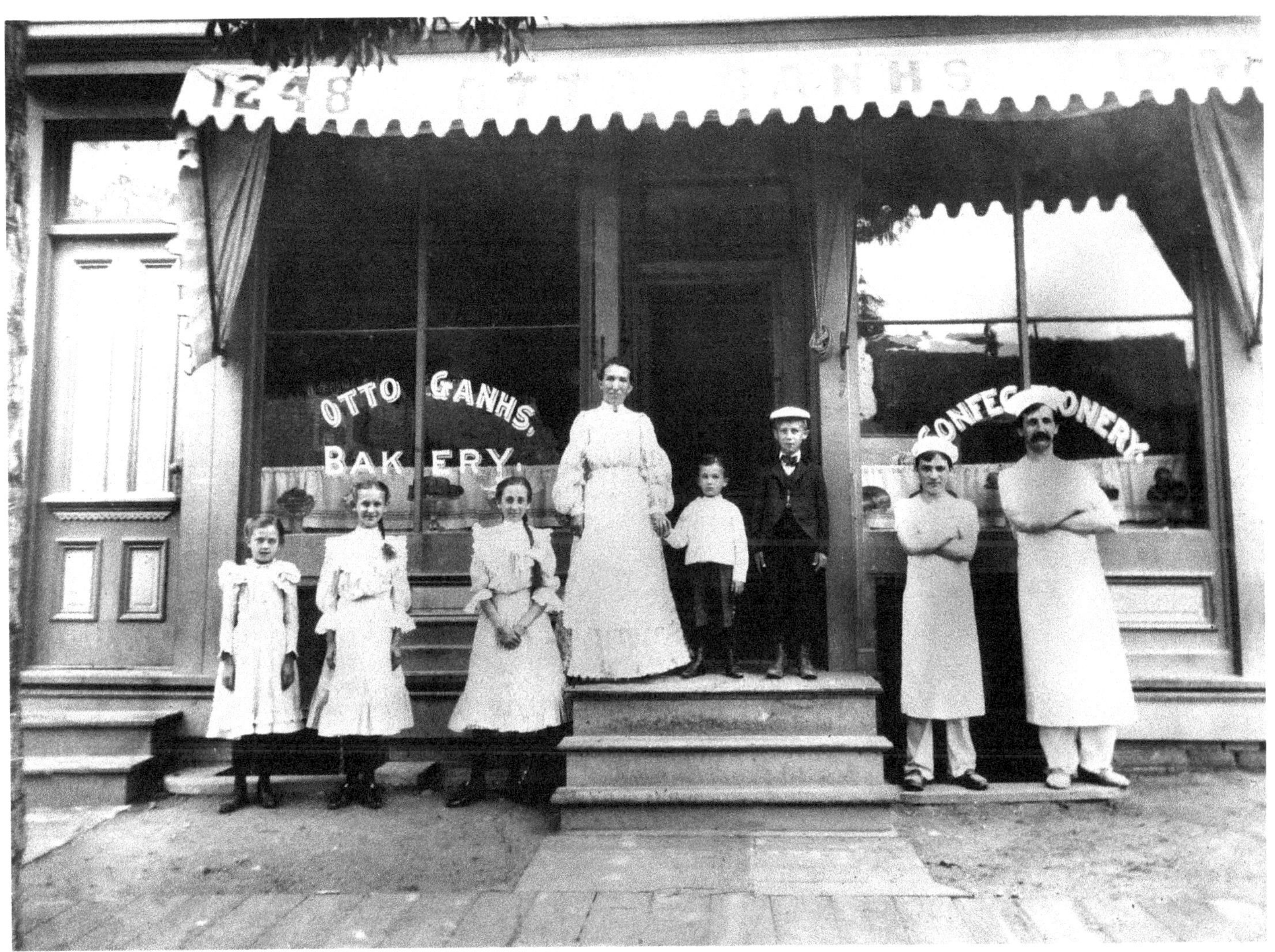

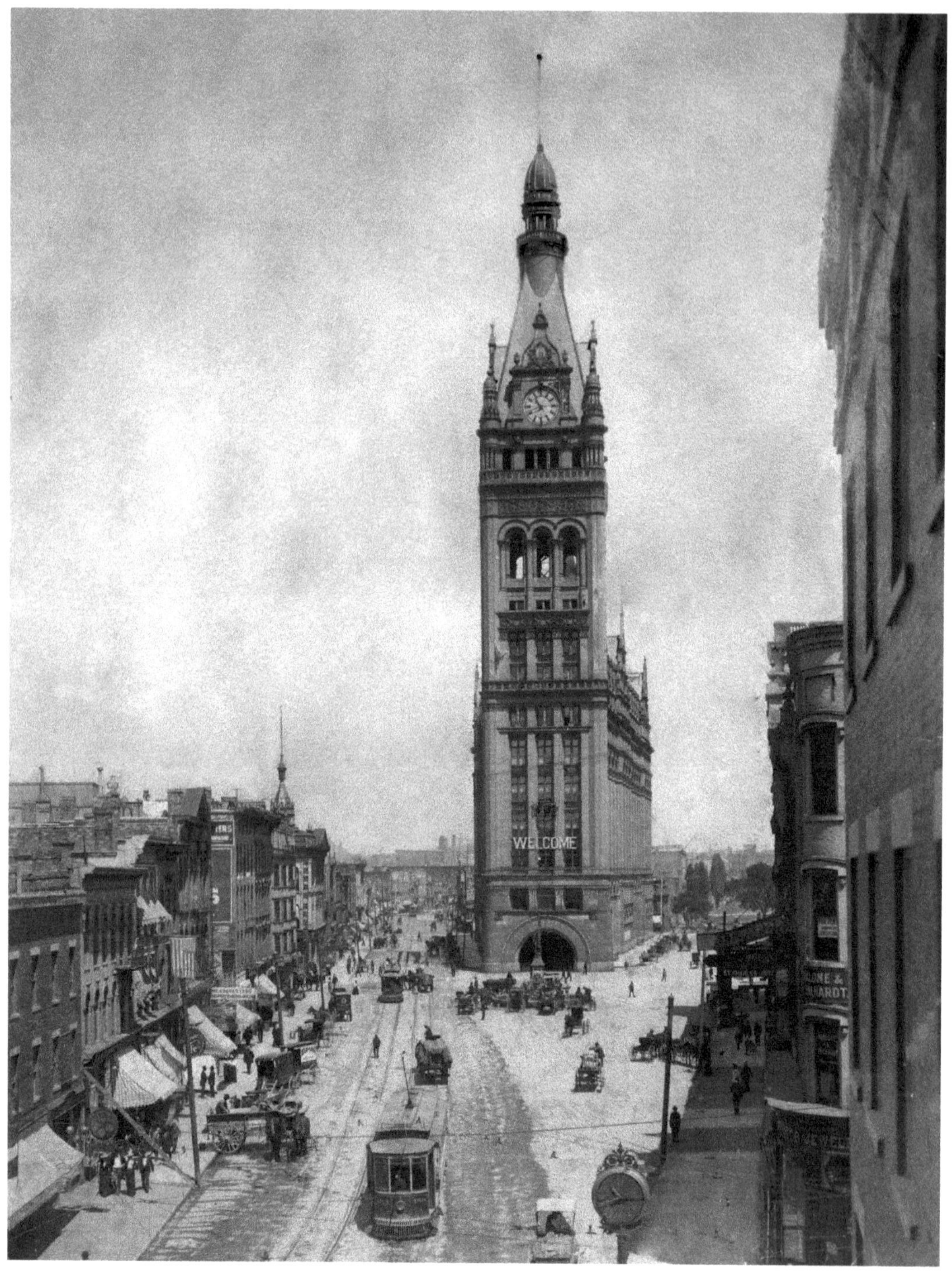

Milwaukee's City Hall was constructed between 1894 and 1895 and has served as the city hall for Milwaukee ever since. The building was placed on an entire block bordered by Wells Street, Market Street, Kilbourn Avenue, and Water Street. In 1904 it was the tallest building in Milwaukee. It was added to the National Register of Historic Places in 1973 and in 2007 is slated for extensive renovations.

Milwaukeeans panicked when they were informed in 1905 that the president of the 1st National Bank had been arrested for embezzling 1.6 million dollars. As depositors feared for the safety of their money, primary stockholders Charles F. Pfister and Fred Vogel acted quickly, bringing in truckloads of gold and exhibiting it to the public. This act seemed to calm the fears of investors and persuade them that the bank was sound.

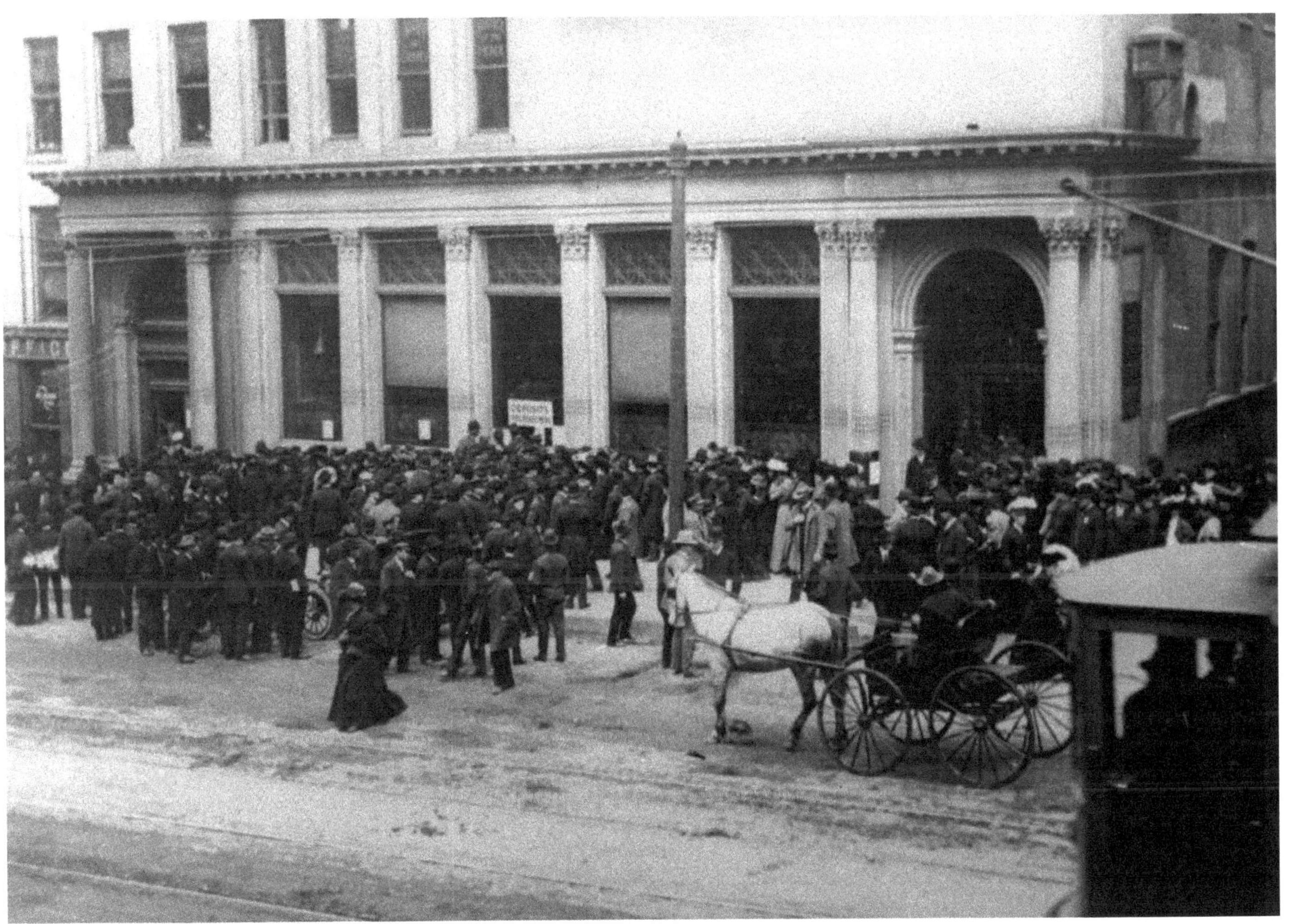

Following Spread: Harley-Davidson started their factory in 1903, but the idea started in 1901 when Harley drew an engine on a bicycle. The company hired their first employee in Milwaukee in 1905. Harley-Davidson is now one of the best-known motorcycle dealers in the world.

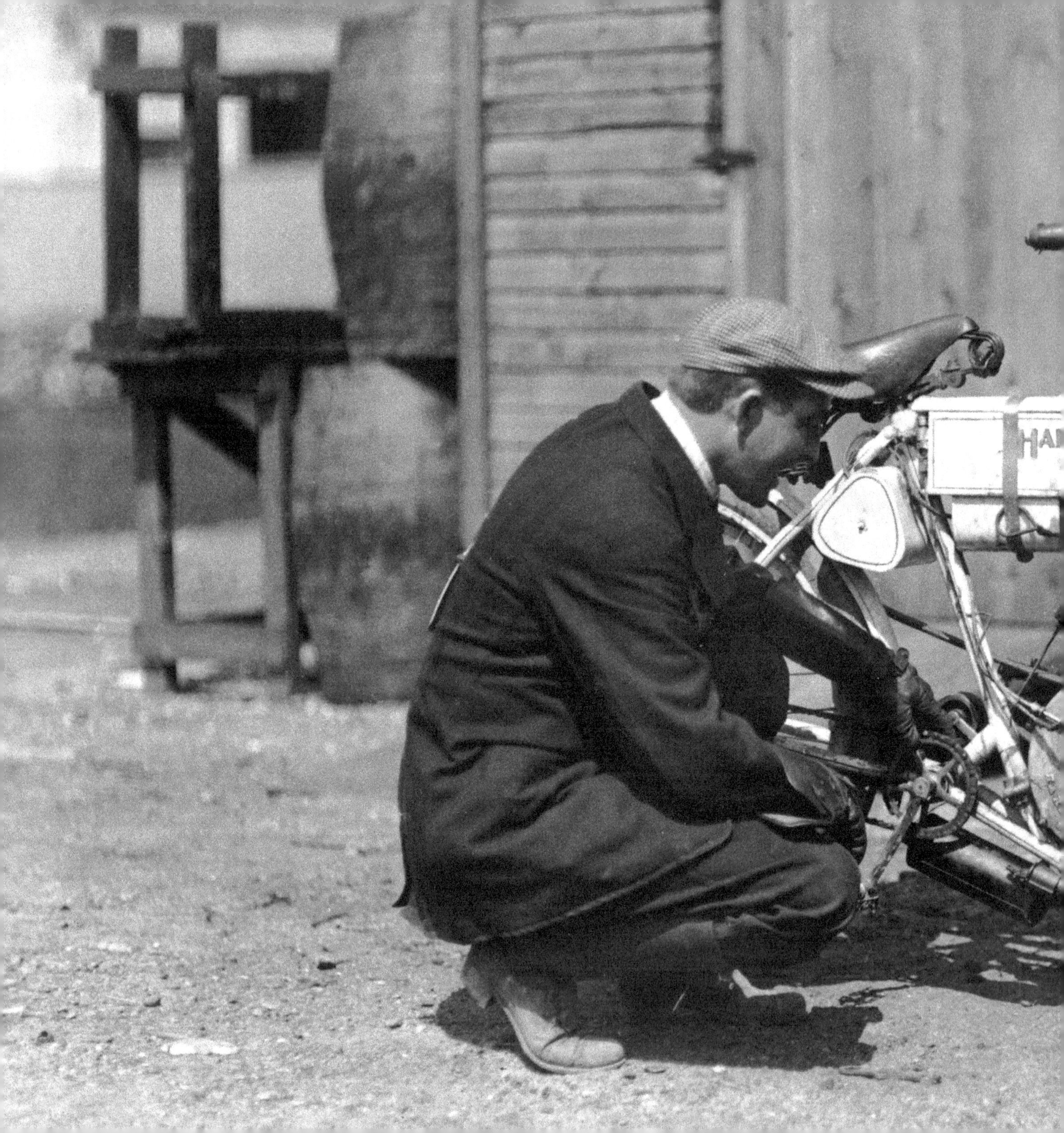

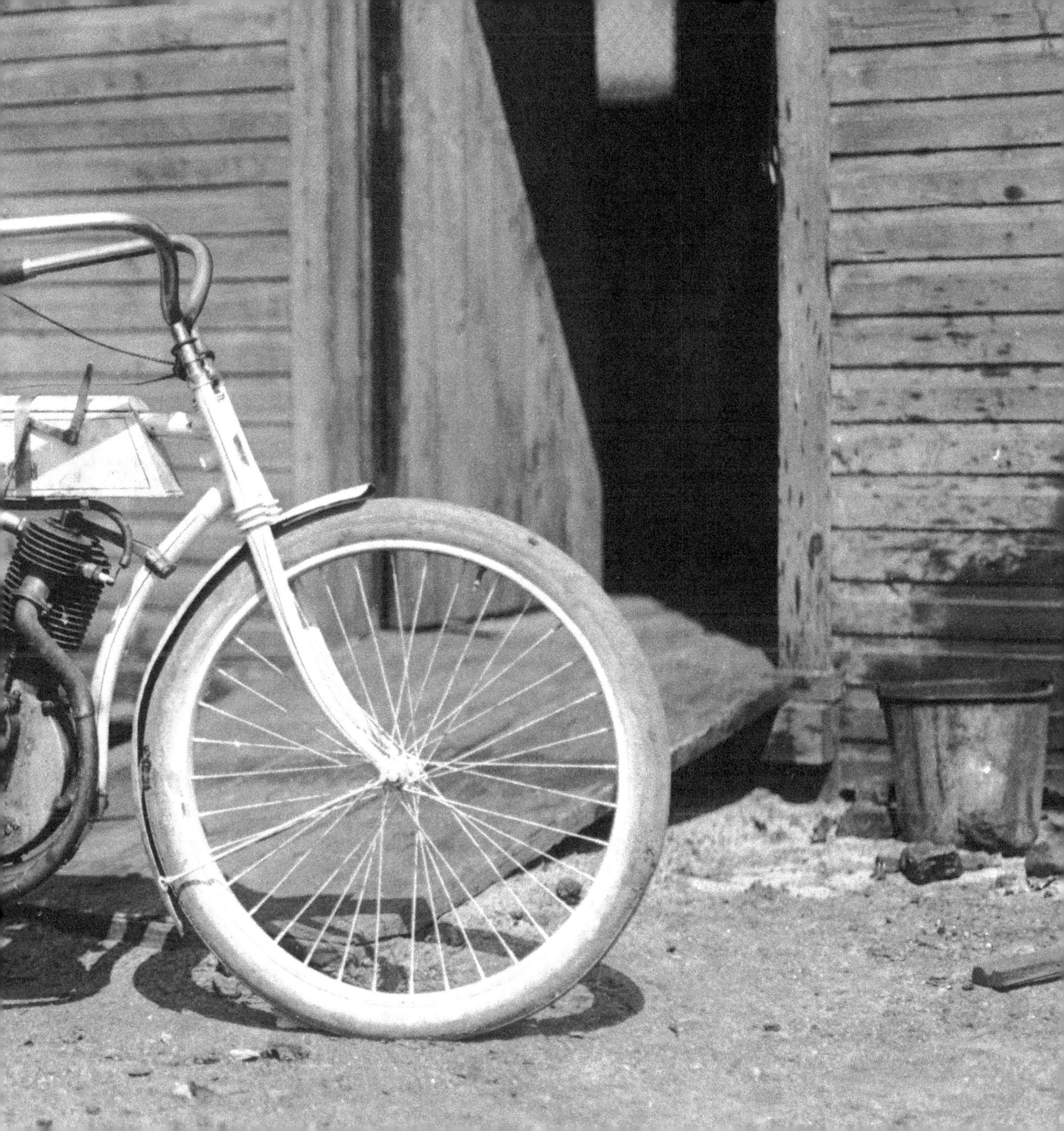

A streetcar is held up by a wagon and horses hauling coal from the Milwaukee Western Fuel Company. Coal was a primary source of fuel in the early 1900s. Most houses were equipped with a coal chute, for storing coal on the premises.

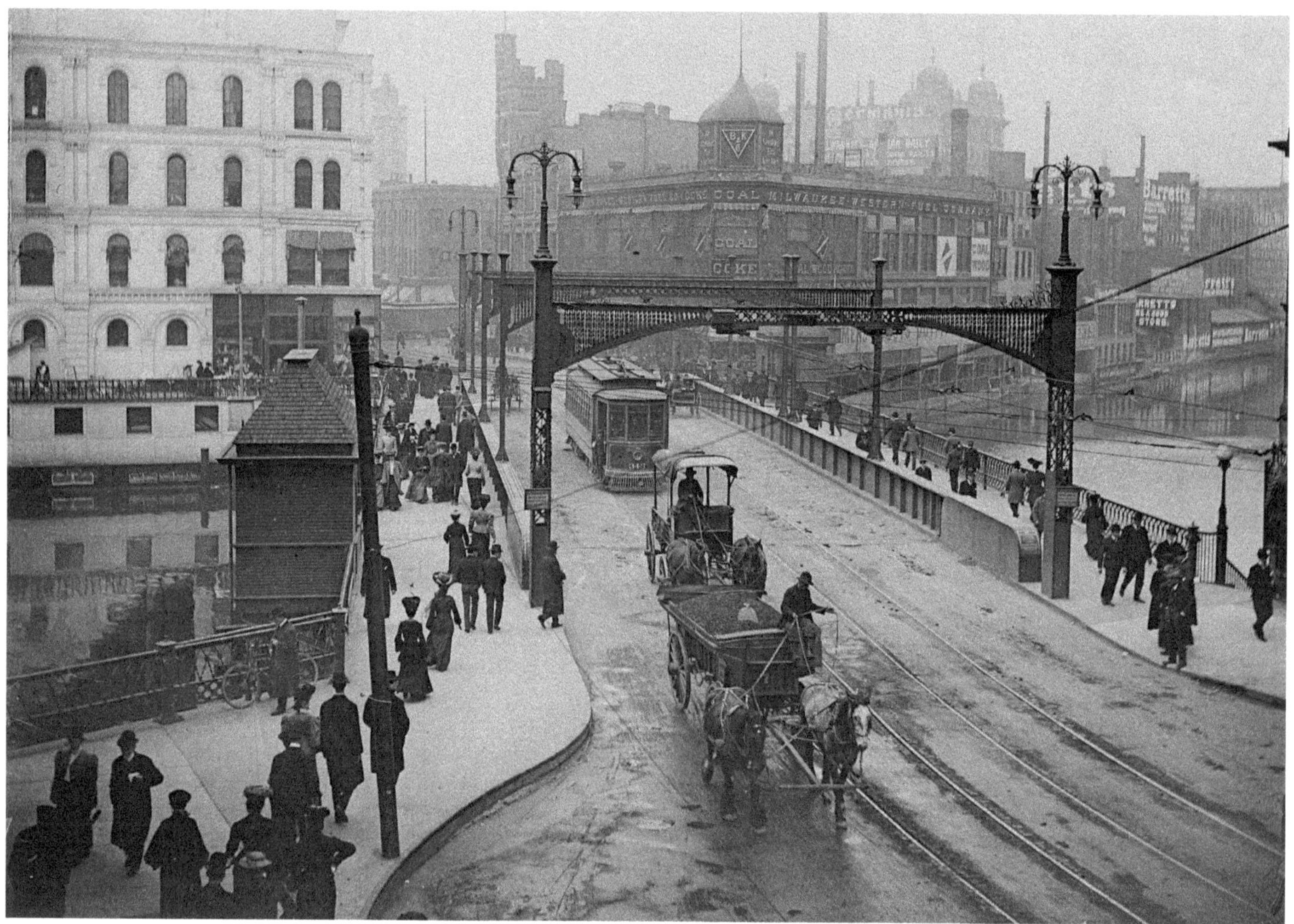

Workers pose for a group shot in 1905, between State Street and Highland Avenue, after paving the street with bricks. The work was arduous and all of it was done by hand. Leftover bricks were stacked on the side of the street to be carried to the next job.

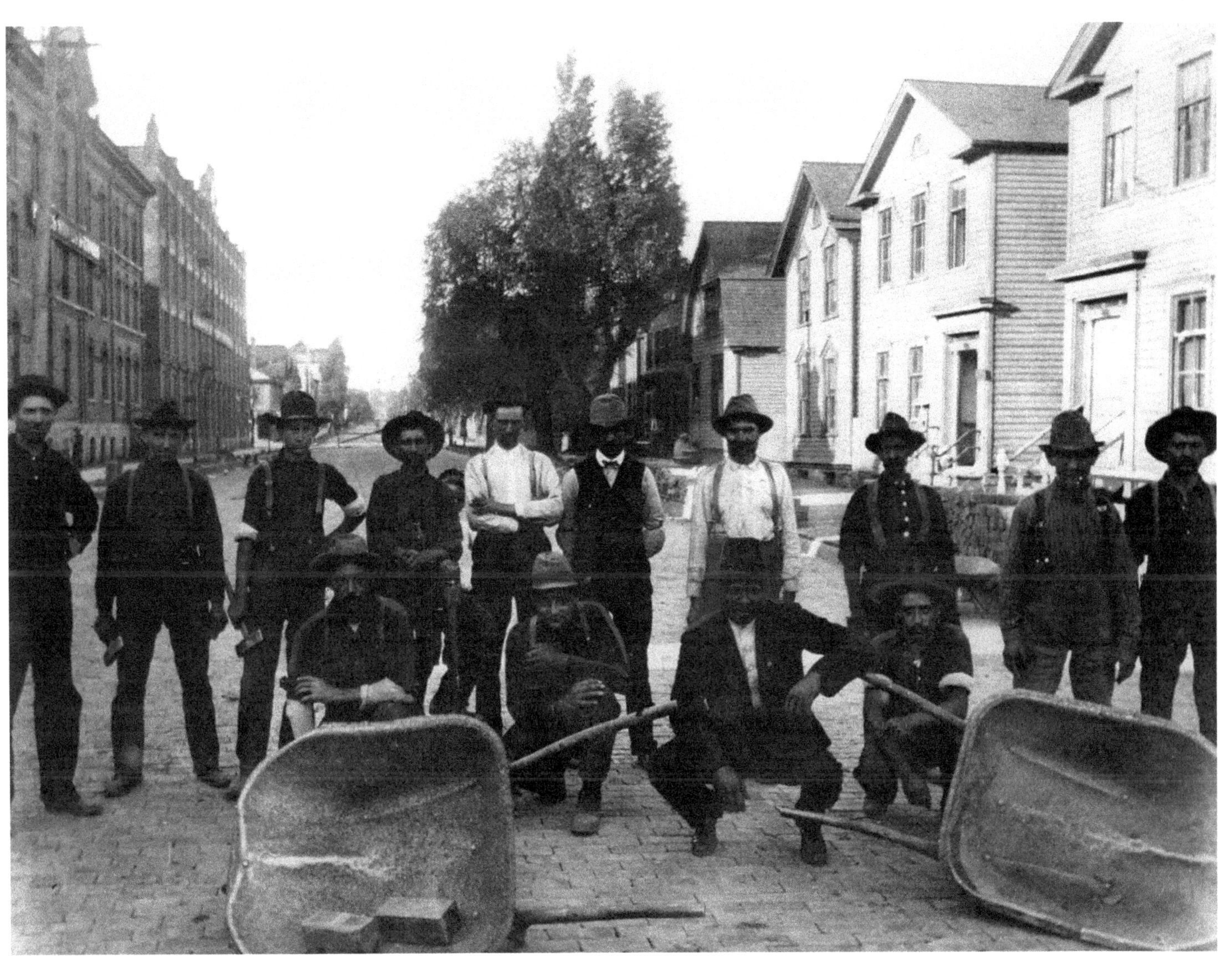

Opening day of the baseball season in 1907 was not met with an overflowing parking lot full of cars. Ball fans boarded streetcars like the one in this photograph to reach Athletic Park (later renamed Borchert Field) and watch their favorite teams play ball.

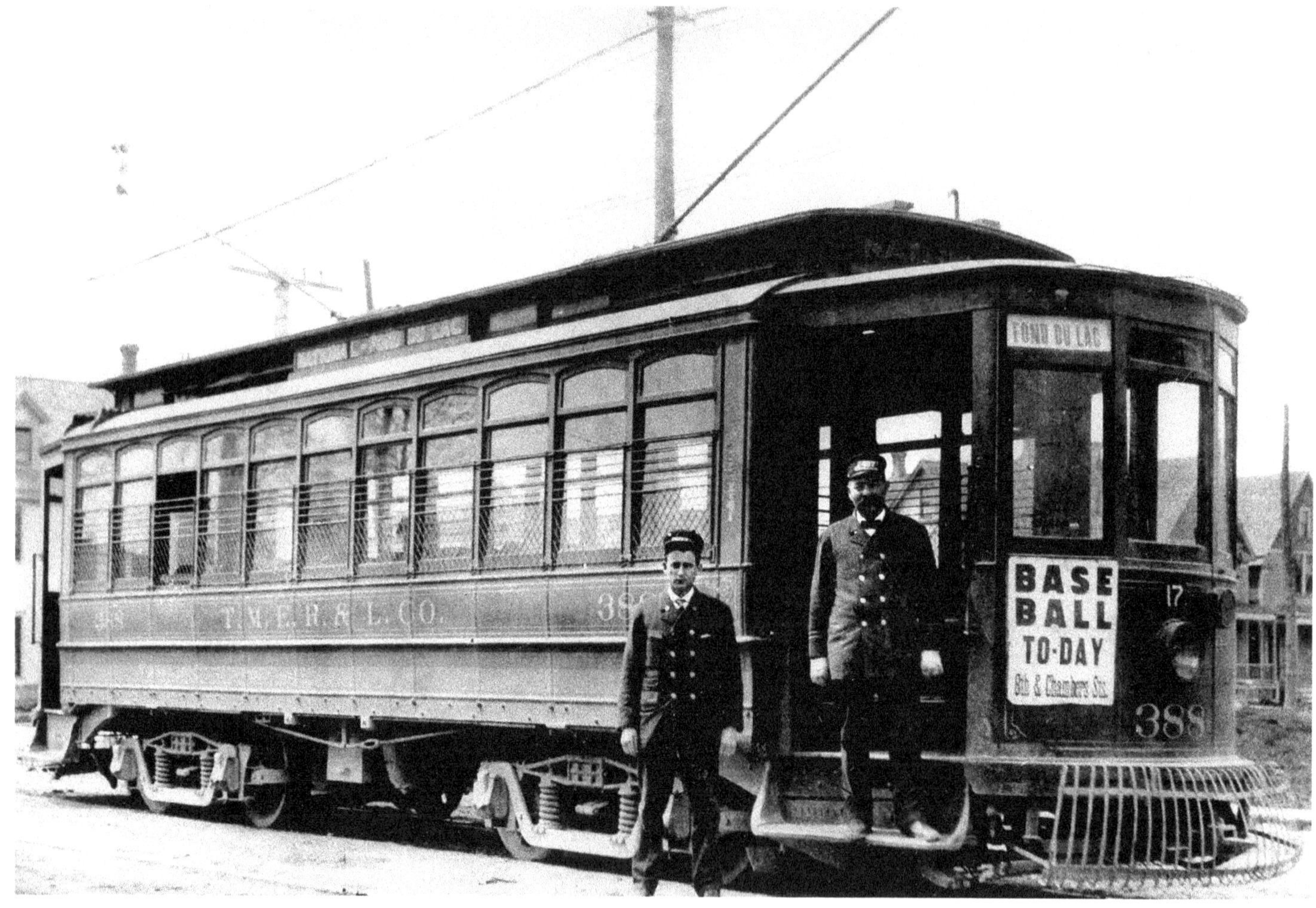

The Milwaukee School of Engineering was founded in 1903. This image, taken in 1907, shows the school's first home on Winnebago Street. As the school grew, the building became too small and M.S.O.E. was forced to move to different quarters. It is now located at 1025 N. Milwaukee.

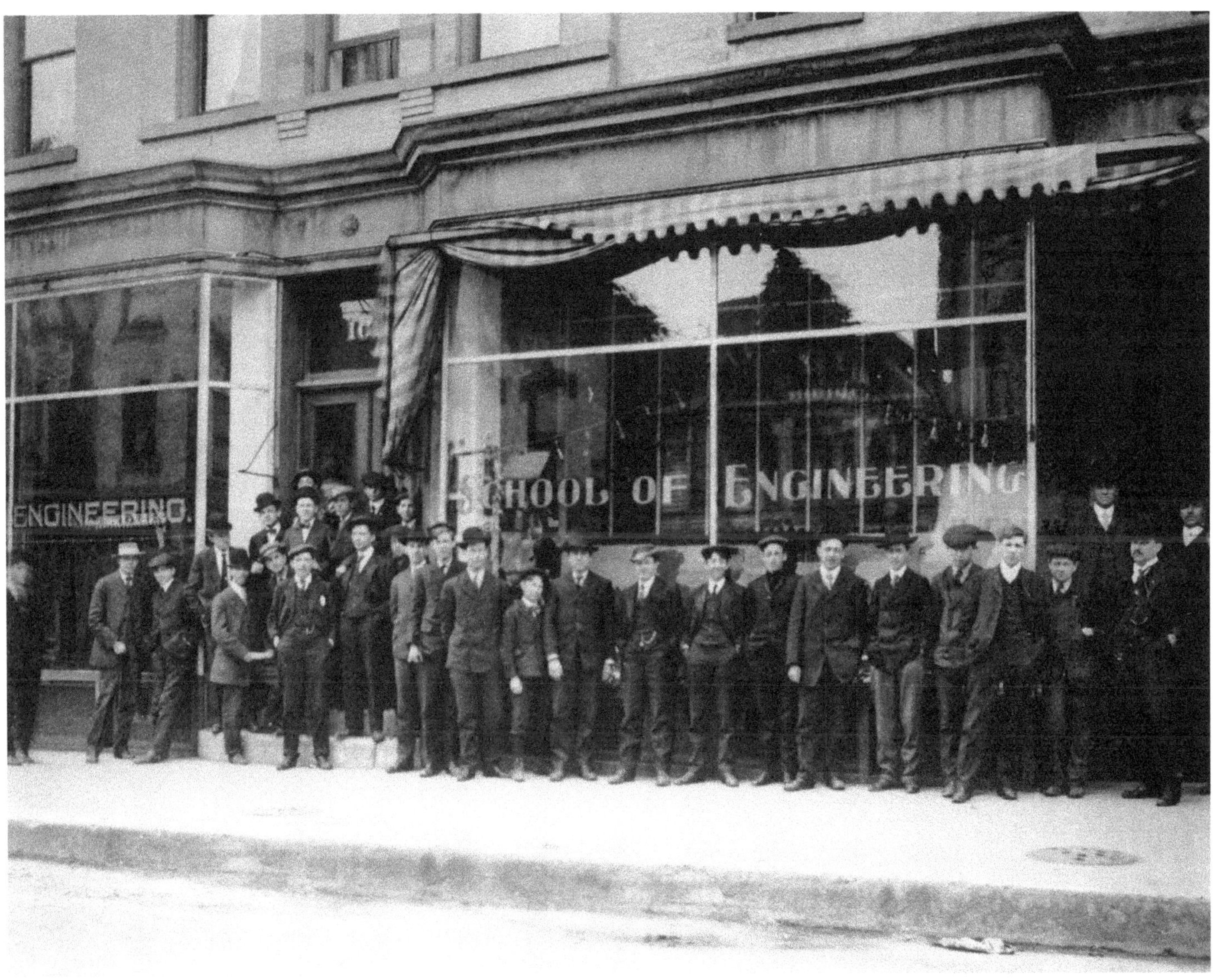

This Corliss steam engine was housed at the International Harvesters Milwaukee Works. Engines like this one were made at Allis Reliance Works. Industries like Allis Reliance and International Harvesters were the core of Milwaukee's manufacturing economy, which also included Harnischfeger, Pfister and Vogel, Allen Bradley, and others.

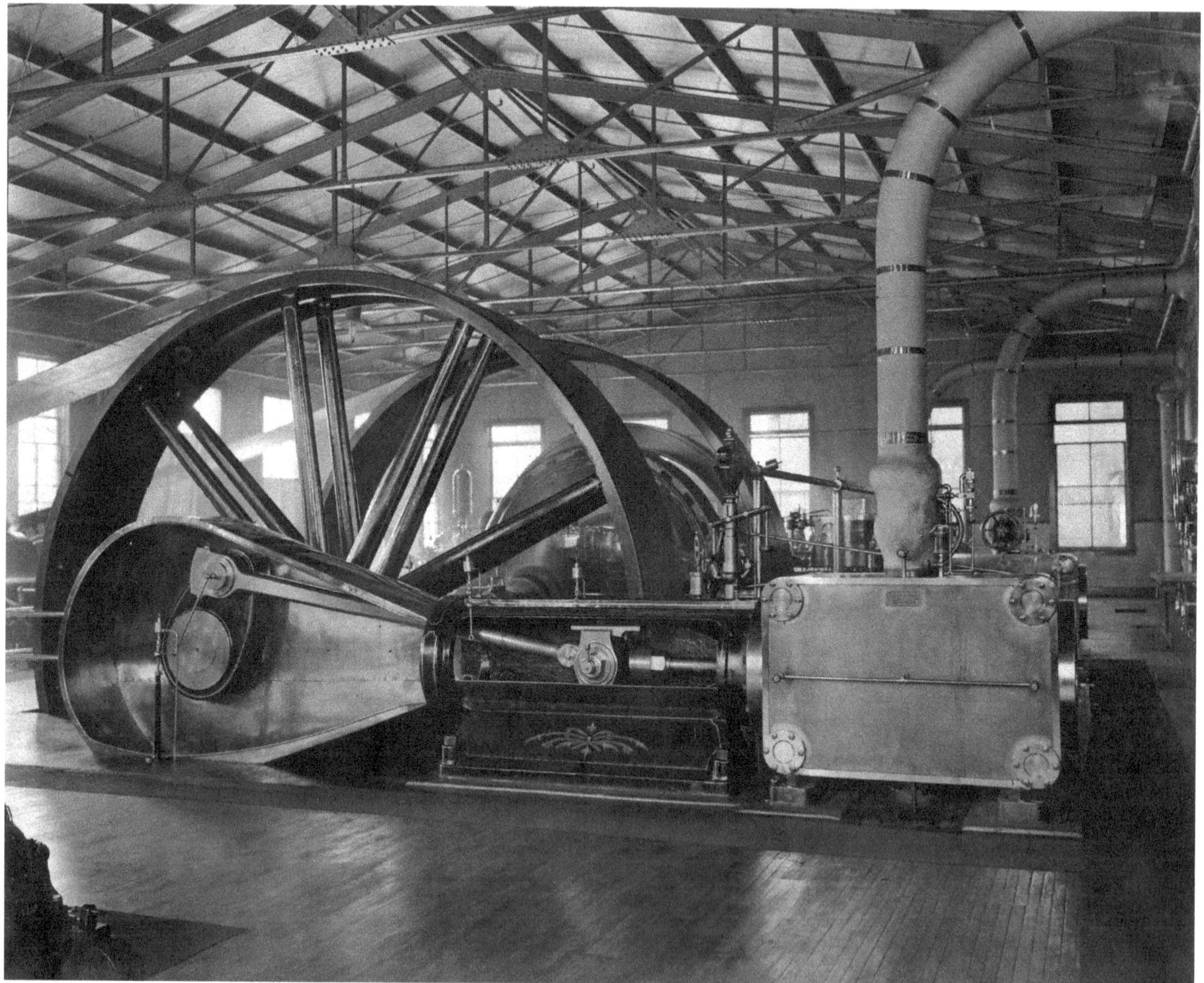

This lively group of people is traveling to the Annual Scottish games in 1909, sponsored by the St. Andrew's society. Cultural celebrations like this one are still very common around Milwaukee, particularly in the summertime.

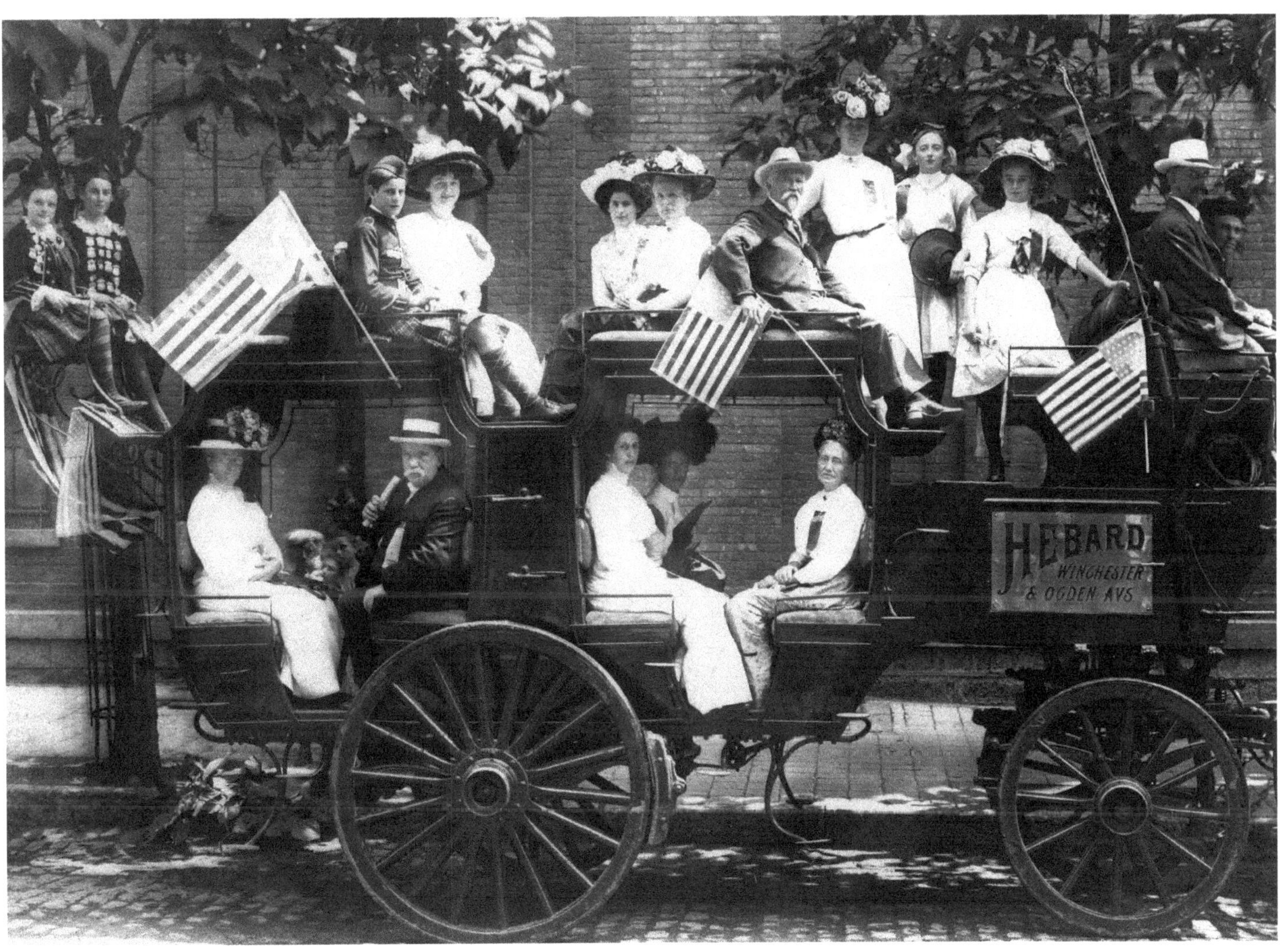

These houses and the sandlot that is there with them sit at the edge of one of Milwaukee's many industrial areas. Rows of well-built houses can be seen in the background. Taken in 1909, this photograph shows boys playing baseball in their spare time.

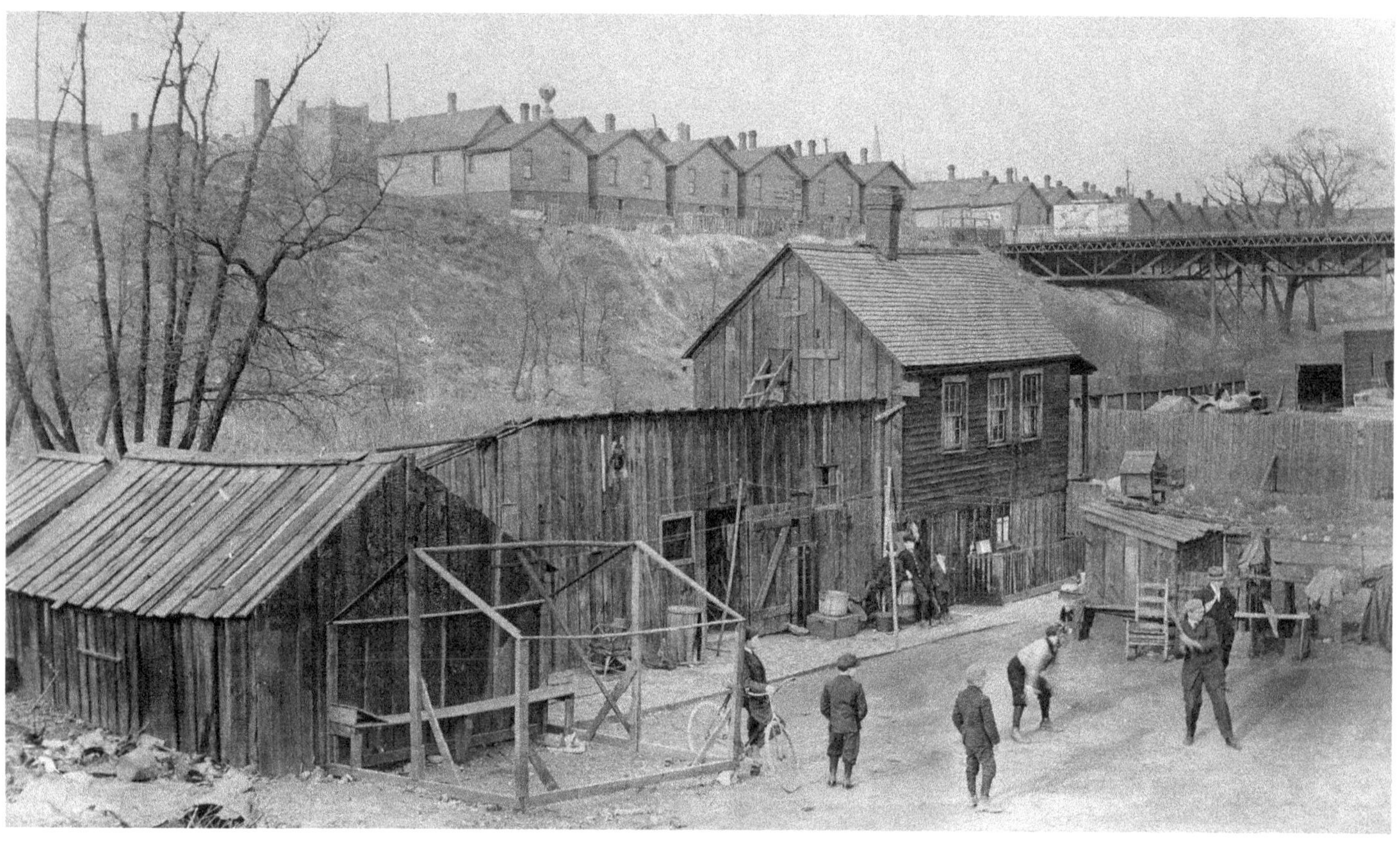

Retzer Bros. Grocers is an example of one of the many neighborhood groceries that existed in Milwaukee. This image, recorded in November 1908, shows the many different items available for purchase, including Gold Medal Flour and Van Houten's Cocoa. The business was located on 1027 1st Street, now 2609 National Avenue, until 1955.

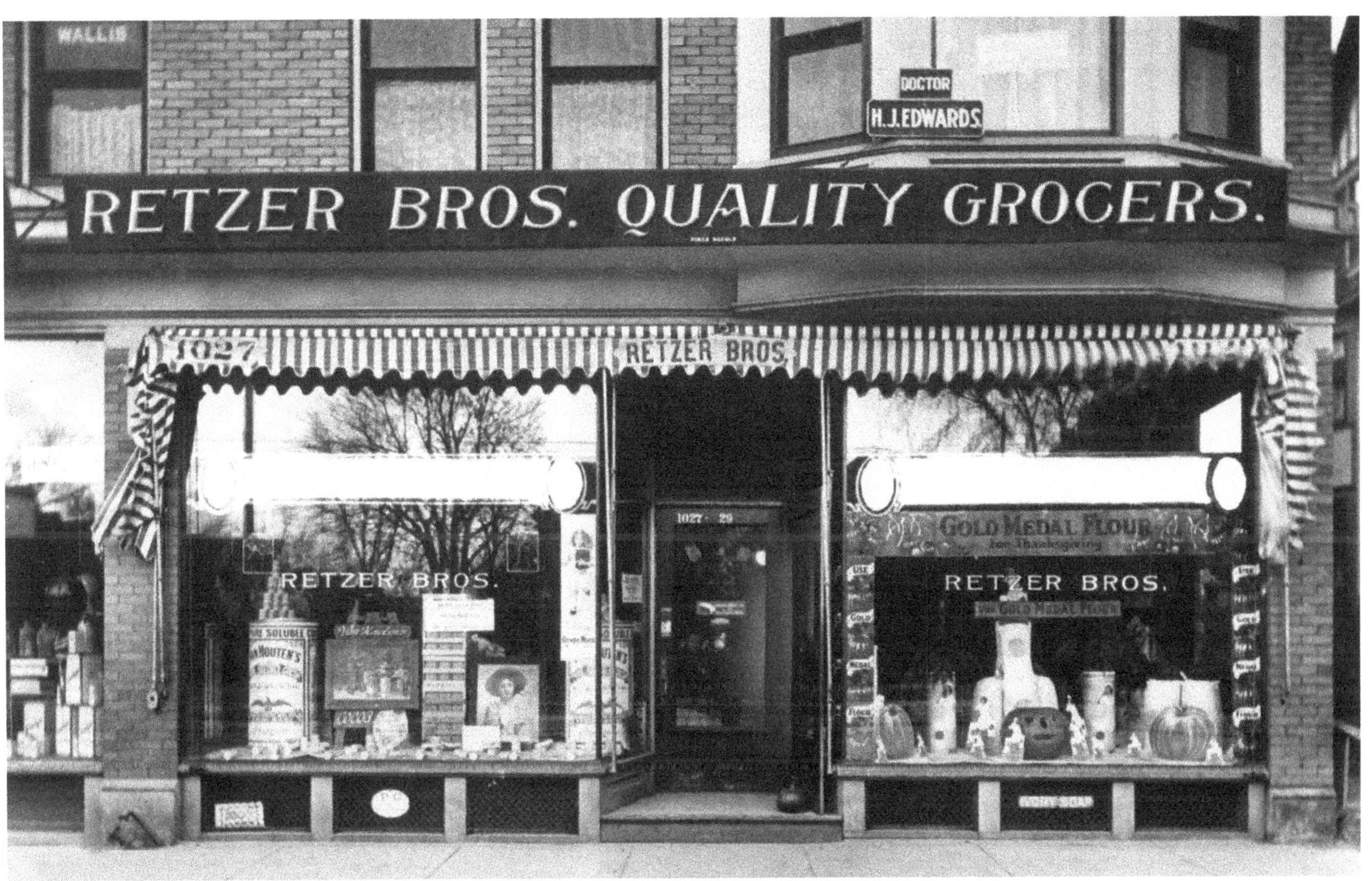

These students are sitting in one of Milwaukee's public schools in 1909. The children's names are written on the board behind them. Many school locations were determined by ward boundaries, often causing two schools to be built within a few blocks of each other.

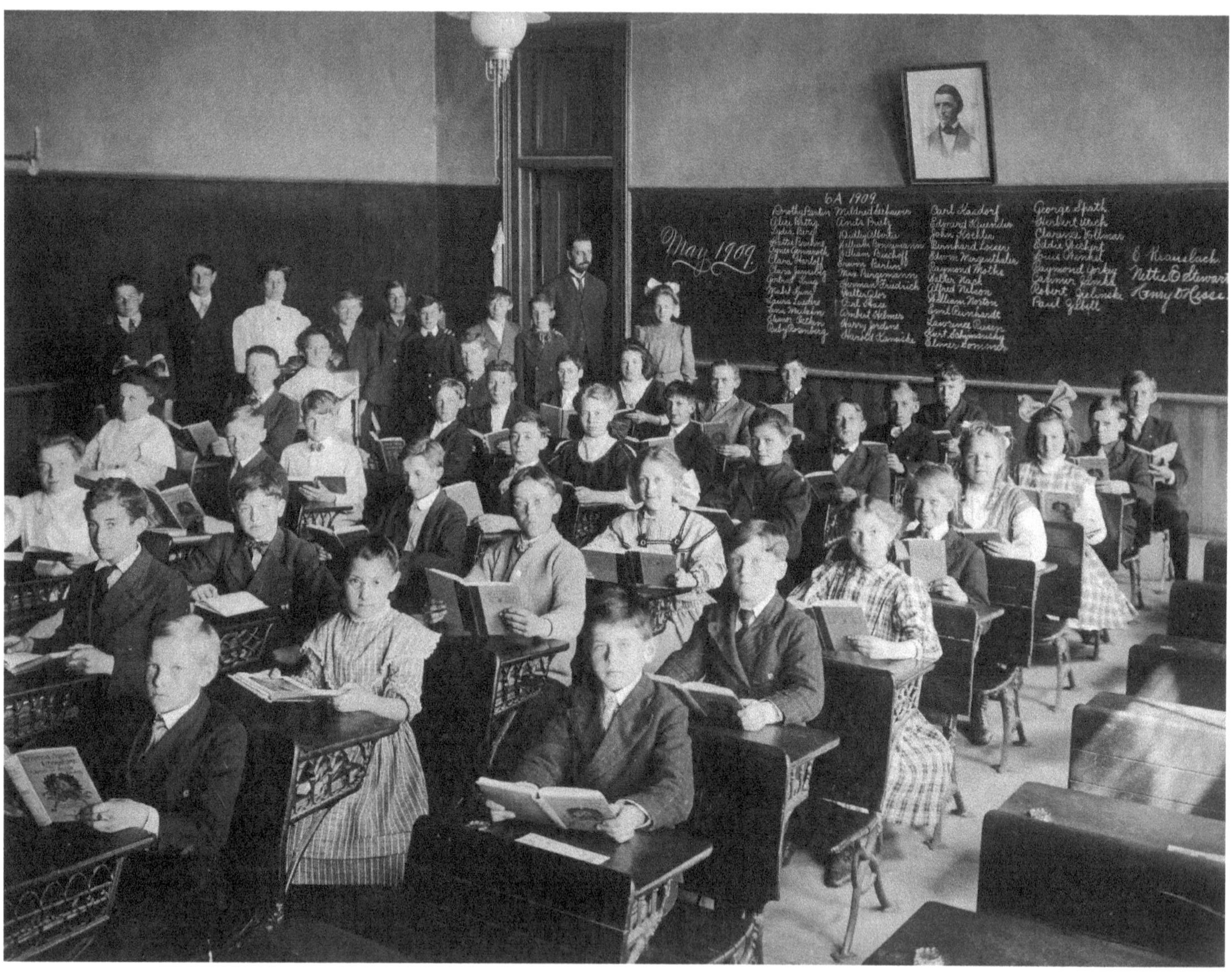

The tugboat *Conrad Starke* approaches a bridge on the Milwaukee River. The industry of the city is visible in the background.

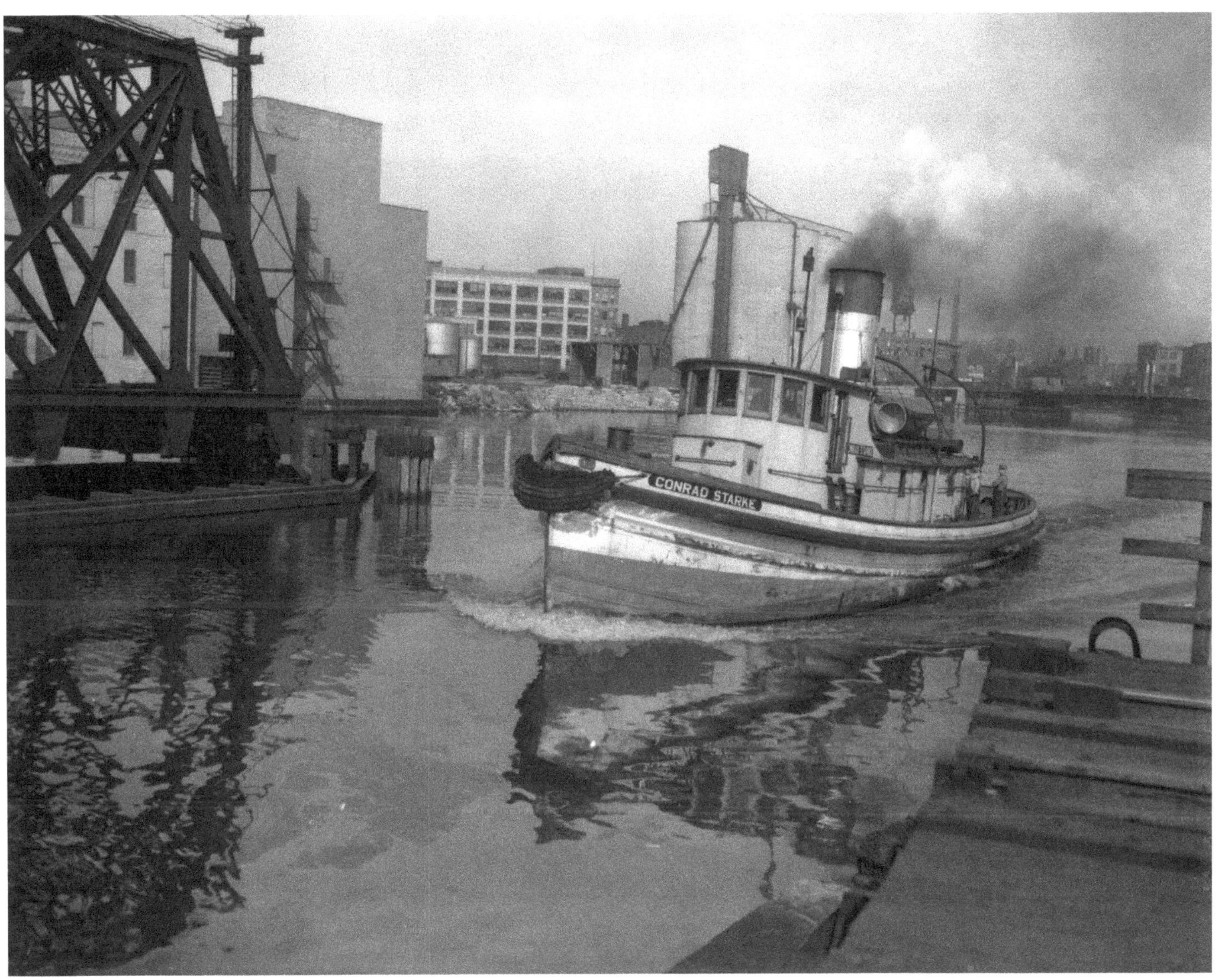

Emil Blaskovics' meat market on 10th Street was not shy about posting prices. In 1910 veal was 8 cents a pound and suckling pigs were 17 cents a pound. The business later moved and became a poultry wholesaler.

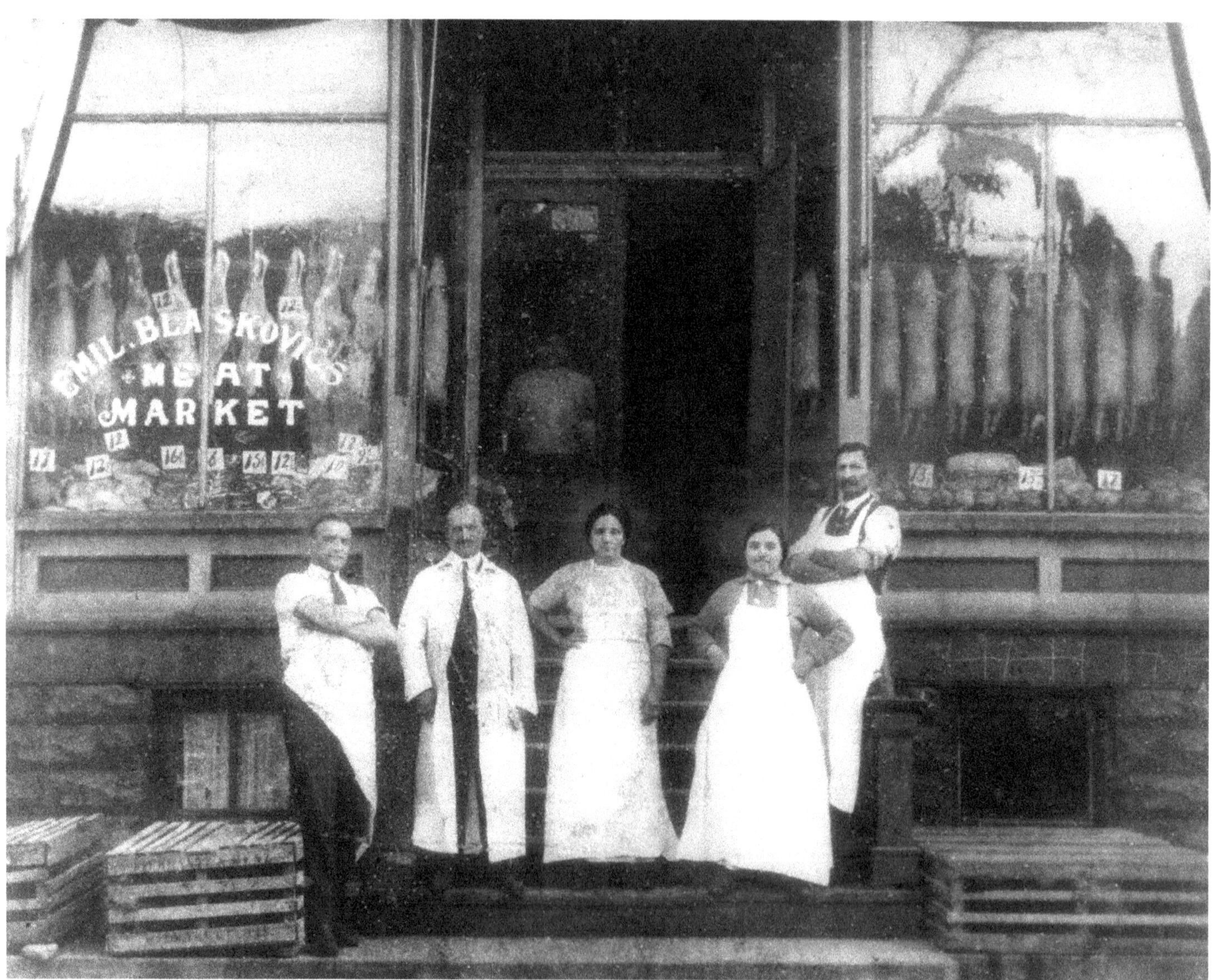

Wagons, streetcars, and automobiles are visible in the background in this photograph, taken on a rainy day in downtown Milwaukee.

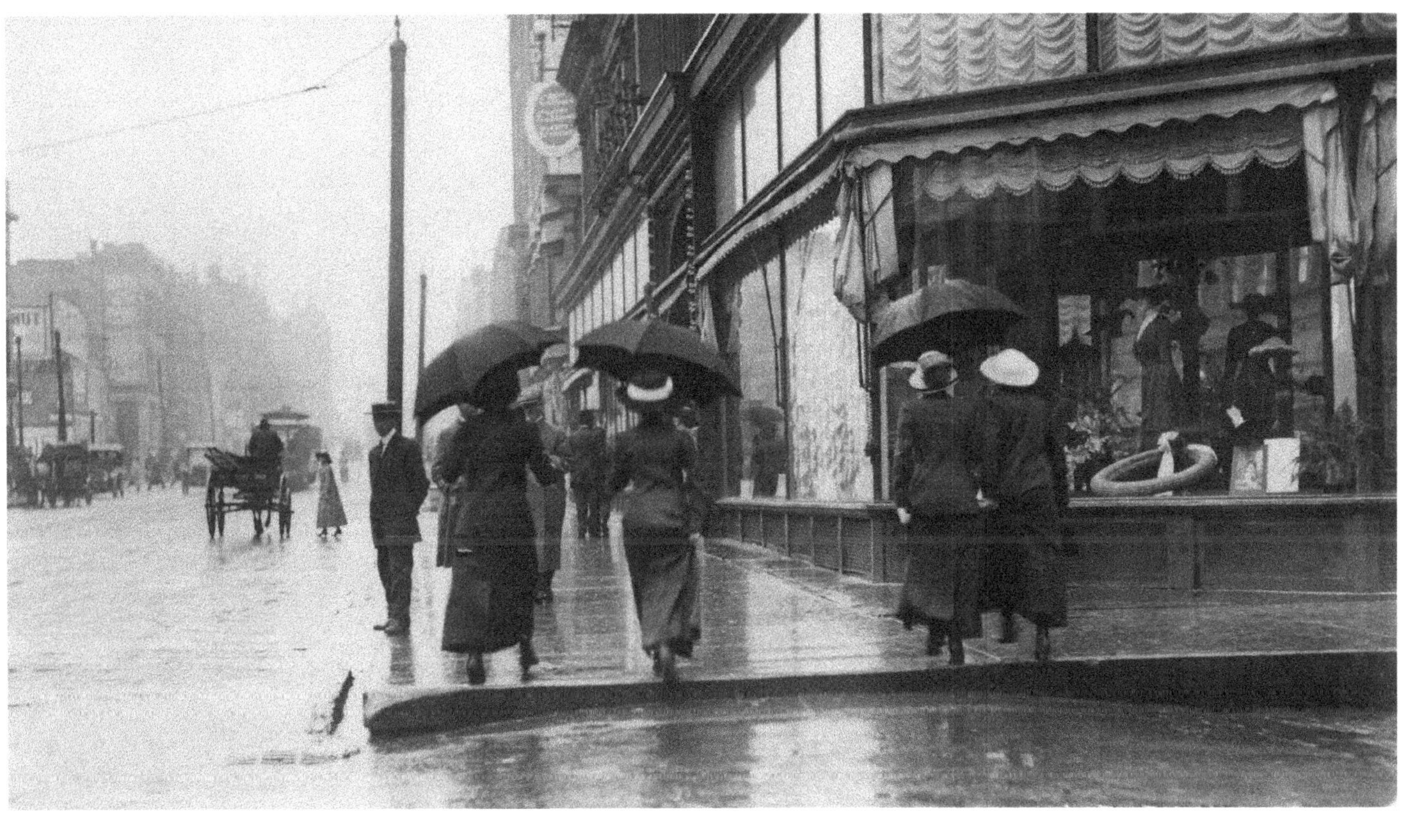

An iceboat ventures onto an area lake. Wisconsin is still a popular destination for those wishing to engage in this form of recreation. Near the turn of the century, however, iceboating was a mode of transportation as well as recreation.

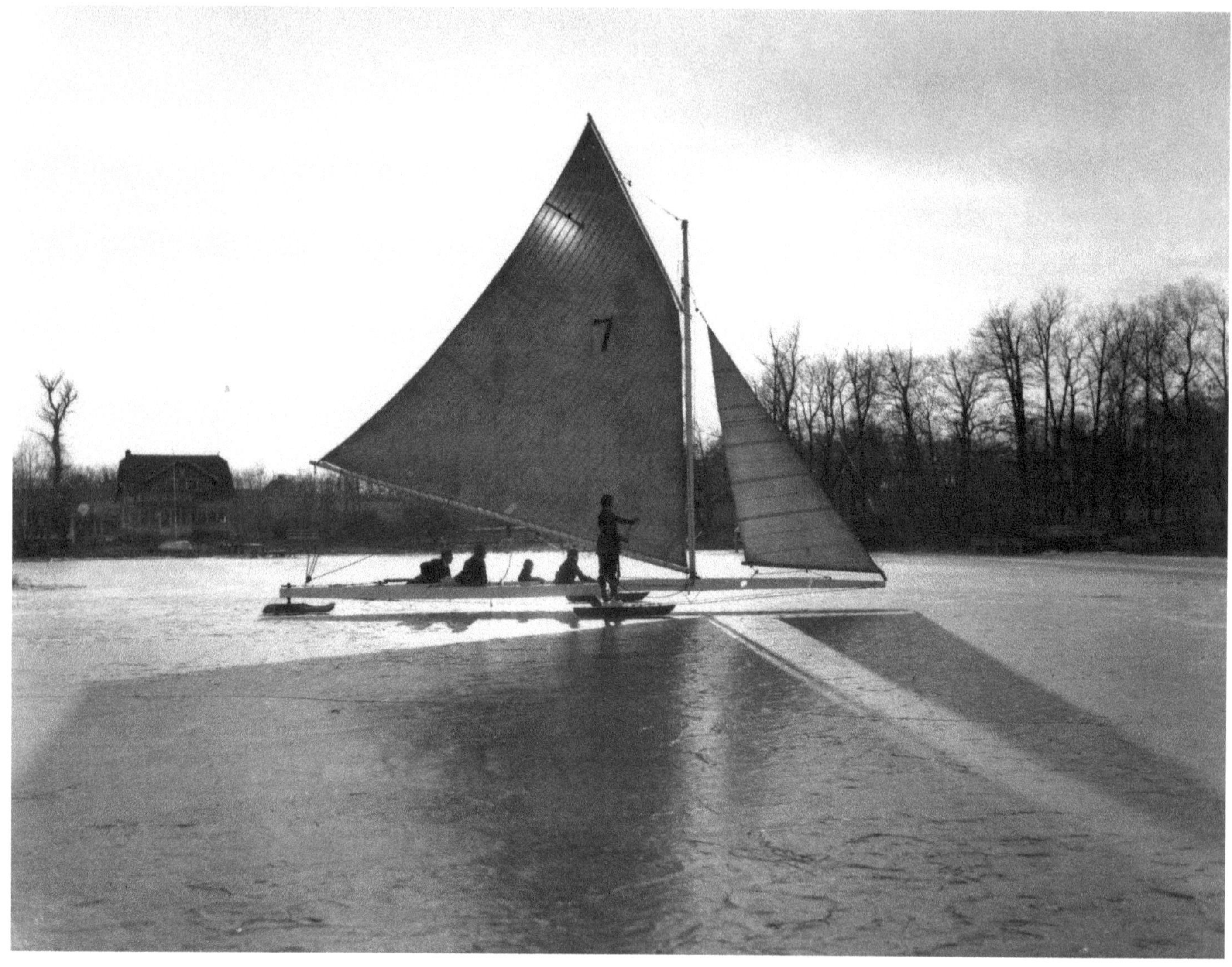

The loading docks in Milwaukee were never a quiet place. Wagons, horses, people on the move, and the sounds of workers hauling boxes were almost always present.

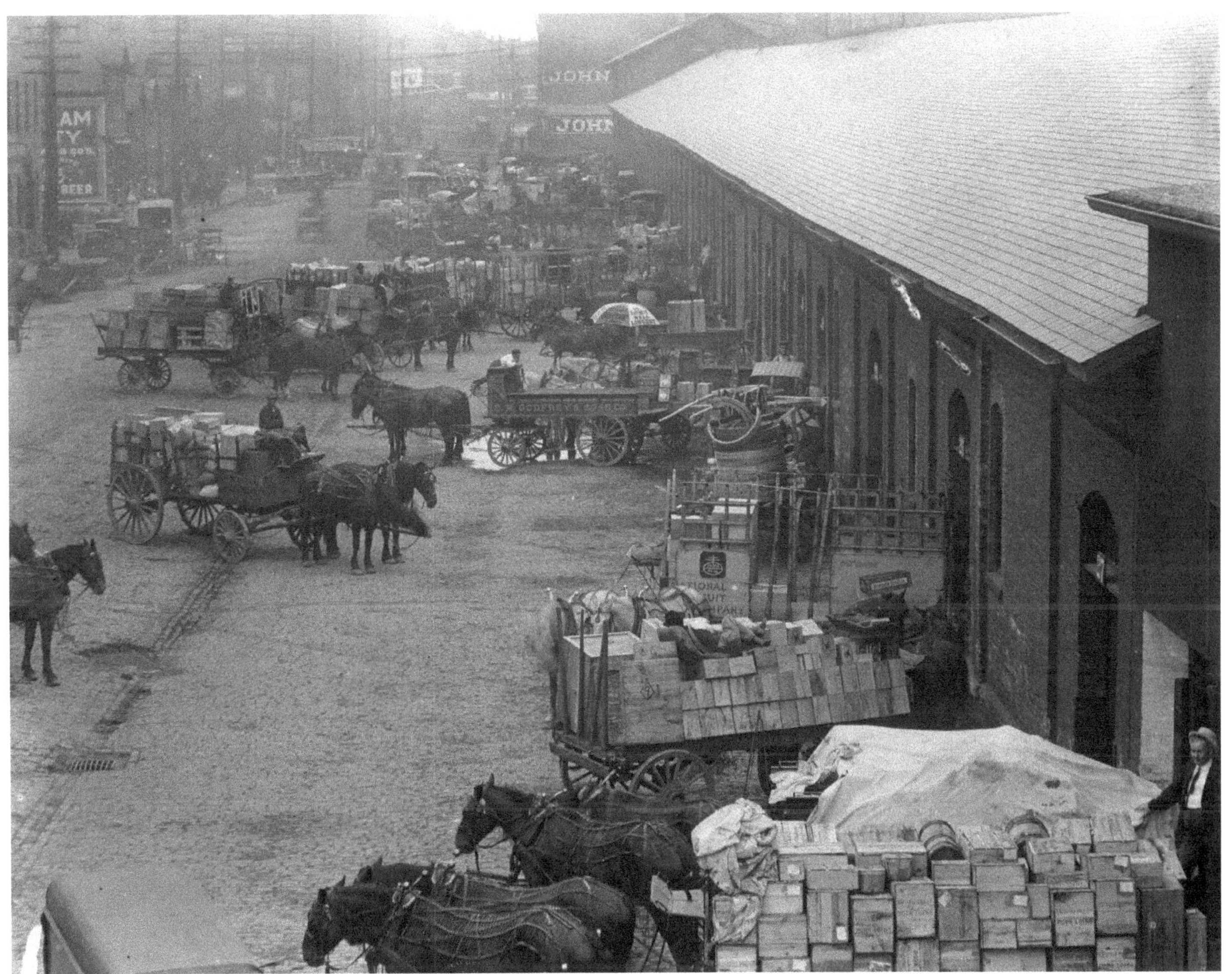

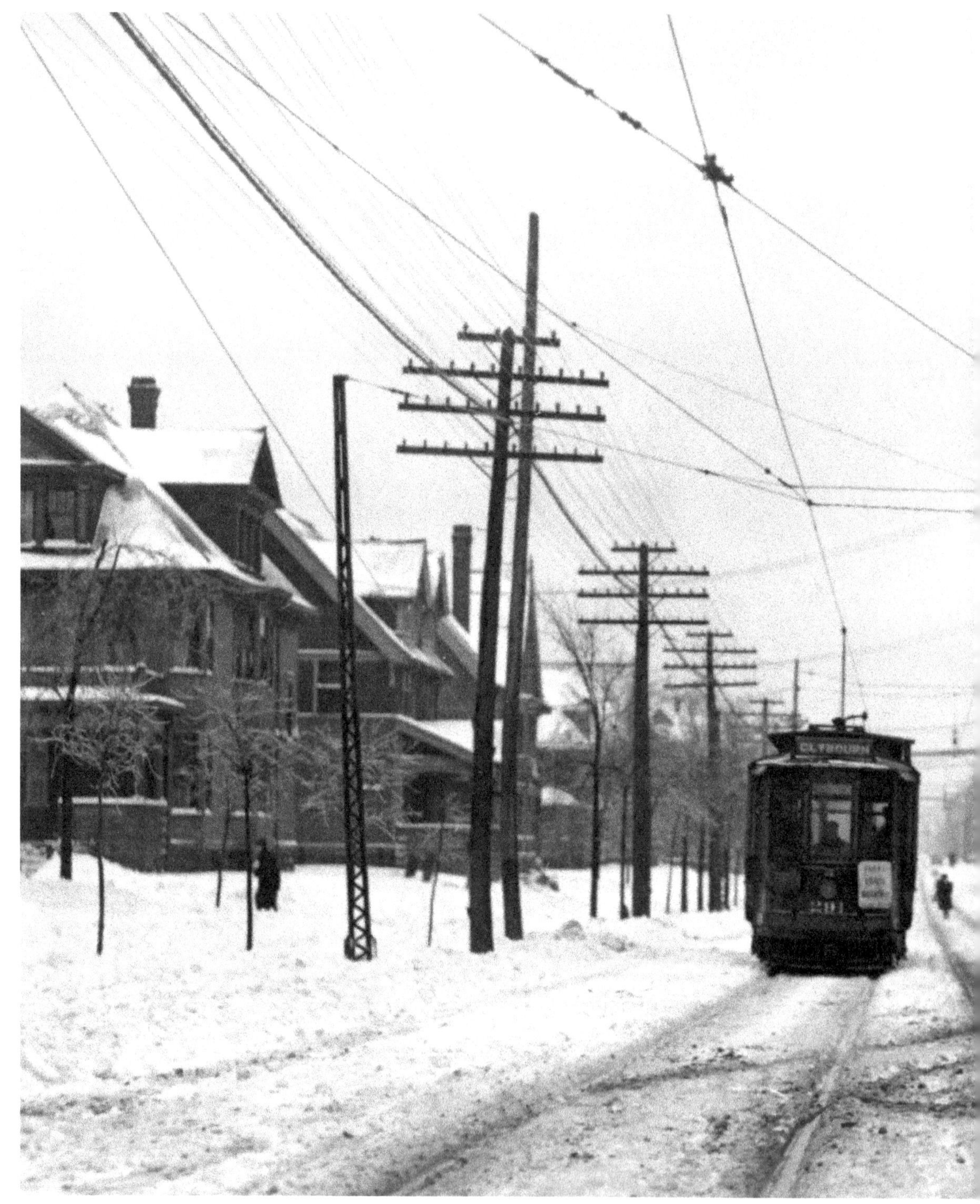

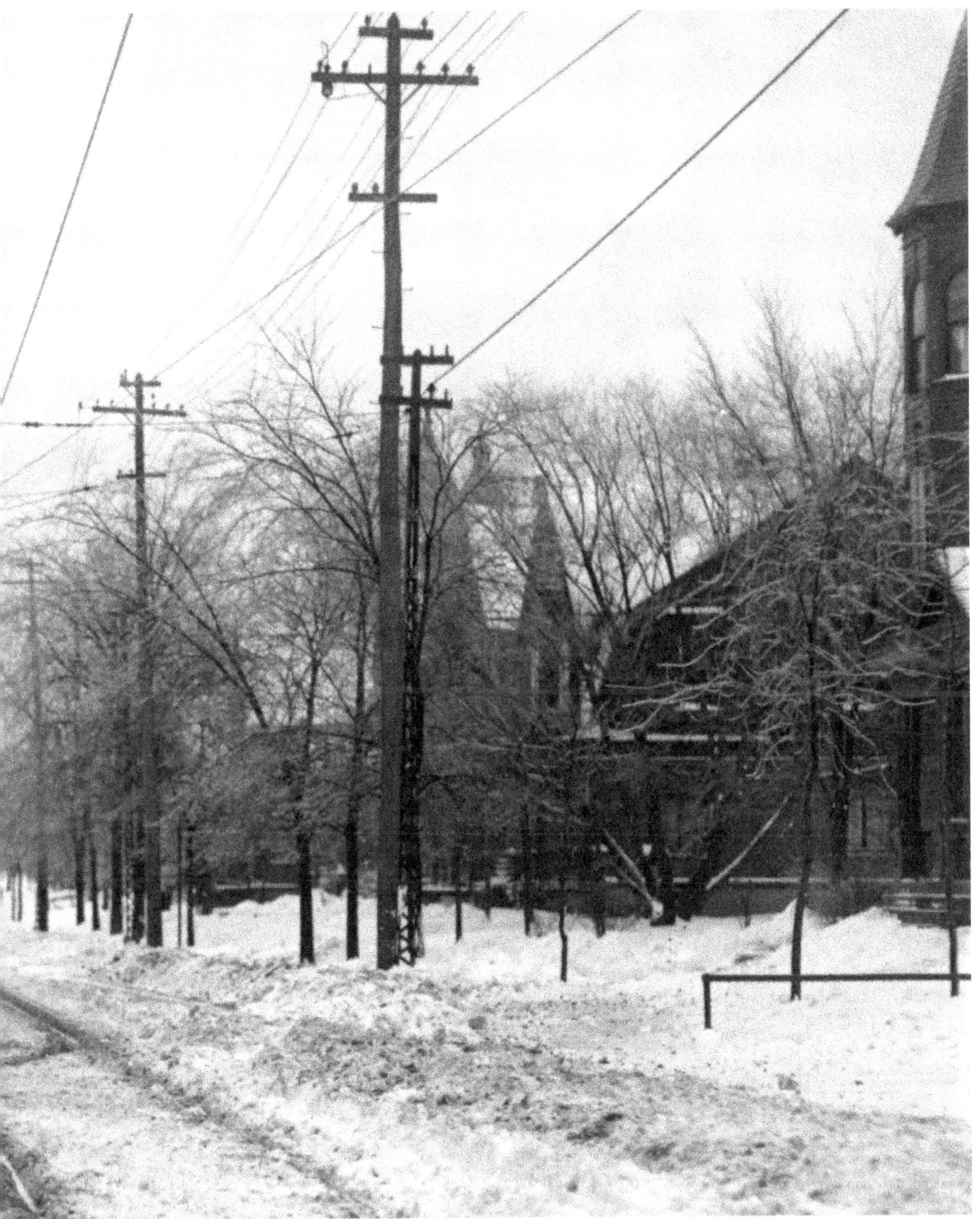

This photograph of a streetcar offers a glimpse into cold Wisconsin winters of a bygone era. Electric streetcars in Milwaukee began service in 1890 and plied their routes until 1958.

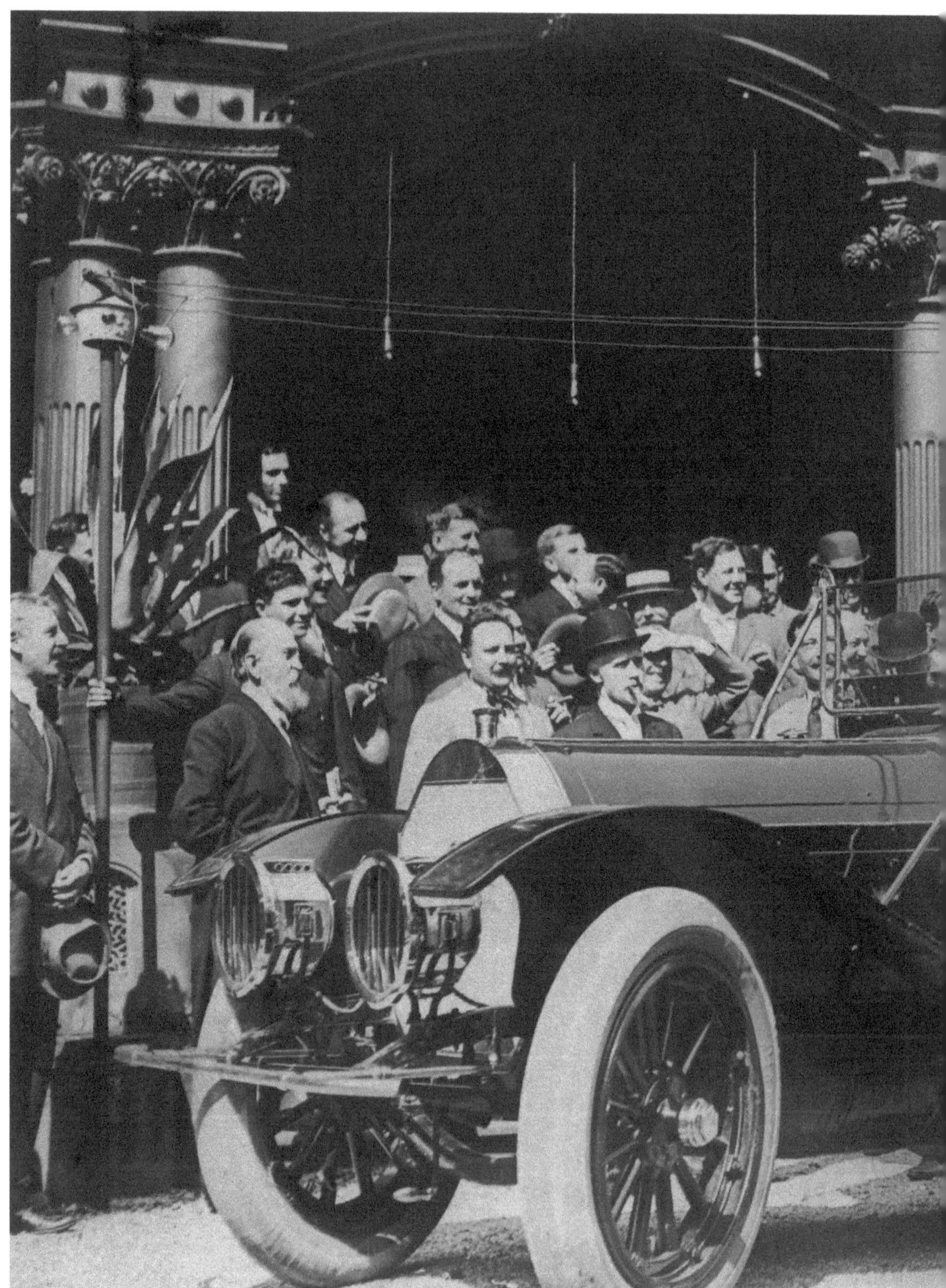

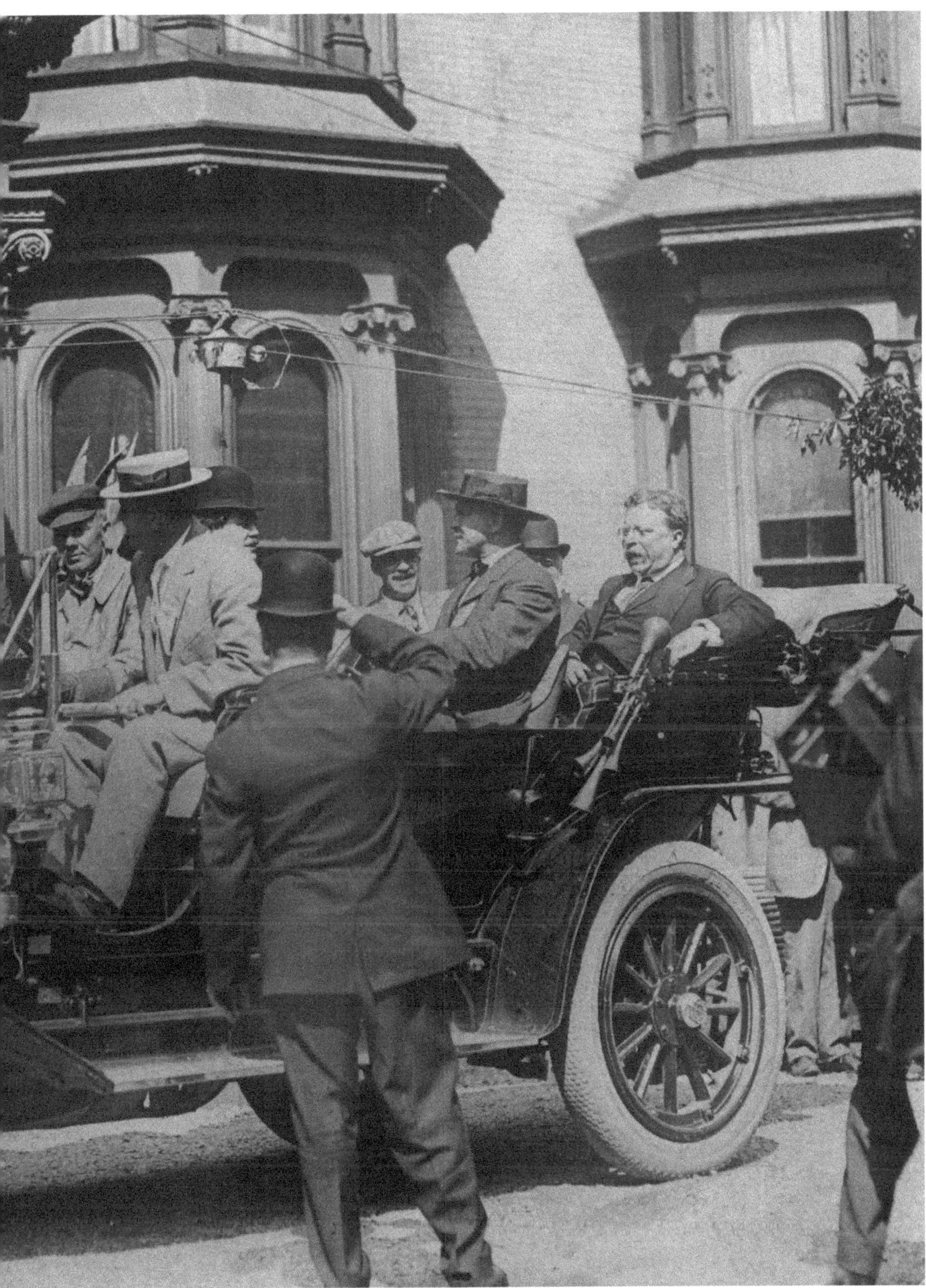

Teddy Roosevelt visited Milwaukee in 1910. This image shows him in front of what was then known as the Deutscher Club, a club founded to promote German-American awareness, reflecting the large German population that had settled in Milwaukee. During his presidency, Roosevelt had earlier visited and spoken at the club in 1903. Known today as the Wisconsin Club, the house once belonged to Alexander Mitchell. It is located at 900 West Wisconsin Avenue.

Teddy Roosevelt is seen leaving the train station in 1910 accompanied by the governor, the police sergeant, and the father of the highway system in Milwaukee, Frank Cannon. A mere two years later, an attempt would be made on Roosevelt's life during a campaign visit to the city. The bullet of the would-be assassin entered his chest, but was stopped short of its mark by items, including a speech, that Roosevelt had tucked into his shirt pocket. Declining suggestions that he visit a hospital, Roosevelt delivered the speech the same evening.

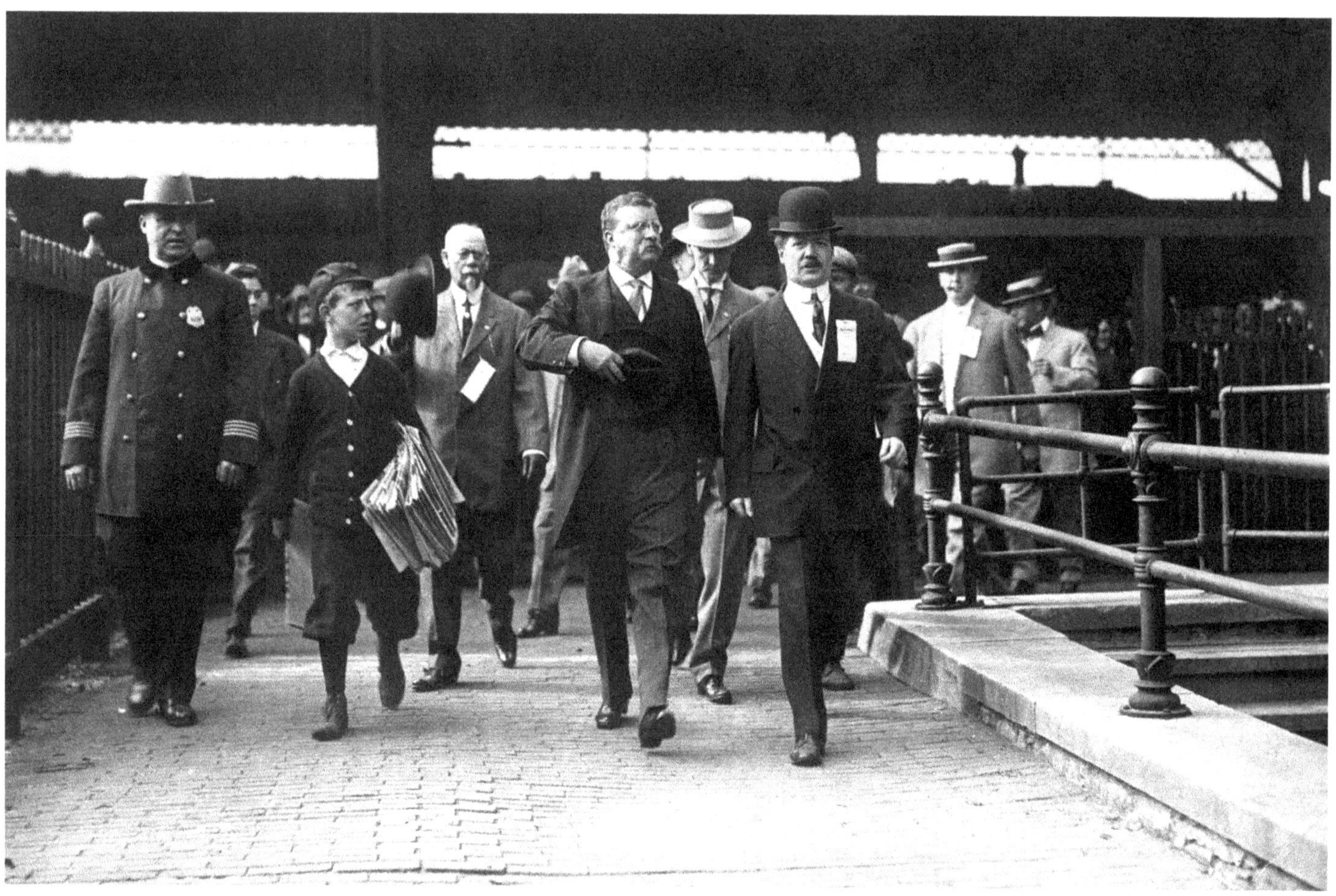

Fire fighters attempt to rescue citizens from a burning building. Similar attempts had been made, with less success, when the Milwaukee Newhall House, one of Wisconsin's largest hotels, caught fire in 1883, some 20 years earlier. At least 70 people perished in the Newhall House fire.

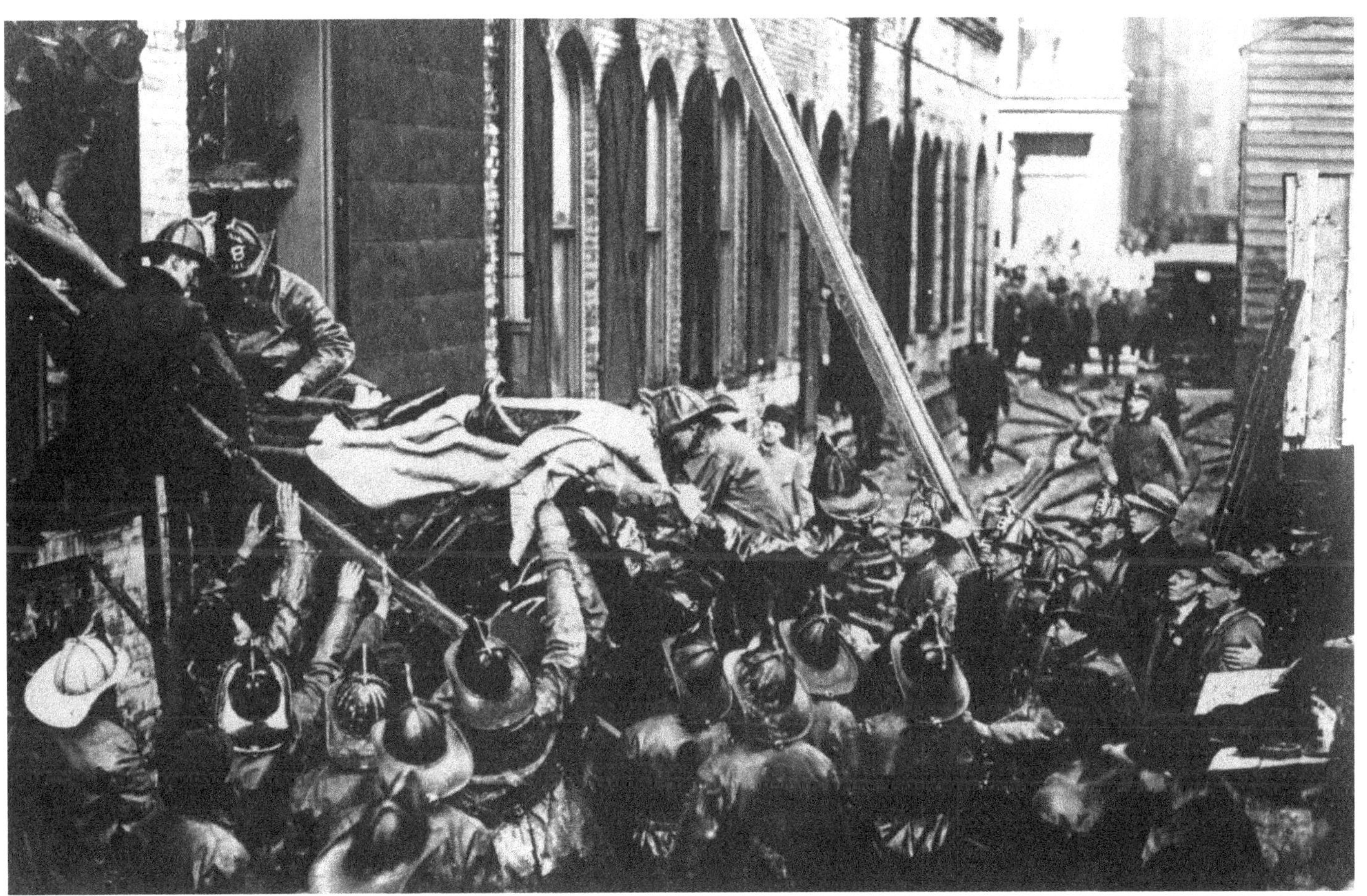

Photographer George Malone poses with his camera in front of an ice formation on the Milwaukee shoreline of Lake Michigan in 1910.

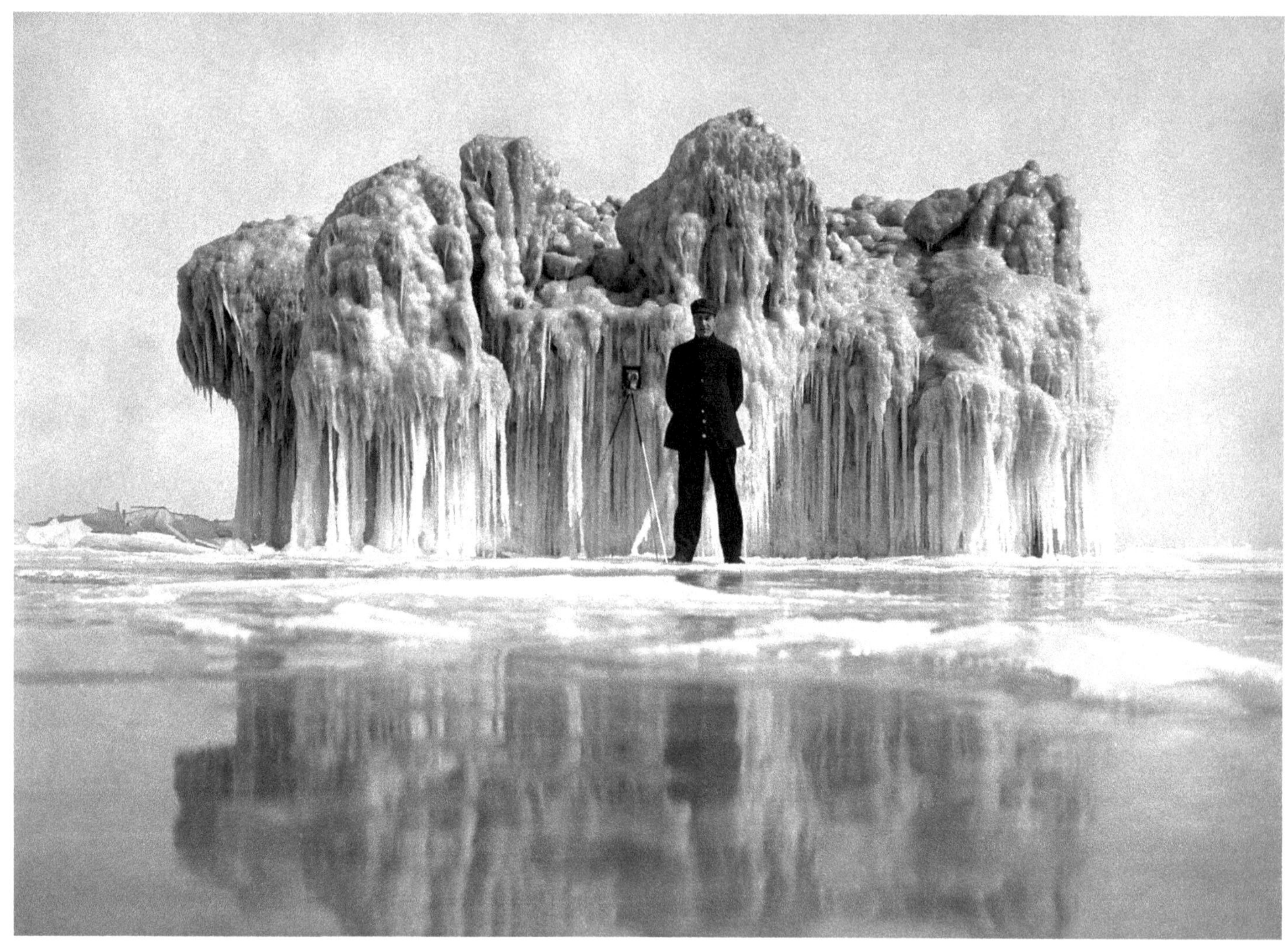

This image of the Grain Exchange Room, recorded in 1910, is an example of the modern-day trading floor. It was housed in the Mackie Building, once known as the Chamber of Commerce, and was used as a location for sampling the wheat that was grown in Wisconsin. The Grain Exchange Room was renovated in 1983 and is now one of Milwaukee's elite reception halls.

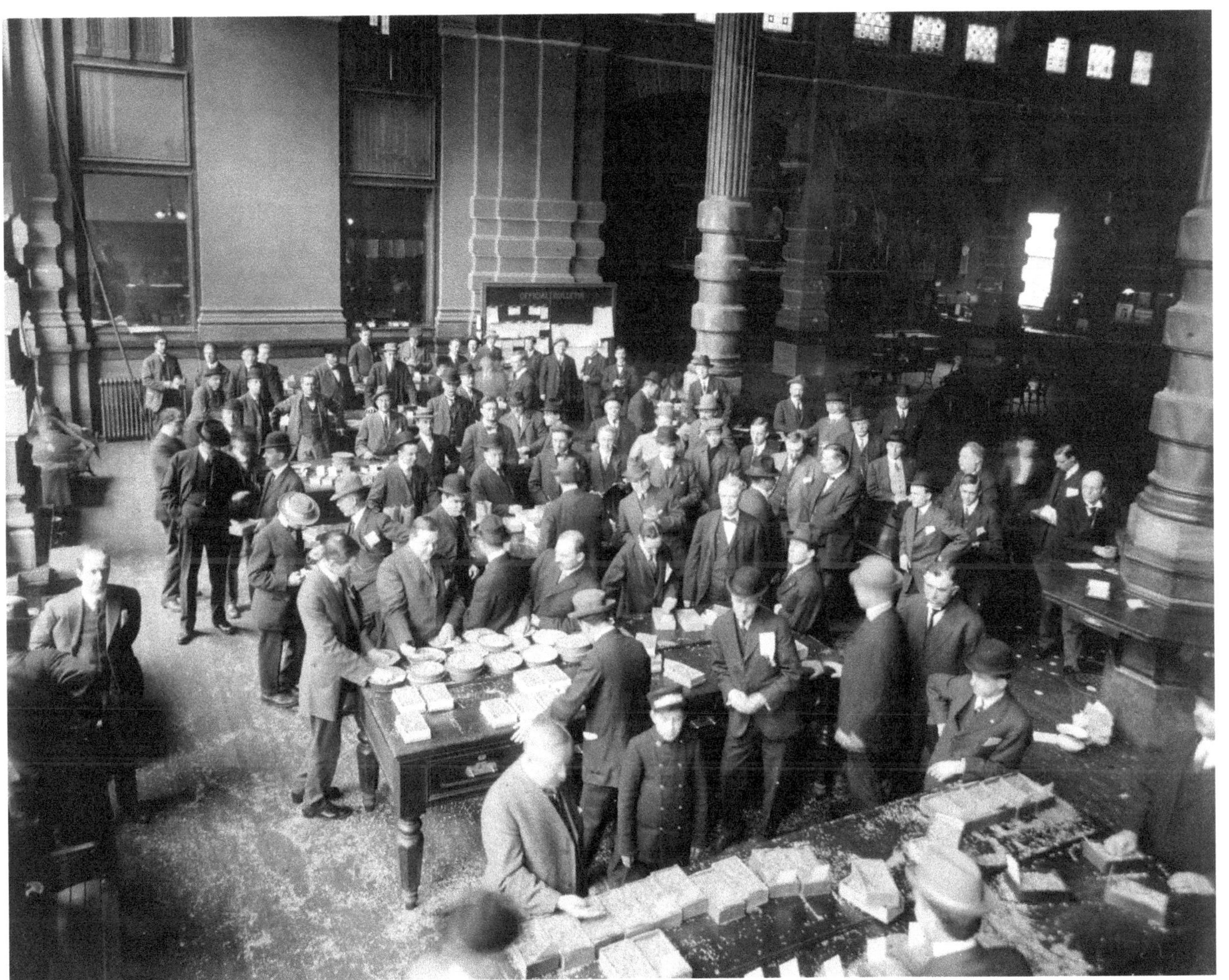

Taken in 1919, this photograph illustrates how gasoline salesmen pursued their trade. Their trucks filled with gasoline, they would visit local filling stations to make the sale.

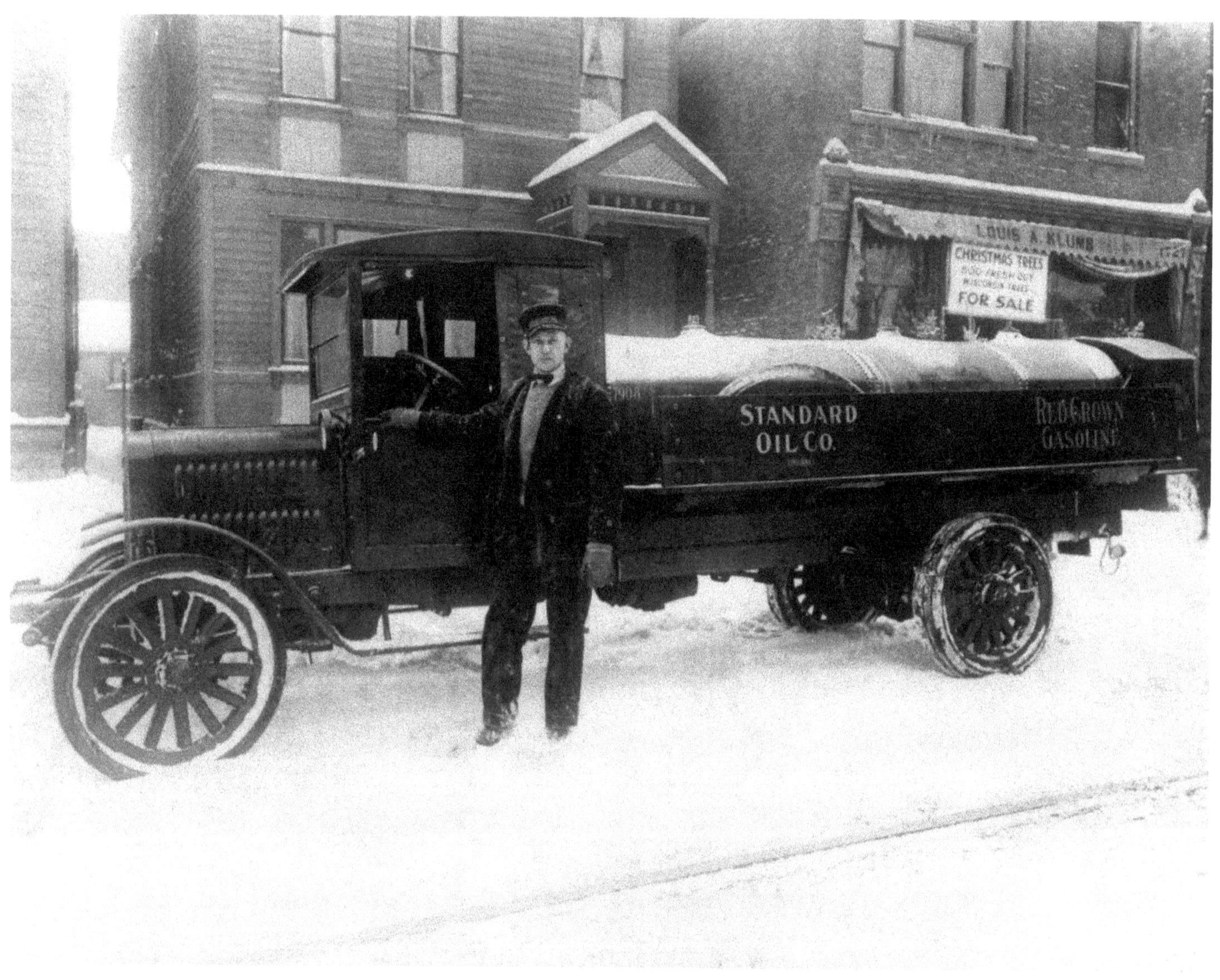

The beach is always a popular summer destination offering an escape from the heat. This beach on Lake Michigan offers a respite as well as a chance to socialize with other Milwaukeeans and show off the fashions of the 1910s.

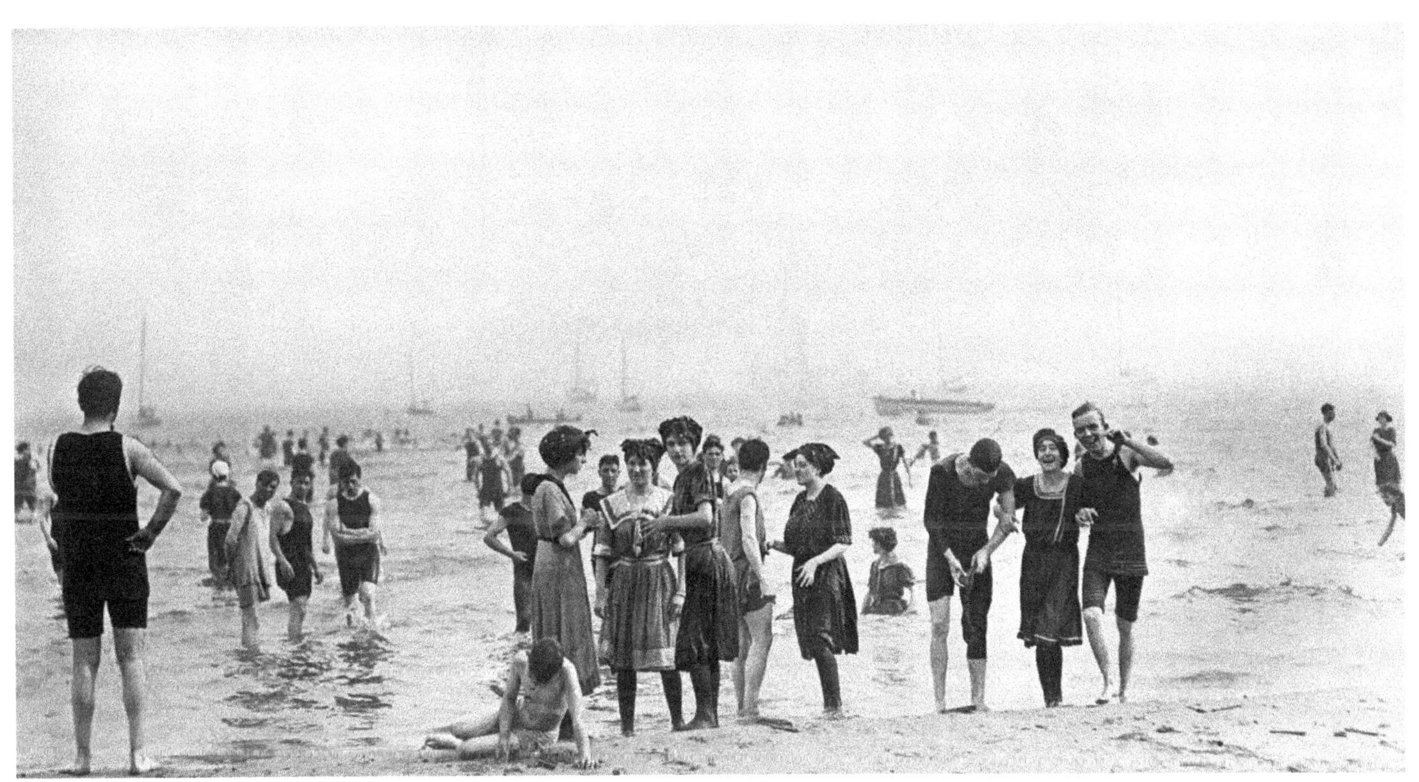

On the day this image was recorded, John Kaminski, the first licensed pilot in Wisconsin, was scheduled to fly his Curtiss pusher from the Wisconsin State Fairgrounds on 640 S. 84th Street. Today the fairgrounds are home not only to the state fair, but also to various special events including the World Beef Expo and the Milwaukee Journal Sentinel Sports Show.

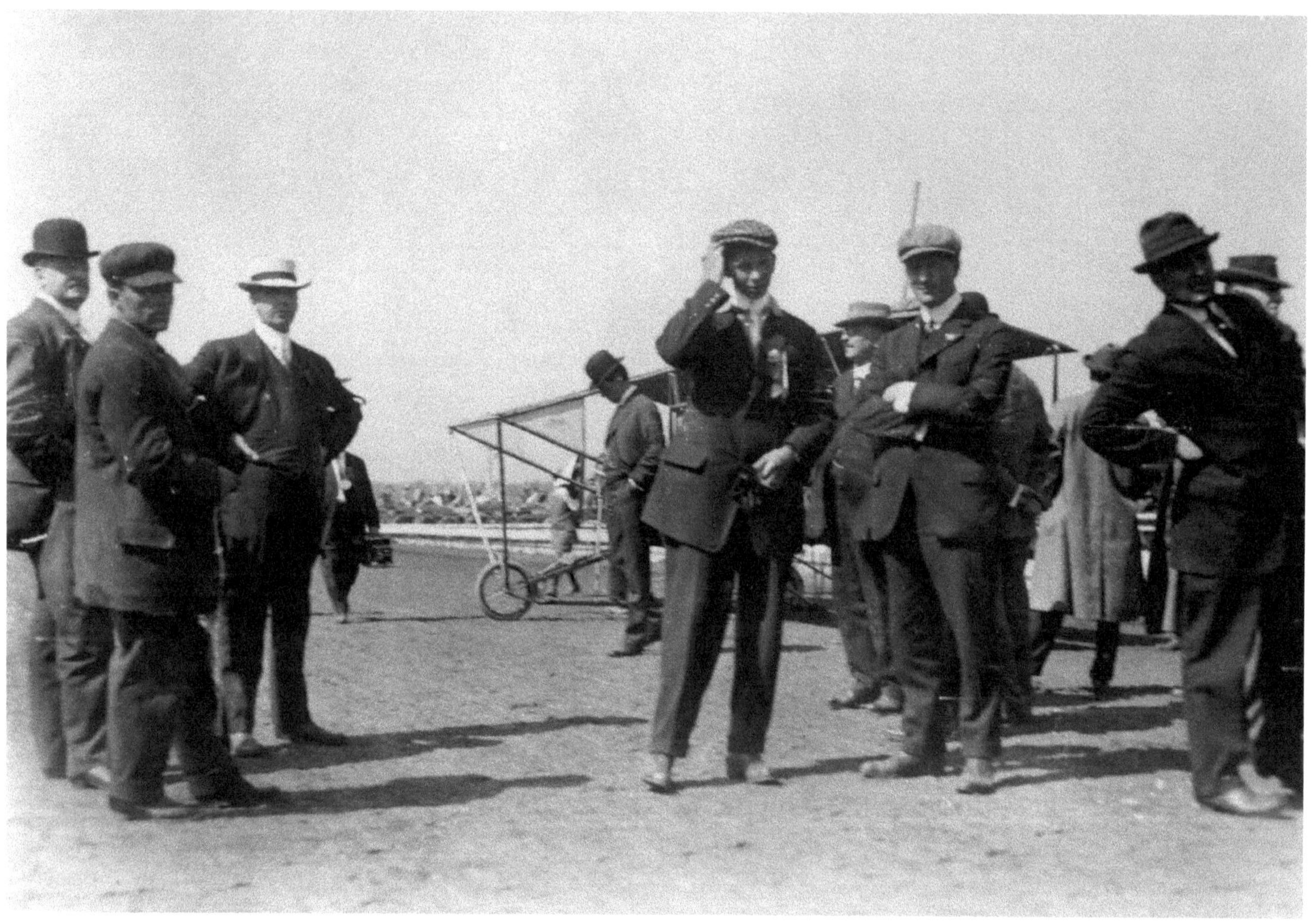

The Wright Model B flyer visible in this 1912 photograph is believed to have been flown by Farnum Fish. Fish, an early aviator, primarily on the West Coast, spent much of his time flying as an exhibitionist and giving passenger rides and flying lessons.

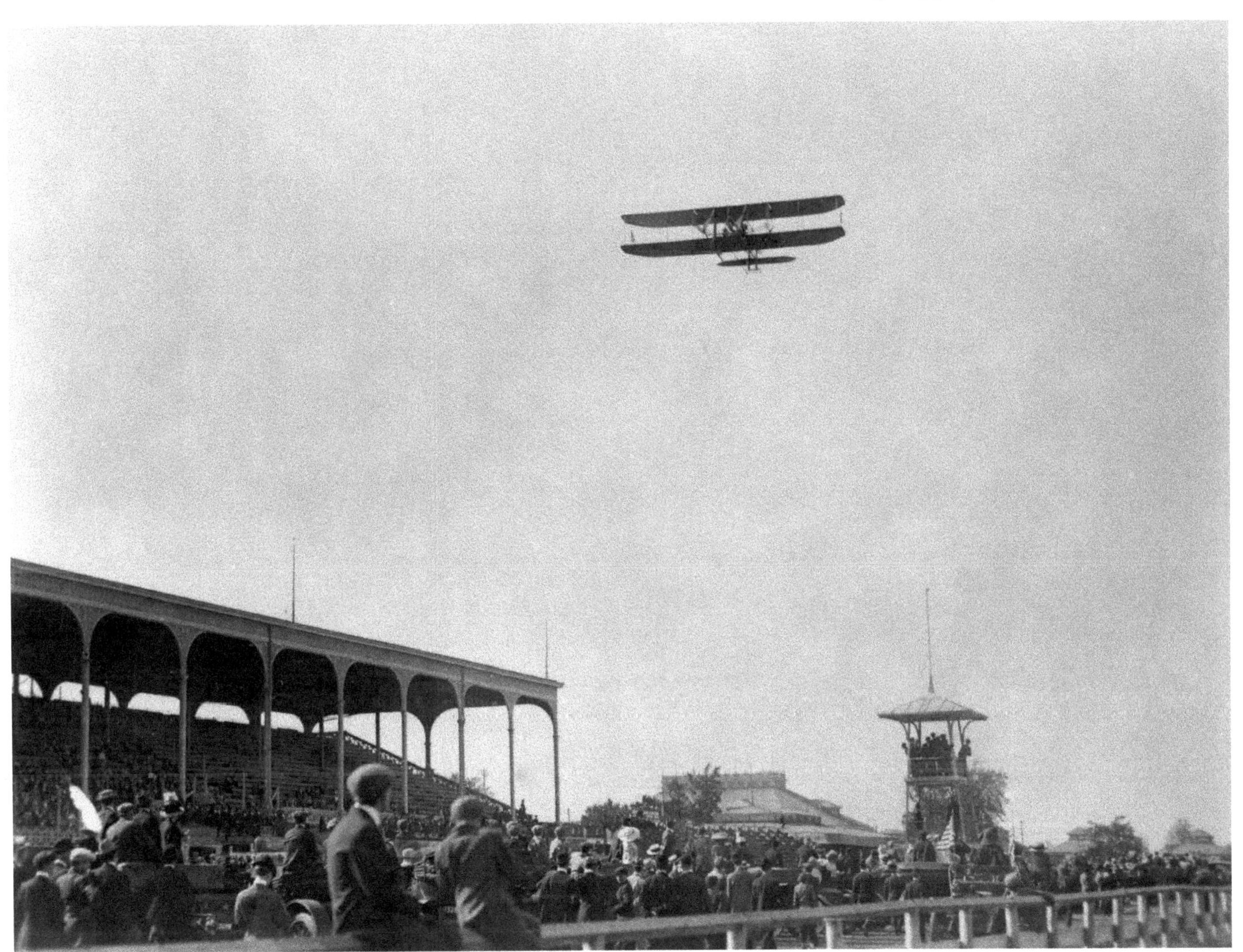

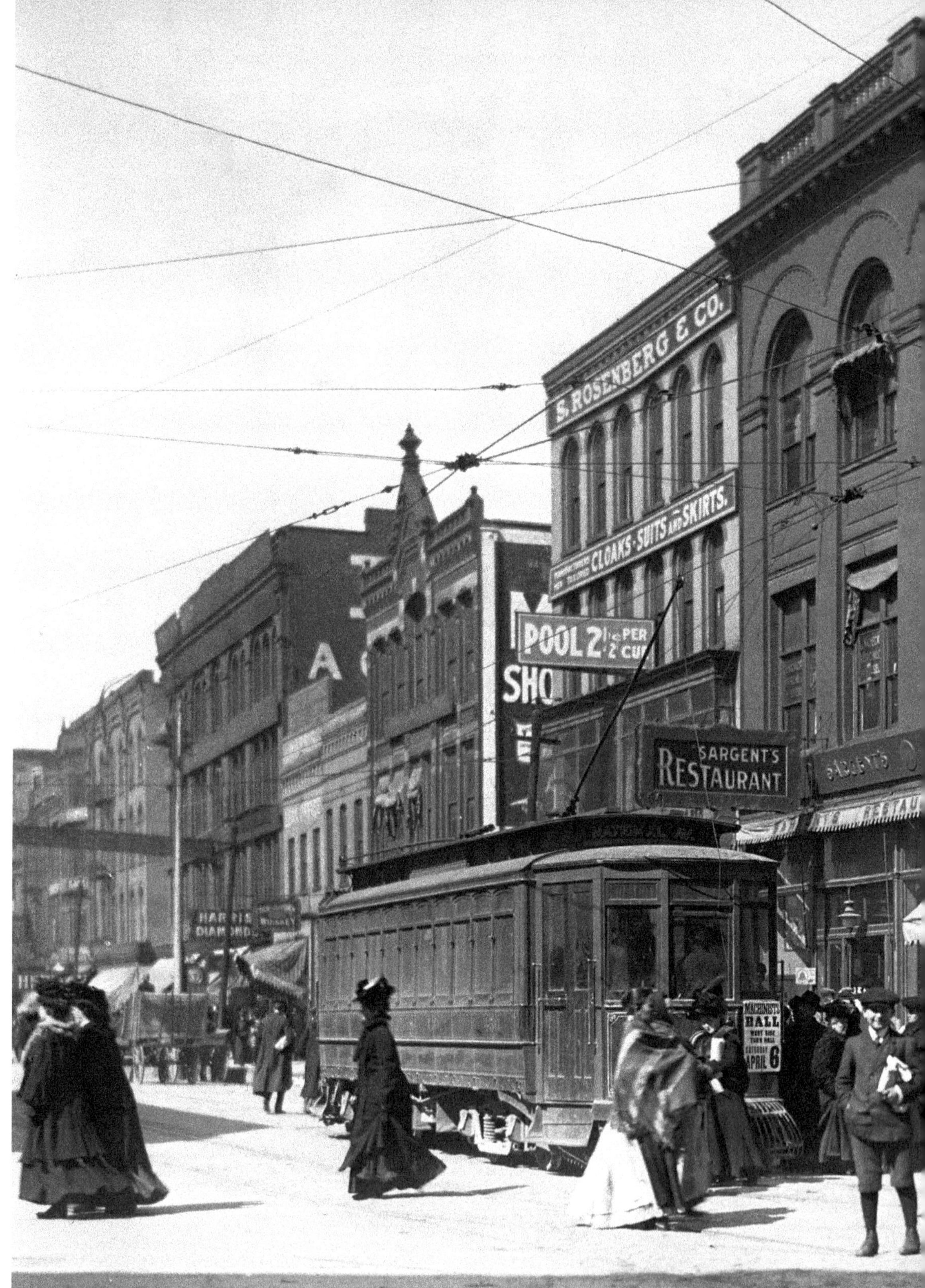
S. ROSENBERG & CO.
CLOAKS · SUITS AND SKIRTS.
POOL
SARGENT'S RESTAURANT
APRIL 6

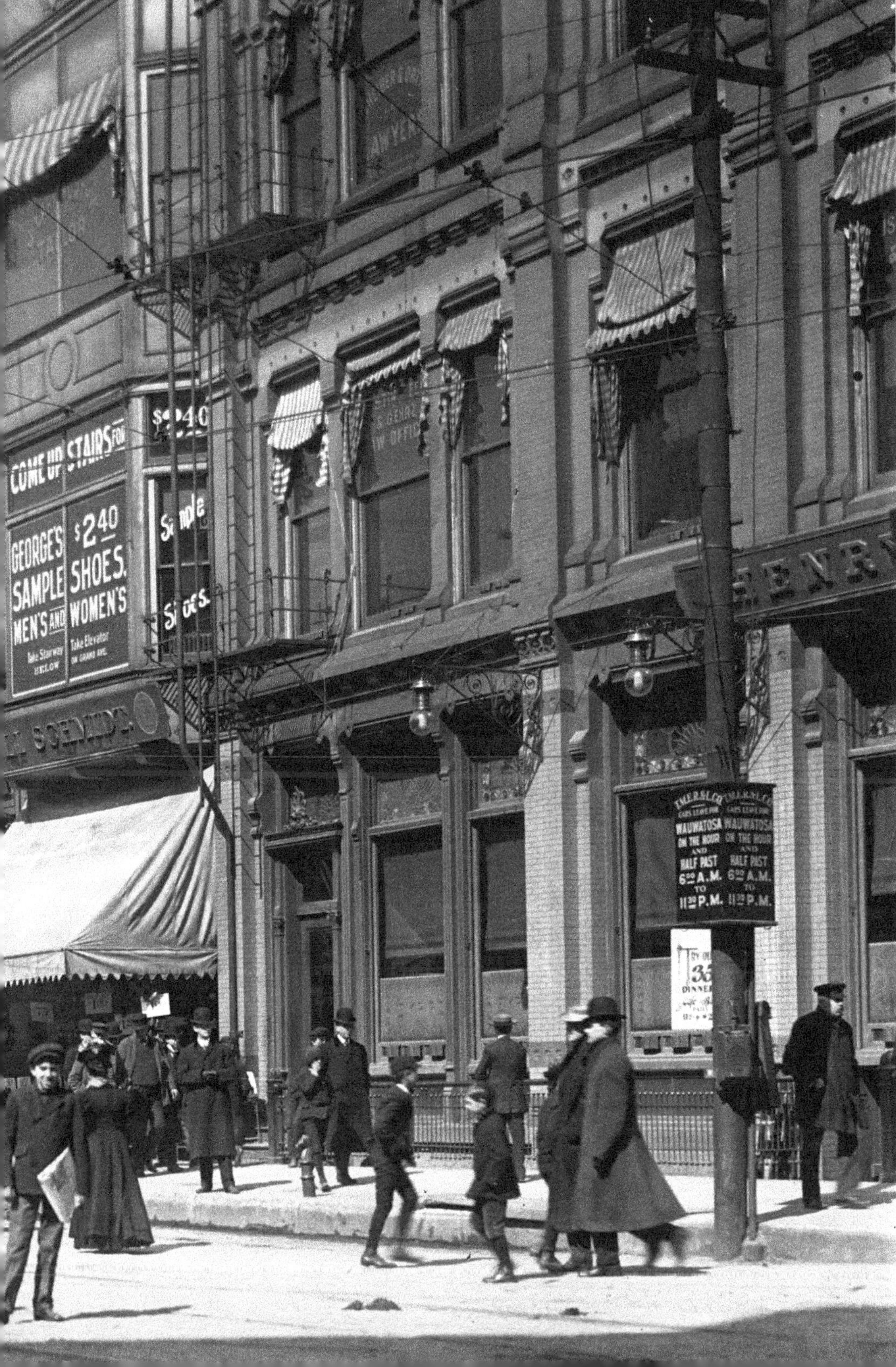

This view of West Water Street in 1912 offers a glimpse into the Water Street that once was, filled with pedestrians and streetcars. Now called Plankinton, the street is home to numerous restaurants and hotels.

The W. S. Seaman Co. manufactured automobile bodies for other companies, including Chalmers, Chicago-Electric, Ford, and Cadillac. It was purchased by the Nash Motors Co. in 1921.

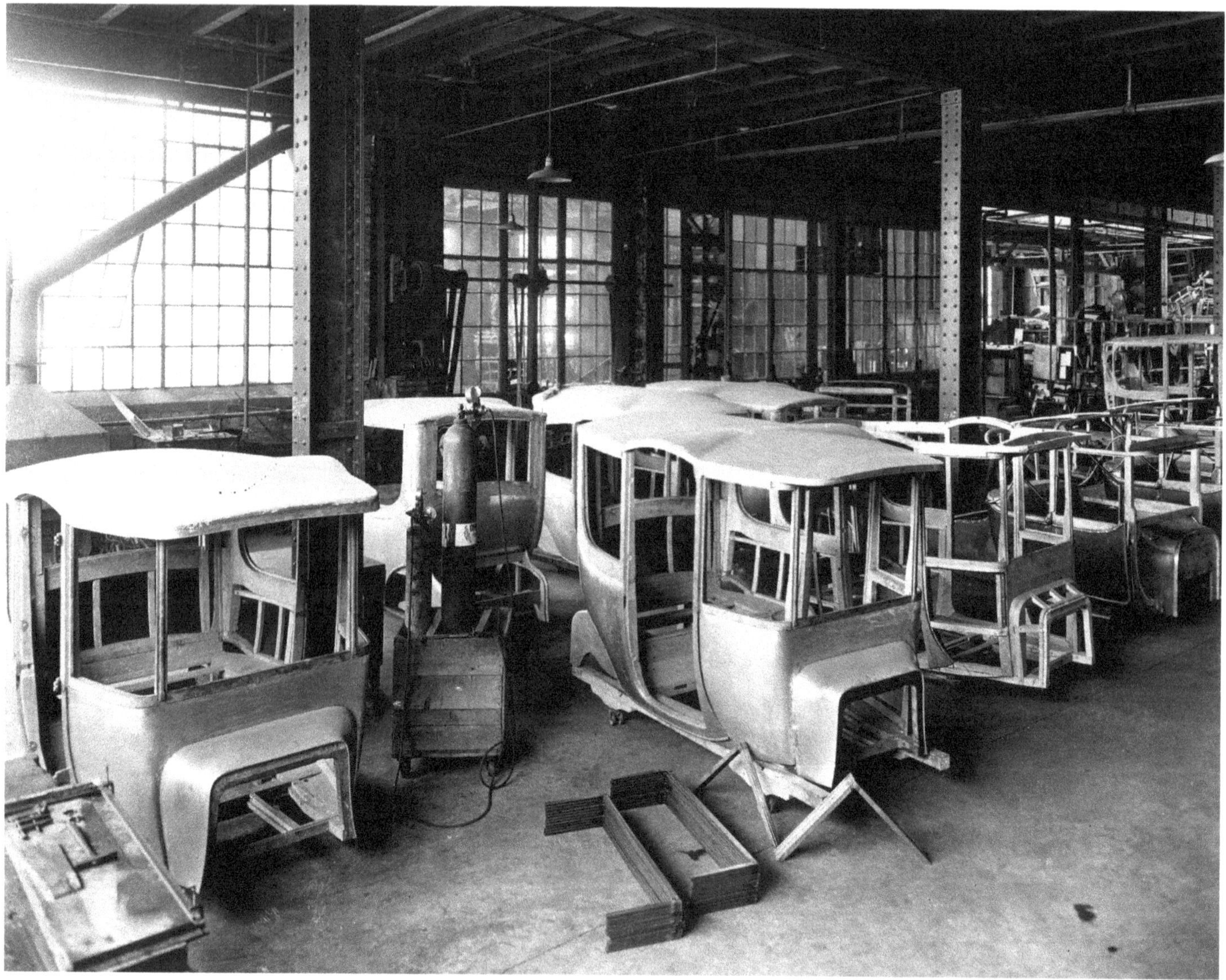

This photograph offers a peek into a local bar in 1914. Although the decor and the drinks have changed, the corner bar is still a place to relax and catch up on the goings on in the neighborhood. One more thing has changed about the local bar—the prices. In 1914 a shot of whiskey was a nickel.

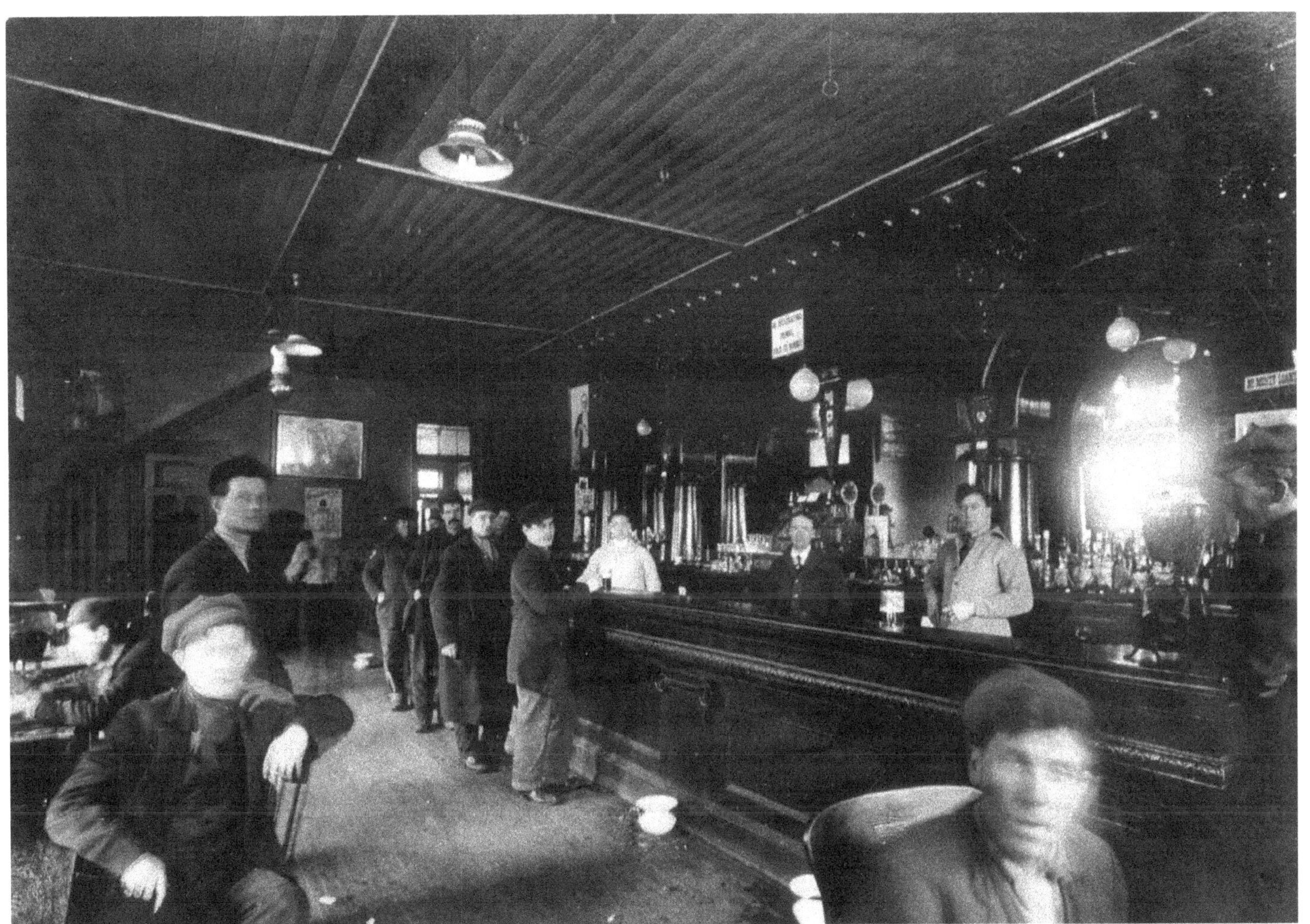

The Quality Biscuit Company was a prominent business in the city. Shown here is a Packard, a company truck, in 1914. Quality Biscuit was acquired by the United Biscuit Company of America in 1928, along with two other biscuit companies from the Northeast and the Midwest.

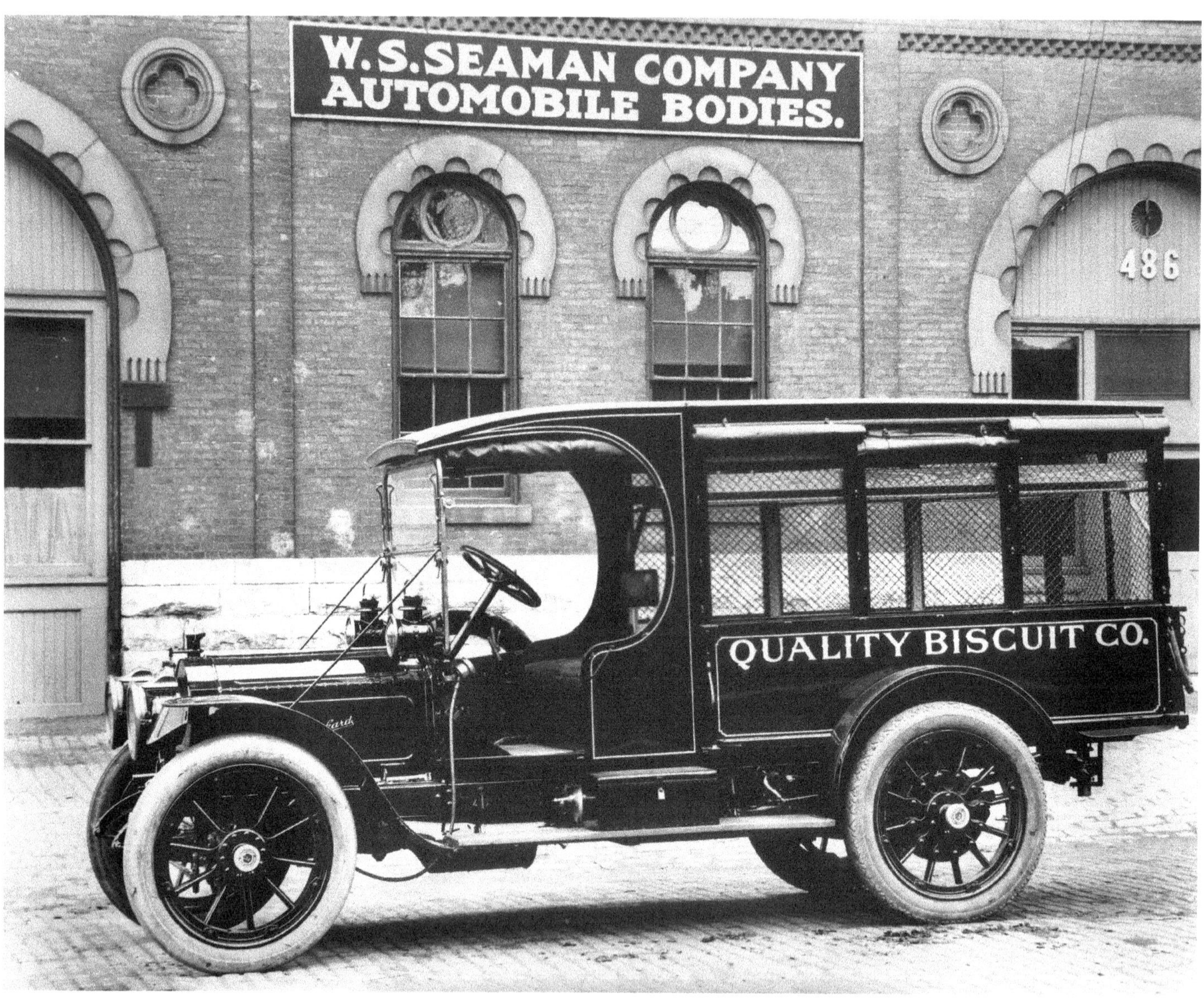

One of the best-known breweries in the world was started in Milwaukee in 1844. Pabst Brewing, at one time Best Brewing, once made the most popular beer in the city. As the years went by, brewing beer became a big industry, and with the invention of the bottling machine it became very profitable.

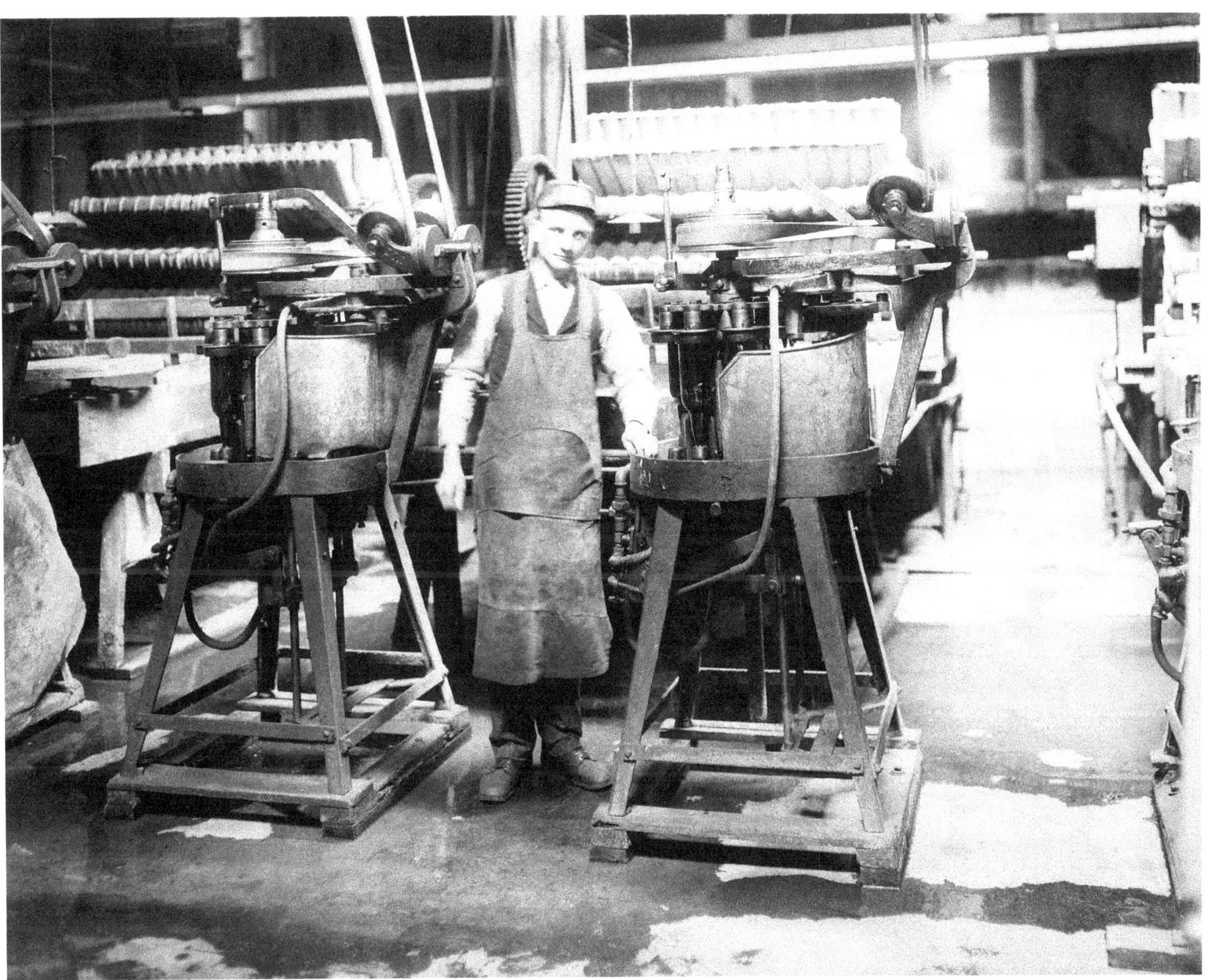

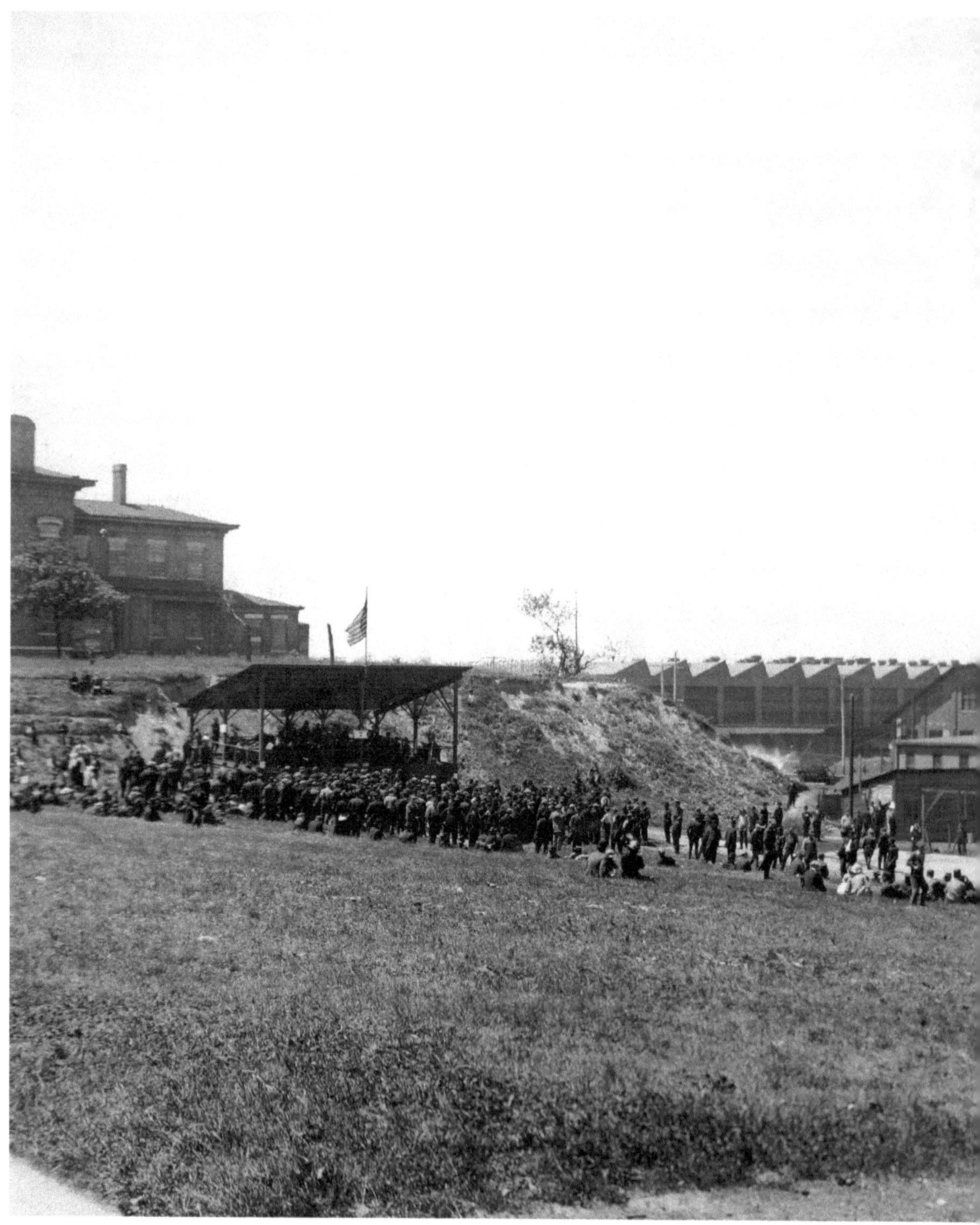

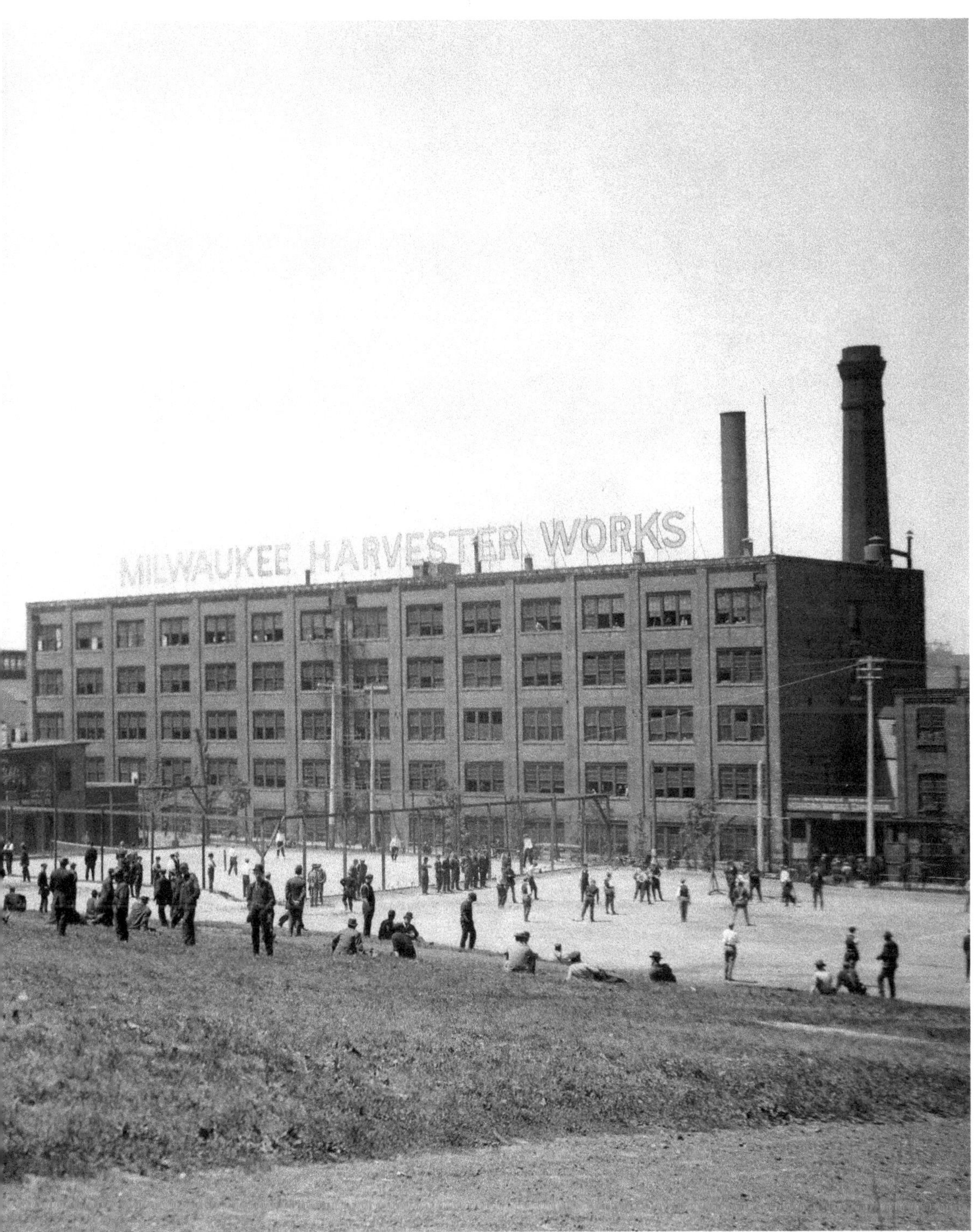

The atmosphere in many Milwaukee businesses was one of family. The workers spent time together outside the factory, as can be seen in this example from the International Harvester Co.

Manufacturing and industry have always been a staple in the Milwaukee economy. Workers here are manufacturing parts at the International Harvester Co.

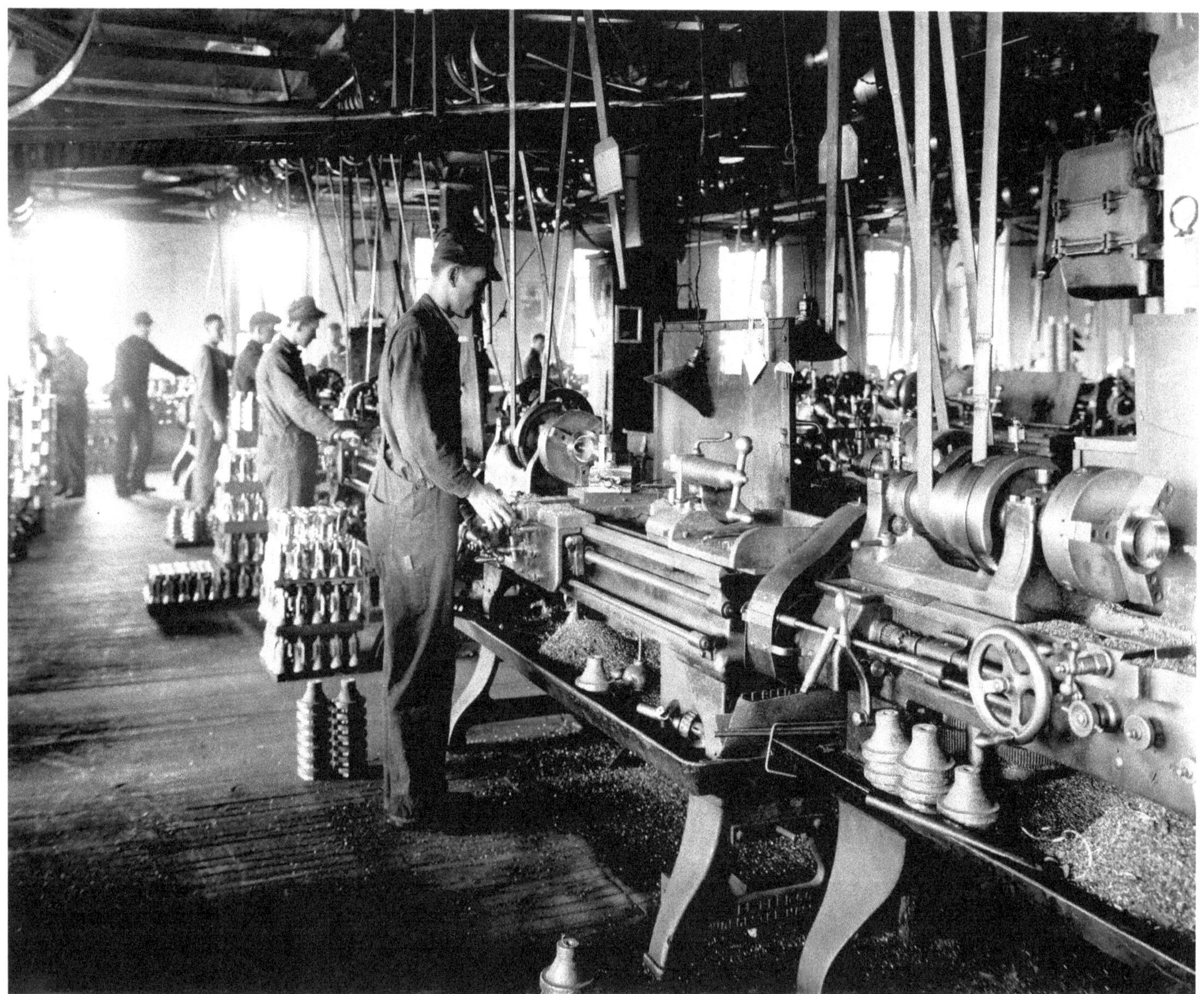

The Teasdale Vice Committee Investigation, an effort spearheaded by Senator Howard Teasdale, used this 1914 image to help identify and prohibit any unsavory behavior in Milwaukee, such as prostitution and liquor consumption.

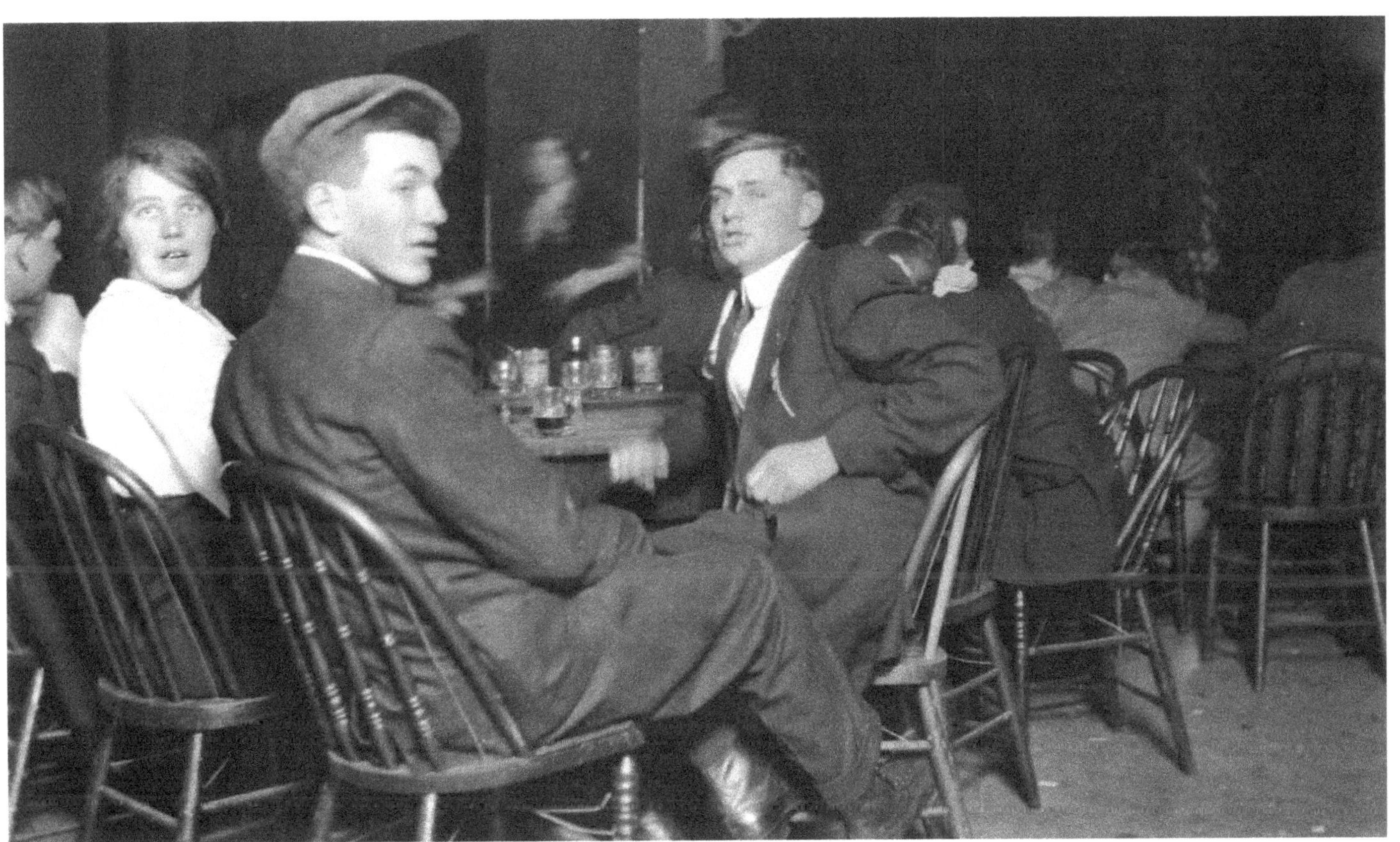

Armour and Co. once had a Milwaukee tie. Philip Armour and John Plankinton, one of Milwaukee's meatpacking magnates, were at one time partners. The partnership dissolved in 1884, and the two businessmen went their separate ways, both maintaining profitable businesses in the meat industry, Armour with his family and Plankinton with Patrick Cudahy.

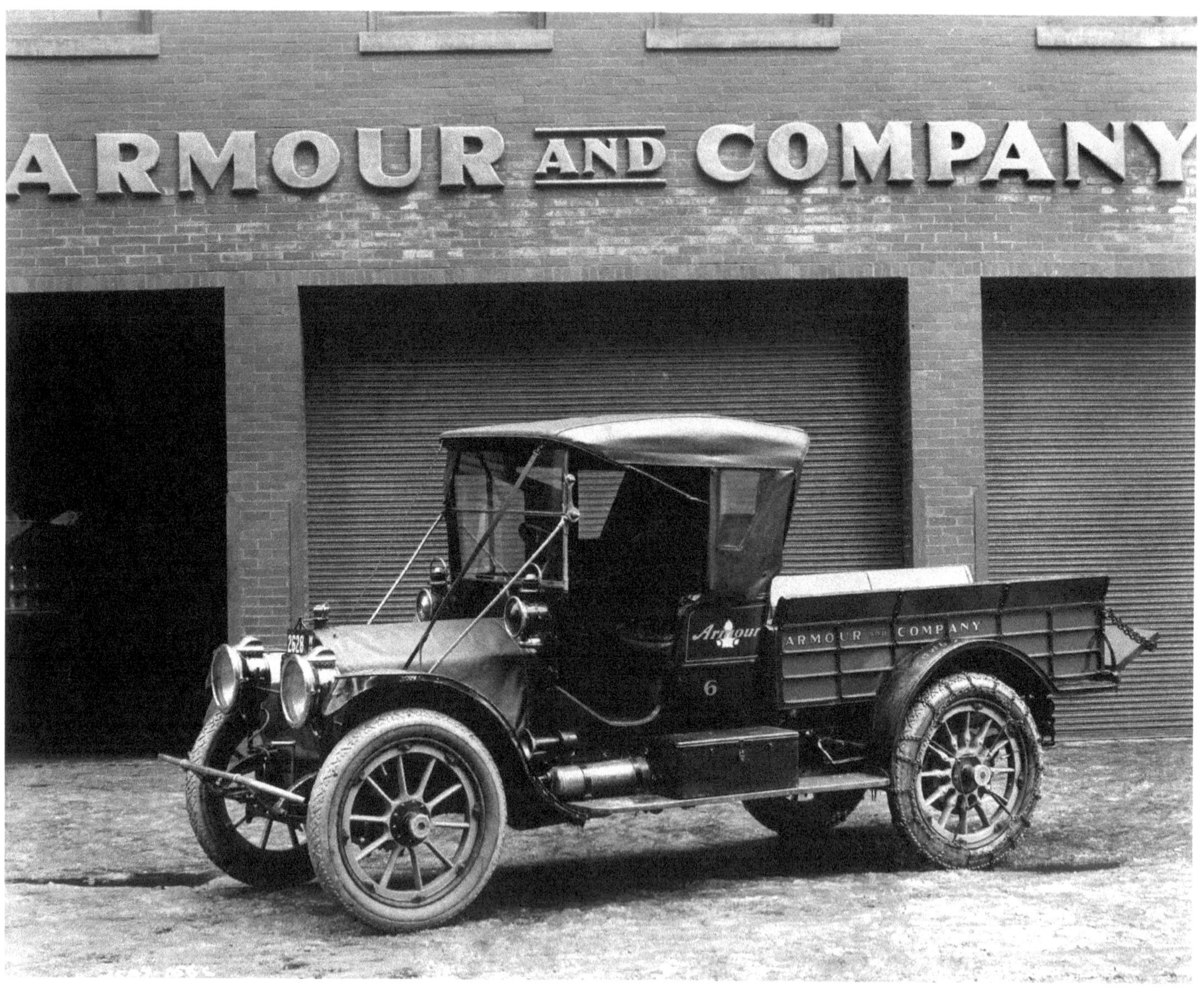

Students at the Continuation School in Milwaukee pose for a photograph in 1915. The school was started in 1912 and emphasized trade skills. Enrollment grew and by 1923 a new building was needed. The name was then changed to Milwaukee Area Technical College.

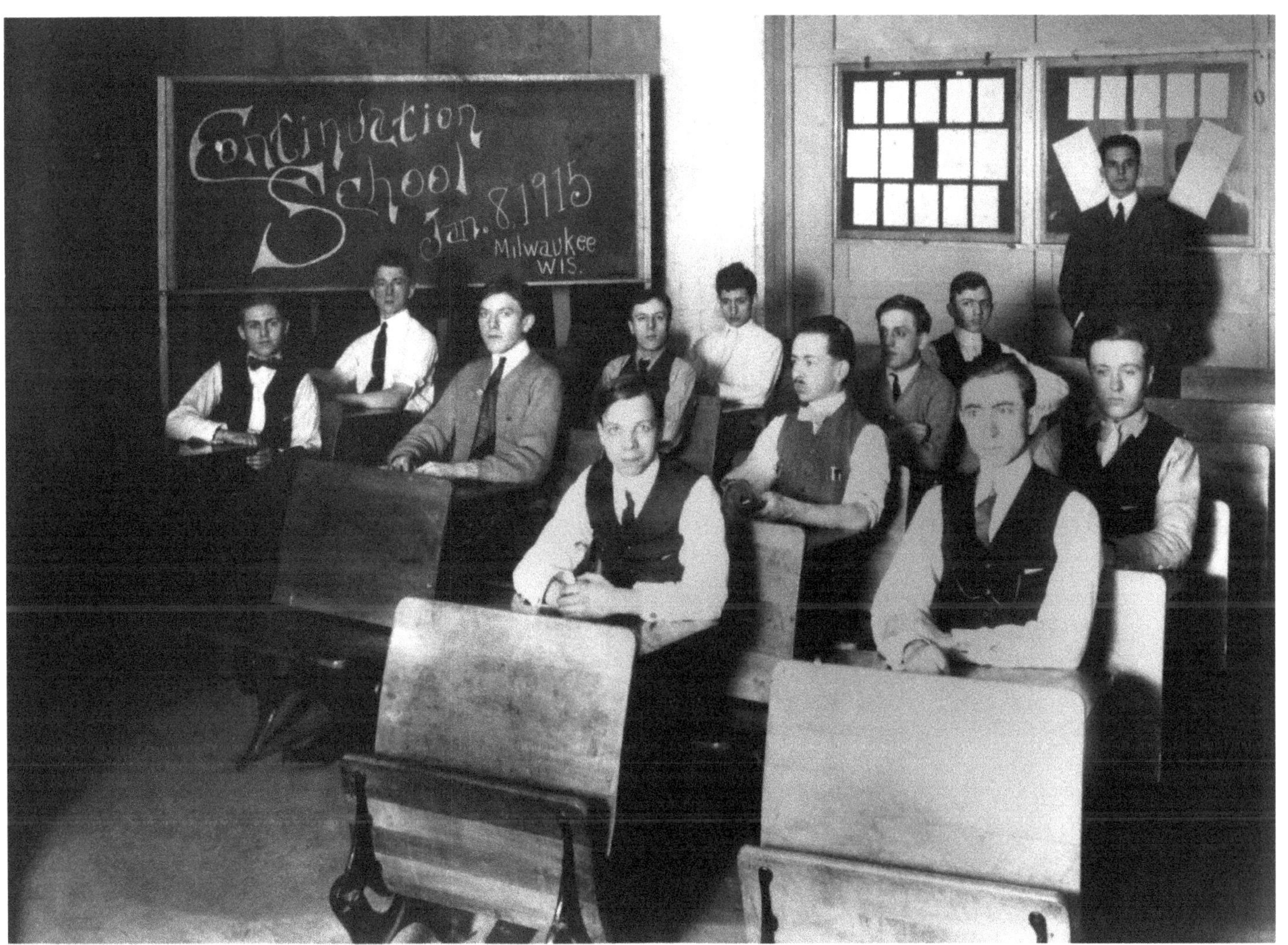

The *Milwaukee Journal* newspaper, started in 1882, existed as an independent newspaper until 1995, when it joined the *Milwaukee Sentinel* to form the *Milwaukee Journal-Sentinel.* The term "Pathfinder," visible on the rear tire of the vehicle, refers to the *Journal*'s 1915 highway information team.

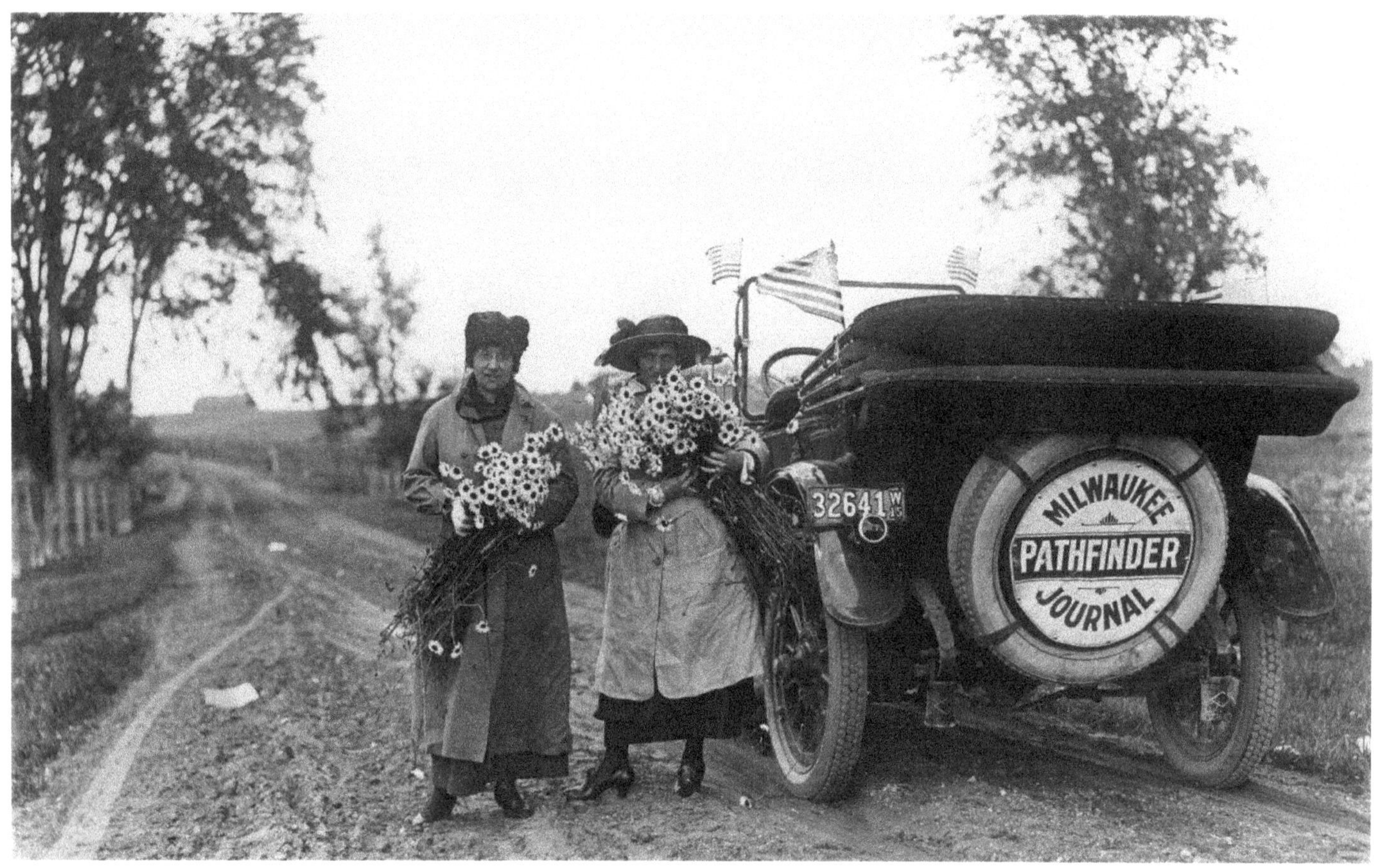

Like the local grocer, butcher, and tavern, the local bakery and confectionery was a staple in most Milwaukee neighborhoods. Jens Confectionery was located at 1503 Green Bay Avenue and offered customers an opportunity to sit at the counter and enjoy a dish of Luick ice cream at the cost of a nickel or a dime.

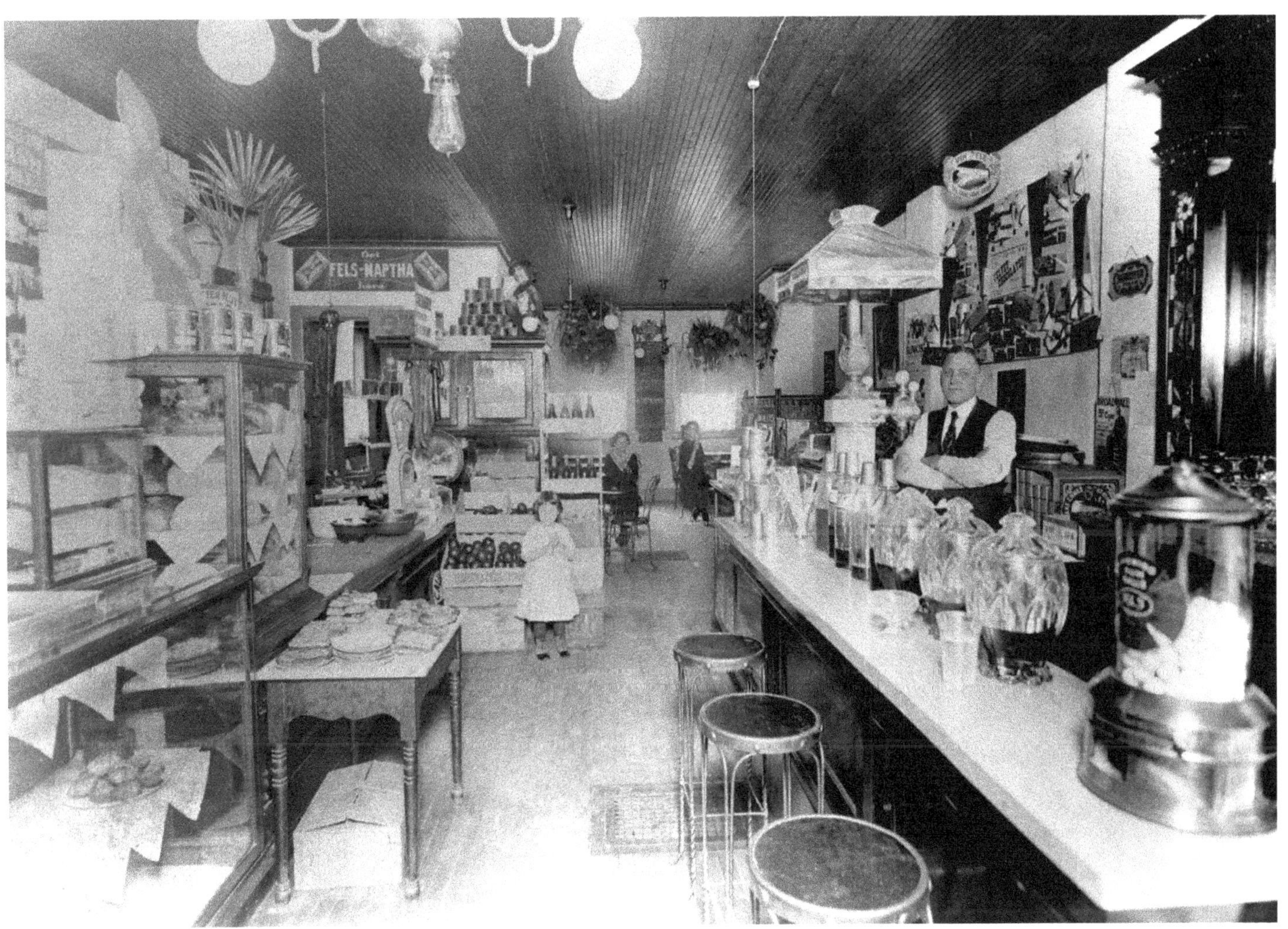

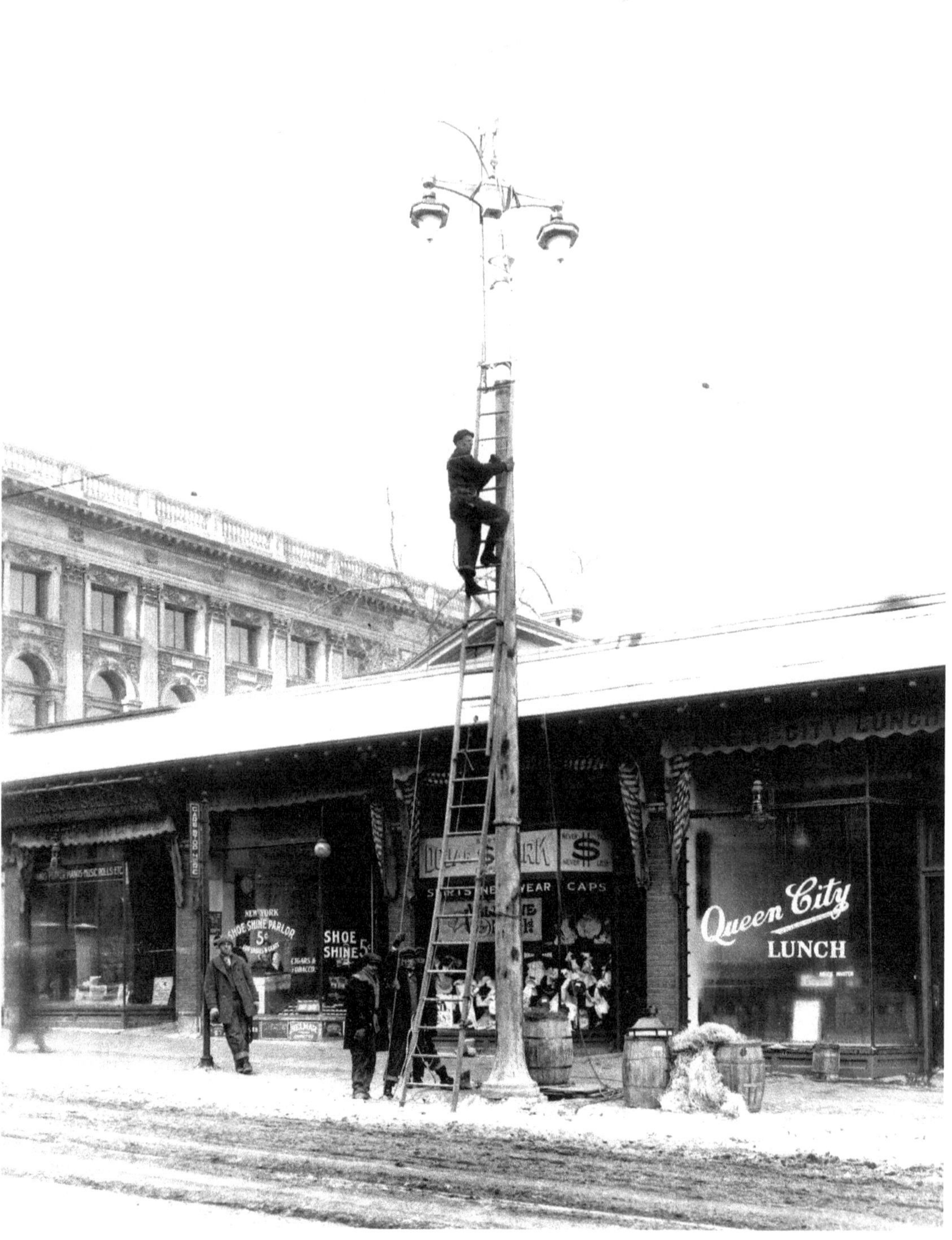

Workers on Grand Avenue are working on the streetlight around 1916. The Central Library is visible in the distance. Queen City Lunch was a popular stop after getting a shoe shine at the New York Shoe Shine Parlor.

Troops train behind the old post office in 1917, which was located in the Federal Building at 517 E. Wisconsin Avenue. The sergeant in this image had just returned from Mexico and was given the job of training the new recruits. At this time, many new soldiers were recruited at the Plankinton Arcade, which is now home to shops and offices.

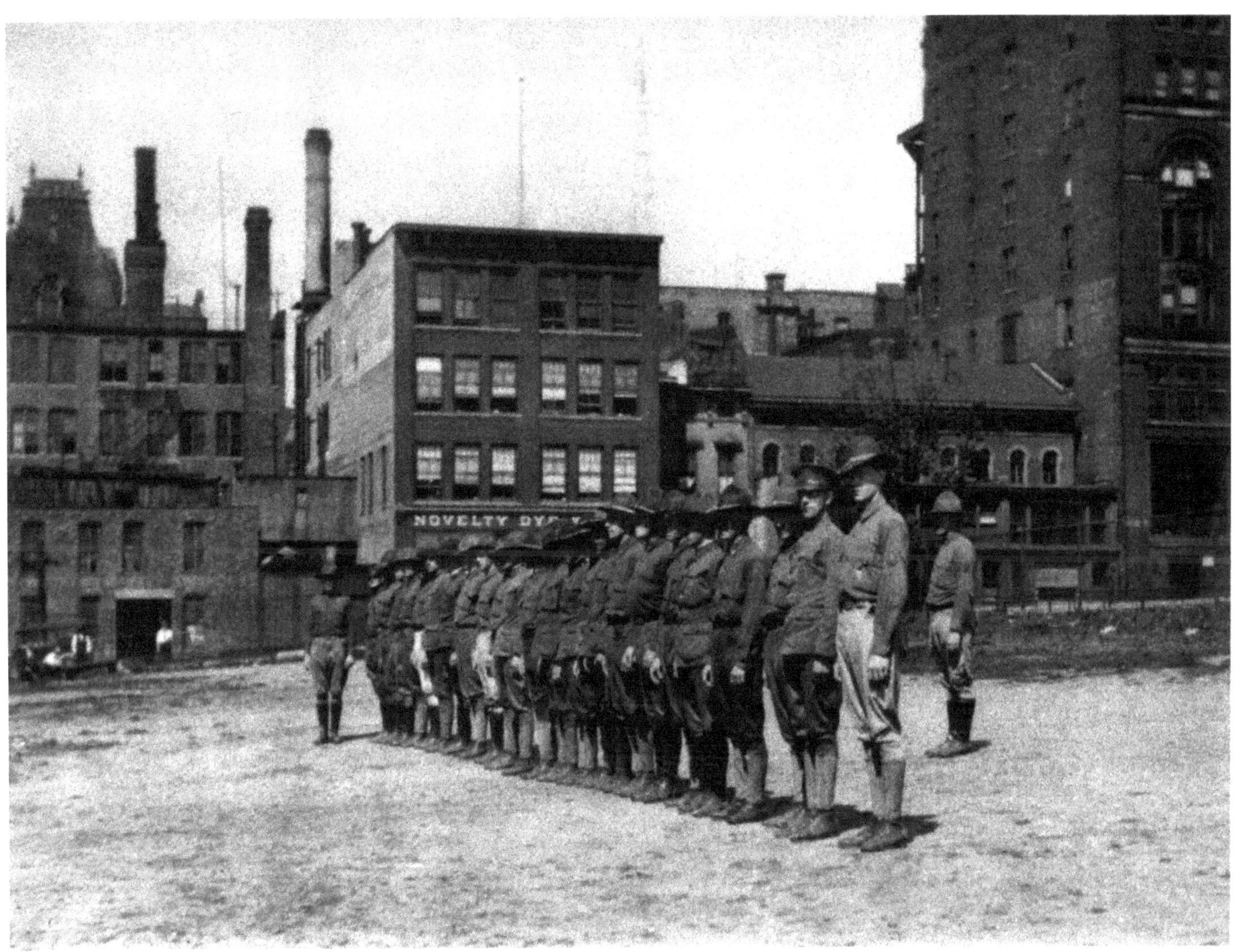

The *Christopher Columbus* was once a popular cruise vessel used to navigate the Great Lakes. This photograph, taken in 1917, shows the damaged ship being towed out of the Milwaukee River. A strong current had overtaken the ship and forced it toward land, causing it to collide with a water tower. The ship was repaired and put back in service a year later. It continued to sail until 1937.

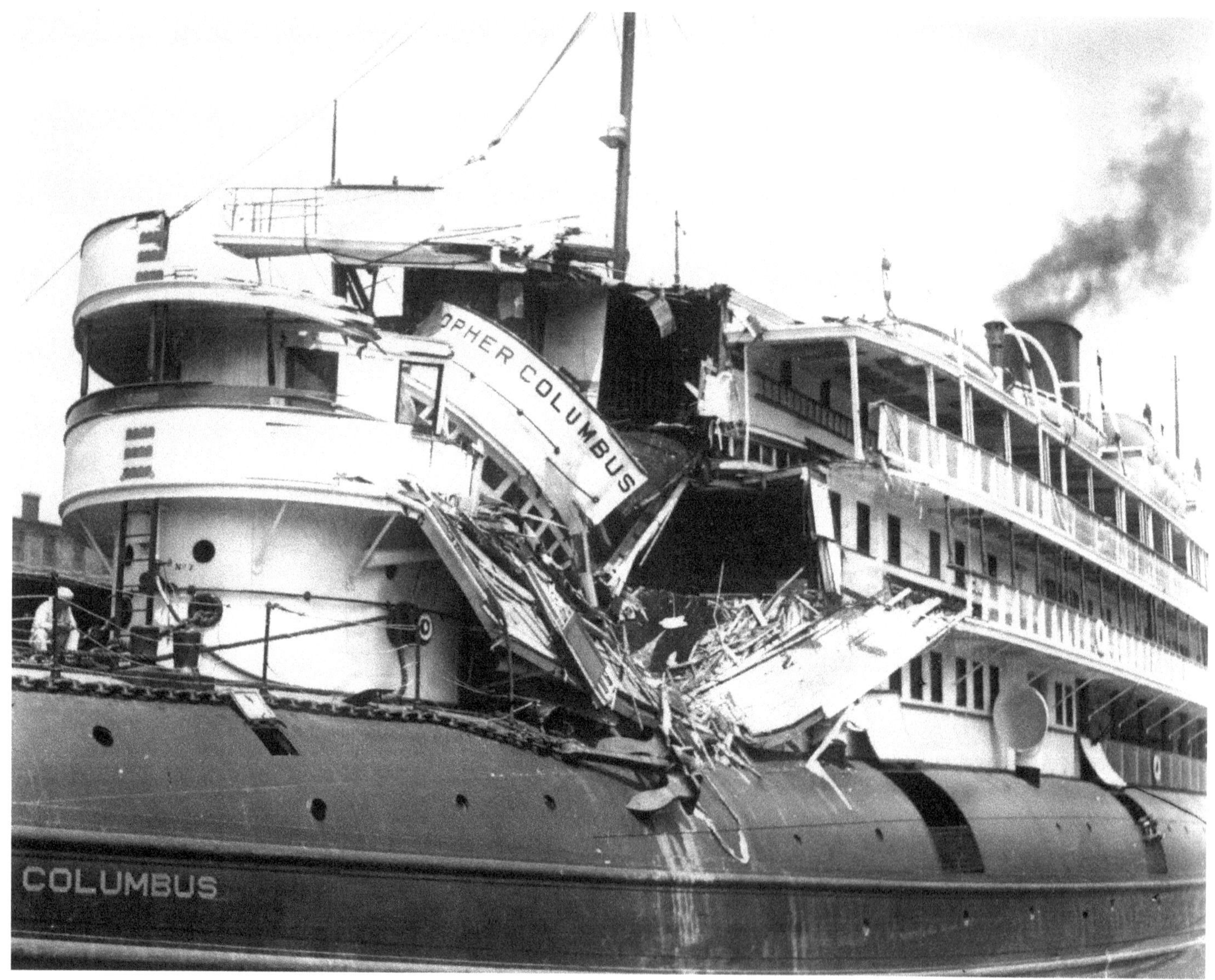

These women are members of the Motor Corps of the National League for Women's Service, started in 1917, which supported the effort at home during World War I.

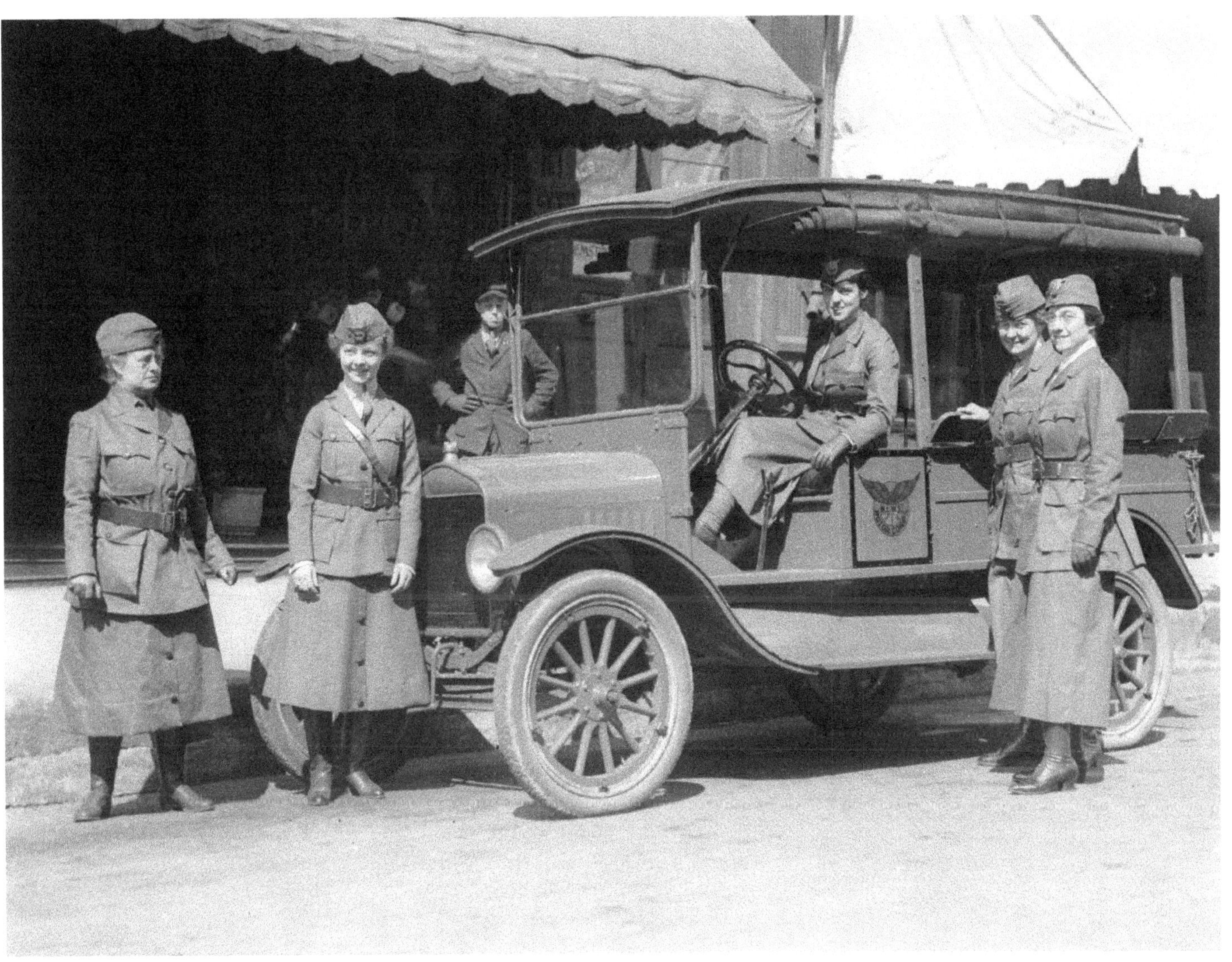

Women work at the International Harvester Milwaukee Works manufacturing cream separators, to help offset a labor shortage as Milwaukee men were called away to duty during World War I.

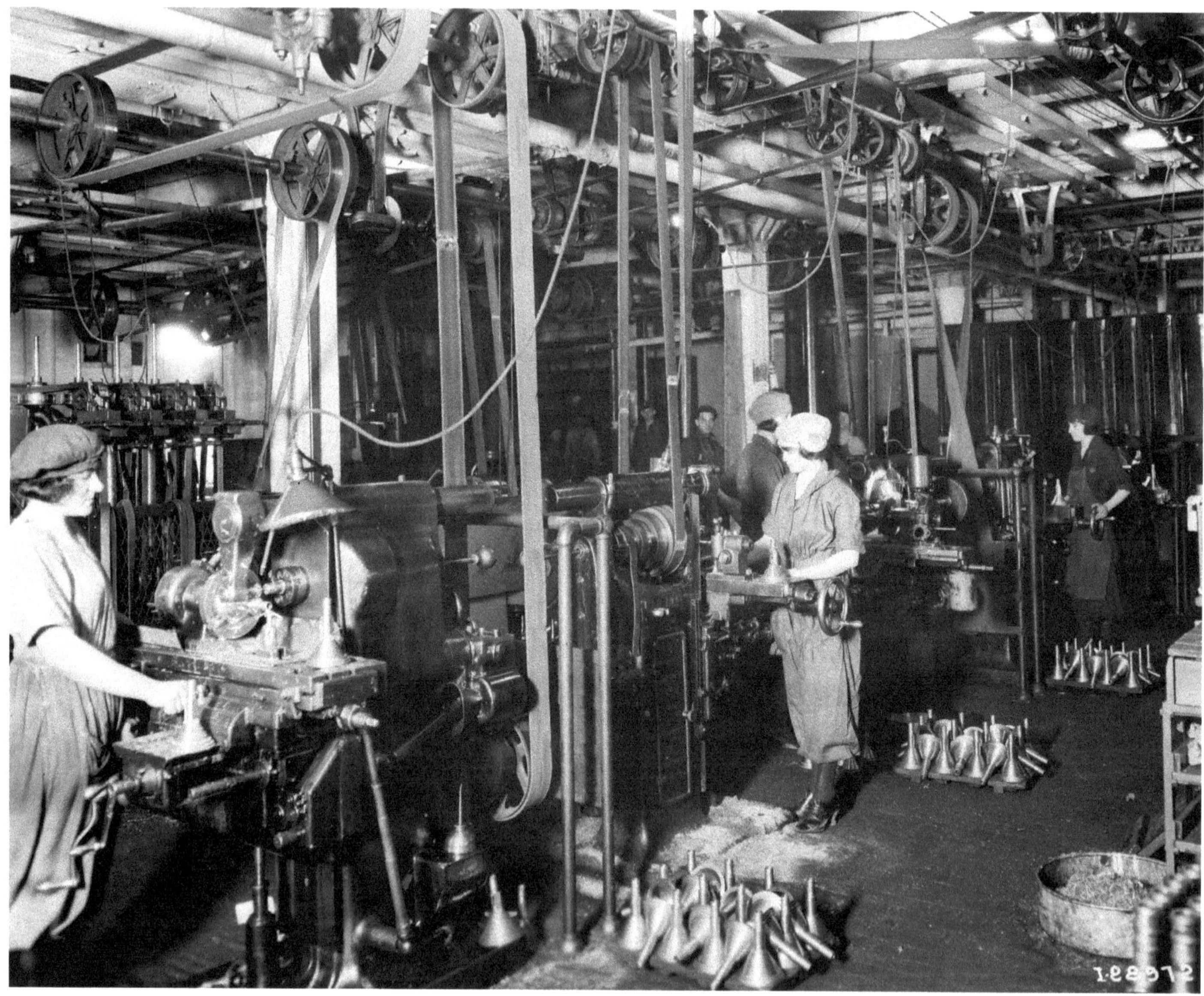

Prohibition and Progress

(1918–1939)

With the end of World War I, Milwaukee entered the era between the two great wars. Citizens of German descent, given the recent carnage, were looked upon with suspicion. To emphasize their status as Americans, many of them Anglicized their names, Johann becoming John, Schmidt becoming Smith. Milwaukee's focus, nevertheless, was on the future, and the city managed to maintain its economy as well as its culture throughout the coming years.

As Prohibition became the law of the land in 1920, the beer brewing industry turned to making non-alcoholic products. Businesses such as Harley-Davidson flourished. Harnischfeger and Allis-Chalmers were also two of the big names of industry in Milwaukee at that time. As technology advanced and the automobile became popular, Milwaukee streets started to become far more crowded. Downtown continued to bustle with streetcars carrying citizens to their destinations.

Golda Meir, whose family had immigrated to Milwaukee from Russia, headed to Palestine with her new husband in 1921, where she would eventually become prime minister of the new state of Israel.

With the stock market crash in 1929 and the coming of the Great Depression, the future looked uncertain. Local government under Mayor Daniel Hoan and New Deal federal programs like the Works Progress Administration (WPA) were especially effective in providing jobs, some of them make-work, some of them invaluable. Work-relief crews built roads, bridges, and the city's county parks designed by Charles Whitnall.

Prohibition came to an end in 1933. On April 7, at 12:01 A.M., the Milwaukee breweries—Miller, Pabst, Schlitz, Blatz—were set to brew beer for anyone who wanted it. With the reintroduction of legal alcohol, especially beer, came a renewed interest in the German heritage of Milwaukee.

Milwaukee continued to grow as a city, and with the coming of World War II, the city was fully braced for the new challenge.

A typical grocery store in 1919 Milwaukee carries fresh produce, canned, and packaged goods, as well as oil lamps and kerosene. Herman Bauman, the proprietor, had two wagons in order to make deliveries to the homes of his customers.

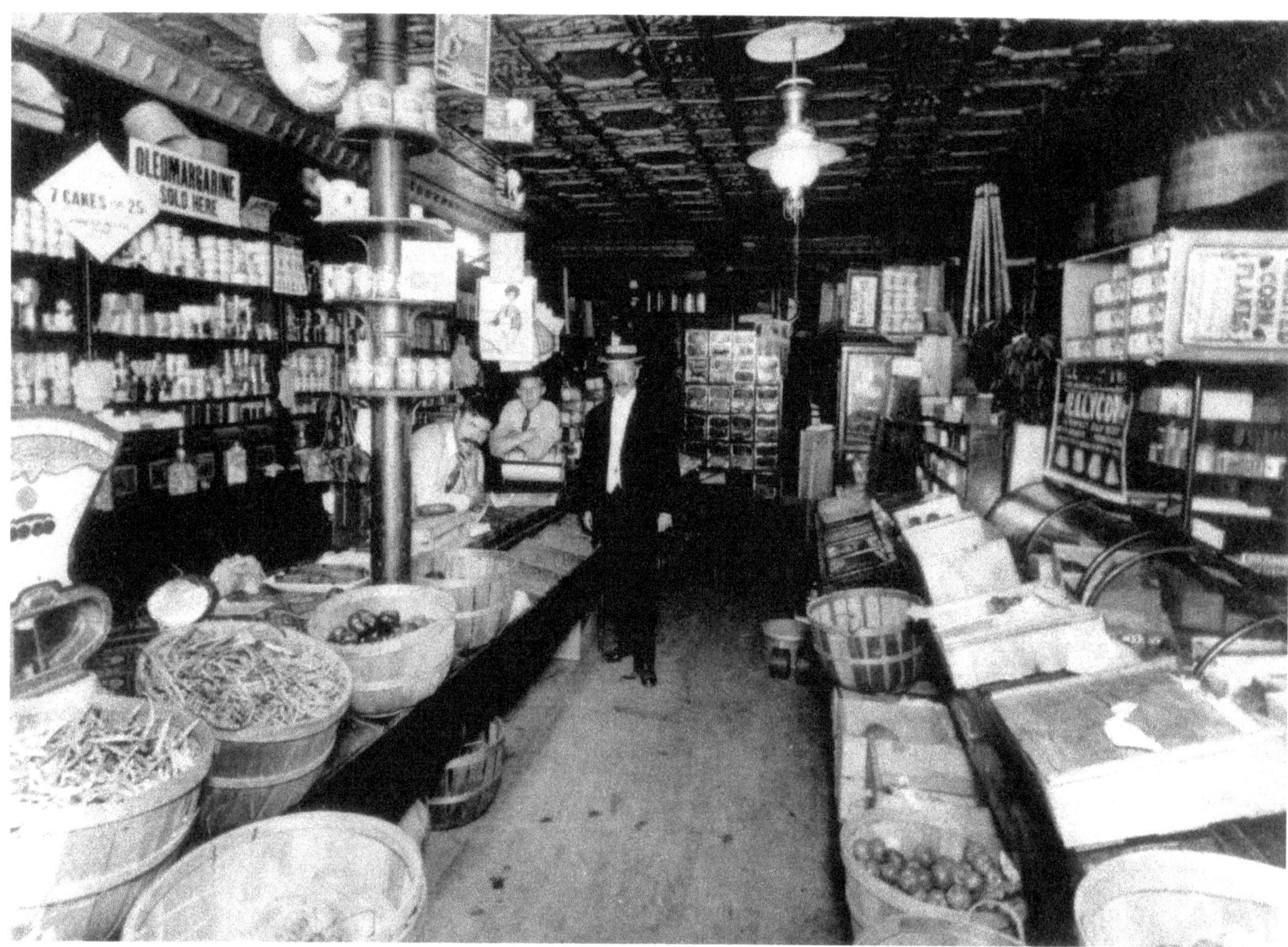

Cracker-Jacks Park, located on the outskirts of the city, was a place to relax, enjoy the outdoors, and picnic. In 1919, Jung Beer, a beer not synonymous with Milwaukee, was actually manufactured in Random Lake, Wisconsin, until 1958.

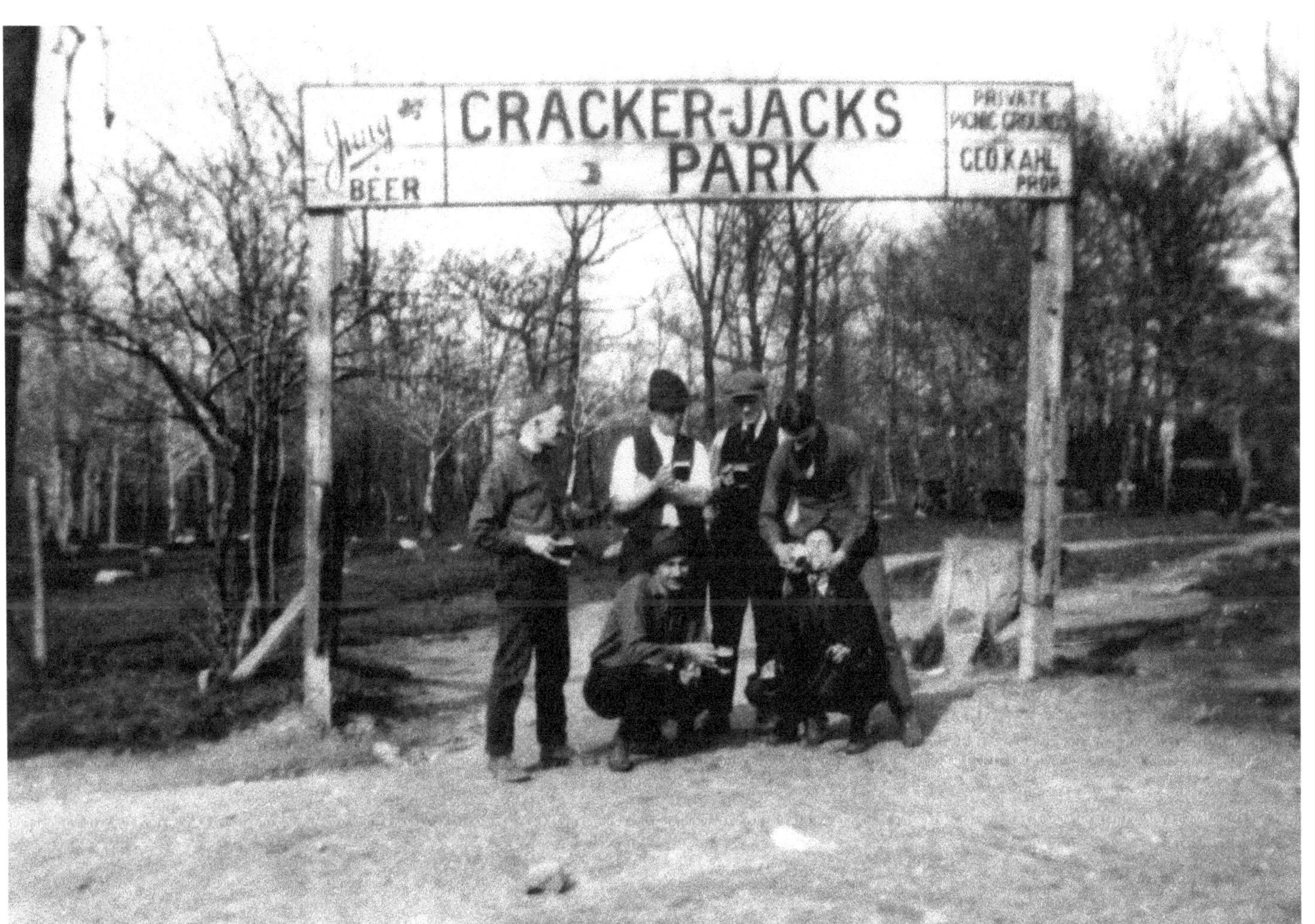

The Prohibition Act, which left the nation dry, left many Milwaukee taverns without an income. The Zahringer Malt Company felt the sting of prohibition as well. Excess malt reached toward the ceilings of this small store. Milwaukeeans would not be put off by the lack of beer for sale. In the end, brewing went from the factory to the home as many people started to brew their own beer during the dry years.

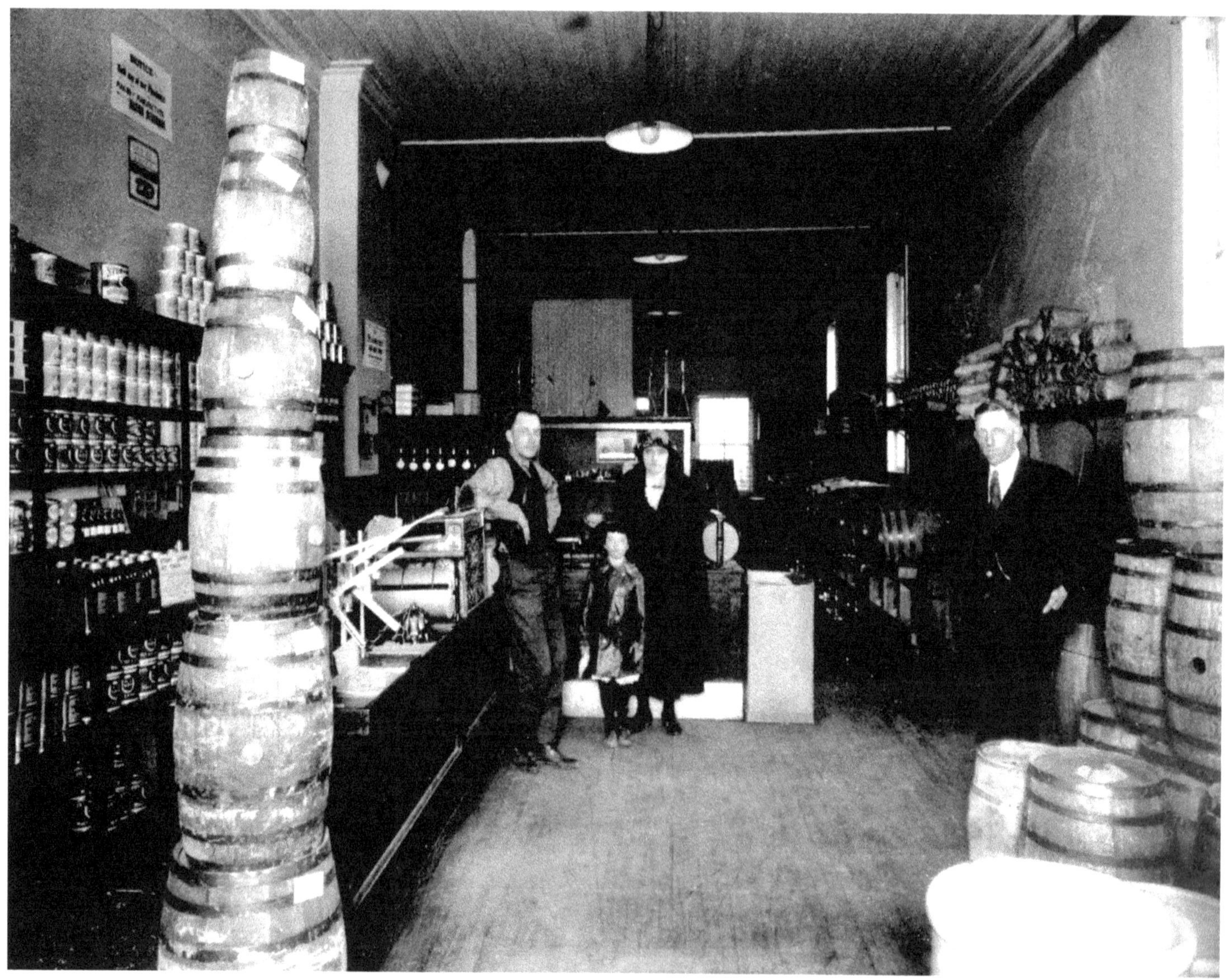

Many Jewish citizens of Milwaukee were present for the "Americanization pageant" that was put on in 1919 to celebrate the blessings the New World had brought to them. This photo offers a scene from the Poale Zion Chasidim, a play depicting Jewish history. Golda Meir, future prime minister of Israel, portrays lady Liberty.

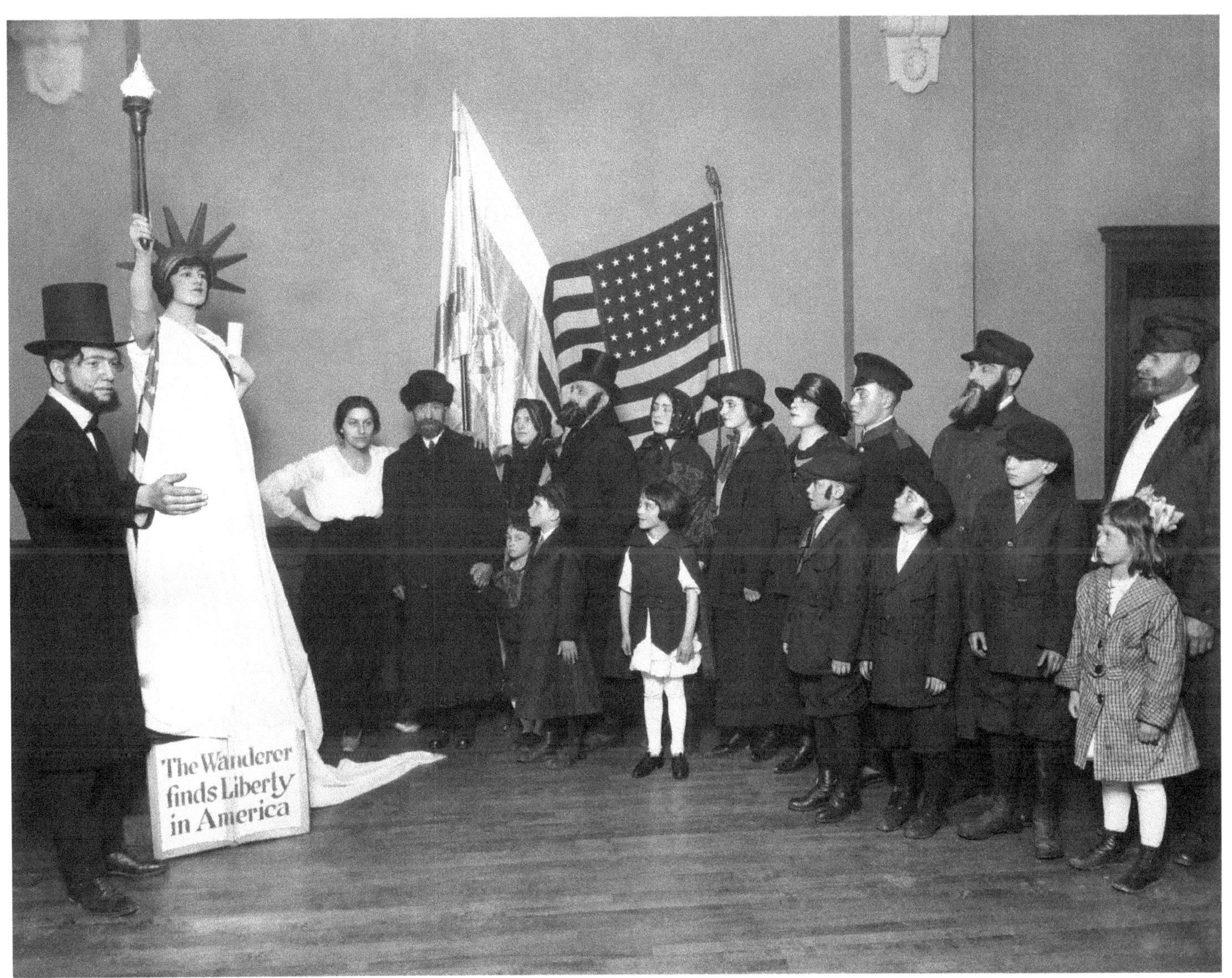

The Great War had ended and the boys were on their way home. Here the 32nd division of the Army parades down a Milwaukee street as the city celebrates the end of World War I with the signing of the Treaty of Versailles in 1919.

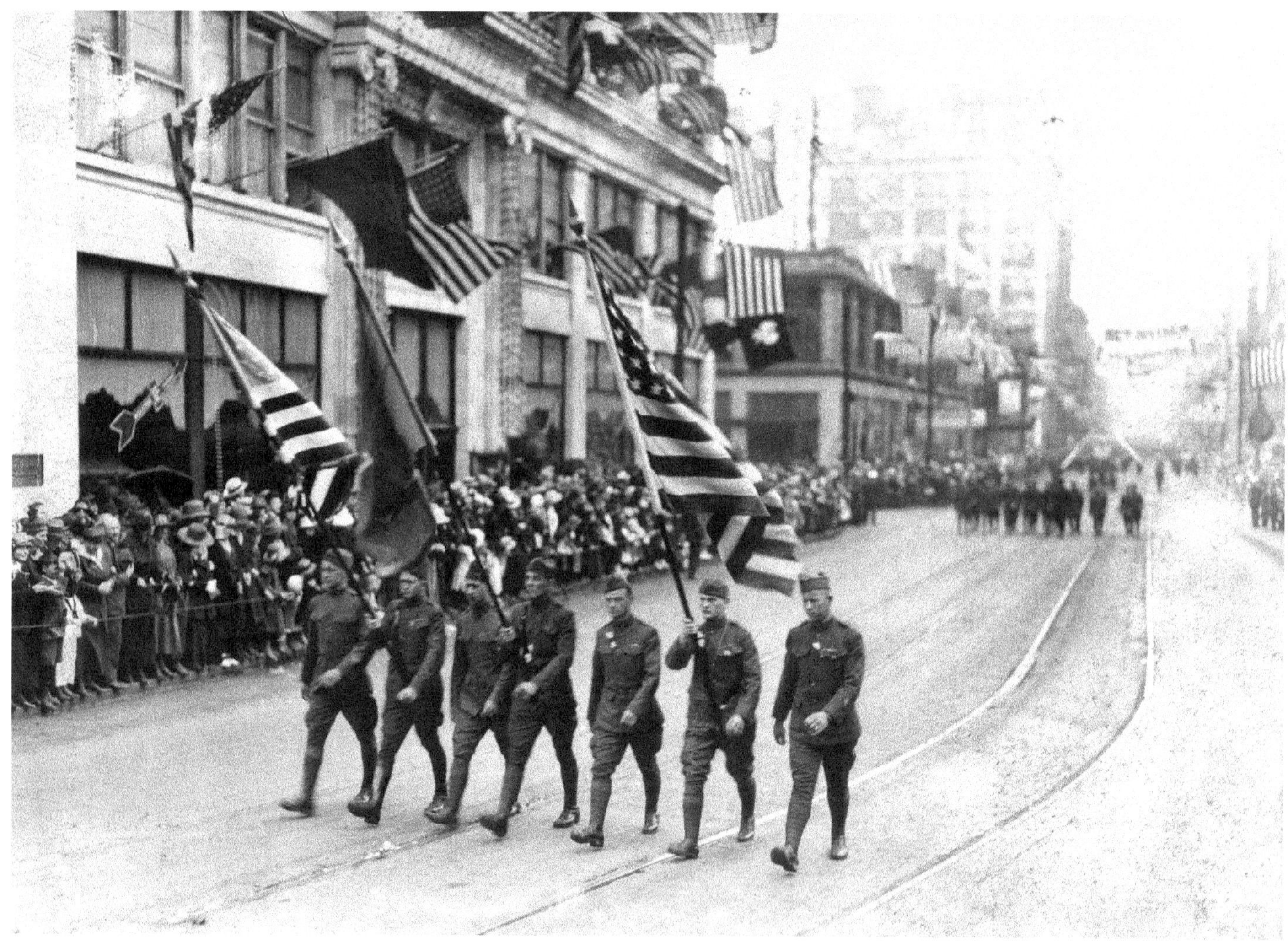

Postal employees picketed in August 1919, demanding a raise to offset the rise in the cost of living.

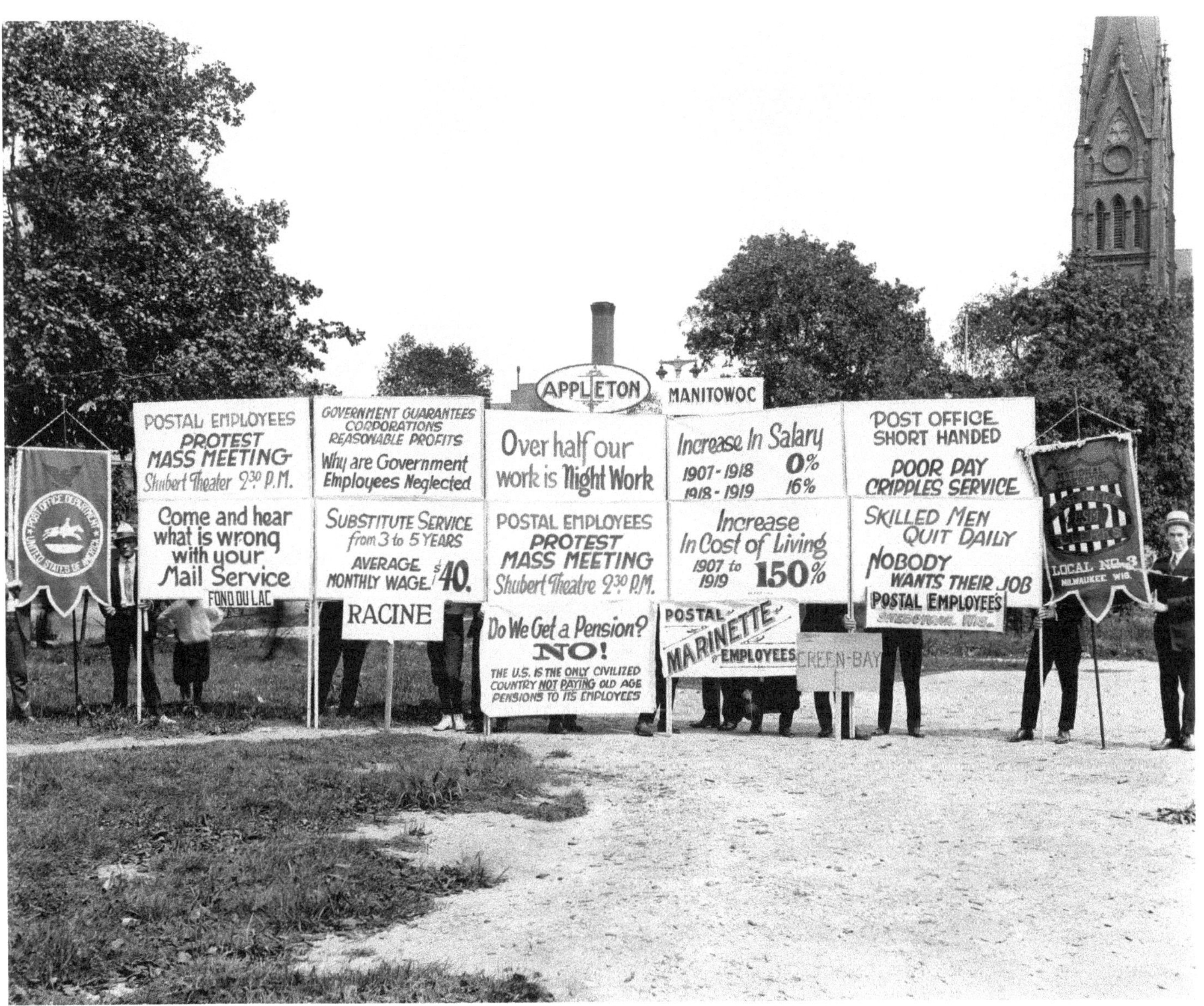

Allis Chalmers was one of Milwaukee's leading manufacturers. Here workers stand beside and atop a plate-steel spiral casing for a hydraulic turbine. The Edward P. Allis Company had joined forces with three other businesses including Fraser and Chalmers in 1901. Over the years the company acquired numerous subsidiaries until its eventual decline. The Milwaukee offices closed in 1999.

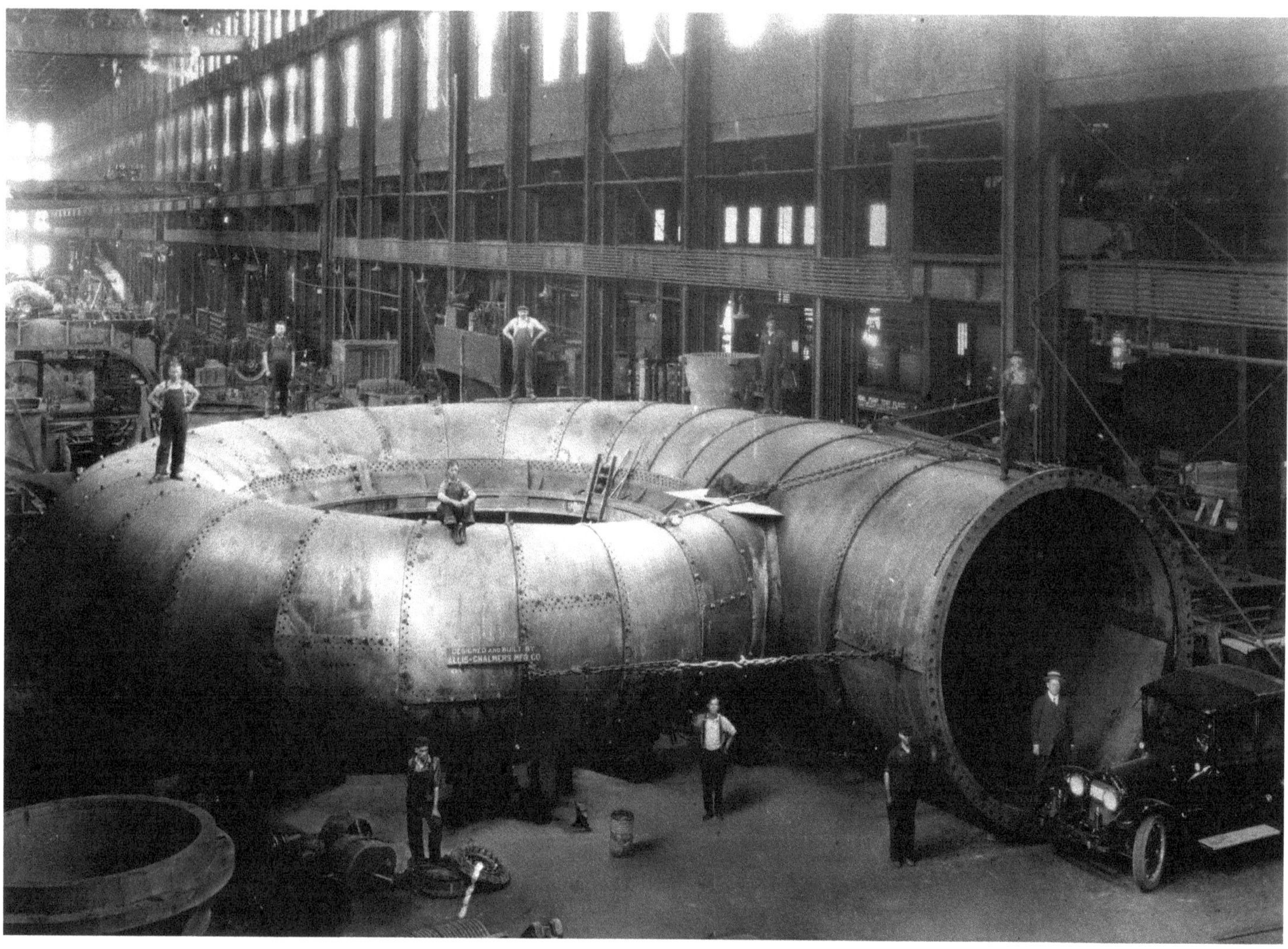

Many companies had their own baseball teams. The International Harvester Company was one of them, and their team is shown here in the late 1910s. Much earlier, in 1878, the Milwaukee Cream Citys, a professional baseball team formed in 1869, beat the Cincinnati Reds 8-5. Baseball has been an important part of Milwaukee society ever since, continuing with the Braves and then the Brewers.

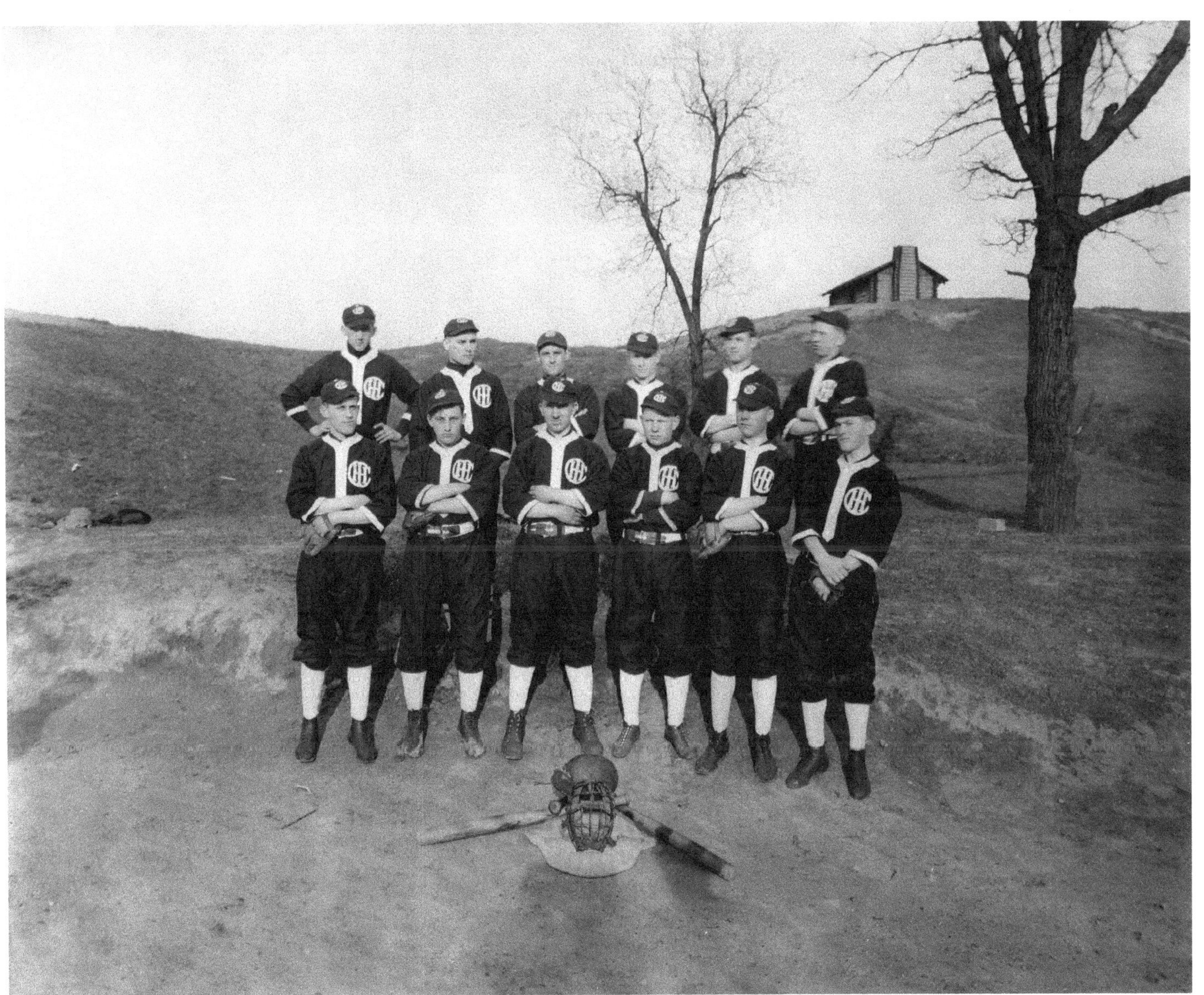

The Alfred W. Lawson Air Line has a new airplane in 1920, the Lawson Midnight Airliner. The planes Lawson built were meant to carry fairly large numbers of passengers. In 1919 Lawson flew a demonstration flight that took him to New York, then to Washington, D.C., and back to Milwaukee while carrying fifteen passengers.

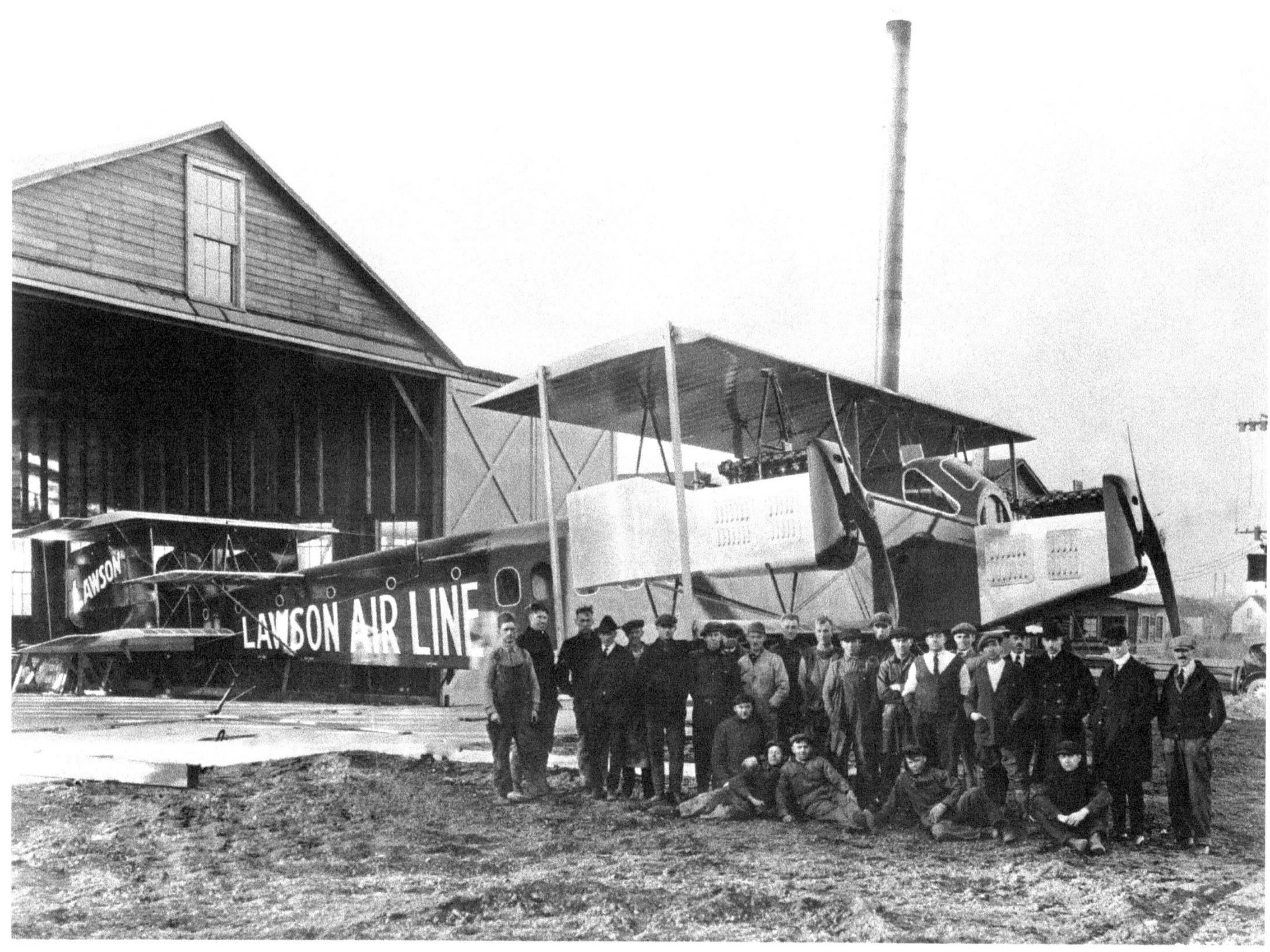

Founded in 1901, the Heil Company was a leading manufacturer of steel tank cars. Julius P. Heil, the company's founder, also utilized the new skill of welding to devise the first garbage trucks. This photograph, taken in 1921, is of a Highway Commission Truck in Milwaukee.

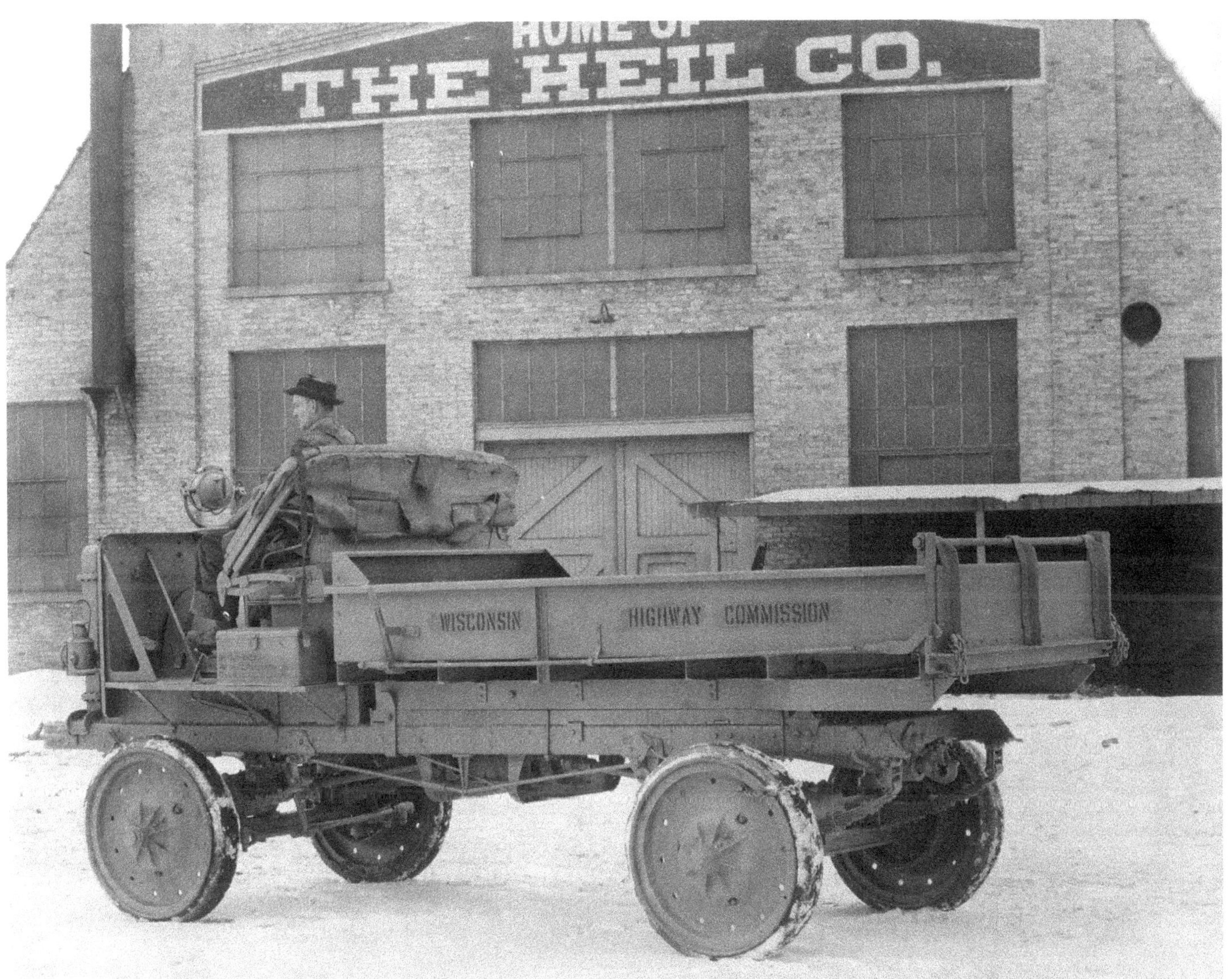

Advertisements for the Orpheum Theatre and the *Milwaukee Journal* newspaper grace this image, recorded in 1922. The number of automobiles plying Wisconsin Avenue has noticeably increased with time.

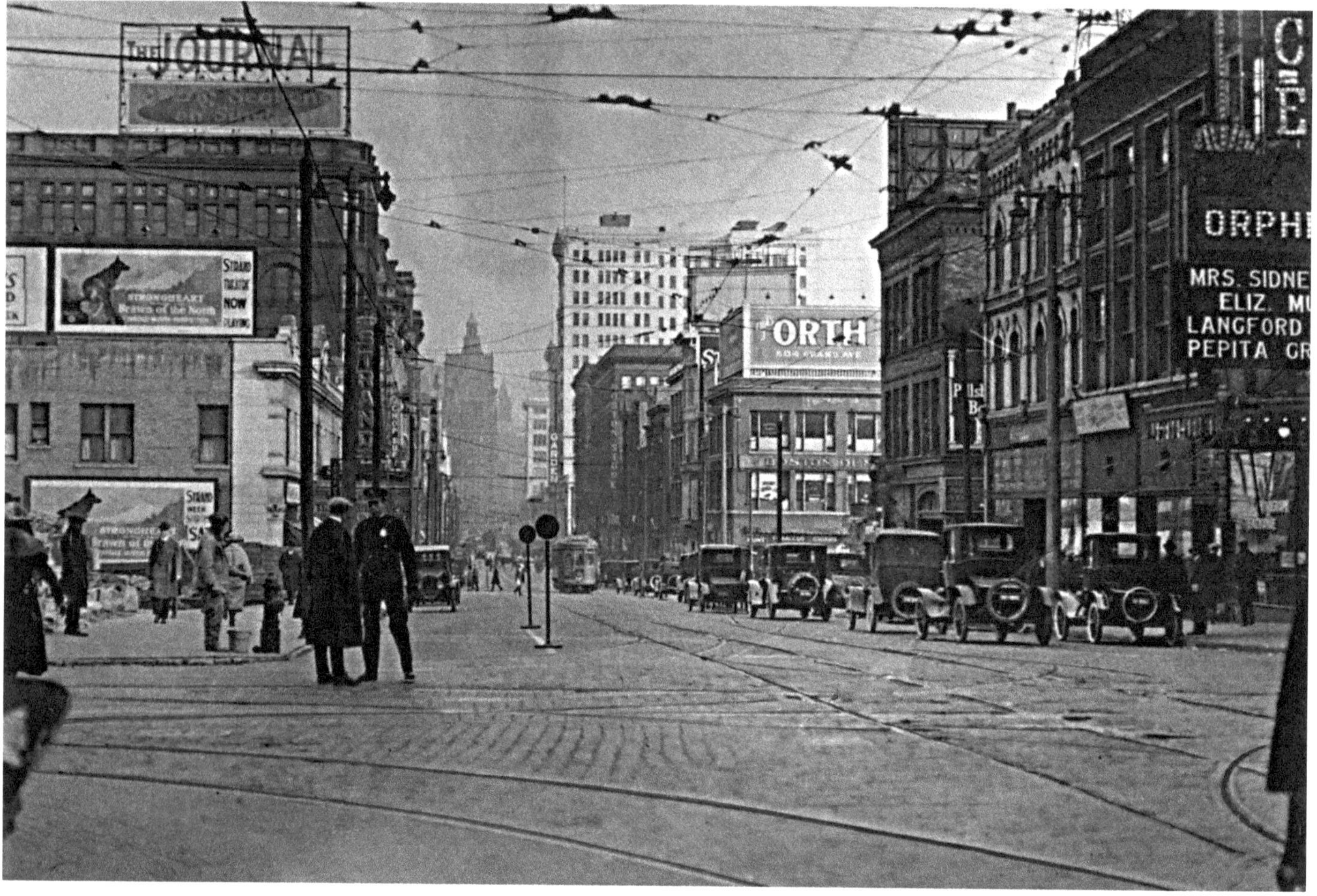

Before there was a branch of the University of Wisconsin in Milwaukee, there was the University of Wisconsin Extension Division. This photograph depicts an exhibit about the WHA radio station, based in Madison, displayed at the Milwaukee Auditorium.

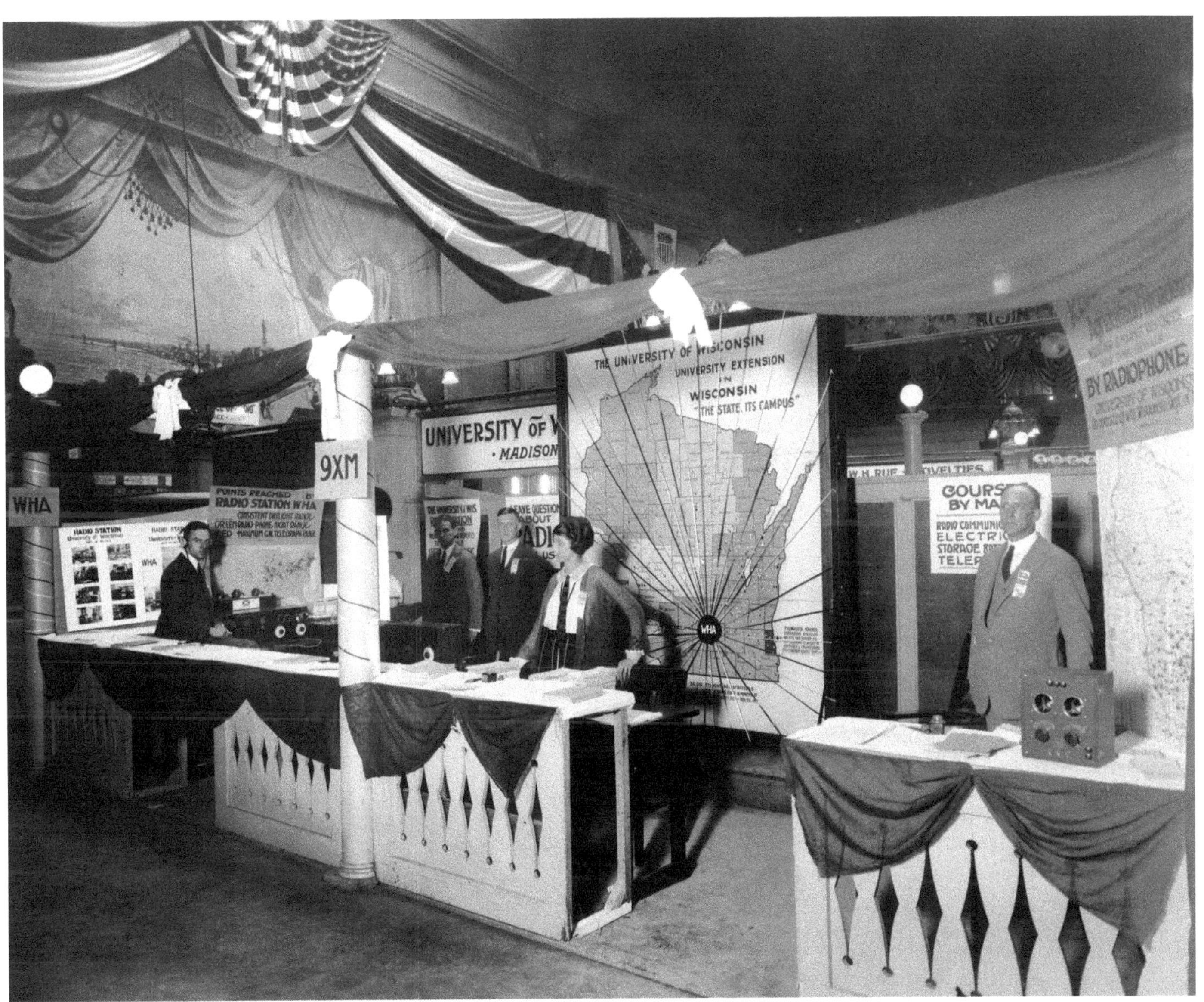

Milwaukee street names have changed quite a bit over the years. Between 1927 and 1933, streets like Grand Avenue became Wisconsin Avenue, and Oneida became East Wells.

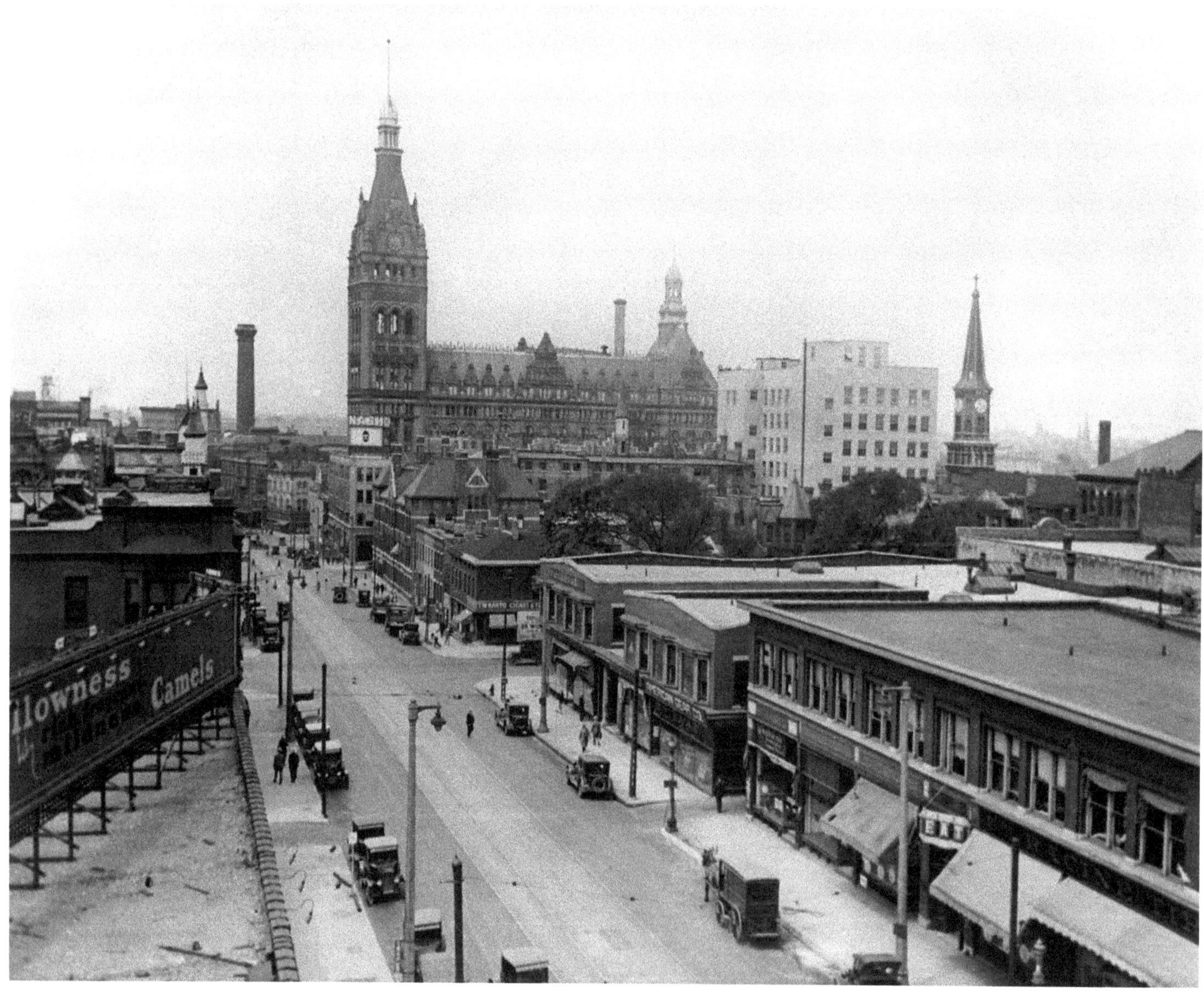

Metropolitan Milwaukee is not the first place many people think of in connection with snow skiing; however in 1925, a ski jump competition was held in Gordon Park, located on the west bank of the Milwaukee River and Locust Street. Warm temperatures in February led officials to consider canceling the event.

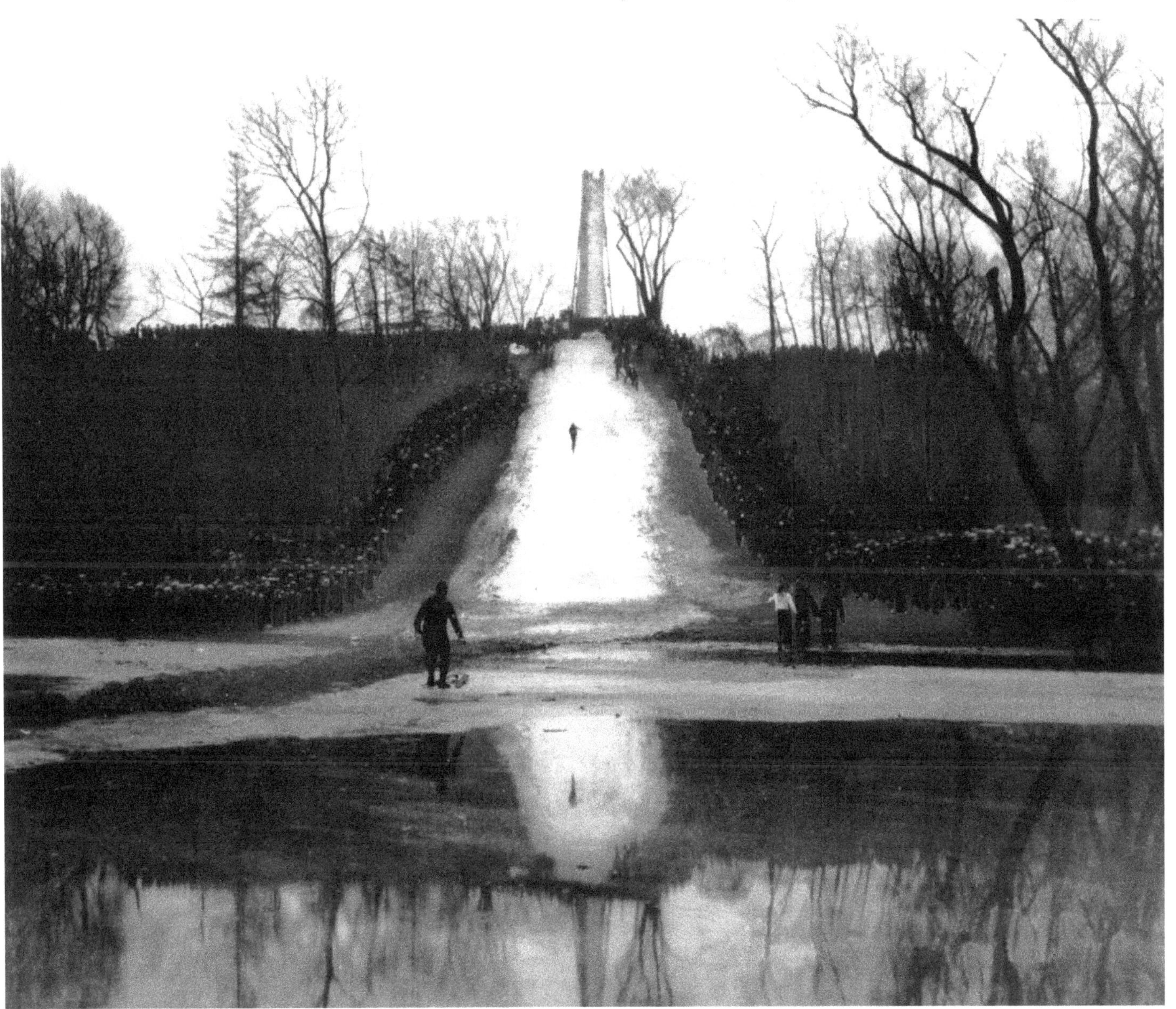

Photographed in December 1924, this tavern, once located on 379 1st Avenue, was a gathering place for the Slovenian population of Milwaukee. Those who frequented the tavern came here to socialize and get advice about becoming American citizens. The sign on the star wishes patrons a Merry Christmas and a Happy New Year.

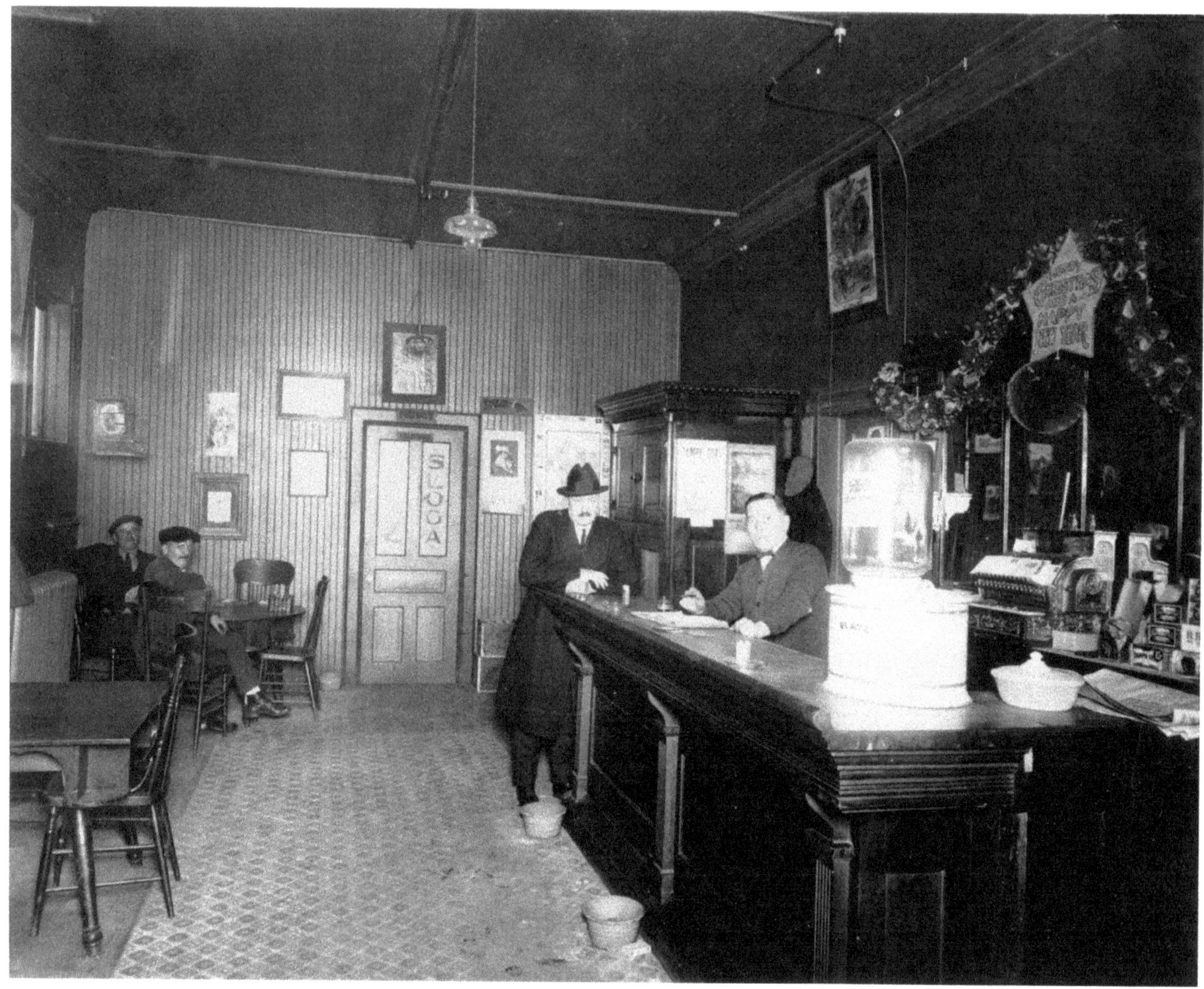

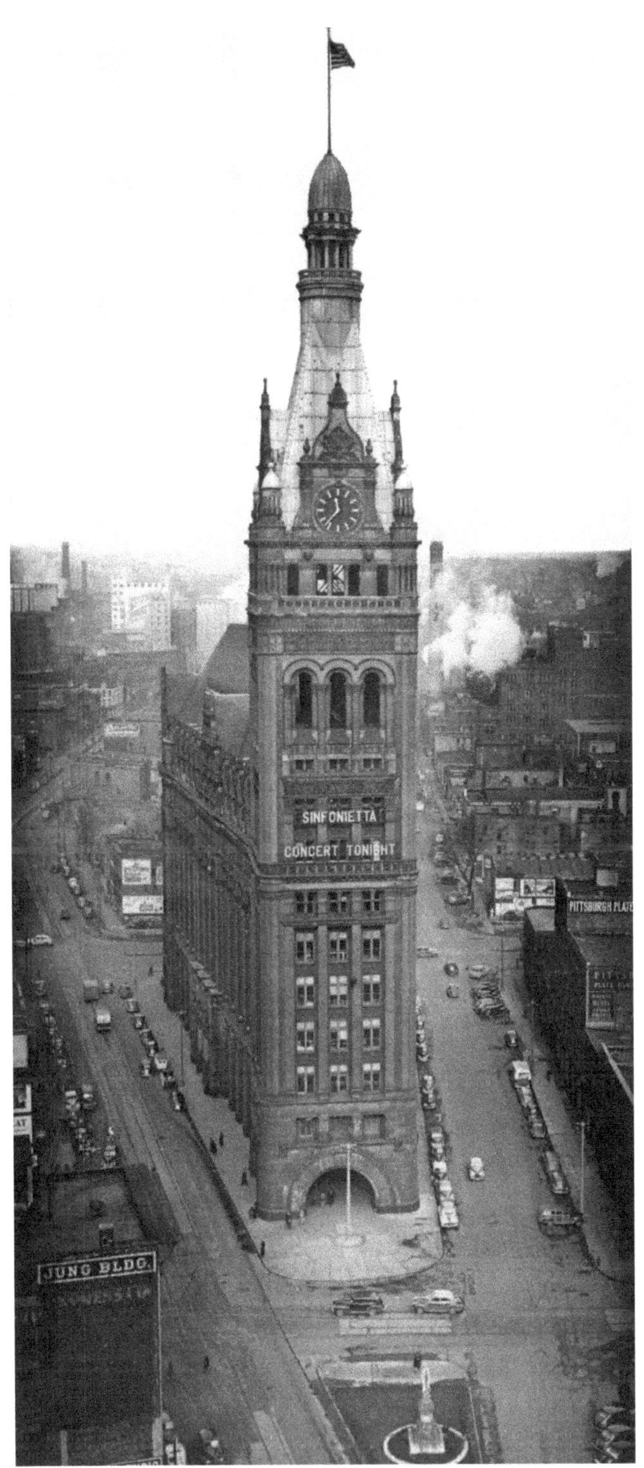

Milwaukee City Hall has always been an imposing building in Milwaukee, particularly in the earlier years of its existence. The lettering on the outside reads "Sinfonietta Concert Tonight." Not only was City Hall a place of government, but it was appreciated for its architectural beauty as well.

Median strips and barriers were not the norm when cars began to rule the roads. Turtles, small metal obstacles with lights that directed drivers at night, helped drivers to navigate. This 1924 Dodge is testing the effects of driving over a turtle. Turtles eventually gave way to other forms of traffic control, with the exception of a few that remained on Port Washington Road in the 1960s.

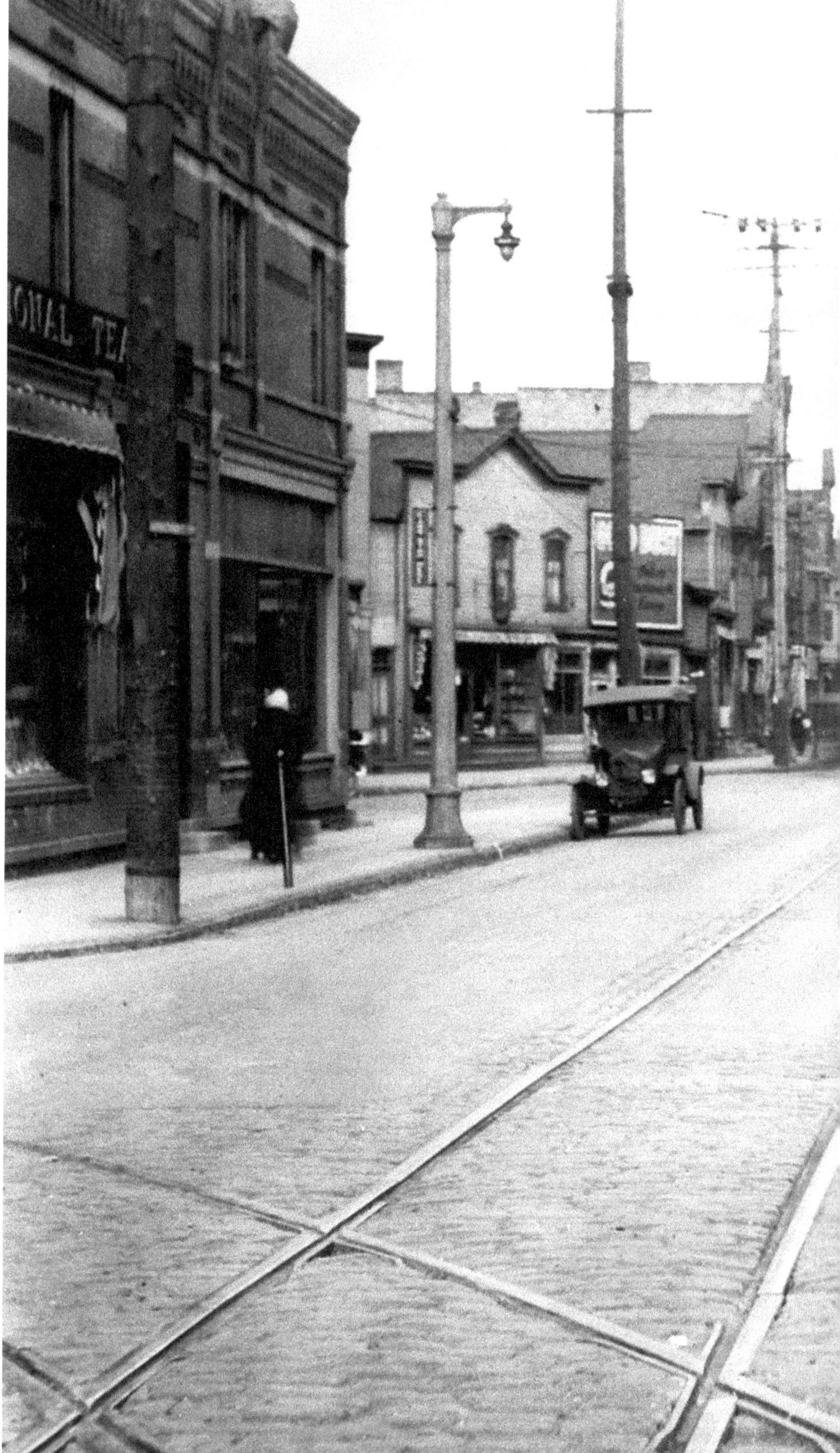

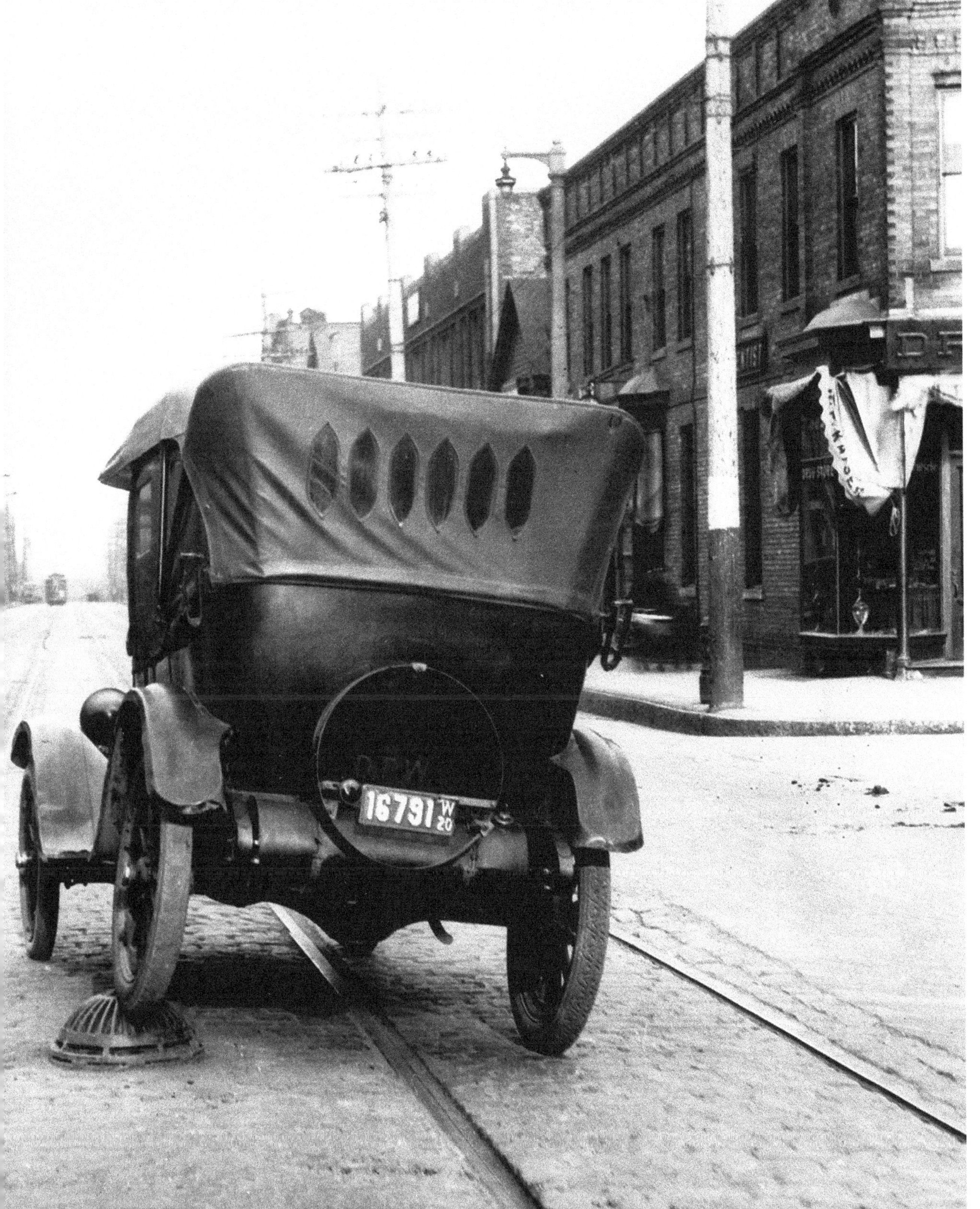
16791 W 20

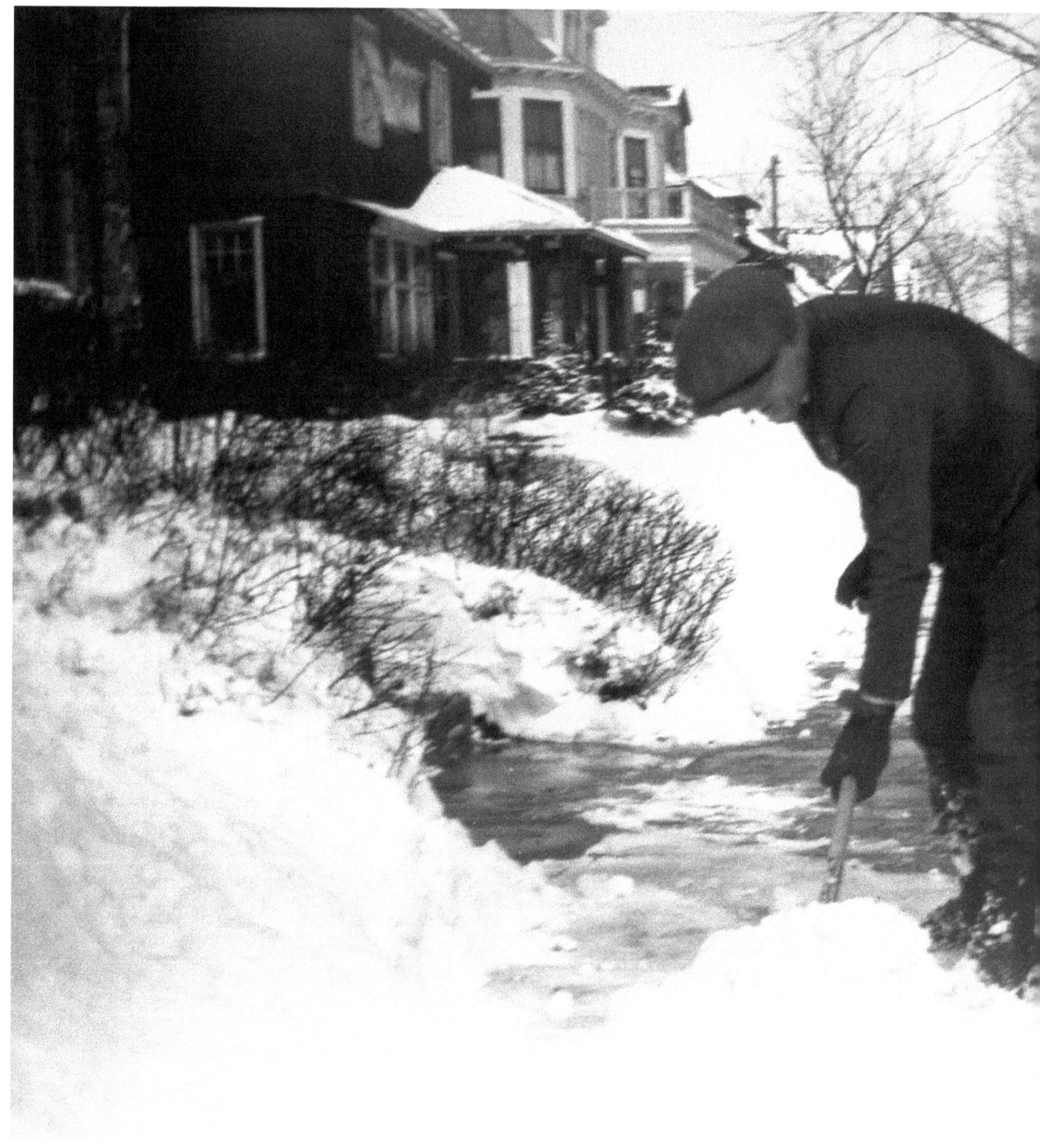

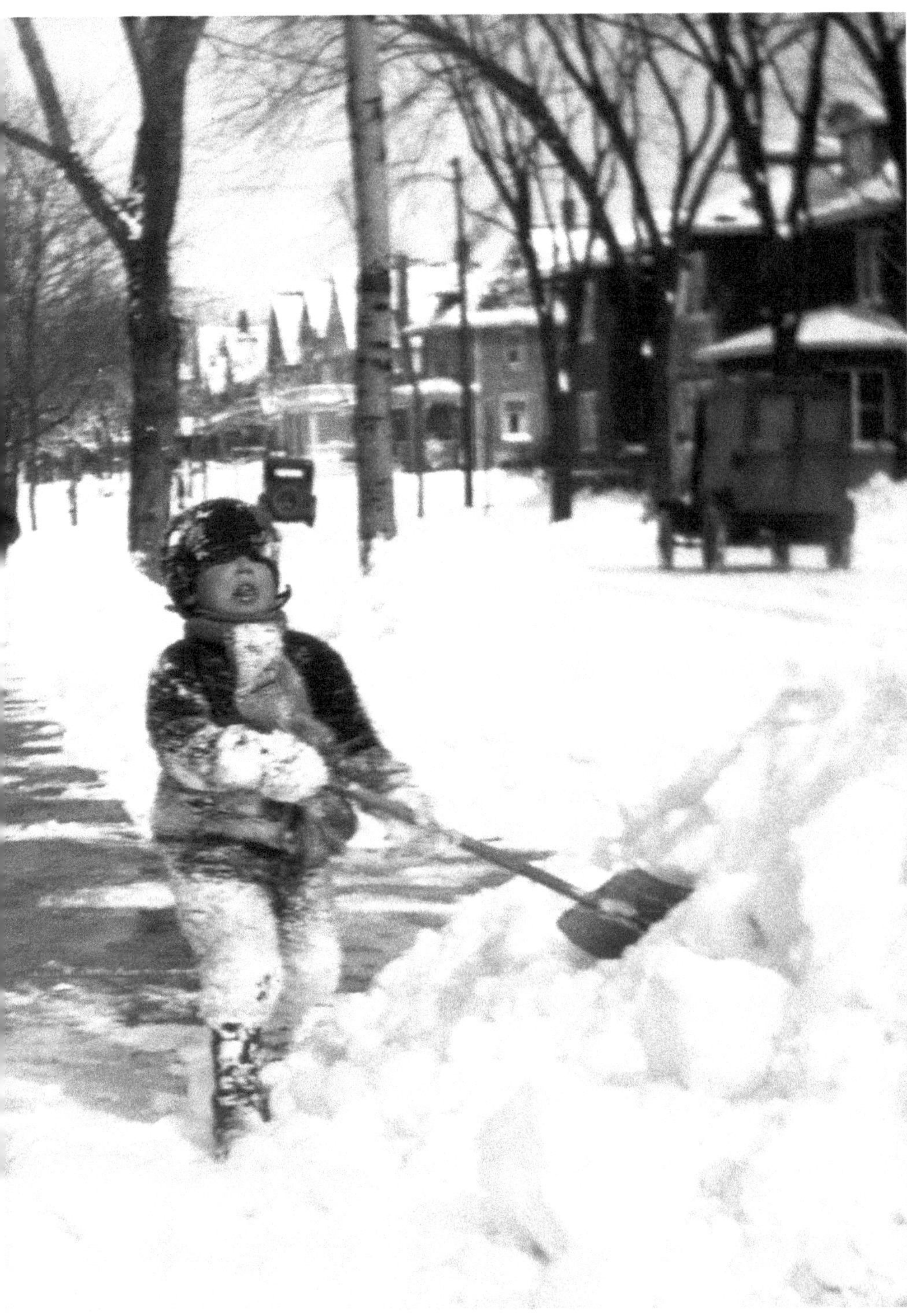

This man and young boy clear the sidewalks of some of the snow that fell on Milwaukee in 1925. Automobiles are visible navigating the slippery roads in the background.

The Atlas Flour Mill was destroyed by fire on December 11, 1926. Atlas flour was a very successful business until the destruction of the mill. No fewer than thirteen fire companies, along with six truck companies and two fire boats, attempted to save the building.

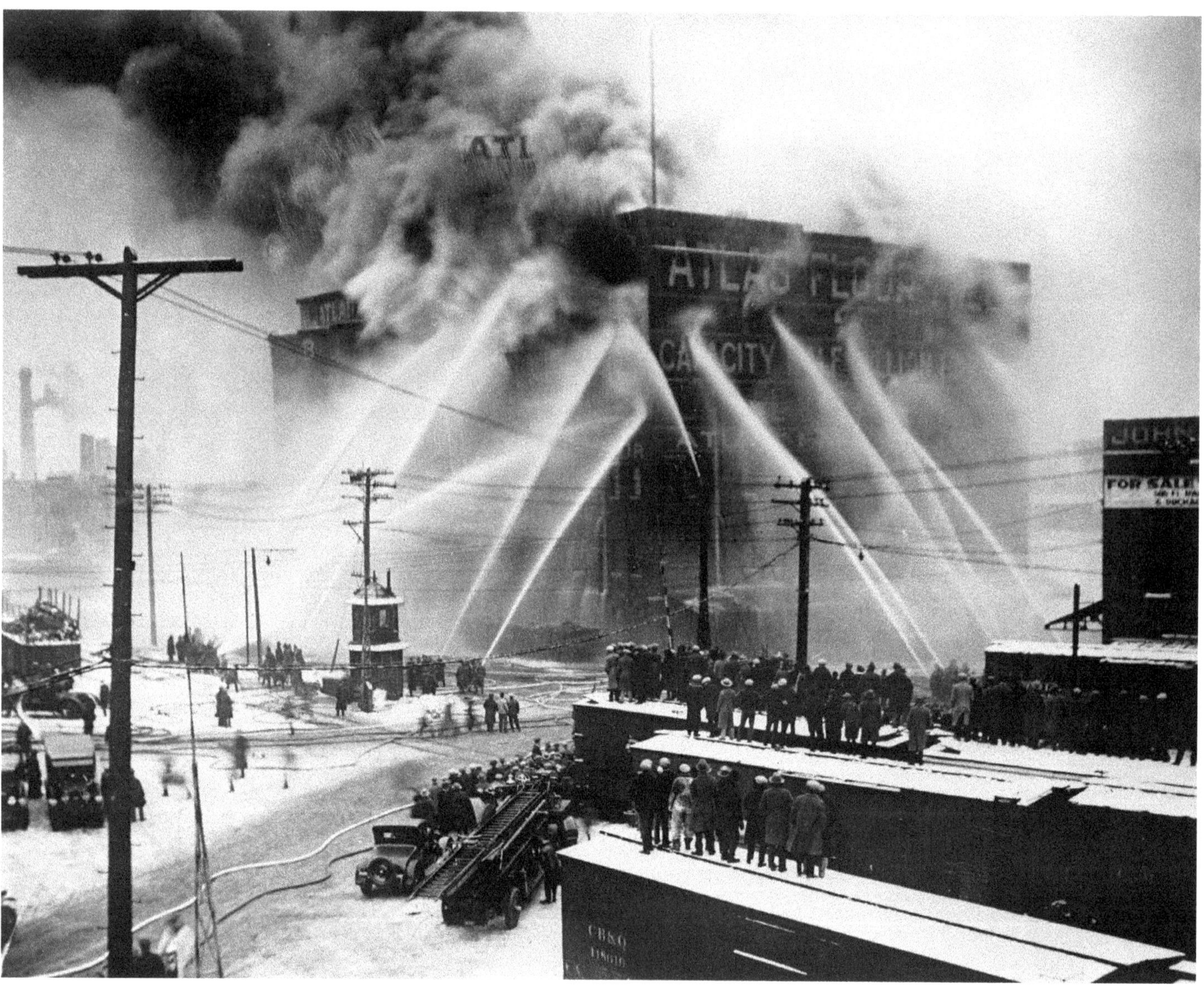

In 1924 when the fraternal order of the Elks decided to build their lodge, they planned it with many recreational activities, such as swimming, card playing, and dancing, in mind. The nine-story building, an imposing landmark located on N. Prospect, was demolished in 1971.

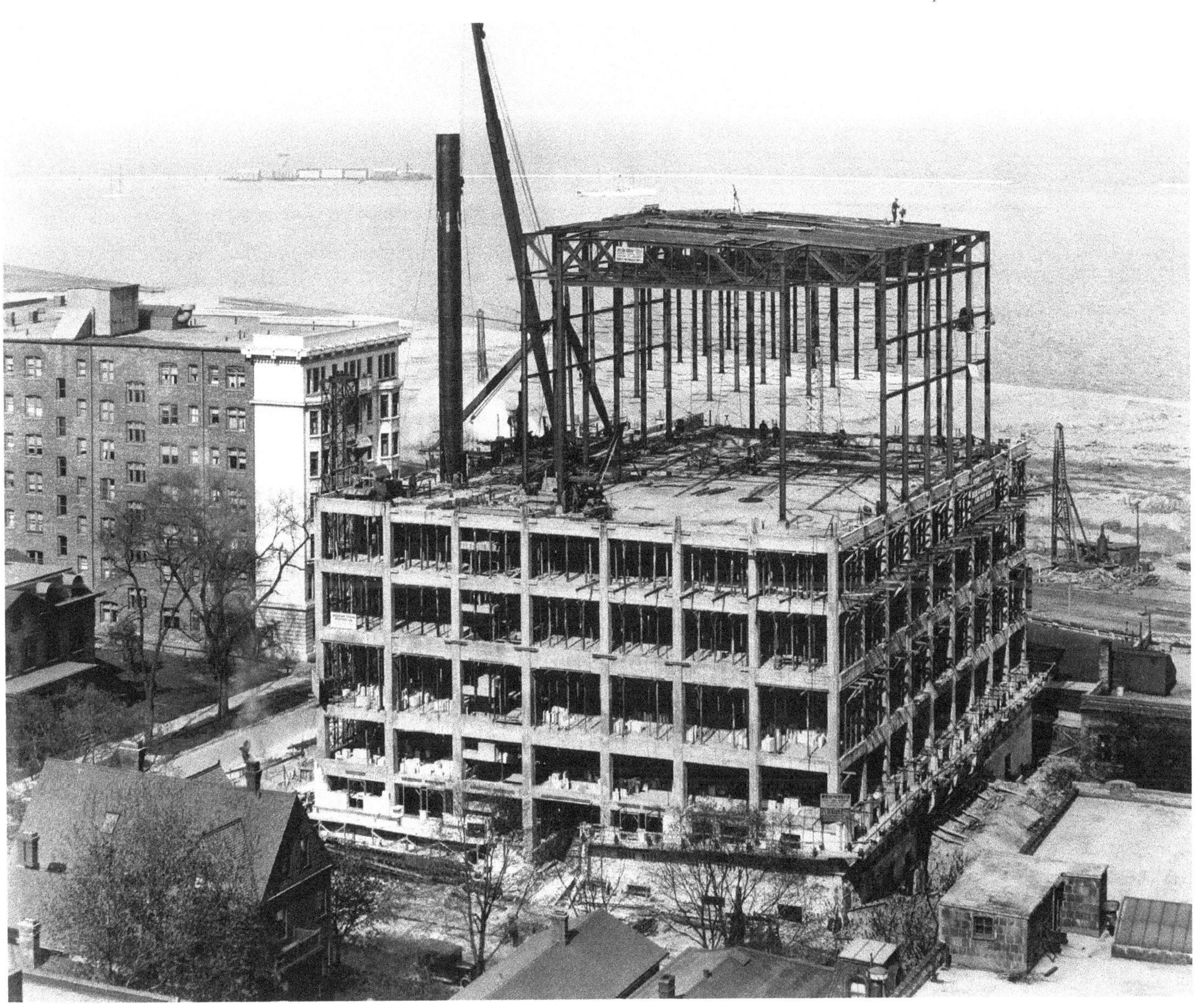

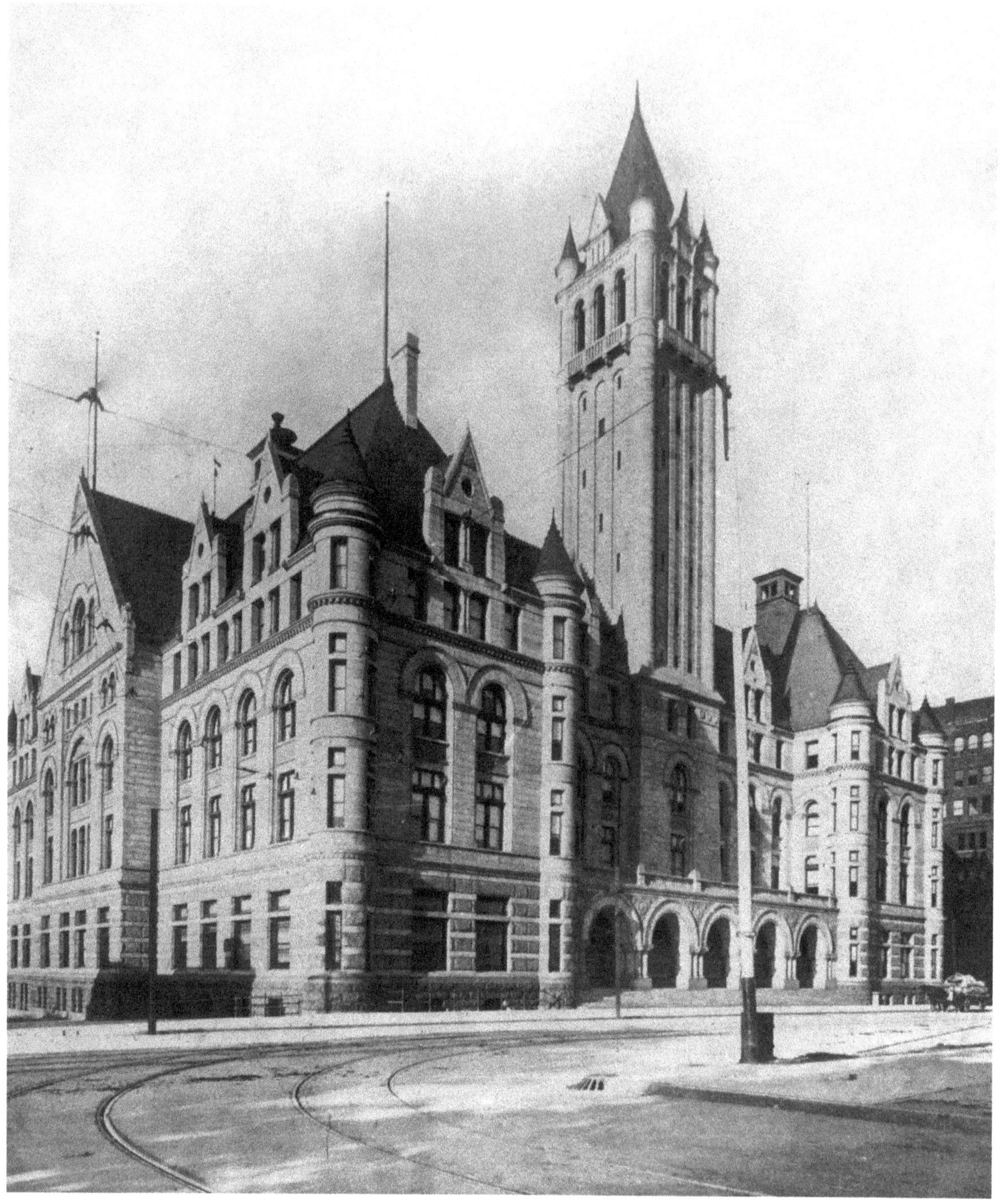

The Milwaukee Post Office, the processing center for the city's mail, was located in the Federal Building, which was built between 1892 and 1899. This photograph was taken in 1928.

Long before the days of armored cars, bank security was a rather simple matter. Here in 1929, Frank Paul unloads the First Wisconsin Bank truck at the Milwaukee Post Office. In 1928 the First Wisconsin Bank celebrated its 75th anniversary, proudly stating that they had 225 adding machines, 55 typewriters, and 33 bookkeepers. Over the years the bank went through many transformations and is now U.S. Bank.

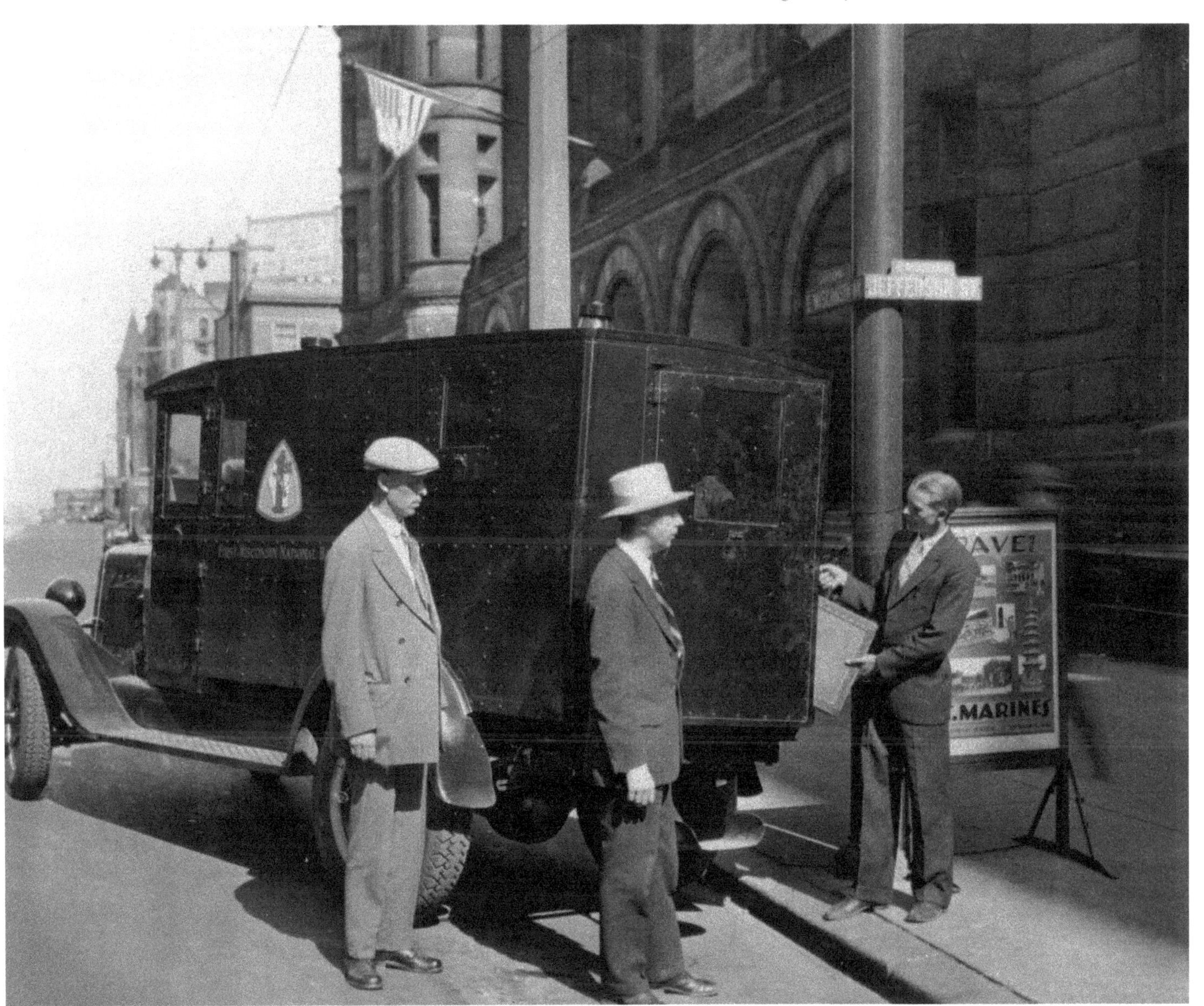

This 1929 view of Wisconsin Avenue shows traffic bumper-to-bumper and women sporting the cloche and other fashionable attire.

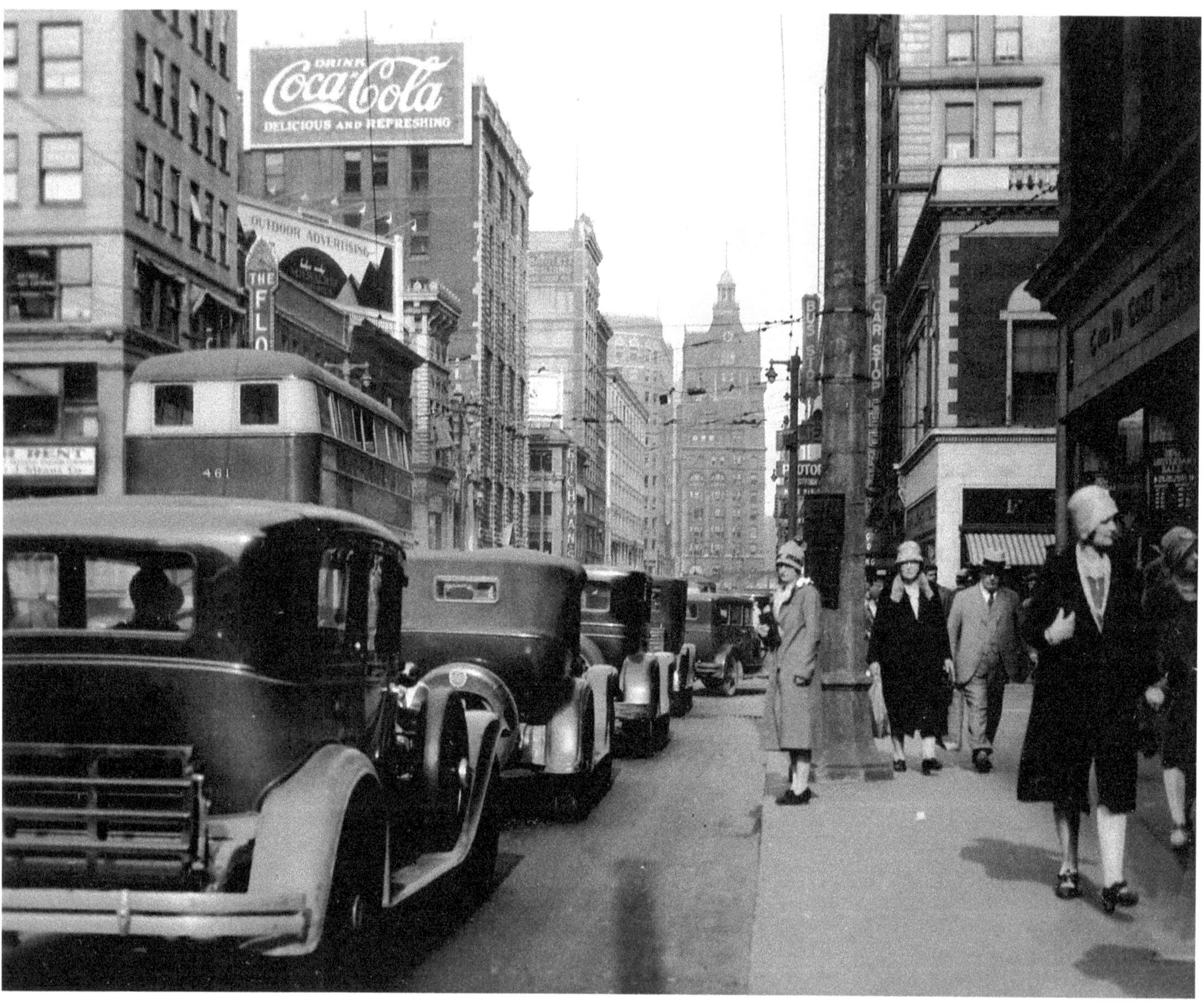

The grocery store of Frank and Ervin Tatera made use of all the modern methods to bring in business, including coupons, competitive pricing, and advertising. This 1929 image shows the interior of the store, once located at 1025 Third Avenue.

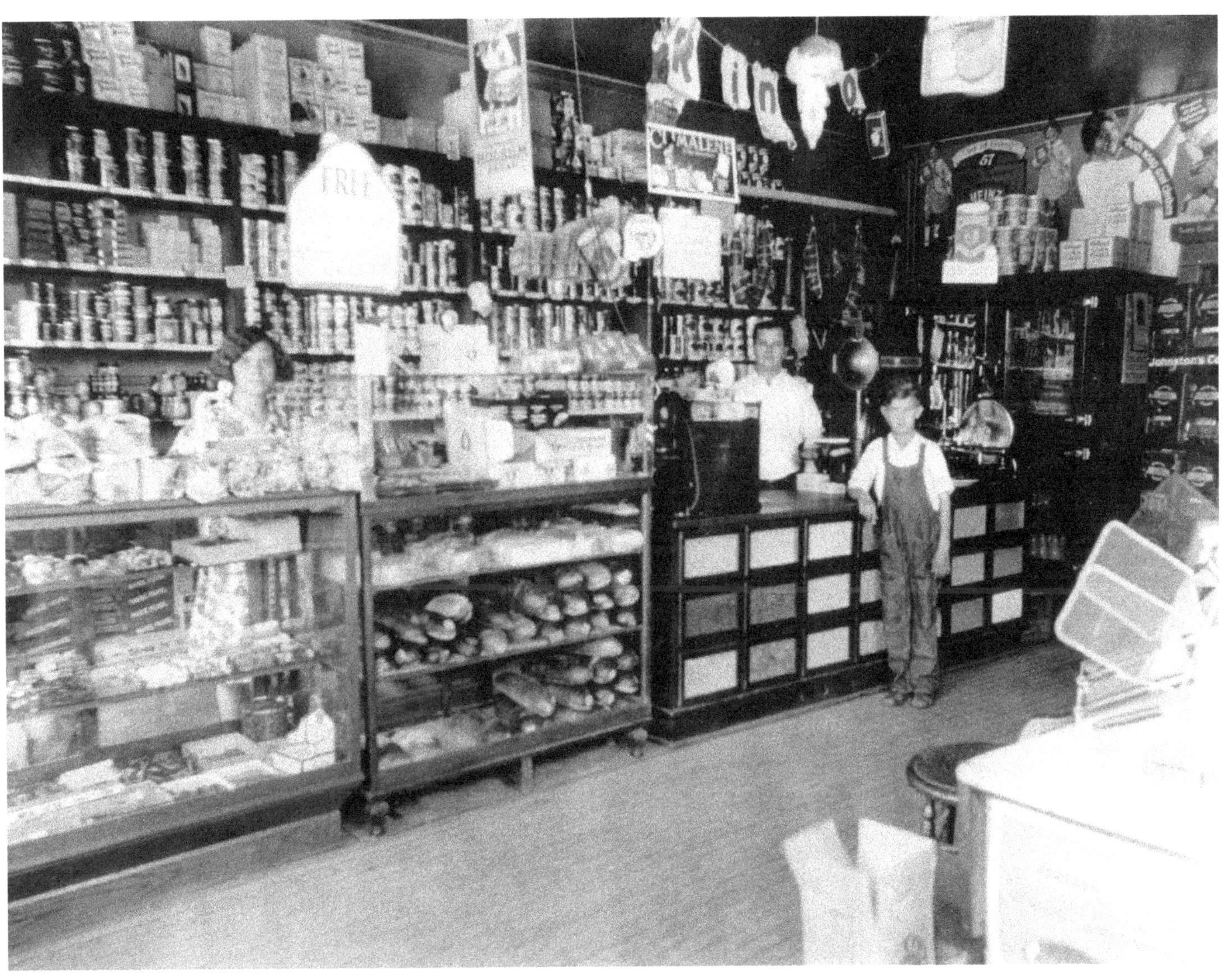

The Loening Amphibian provided air service across Lake Michigan around 1929. It is seen here landing near the shore close to the Chicago Northwestern Depot.

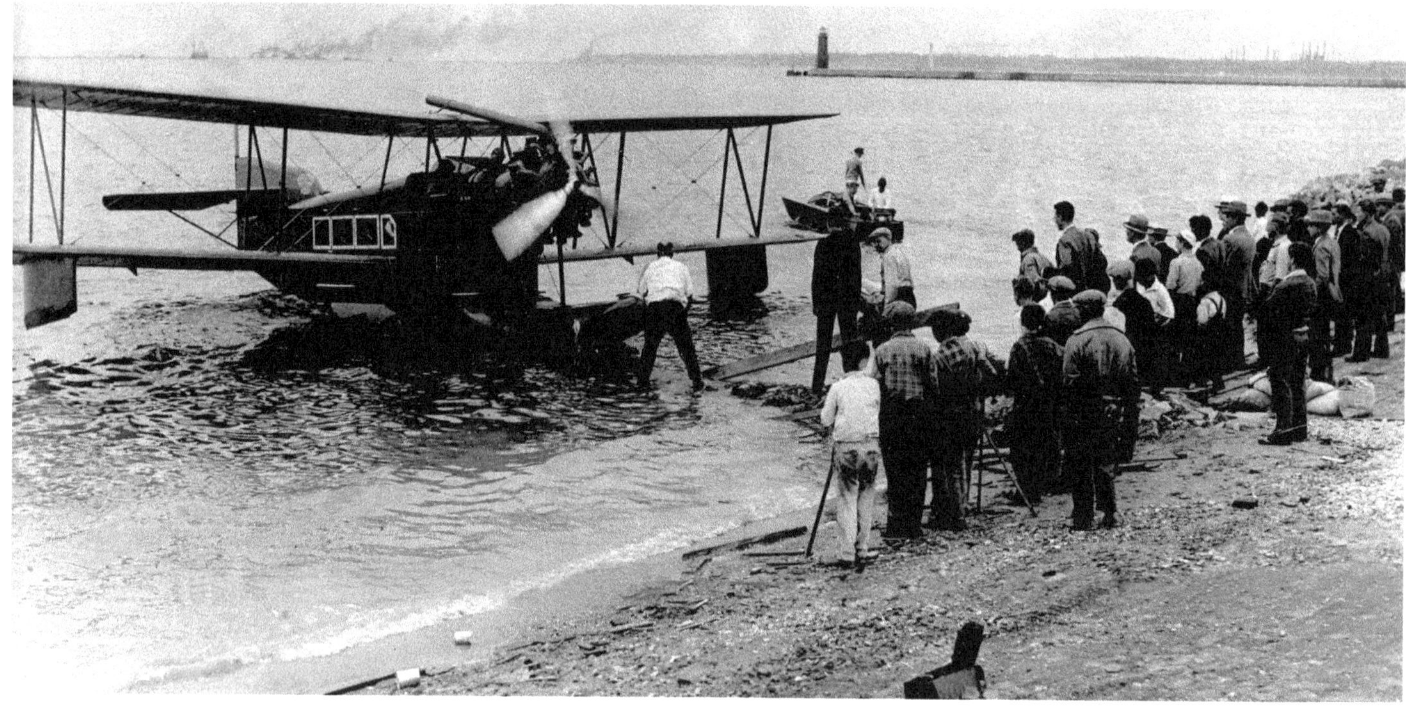

East down Wisconsin Avenue in 1930, Caspari & Virmond advertise shoes and Miller advertises the high life. Although the stock market had crashed the year before, the worst years of the Great Depression still lay ahead.

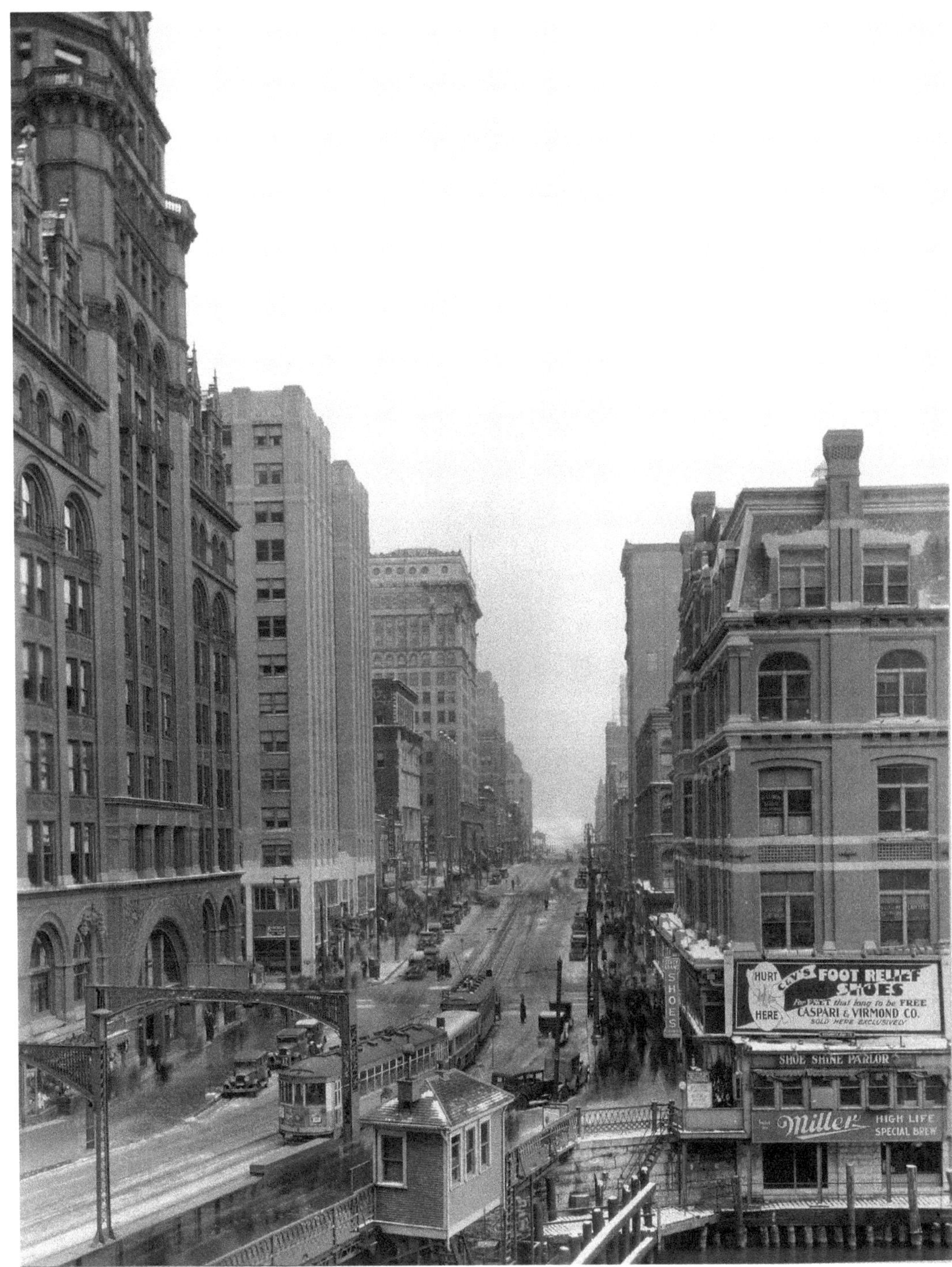

Located at the corner of 4th and Wisconsin Avenue, Espenhain's Department Store advertised itself as the "20th Century Apparel Store." In 1931, signs announce "The End Is Here Everything Must Go" and soon thereafter Espenhain's closed its doors.

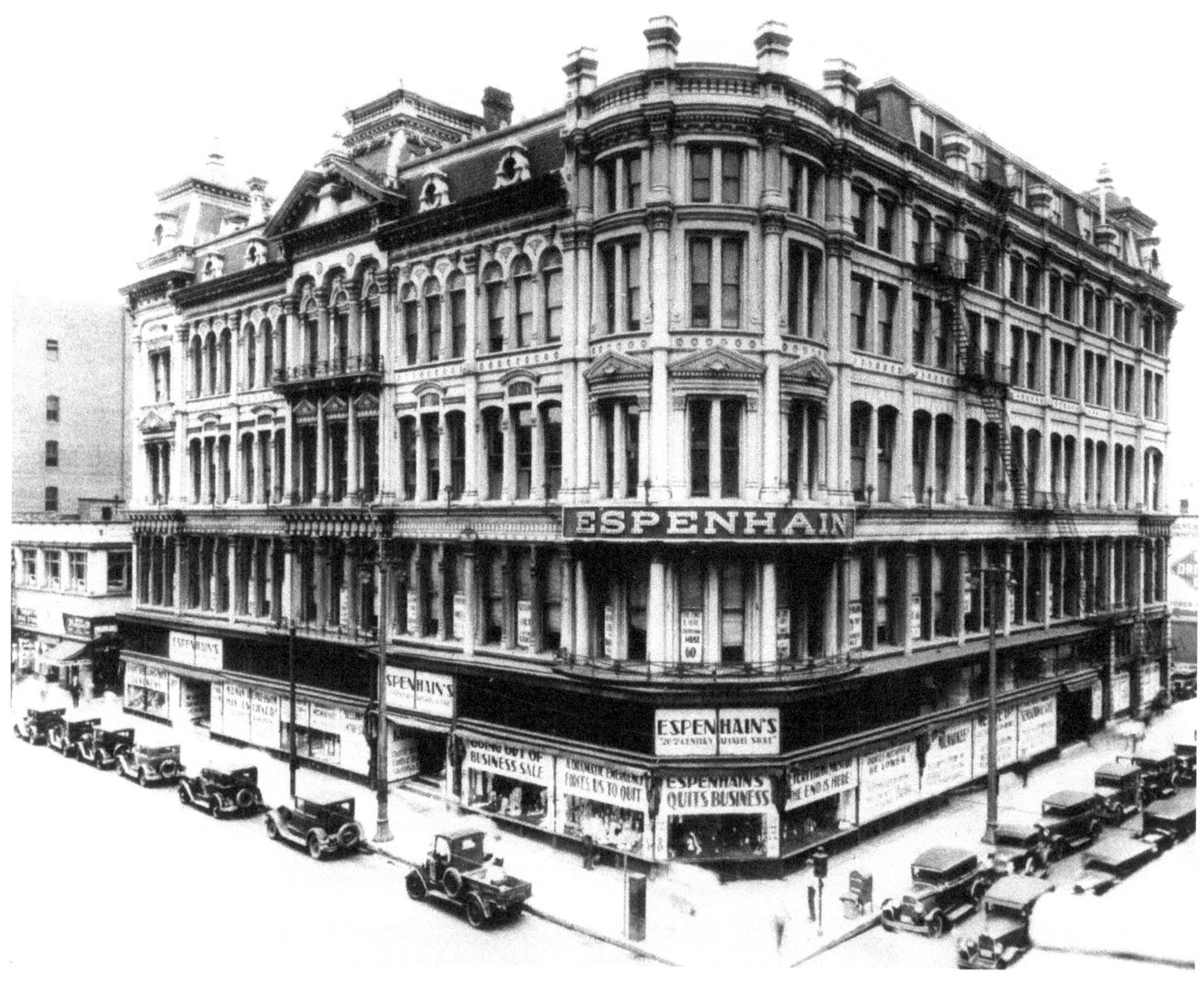

The piers at the swimming parks on the Milwaukee River were popular spots for sunbathing. This pier was located at Gordon Park, also the location of the ski jump.

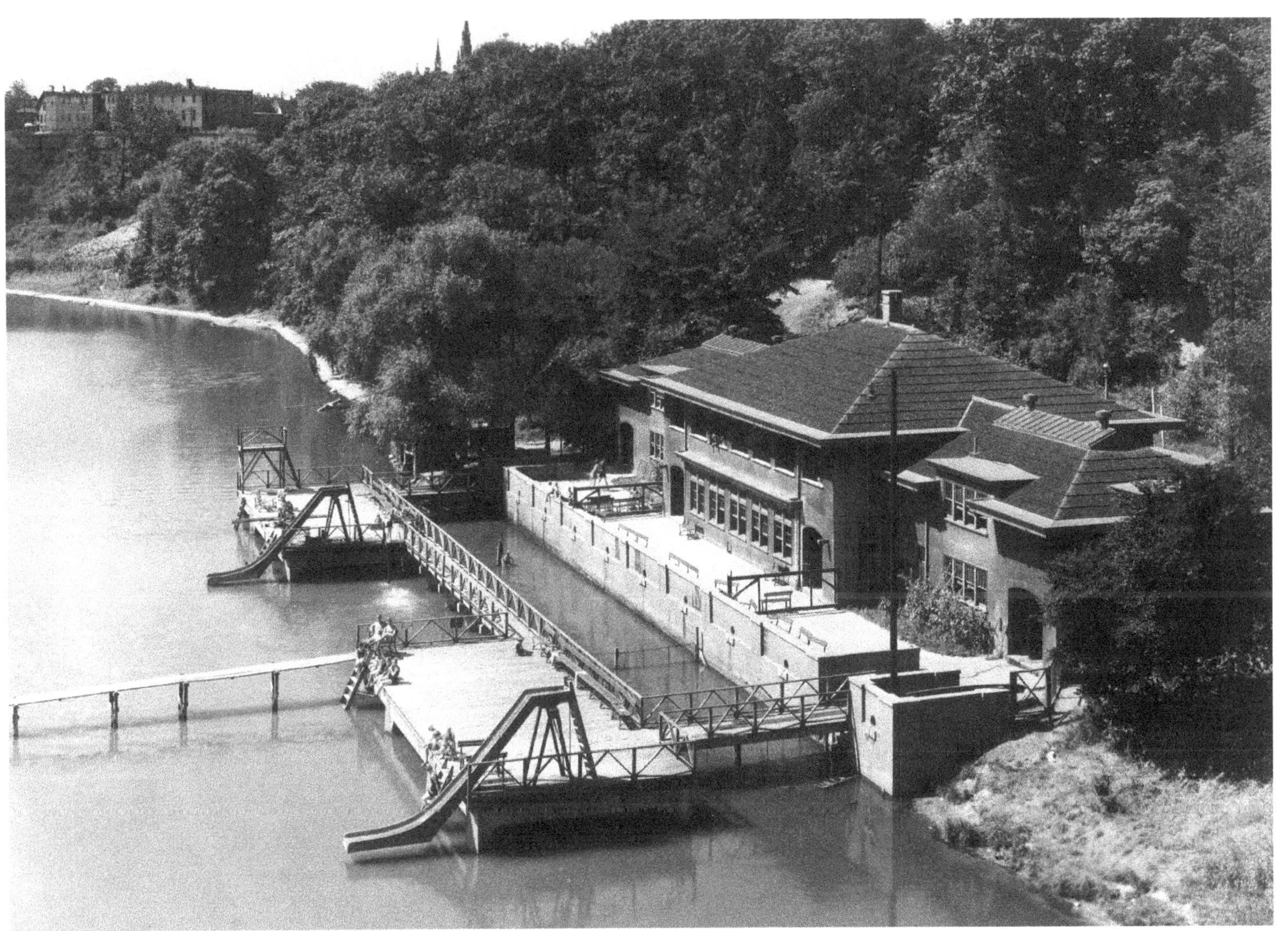

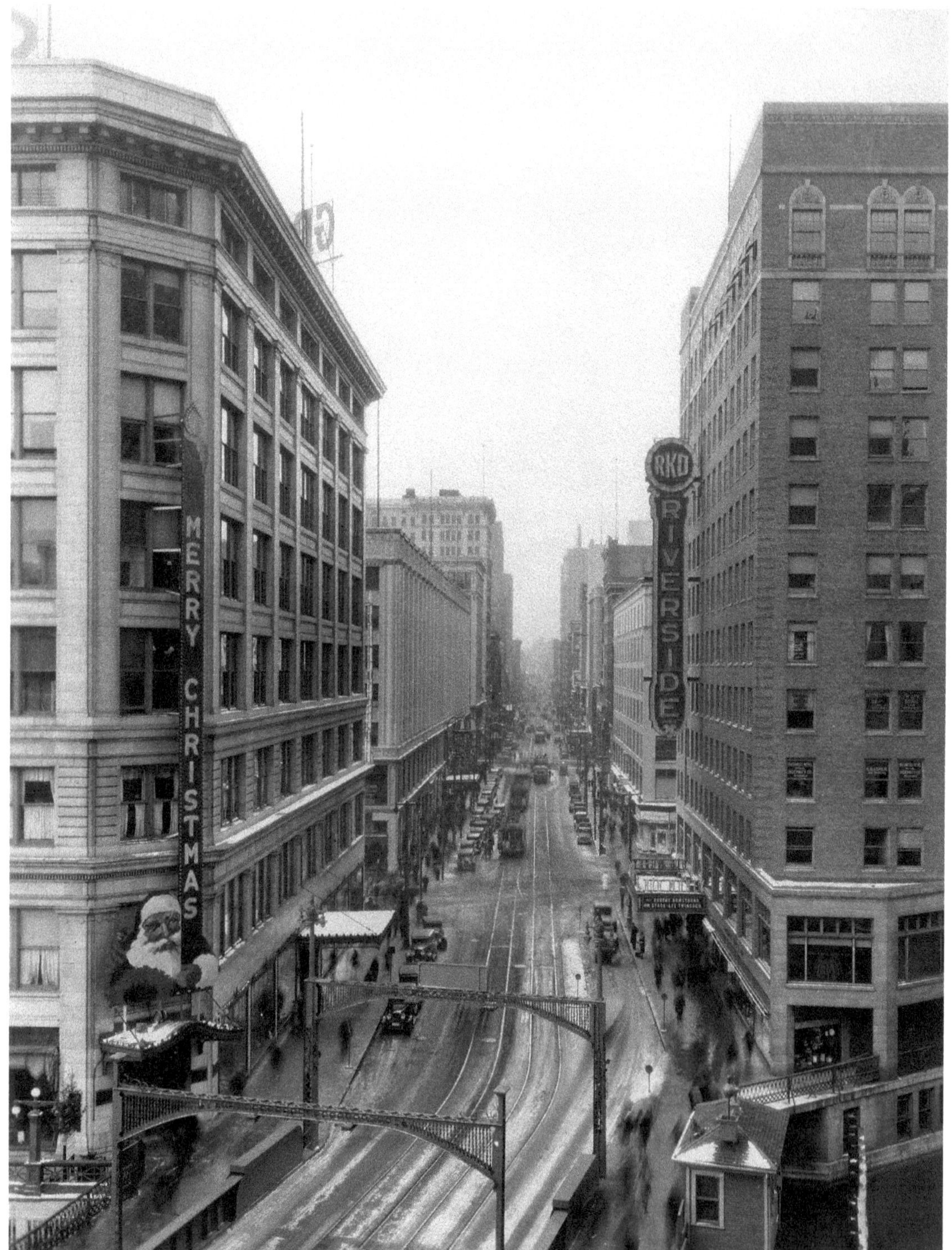

In this view facing west down Wisconsin Avenue in 1930, the marquee of the Riverside Theatre posts concerts and shows. Although the RKO Riverside sign is long gone, the theater remains a popular entertainment venue today.

Arthur Gaspar and Paul Trier are seen here in 1931 at Curtiss Wright Field. The two men would later establish an ambulance service for the area. Gaspar was a funeral director by trade, and Trier, a pilot.

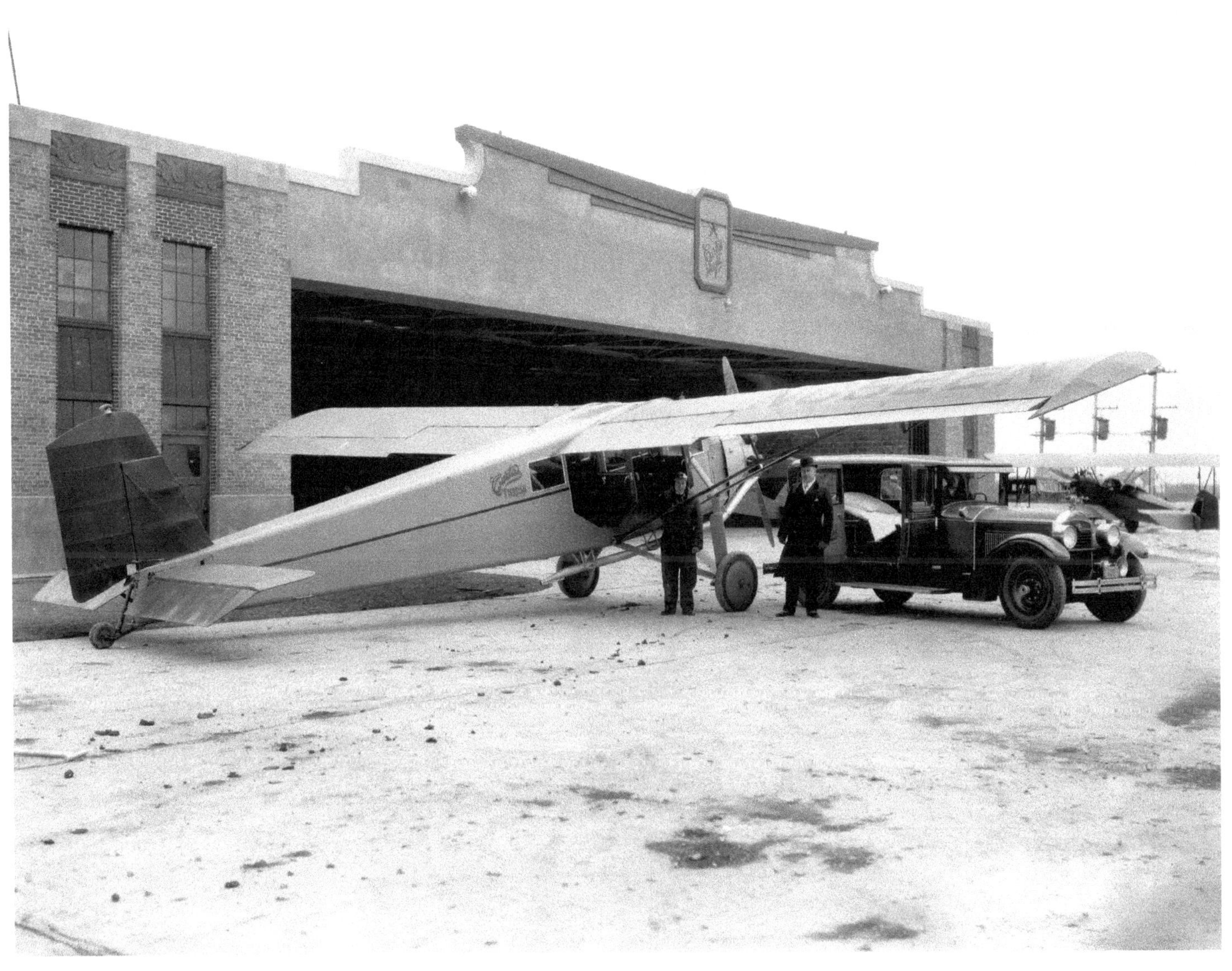

On December 22, 1931, two men and a truck loaded with toys are likely on their way to visit with children. Organizations such as the Marines still collect toys around Christmas time to give to children in Milwaukee.

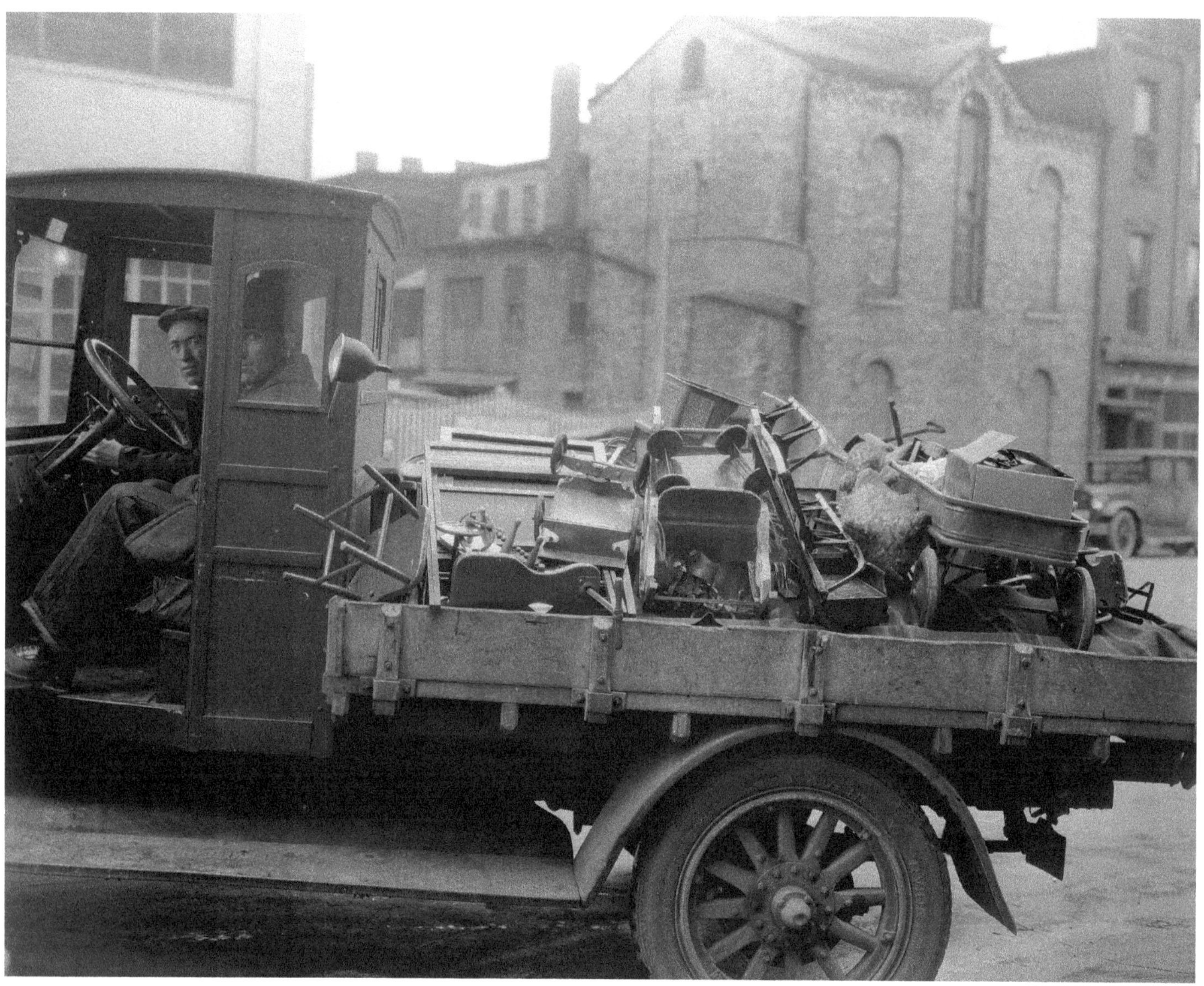

After twelve long years of prohibition, Schlitz brewery was able to begin shipping beer on April 7, 1933, at 12:01 A.M. Other Milwaukee breweries, such as Pabst, Miller, and Blatz, offered similar shipments of beer, now legally able to make their product.

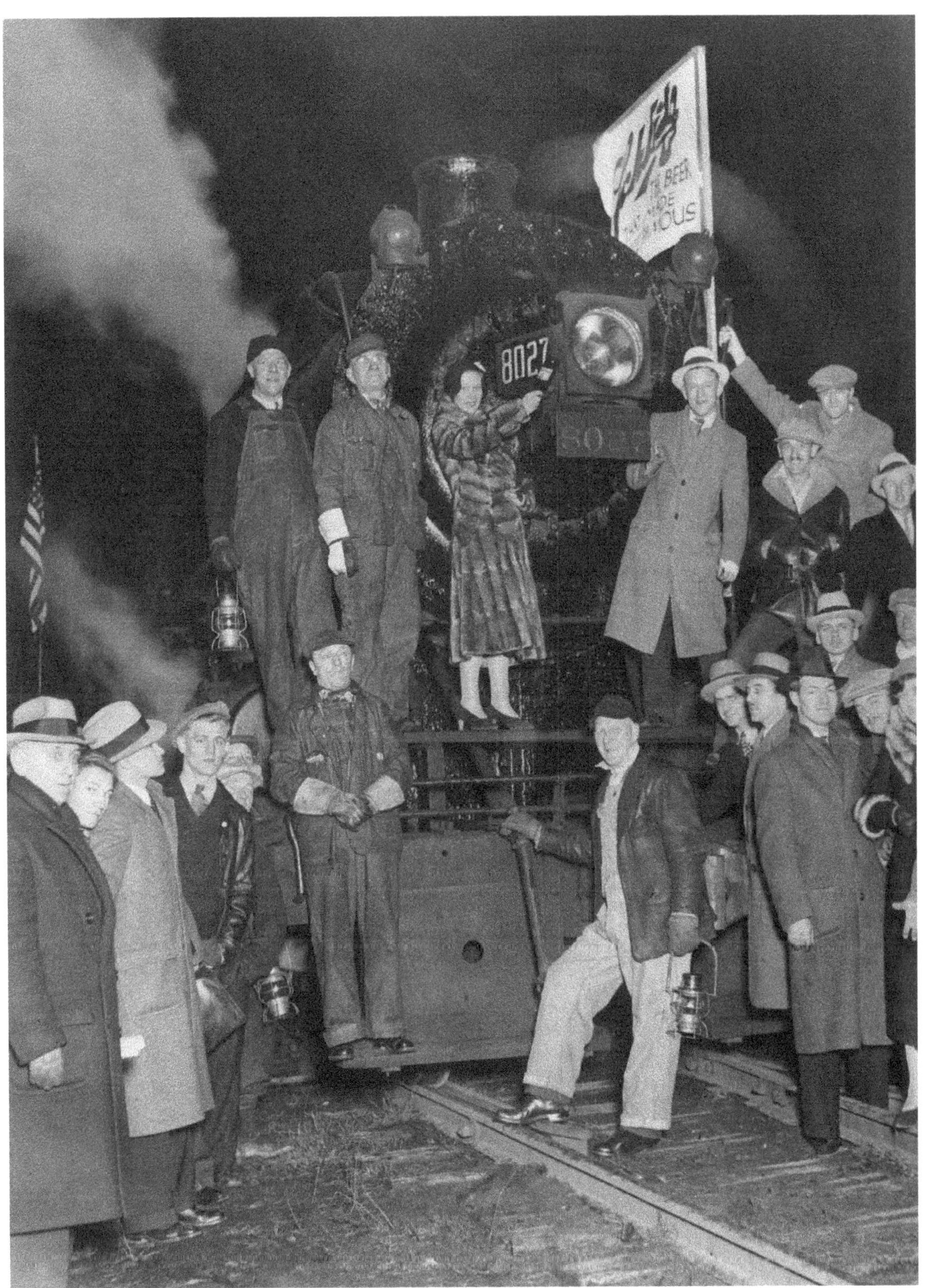

In 1934, picketing workers of Geuder, Paschke and Frey overturned a police vehicle with two officers inside. The officers were attempting to aid office workers to enter the building when chaos ensued and the striking workers became violent. This was not the first, or the last, that Milwaukee would see of violence from striking workers.

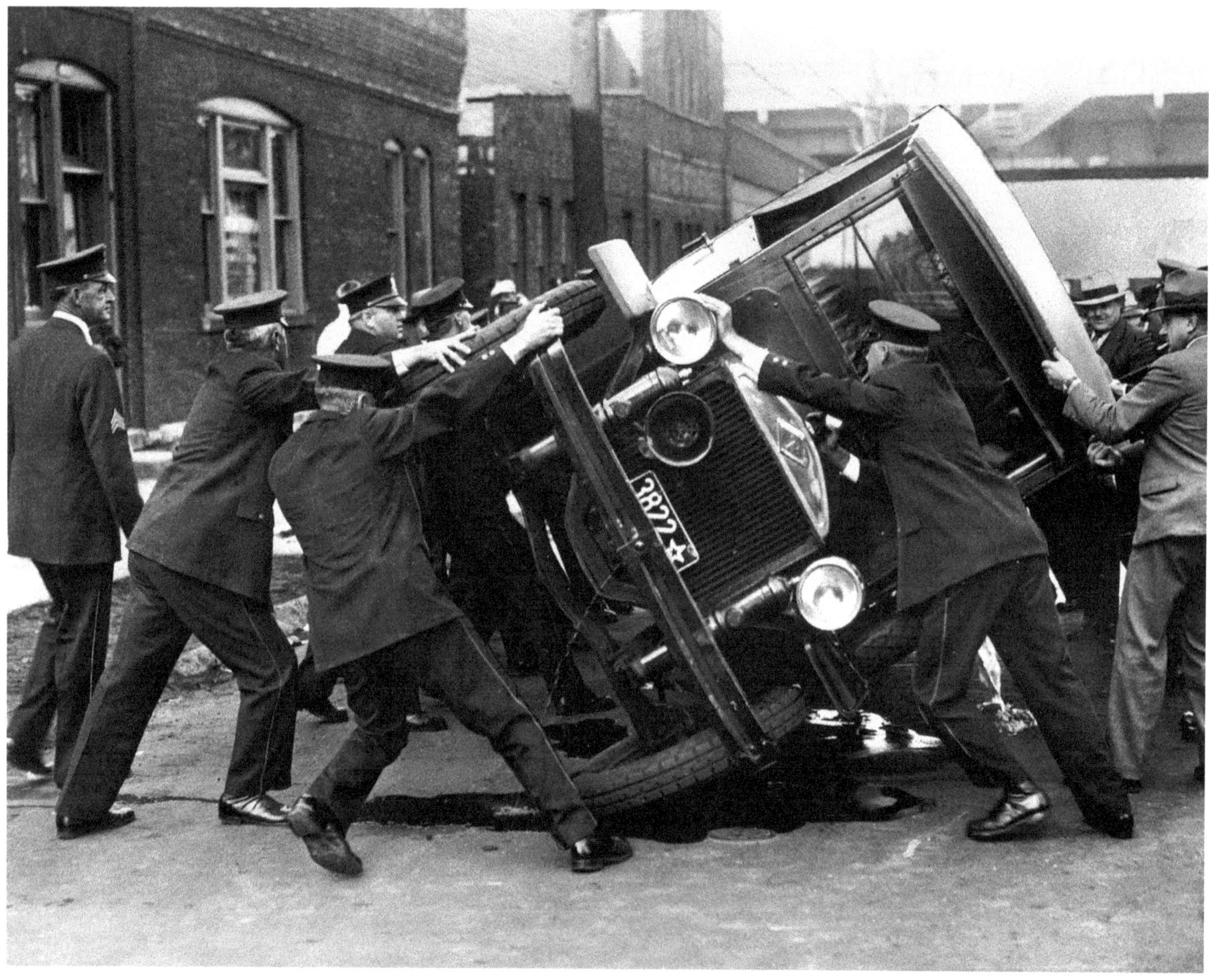

This rail yard worker is riding an industrial tractor through the railroad yard of Miller Brewery. Two refrigerated cars can be seen outside the factory building. The refrigerated cars of beer barons Schlitz, Blatz, Miller, and Pabst helped maintain the quality of the product by keeping it cold.

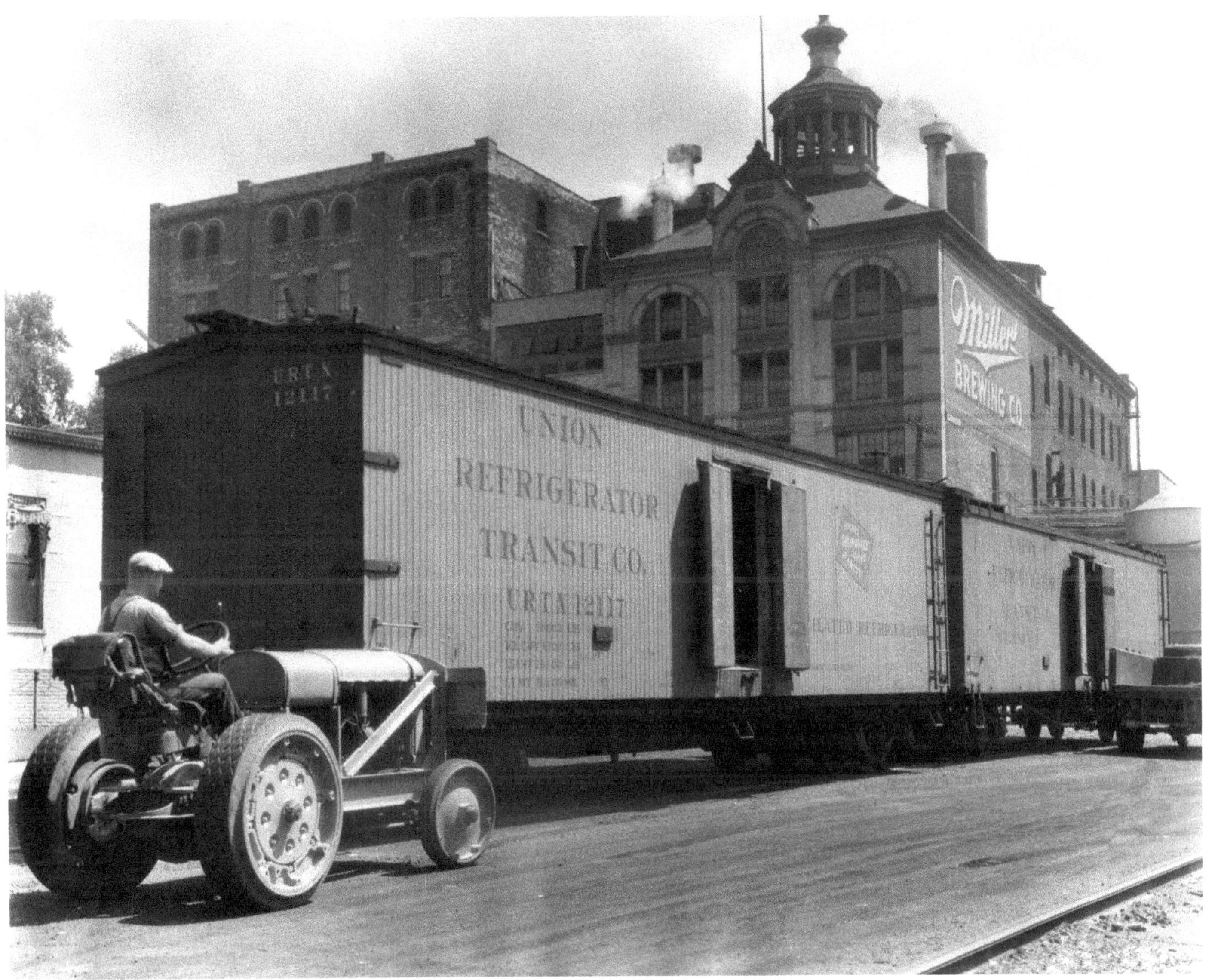

The days of the iceman are long gone, but in this 1938 photograph an iceman is delivering a block of ice to a downtown office building. The man worked for the Wisconsin Ice & Coal Company, delivering ice and coal to homes and businesses.

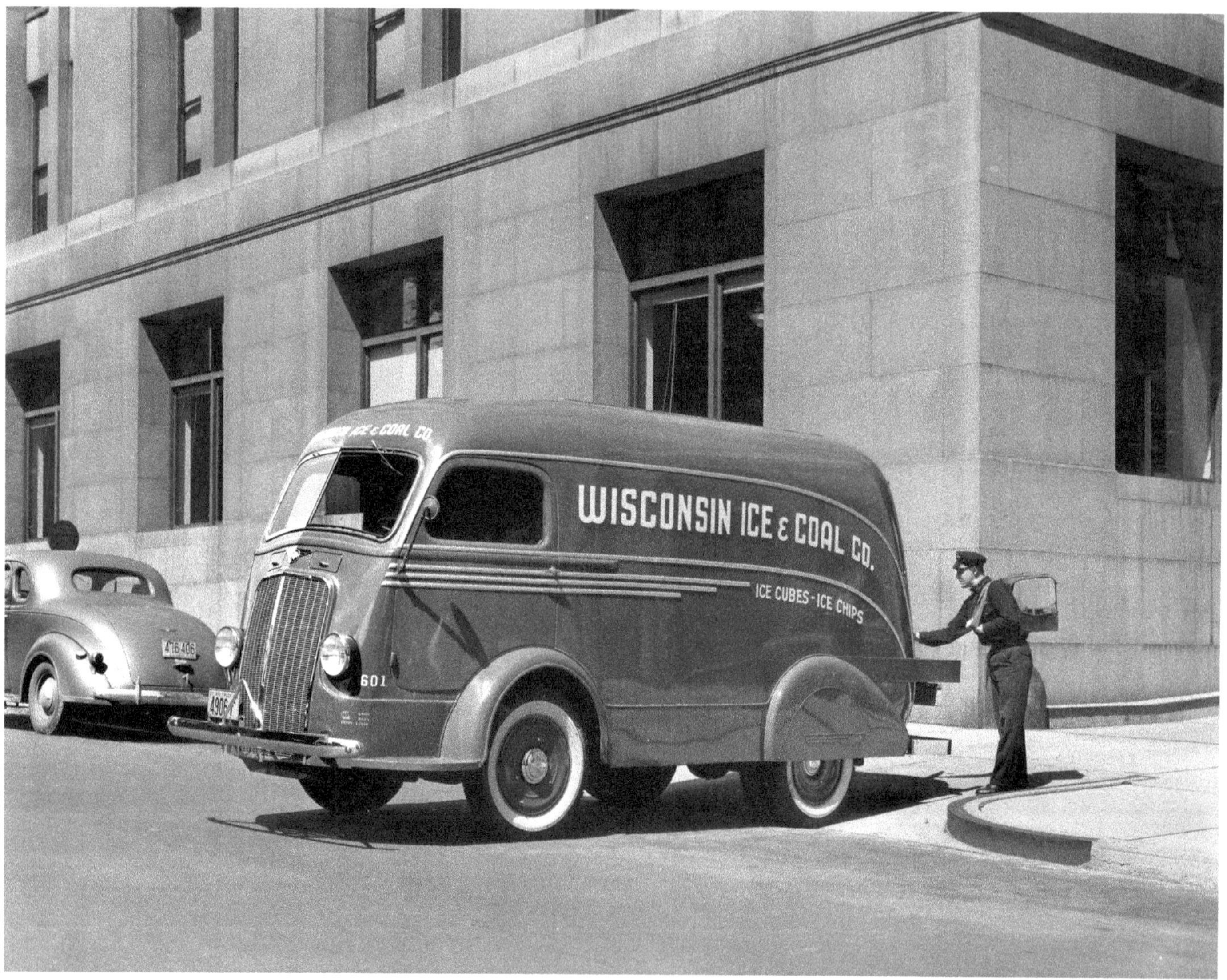

Industry has always been a part of Milwaukee. Here molten metal is poured into a mold. Workers of the Milwaukee Works foundry endured extreme temperatures each day.

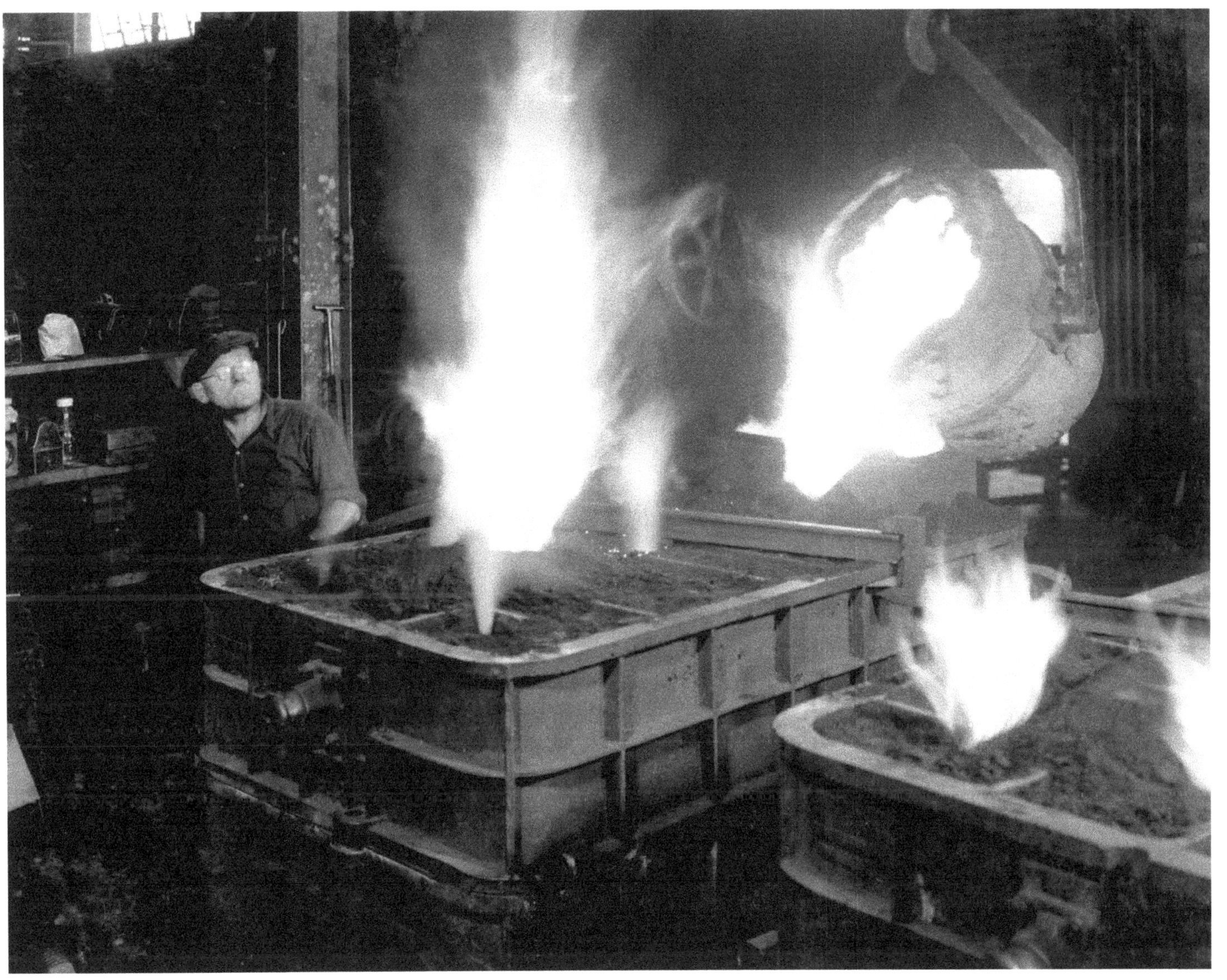

Fresh milk is being delivered to the Hotel Juneau, located at 807 E. Wisconsin, which advertises its rates at $1.50 to $2. The truck was owned by the Golden Guernsey Co.

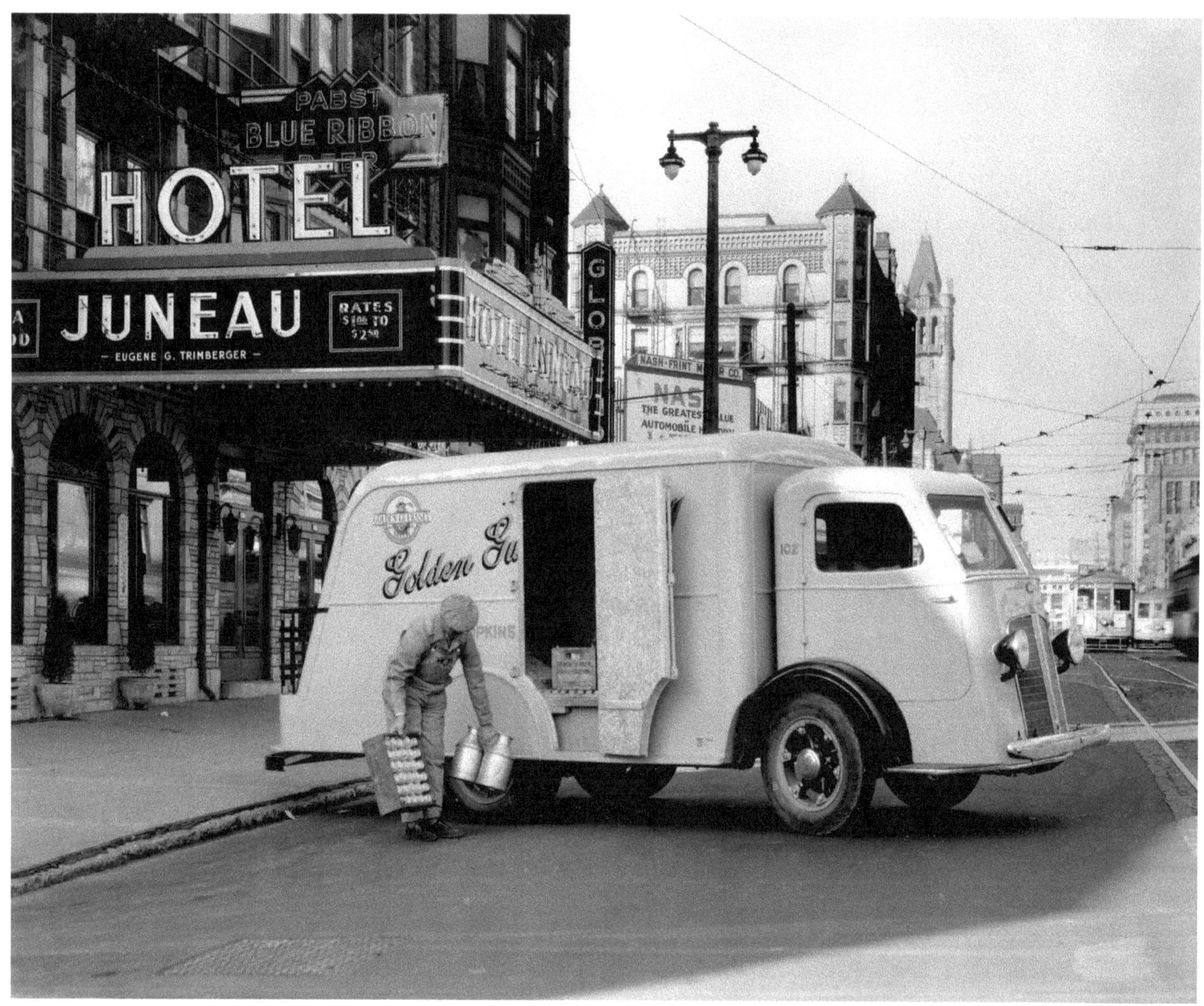

The Goodyear blimp was once a fixture in the Milwaukee air. This particular blimp, named the *Reliance,* started flying above Milwaukee in 1935. It was a form of advertisement, also permitting six passengers at a time to "go for a ride." The U.S. military utilized blimps like the *Reliance* as observation stations. They are now predominantly seen above sports stadiums and large city events.

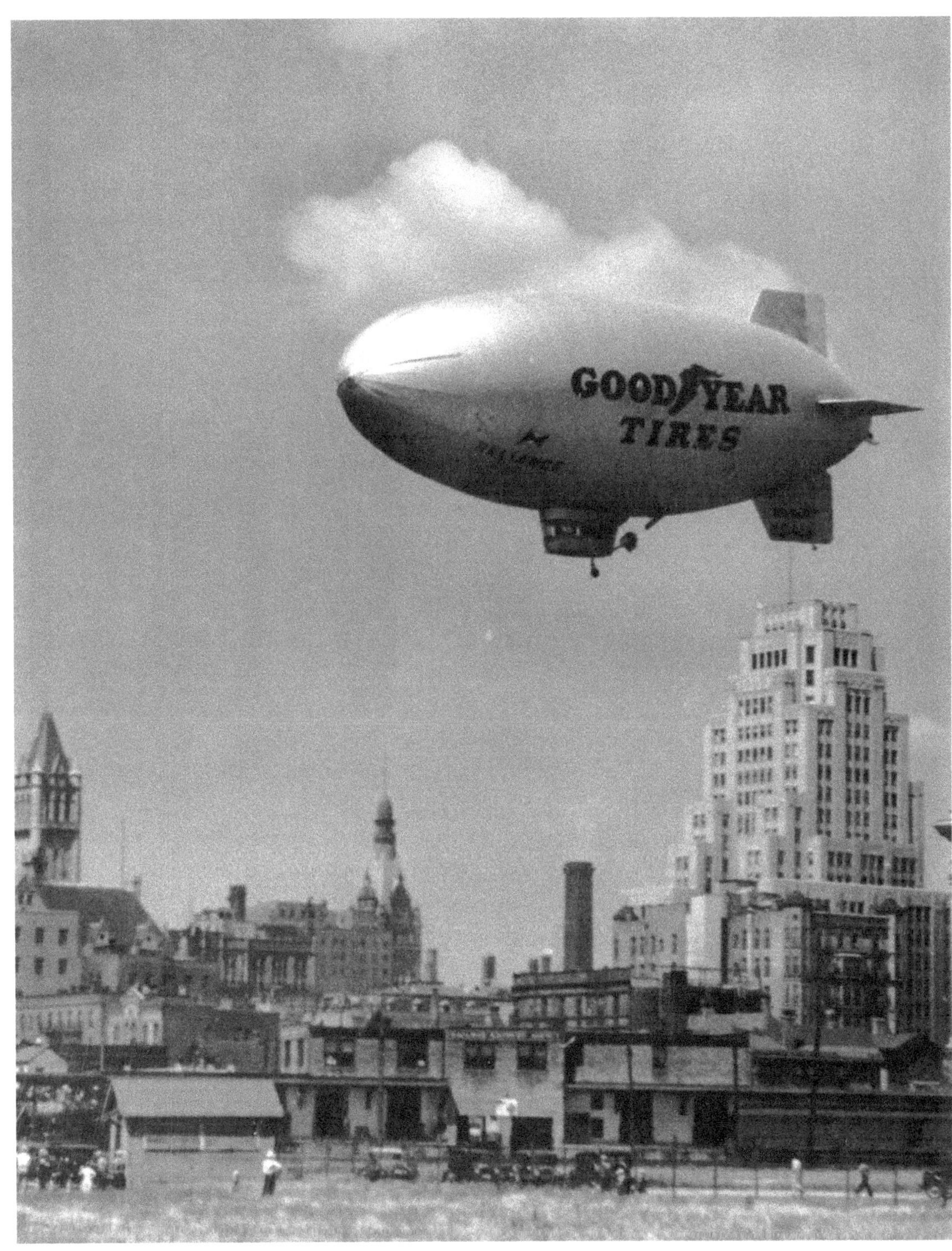

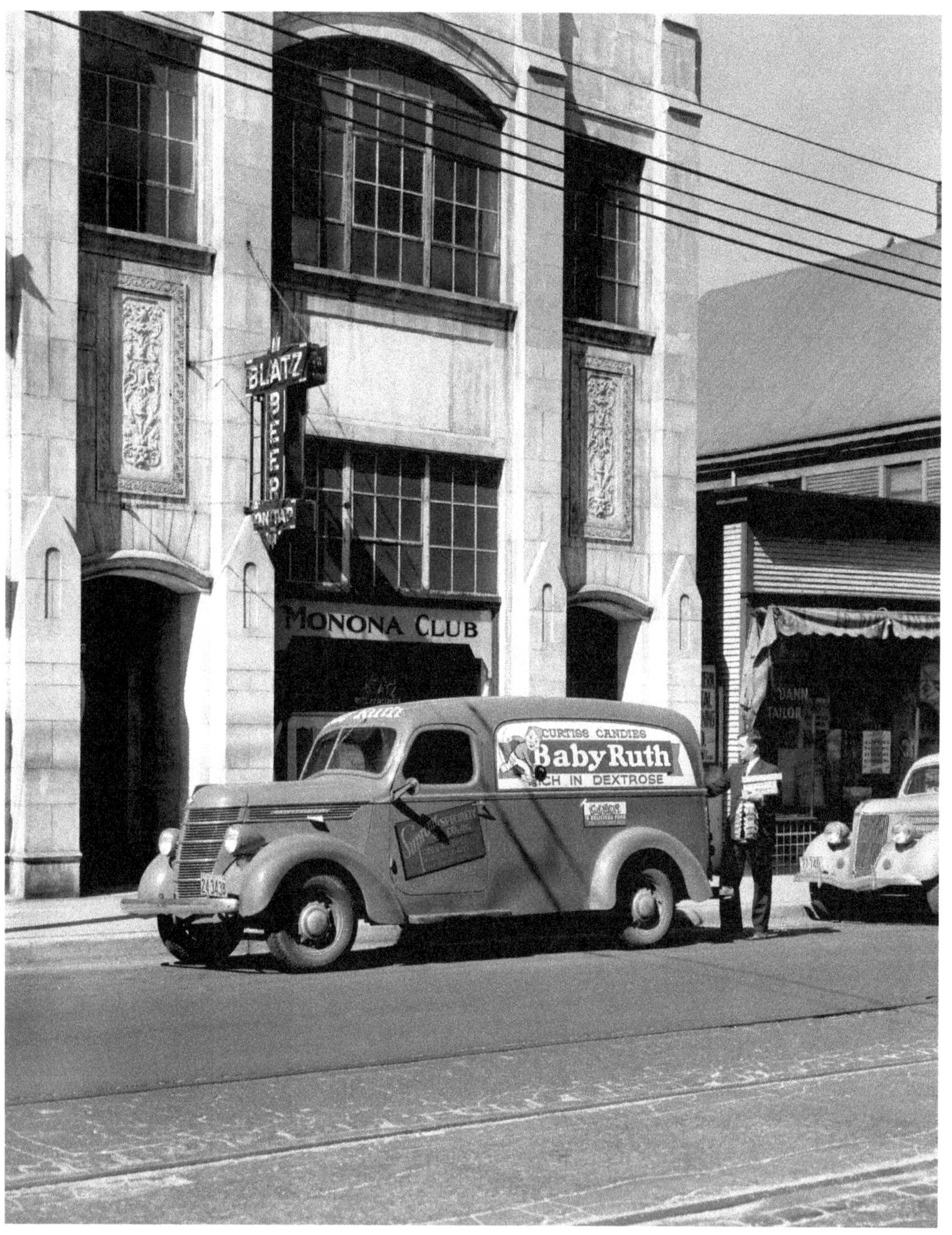

Candy bars "rich in dextrose" are delivered to the Monona Club in 1938.

Shown here in 1939, George Jung was a railroad speed recorder for the Milwaukee Road. Helping to monitor the accuracy of the speed recorders on the engines, his job was very important to the railroad industry's business records and the safety of the engine and its cargo.

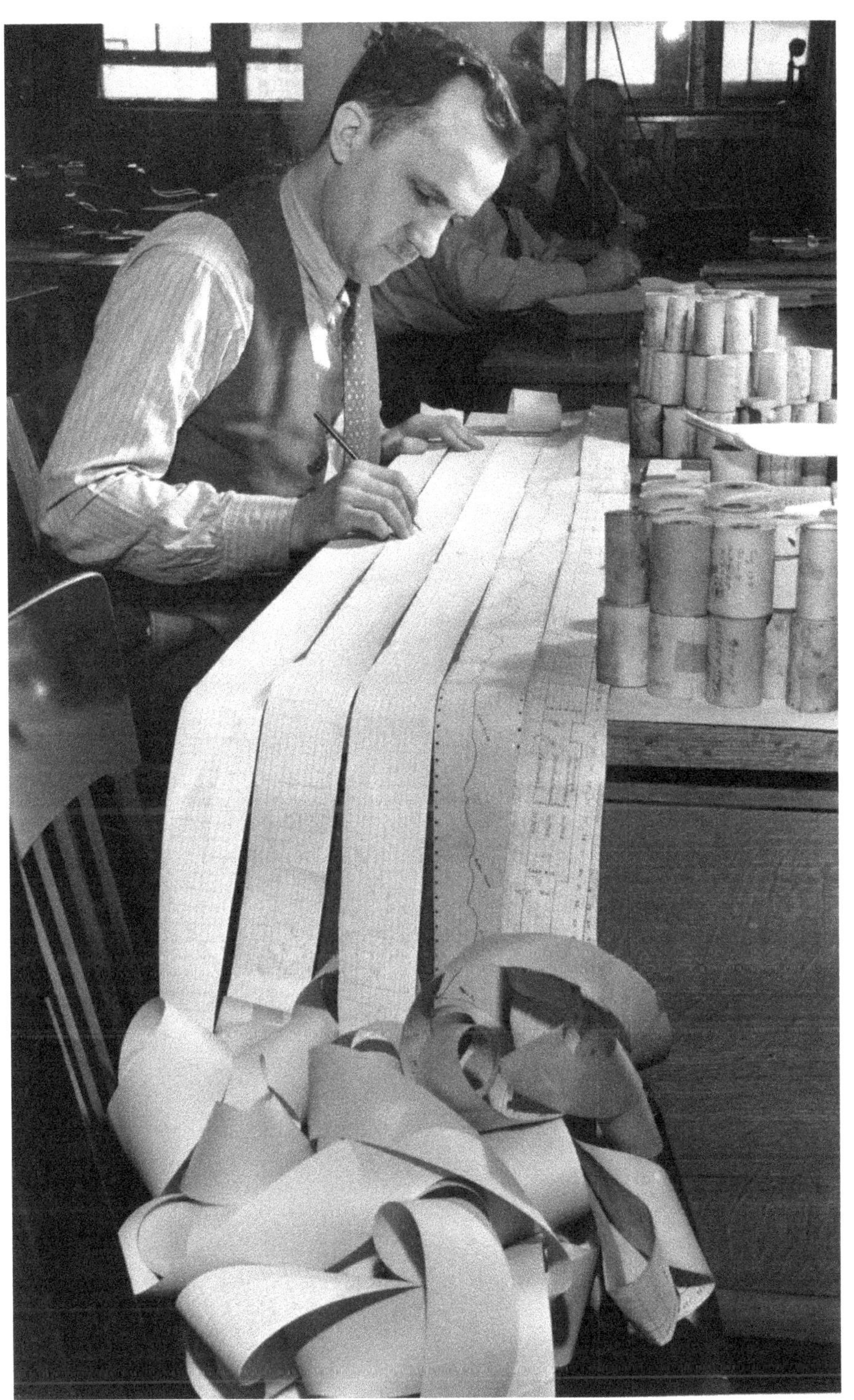

Wadham's Gas Station, located at 27th and Wisconsin, was not a typical 1930s-style station. The oriental roof grabbed the attention of drivers, alerting them to the station's presence, something that other, more traditional stations did not do. Wadham's stations popped up all over Milwaukee until they were eventually purchased by the Mobil Oil Co.

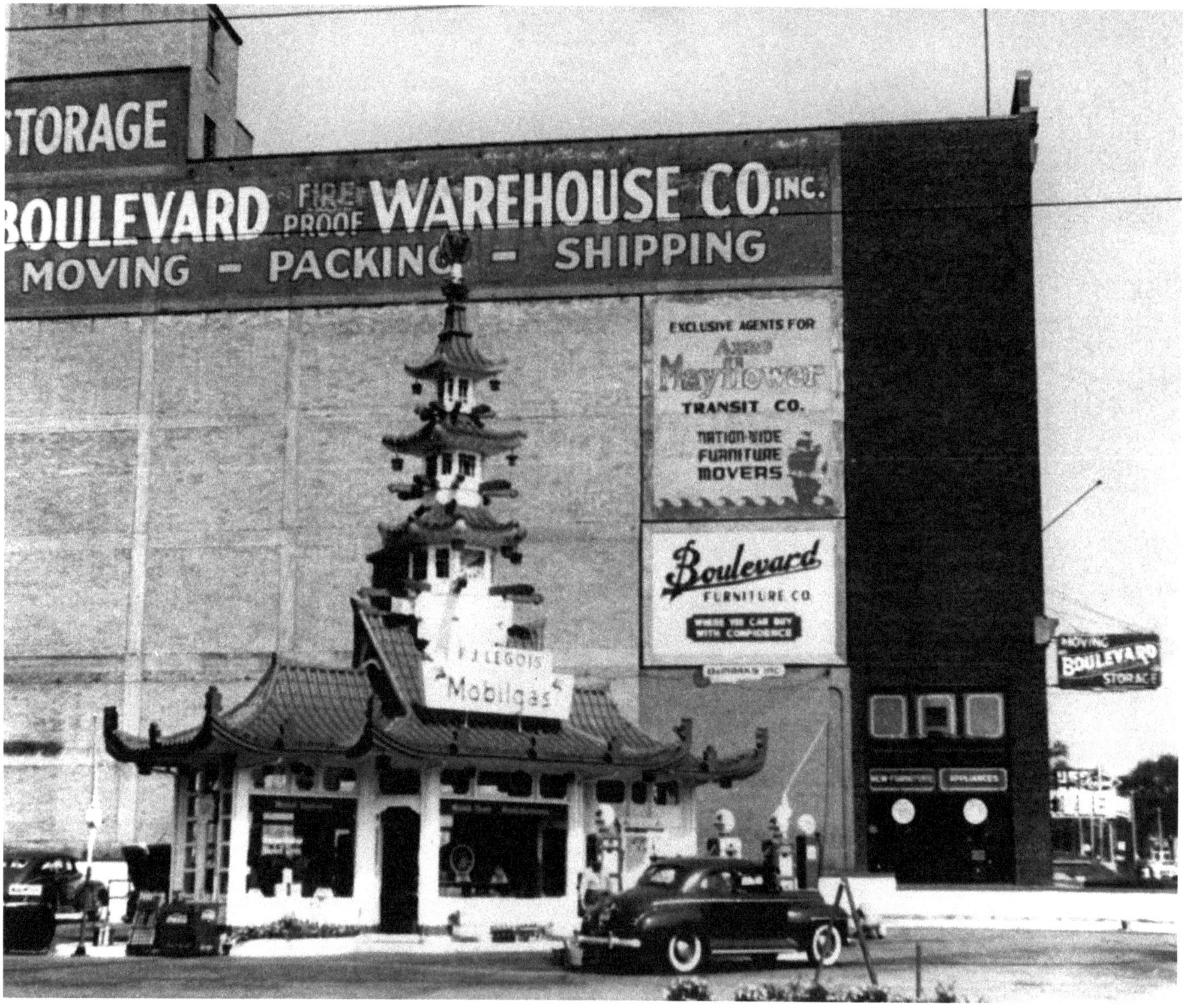

Students board an International D-300 school bus in the city in 1938.

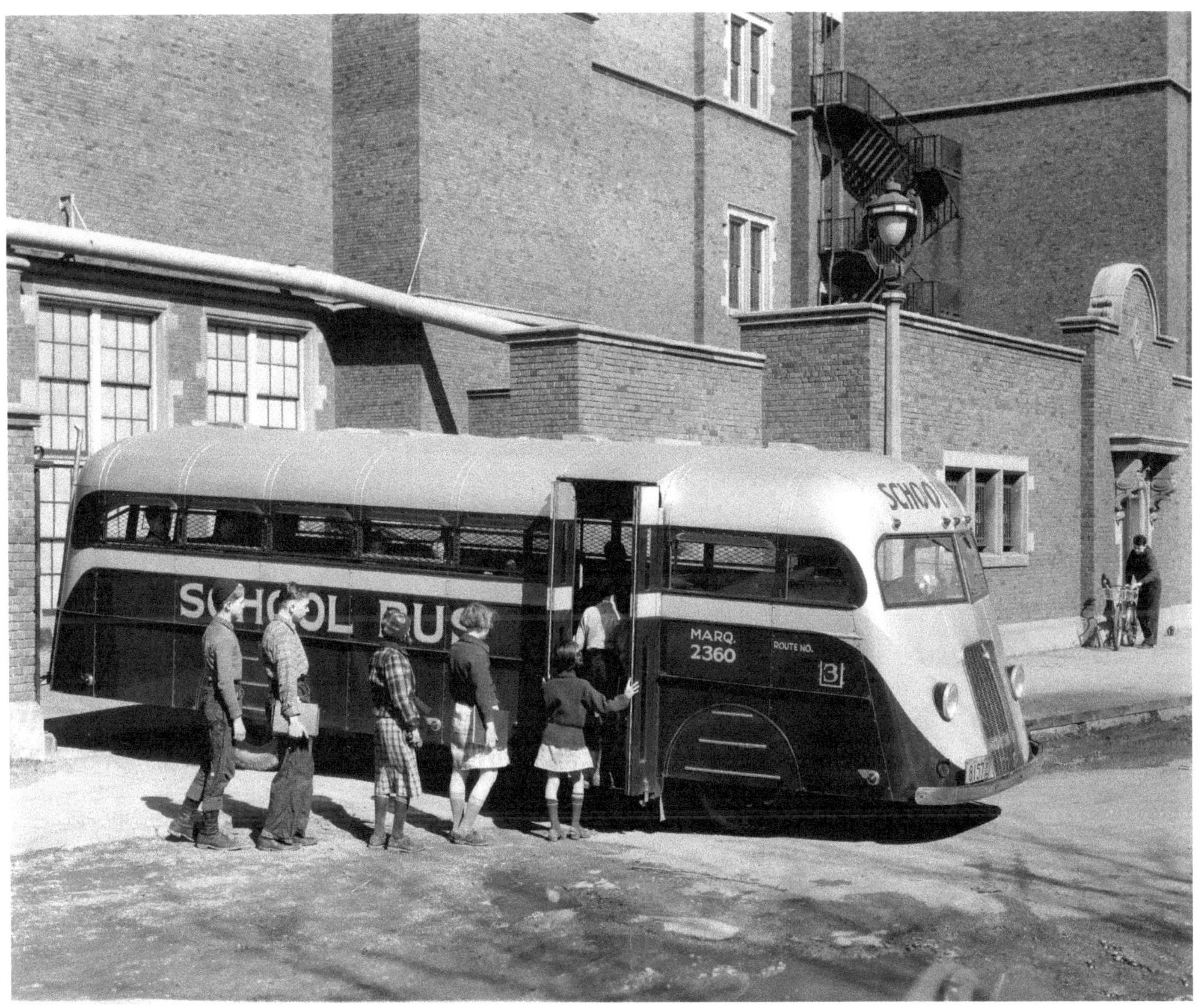

The intersection of 12th and Wisconsin looks quite different today. This photo, taken in the late 1930s, offers a glimpse into the architecture of downtown Milwaukee at that time. While new buildings were constantly going up, the older ones were left to "look up" at the new high-rise buildings around them. The neighborhood is now primarily part of the Marquette University campus, including Carpenter Hall.

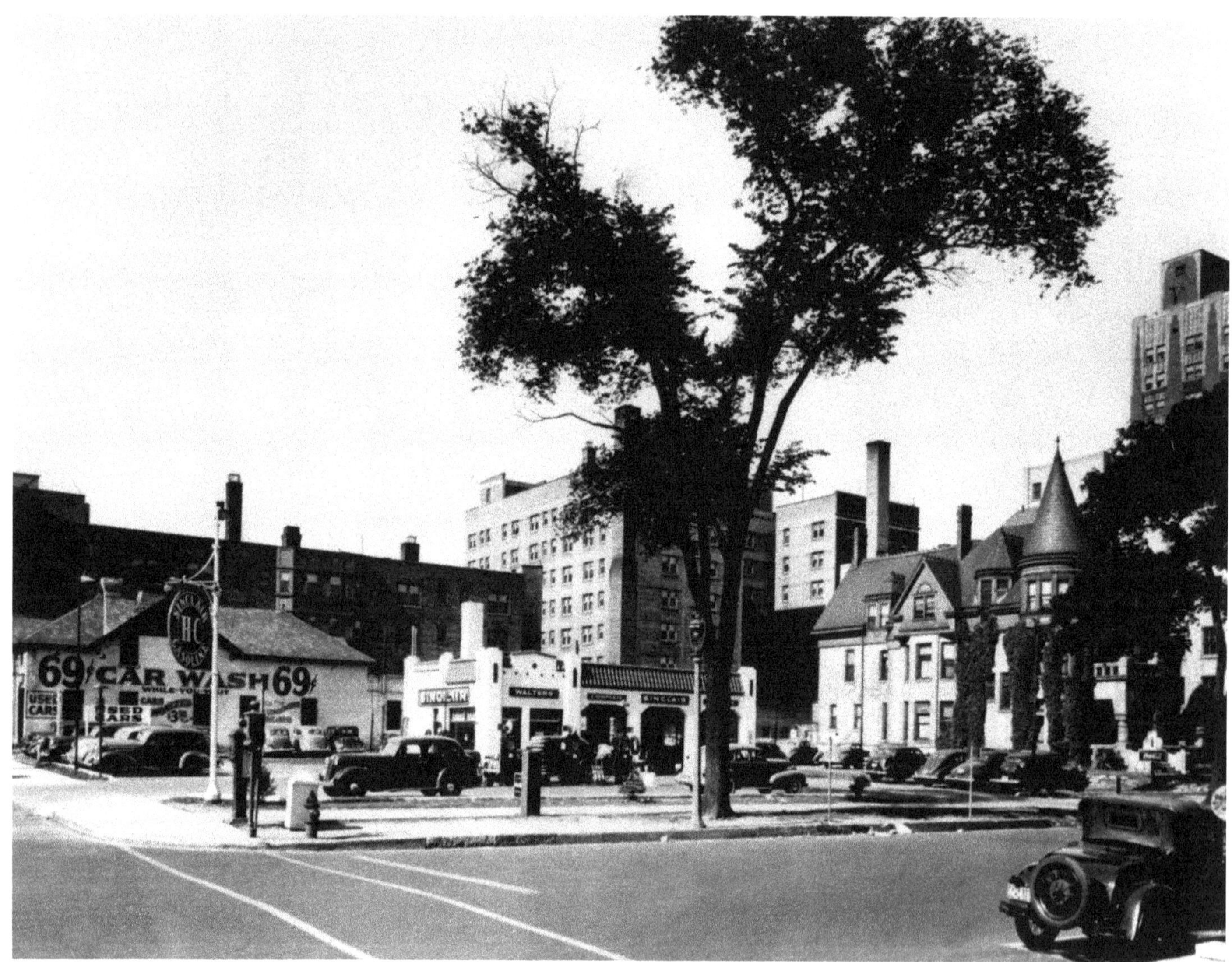

Boy Scouts parade over the Wisconsin Avenue bridge, crossing over the Milwaukee River in 1938. The parade was part of Boy Scout Day at the Wisconsin State Fair. The state fair has been hosted at the Wisconsin State Fairgrounds in what is now West Allis.

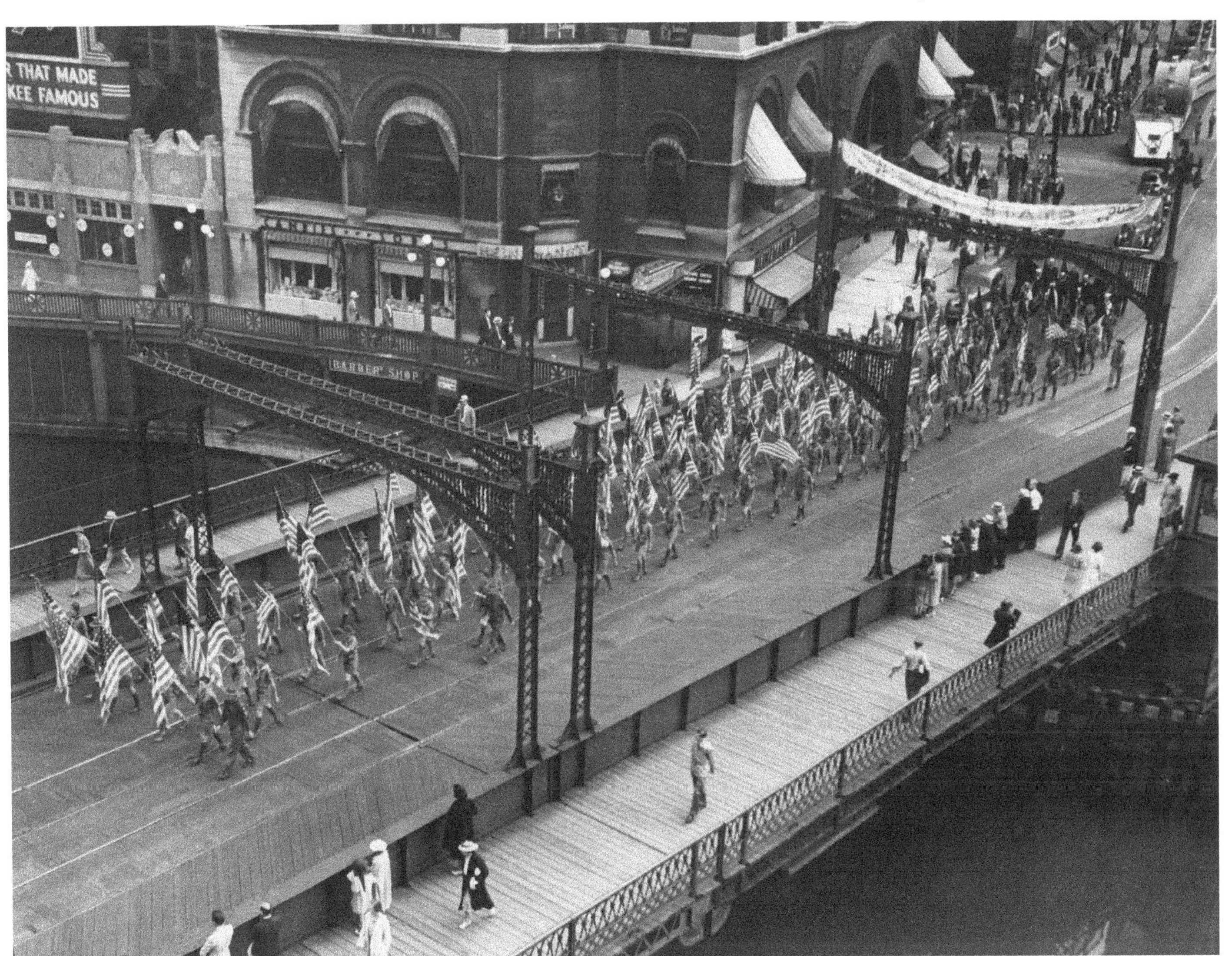

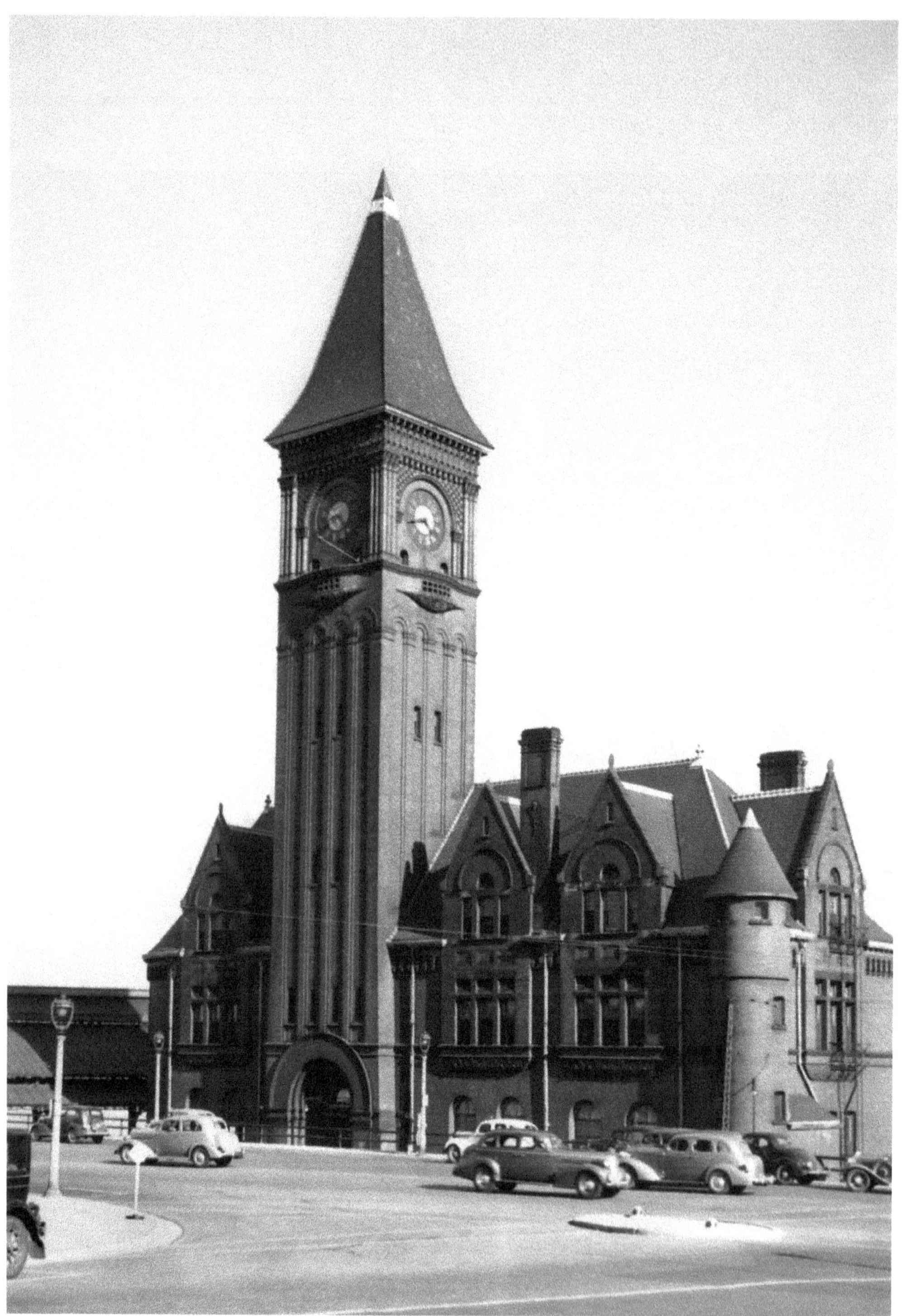

This station was one of two that replaced the original union station on Reed Street. It was built in 1899 and was a fixture in the Milwaukee railroad industry until 1968.

War and the Future

(1940–1969)

As World War II began, Milwaukee's industrial and manufacturing companies retooled for war production. Milwaukee became a center for wartime business. Milwaukee's mayor, Carl Zeidler, chose to join the navy in support of the war and was lost at sea defending the nation. The city participated by rationing food, gasoline, and anything that could help the war effort. Many women went to work in the factories to keep production moving at a time when many men were serving overseas.

At the end of the war, manufacturing retooled again for peacetime. Labor disputes still occurred.

The freeway system was built, a very good thing for the gridlock on city streets but not so good for the city's neighborhoods. Houses, churches, and other neighborhood landmarks were purchased and subsequently demolished, leaving the culturally diverse communities of those areas separated and frayed.

Socialism returned to Milwaukee in the form of Frank Zeidler, the brother of Carl. Mayor Zeidler was instrumental in building the freeway system, upgrading the parks, and implementing new mass transit systems. Milwaukee continued to grow and the downtown skyline continued to rise. With the construction of the Milwaukee arena, County Stadium, and General Mitchell Field, the "Cream City" was now a full-fledged metropolis.

Today, summer festivals have become a time to remember the city's diverse immigrants. The Public Museum boasts the world's largest dinosaur skeleton, and the city's skywalk is alone in spanning a river open to river traffic. As the nation's 22nd largest city, home to Marquette University, the Allen-Bradley Clock Tower, and many other attractions, Milwaukee can take pride in many accomplishments.

In 1940, druggists and pharmacists compound different materials for a patient's given prescription. This pharmacy, known as "the Pharmacy," was owned by Max Lemberger.

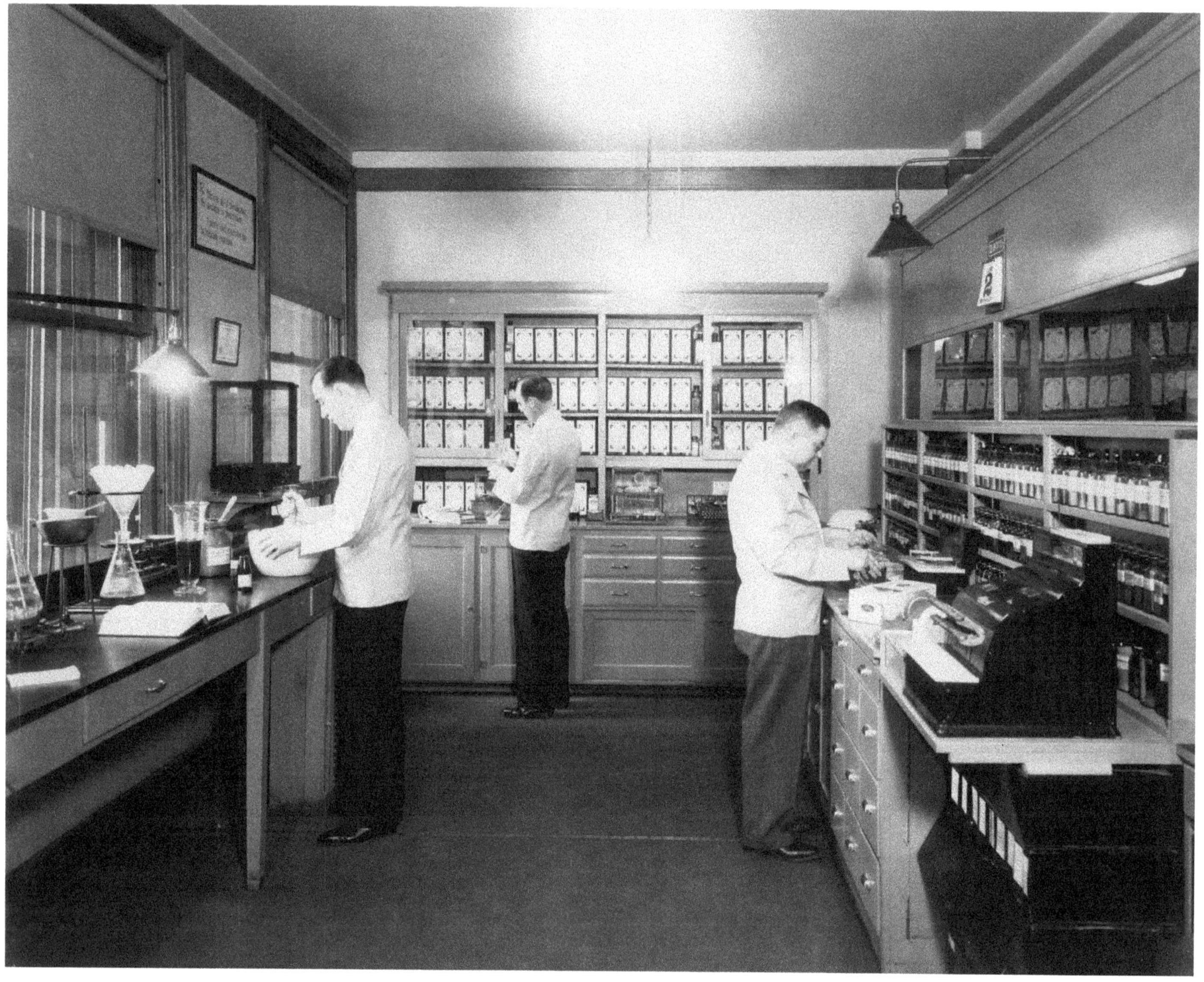

FDR visited Milwaukee in 1940 and toured the Allis Chalmers plant. He is seen here with the governor of Wisconsin, Julius Heil. In 1941 the factory was filled with tear gas when workers shut down the plant and held up production.

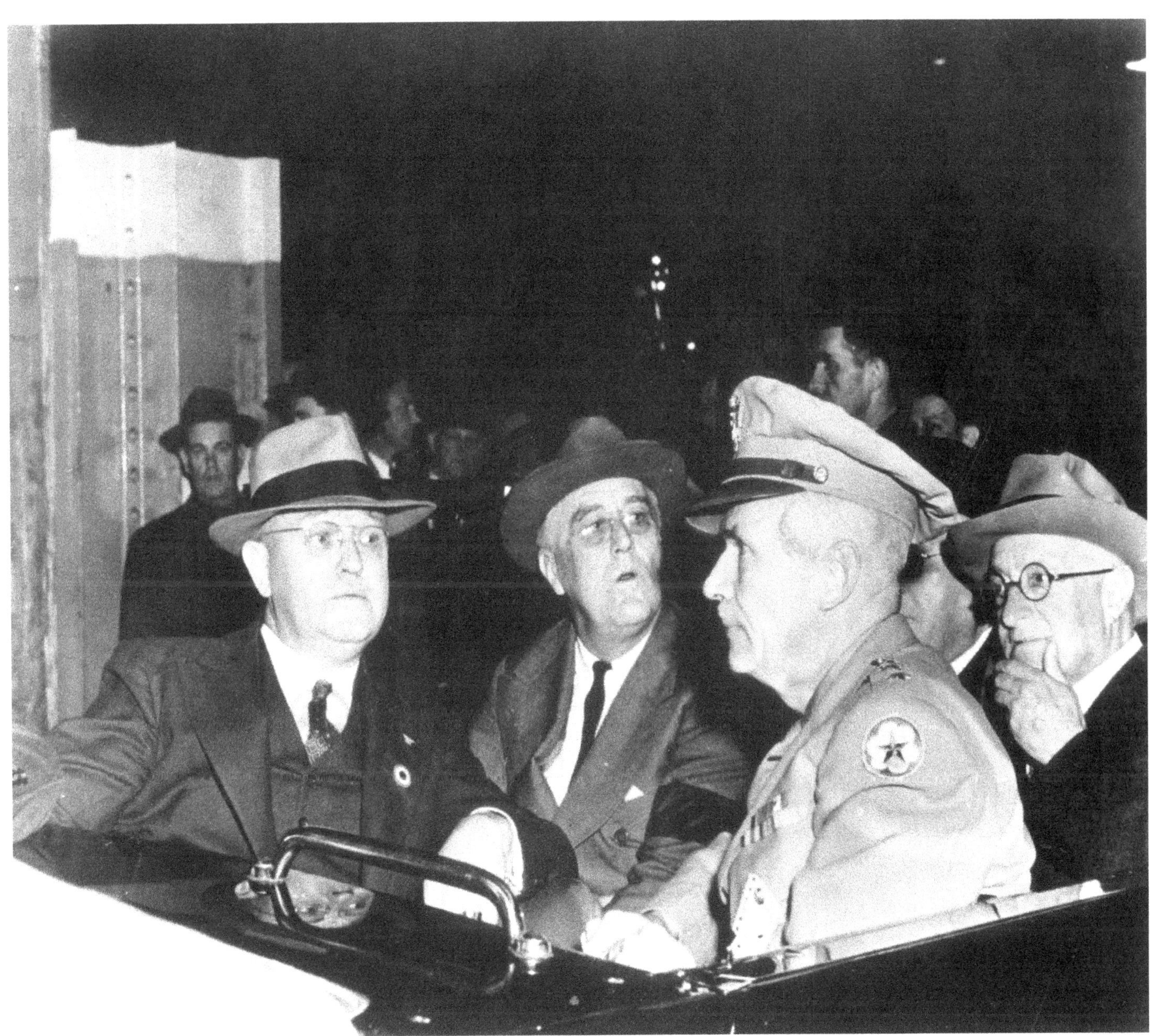

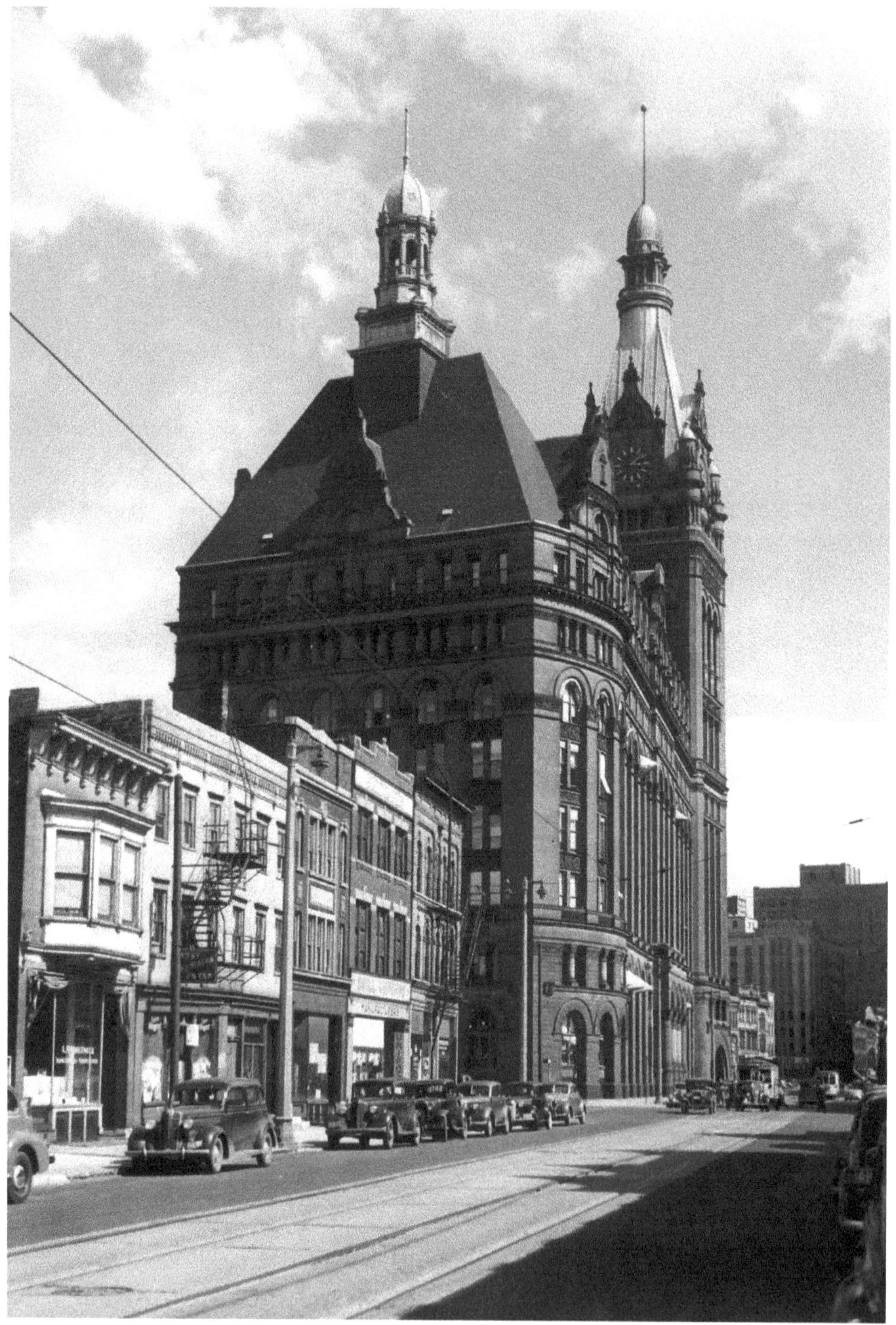

This rear view of City Hall was recorded in 1940. Years of industry and manufacturing in the downtown area and the Menomonee River Valley took their toll on the facade of the building. Restoration has begun and is due to be finished in 2008, returning City Hall to the beautiful building it was when it first opened.

In the late 1930s and early 1940s, "walk" and "don't walk" signals came from the local police officer rather than a light on the other side of the street. Intersections in downtown were crowded with pedestrians walking to their destinations.

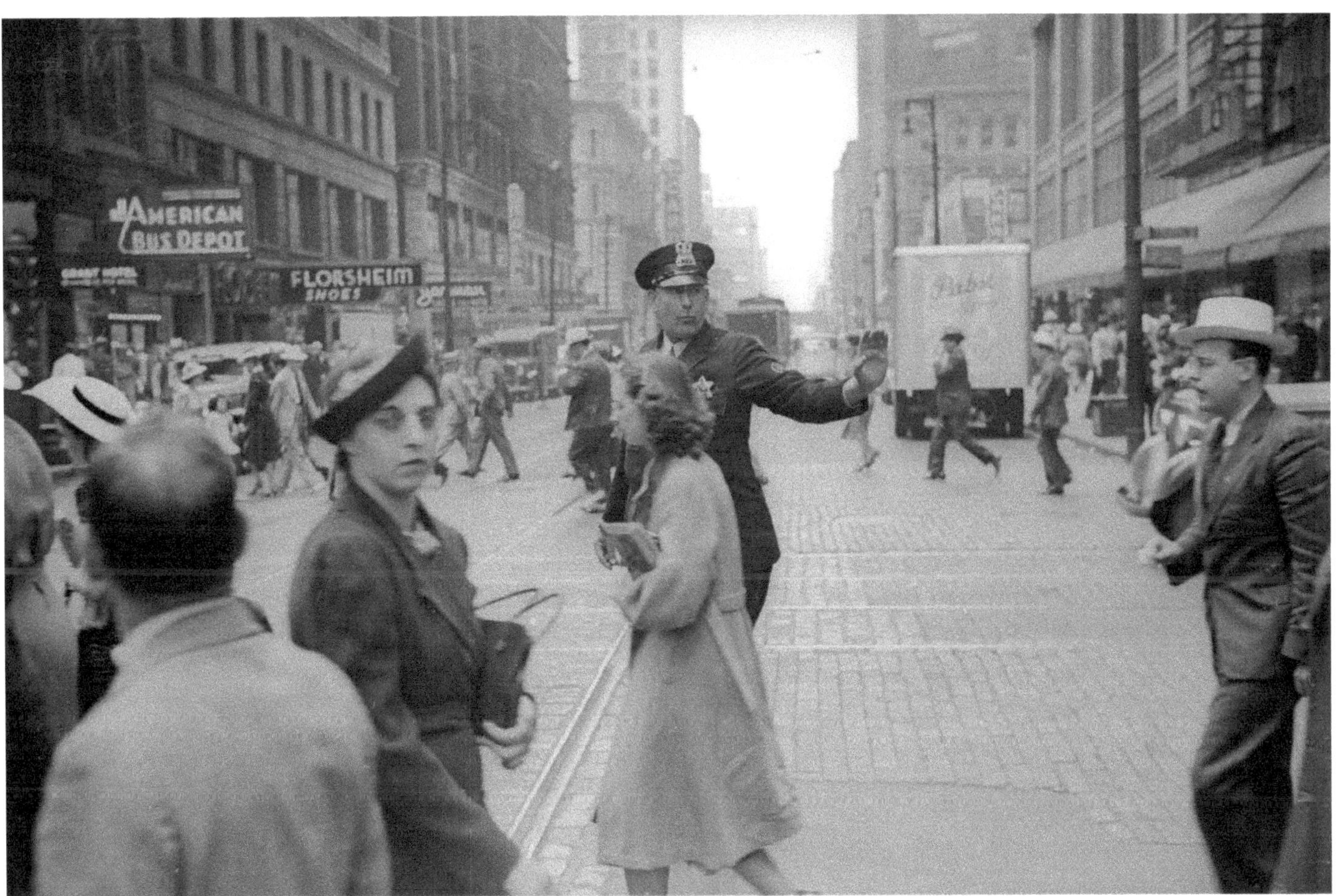

Business at the Milwaukee farmer's market is underway. Today Milwaukee has similar markets scattered throughout the different neighborhoods. Each market carries different produce, appropriate to the cultural makeup of the area. Milwaukee's culturally diverse neighborhoods still thrive, and today's versions of the market seen in this picture allow patrons to take a step back to simpler times.

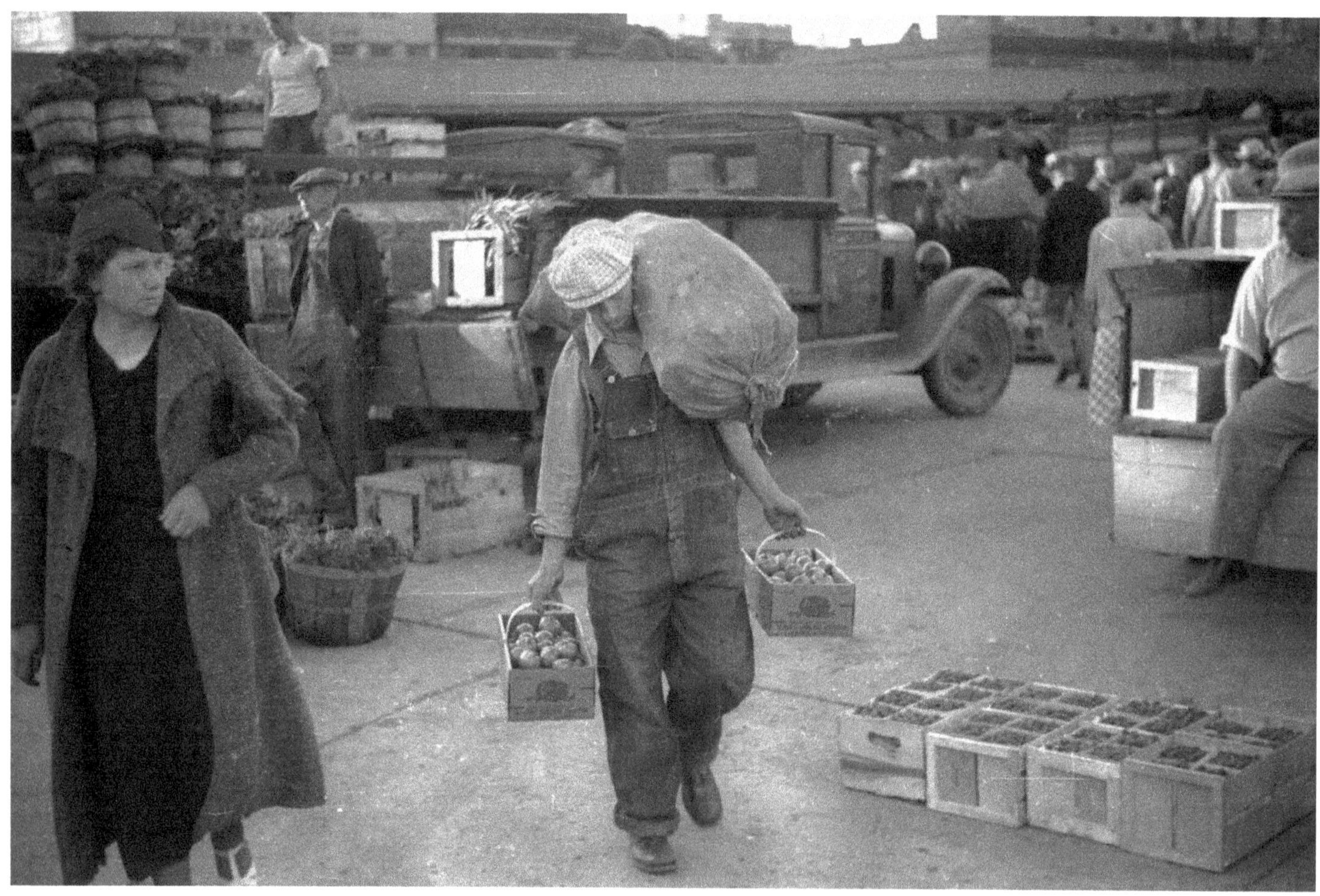

World War II affected every American city and Milwaukee was no exception. On this day, November 30, 1942, coffee rationing went into effect. Gasoline rationing would come the next day.

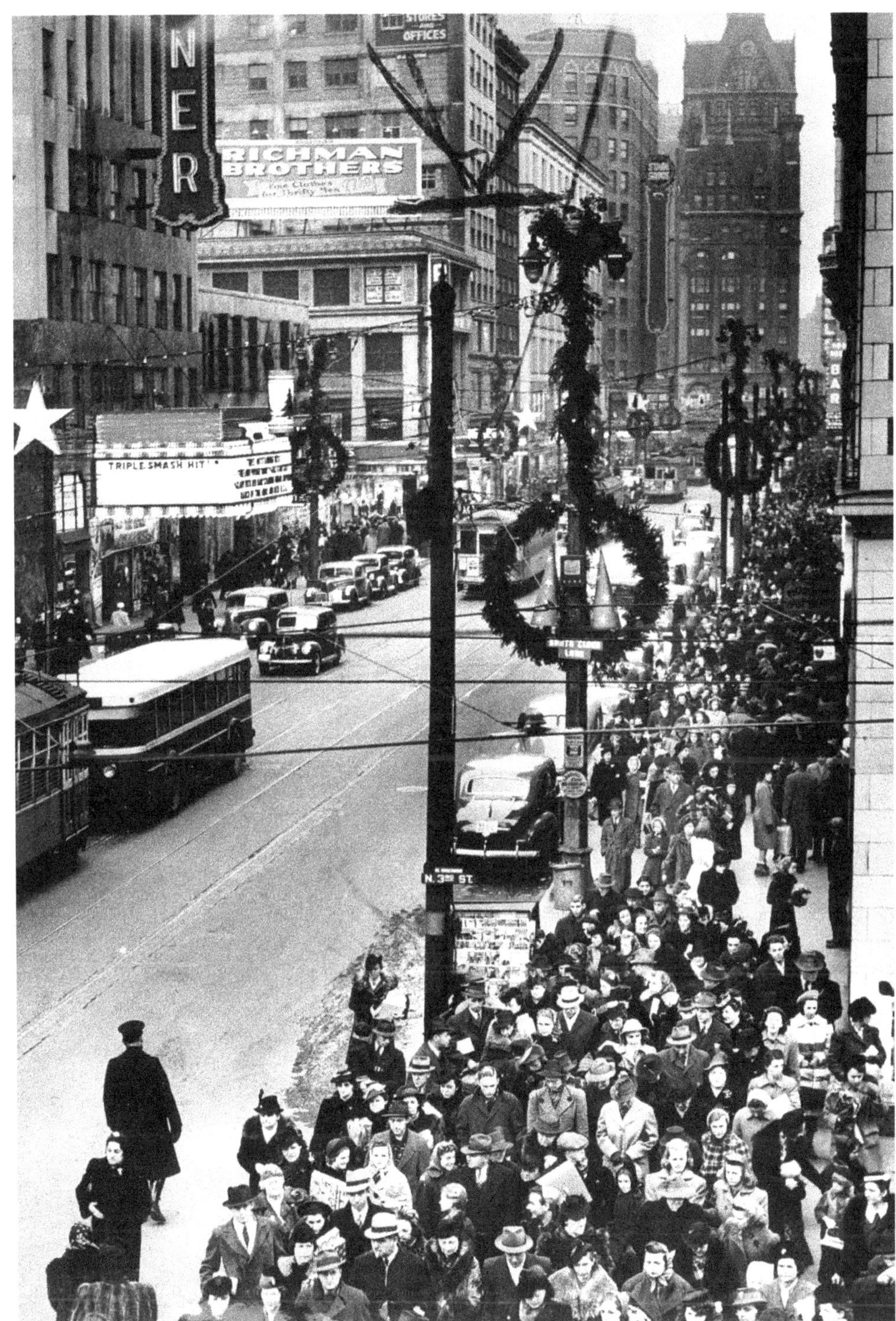

Pedestrians attempt to shield themselves from the rain while automobiles and streetcars vie for the space on the streets.

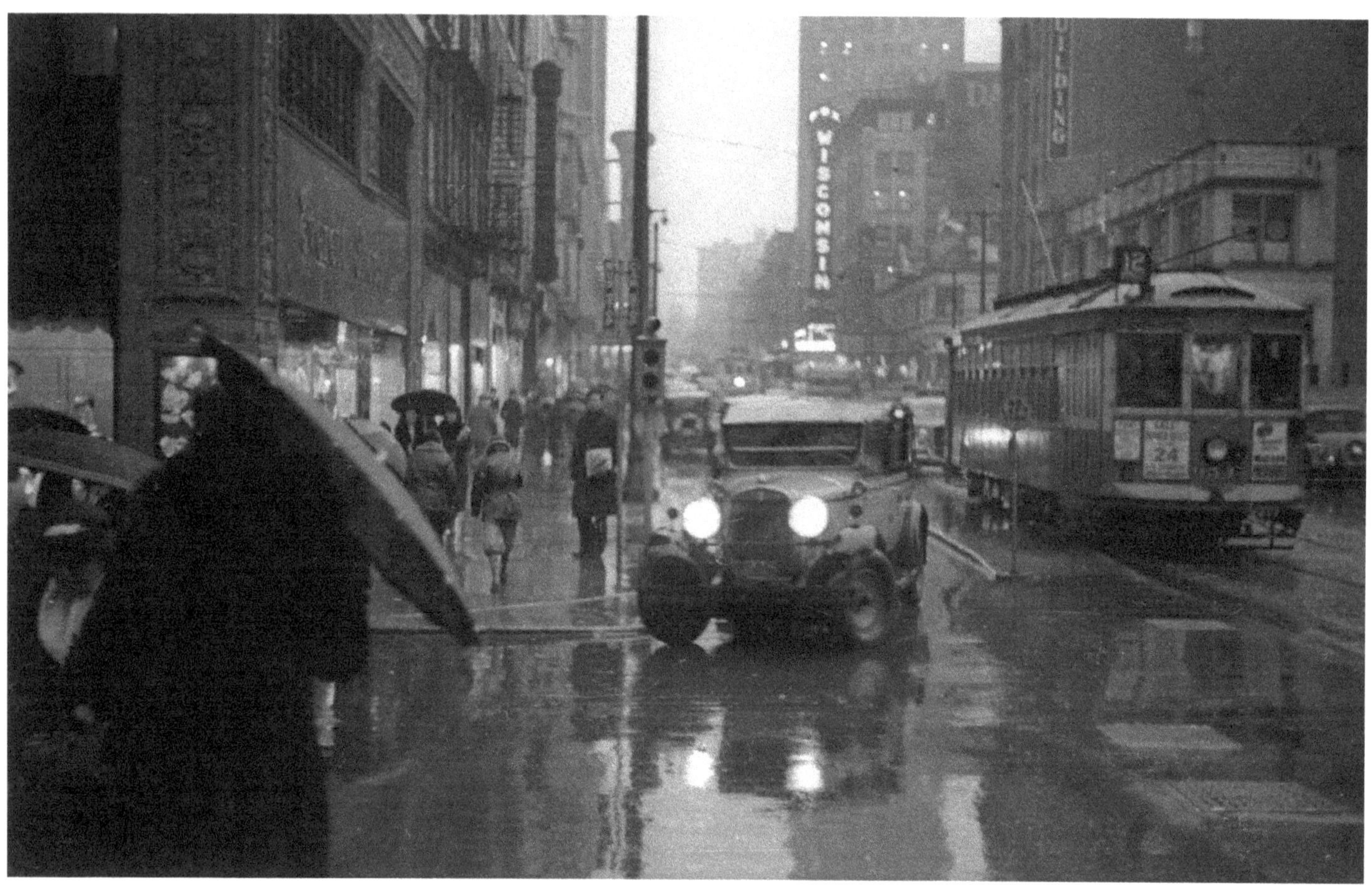

September 3, 1945, offered entertainment that Milwaukeeans had not enjoyed in quite a few years. In the Labor Day parade, citizens and soldiers marched side by side. On the silver screen, John Wayne was starring in *Back to Bataan.* During the depths of World War II, a sense of unity and shared goals were understood as important to the war effort.

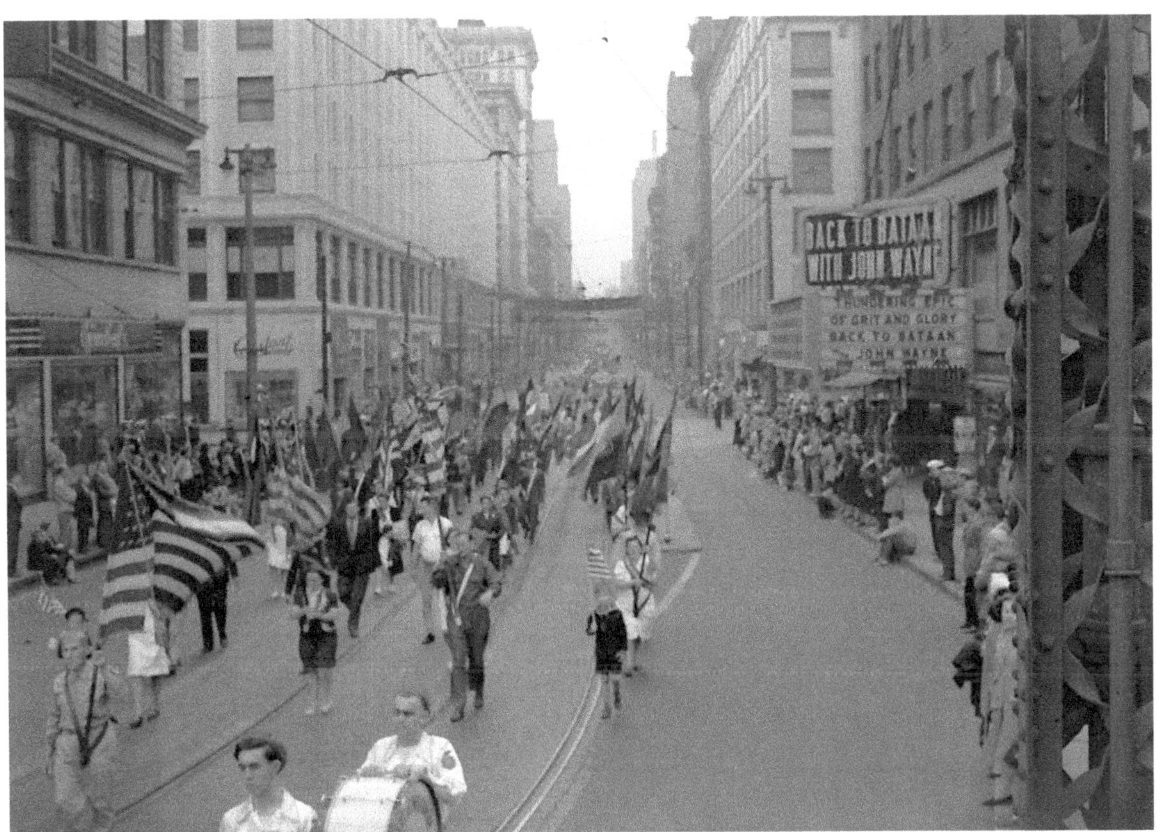

The Milwaukee Vocational School was the next incarnation of the Milwaukee Continuation School, which would eventually morph into Milwaukee Area Technical College. Enrollment flourished owing to a law mandating education.

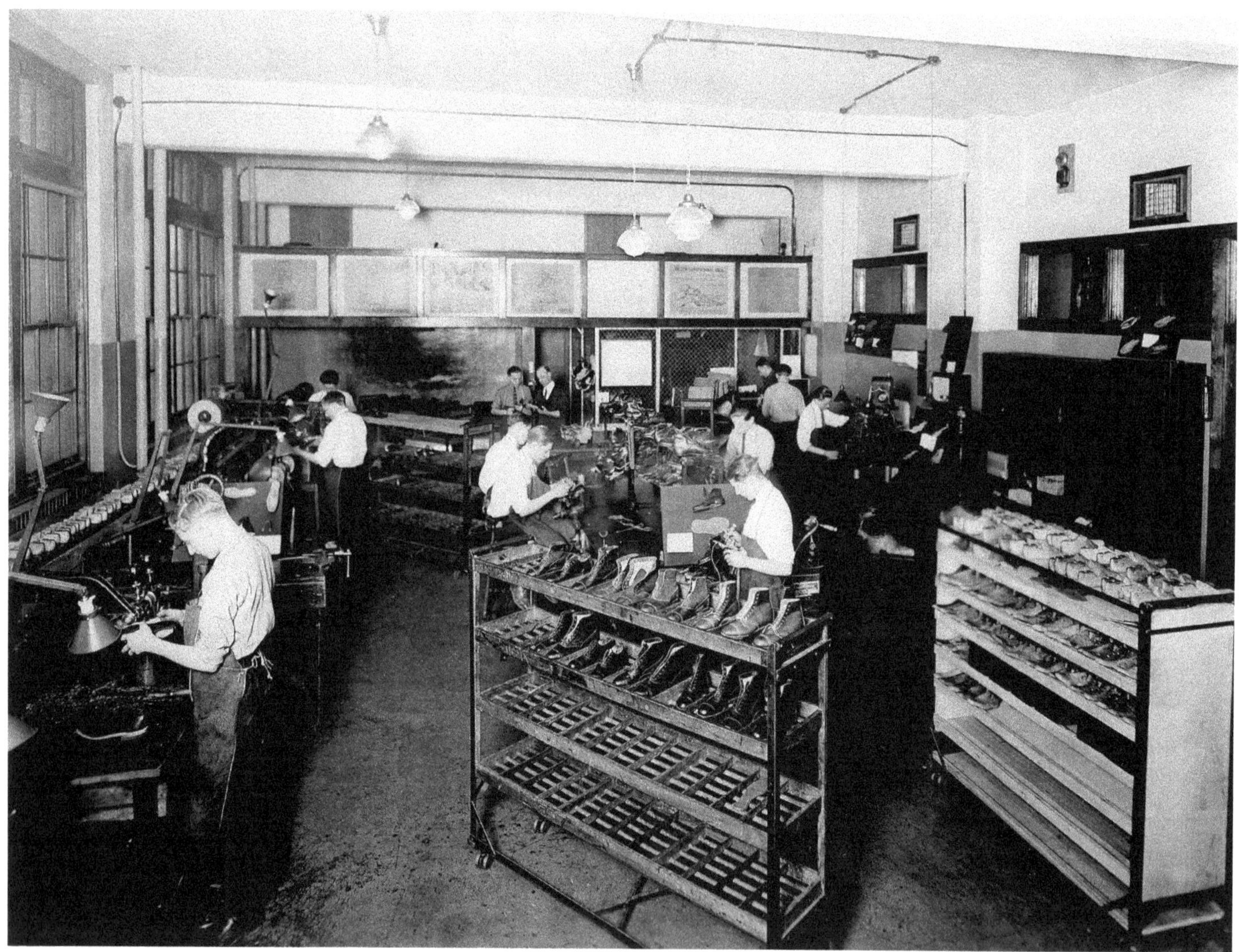

Welding is in progress in the mid 1940s at the Falk Company. Herman Wahl Falk started the company in 1895 to manufacture gear drives for other companies. The Falk Company is located in the Menomonee River Valley.

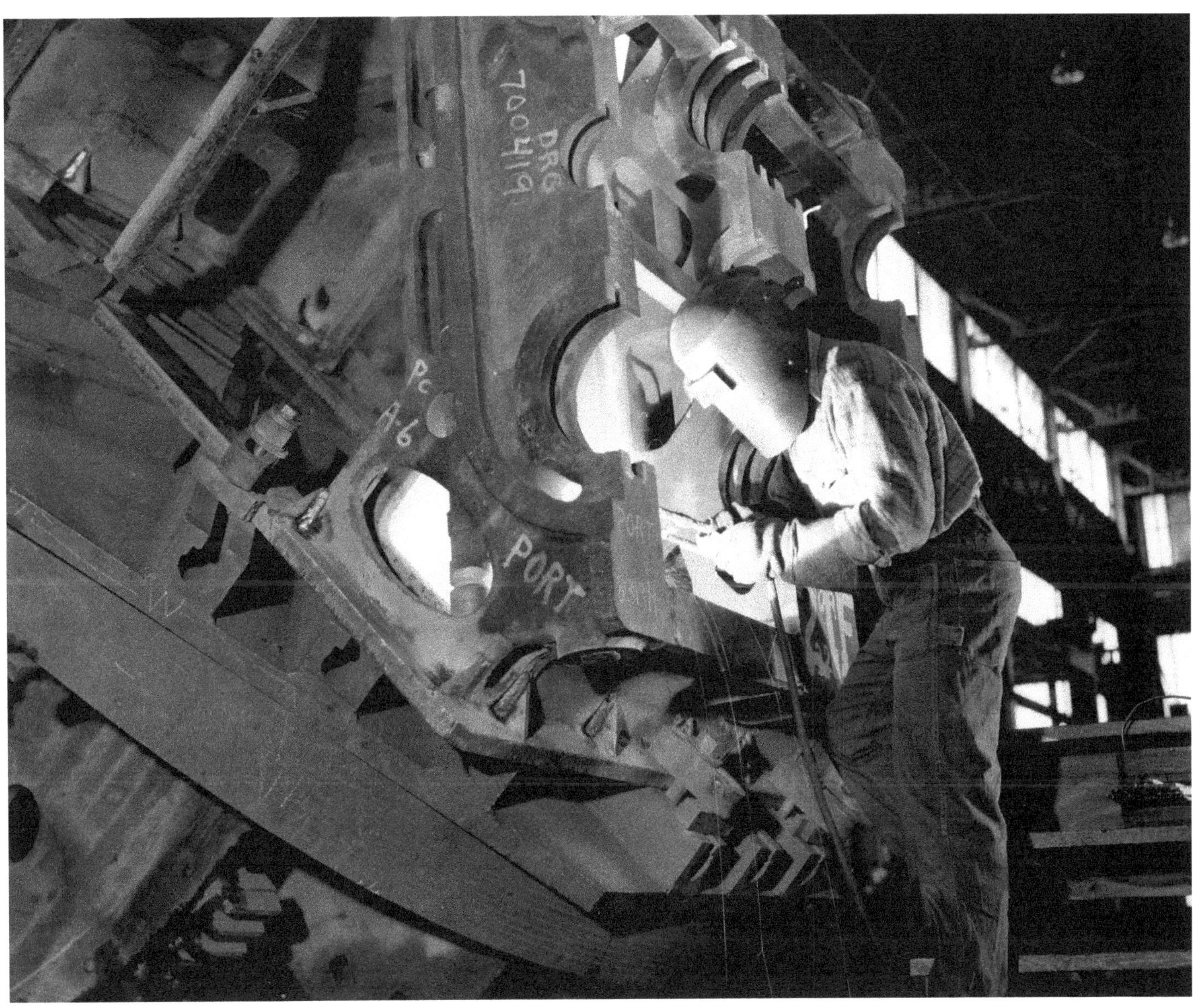

Demonstrators walk up and down Wisconsin Avenue in March 1946 to protest U.S. diplomatic relations with Spain under Francisco Franco during World War II.

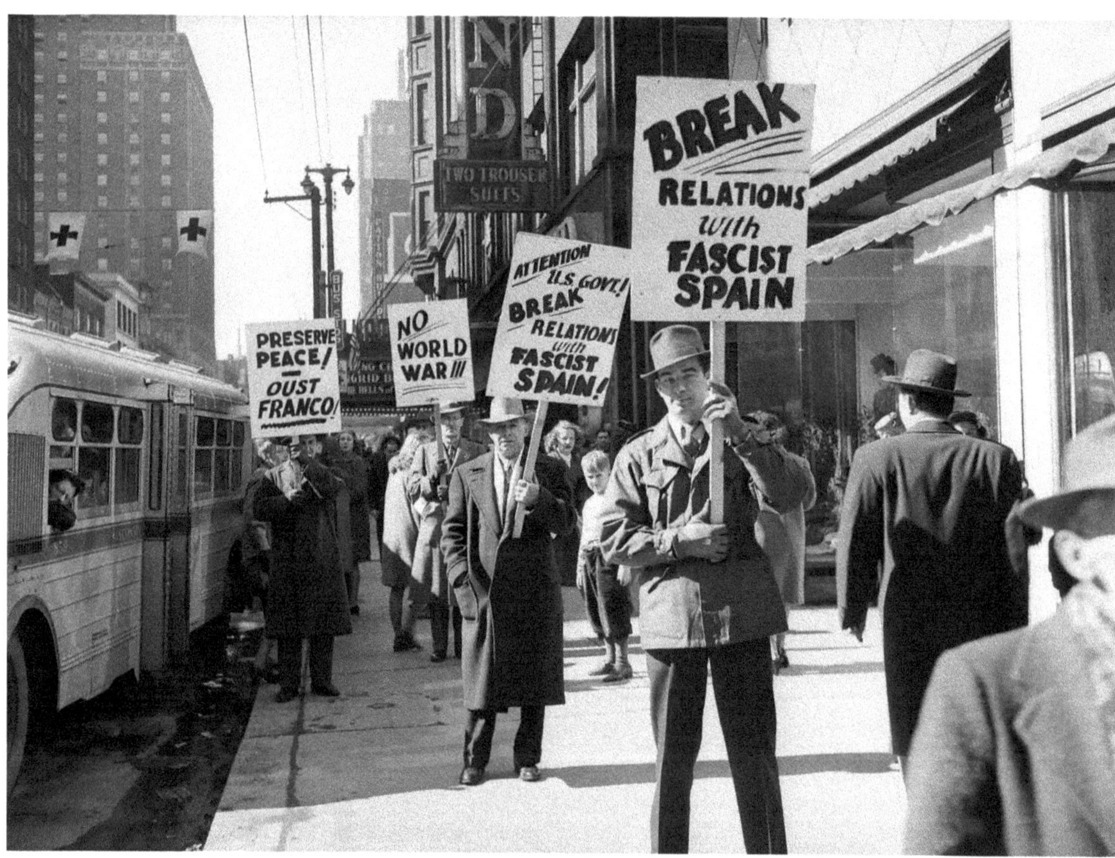

The Milwaukee neighborhood of Bronzeville stretched from North Avenue to State Street and from Third to 12th Street. The Bronzeville Bombers bowling team, pictured here in 1947, placed tenth at the CIO state bowling competition with a total score of 2690.

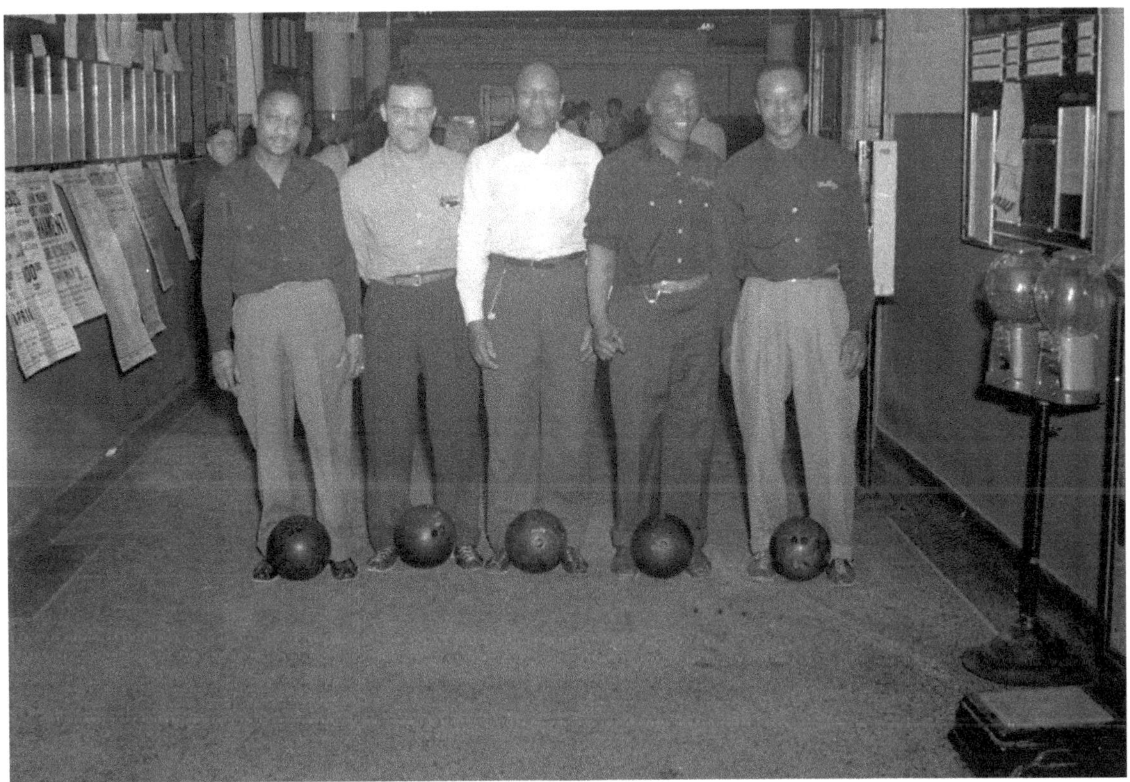

Milwaukee has often been a hotbed for labor disputes, one of which took place in 1946. Workers can be seen here from the Chain Belt Local 1527 receiving support from fellow union workers and offices.

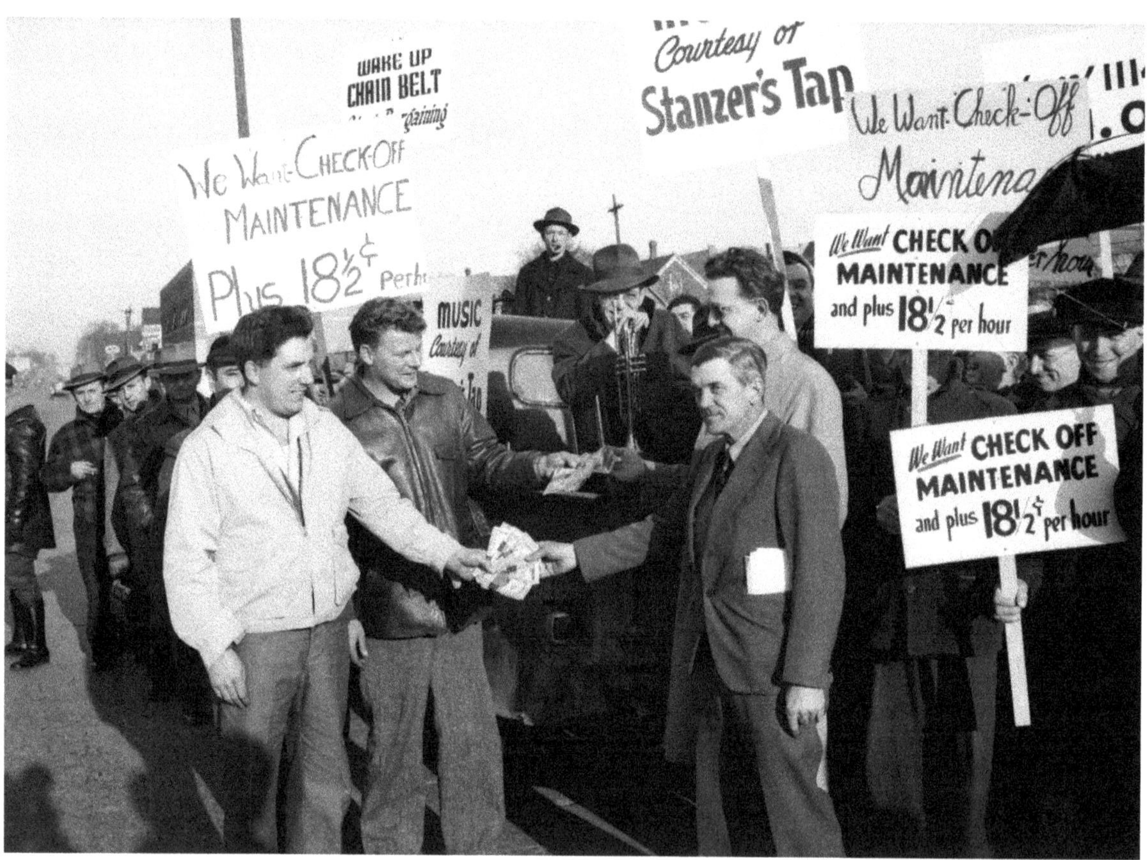

Elsie the Cow, mascot for Borden Dairy, and the very first Alice in Dairyland stand on a parade float in 1948. Alice in Dairyland is an annual contest in Wisconsin in which young women compete to represent Wisconsin and promote its agricultural industry during a one-year appointment to the Department of Agriculture, Trade, and Consumer Protection.

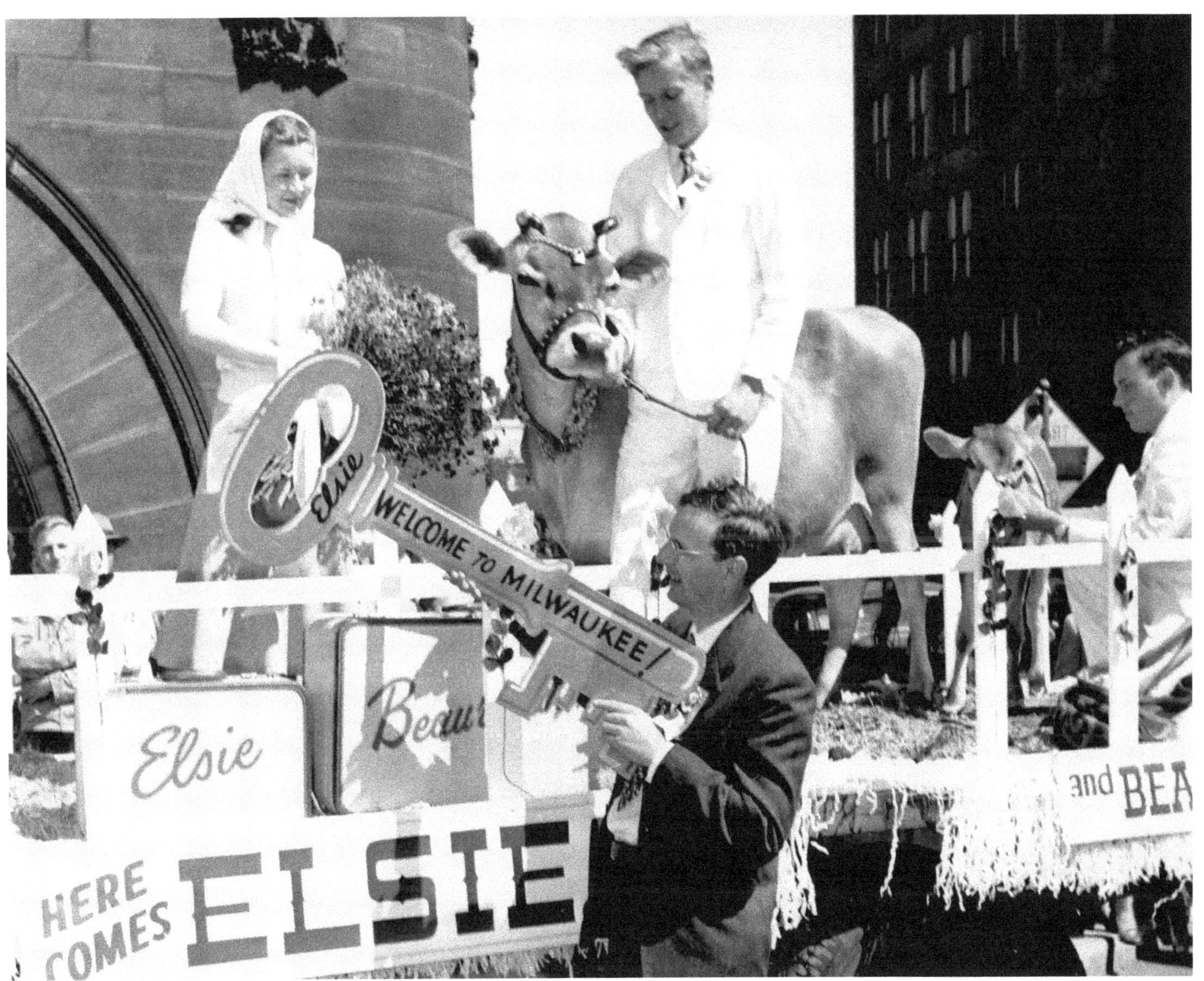

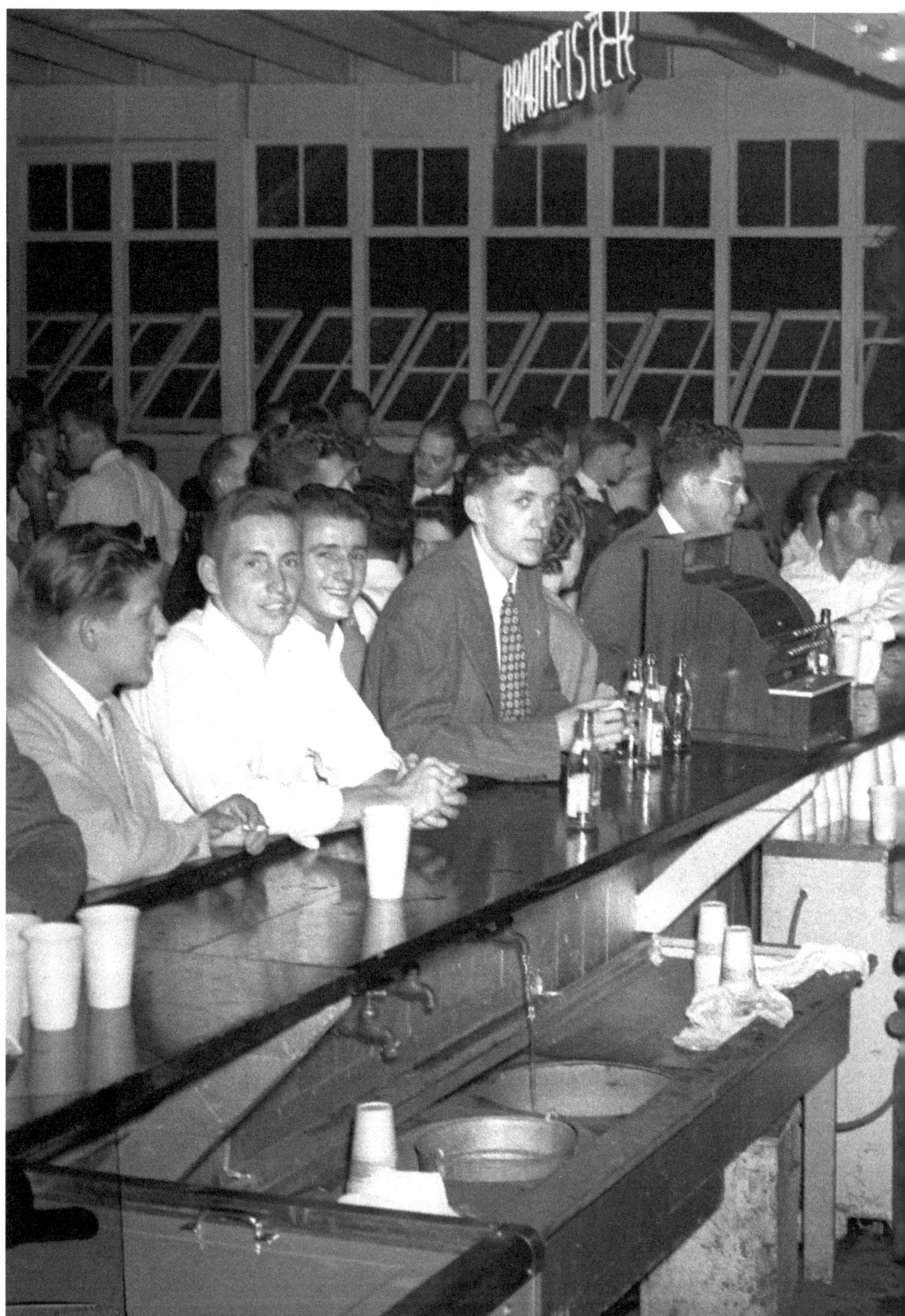
BRAUMEISTER

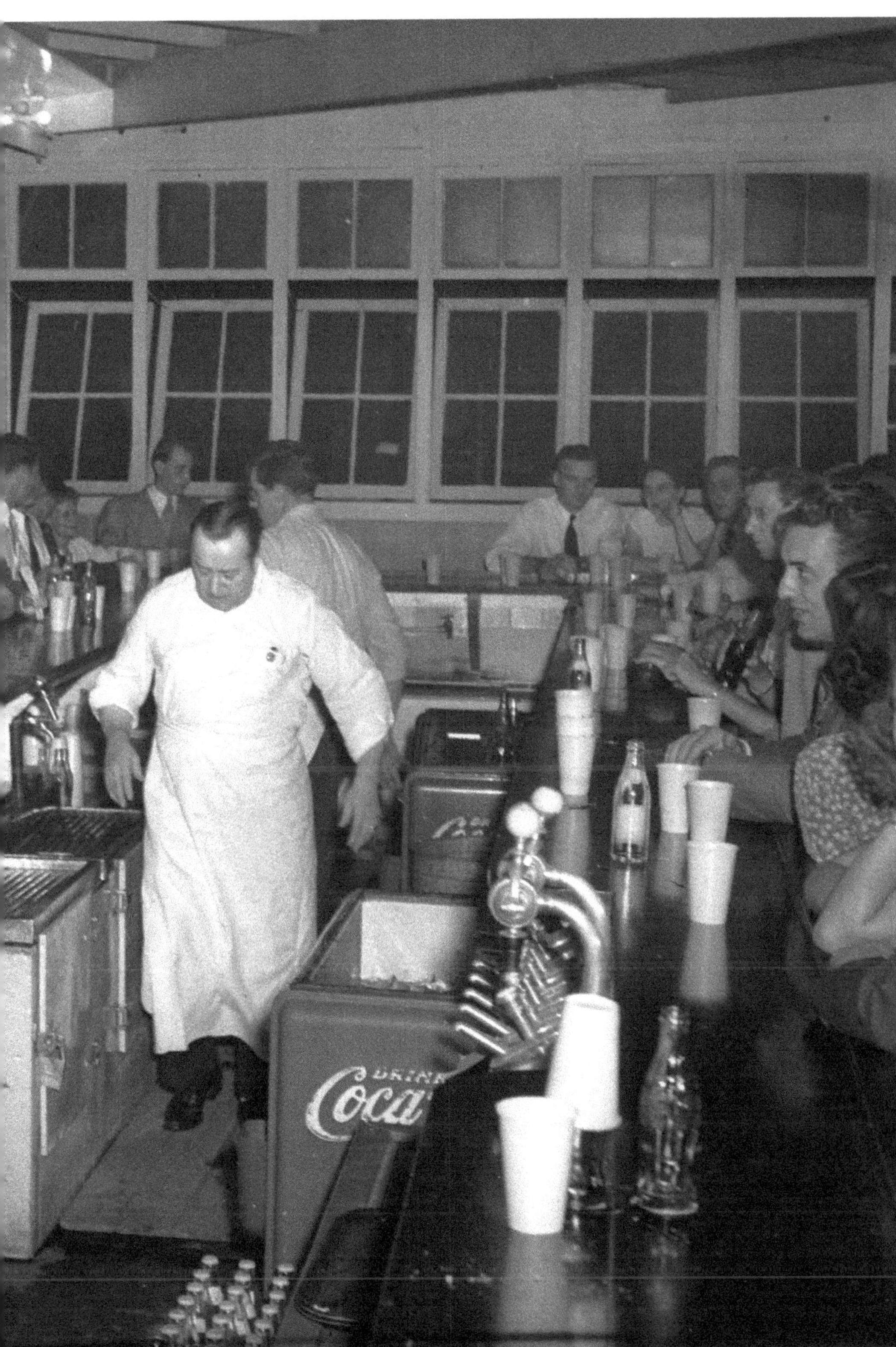

Employees of the Seaman's Body Corporation gather at the annual Union Harvest Dance in September 1947.

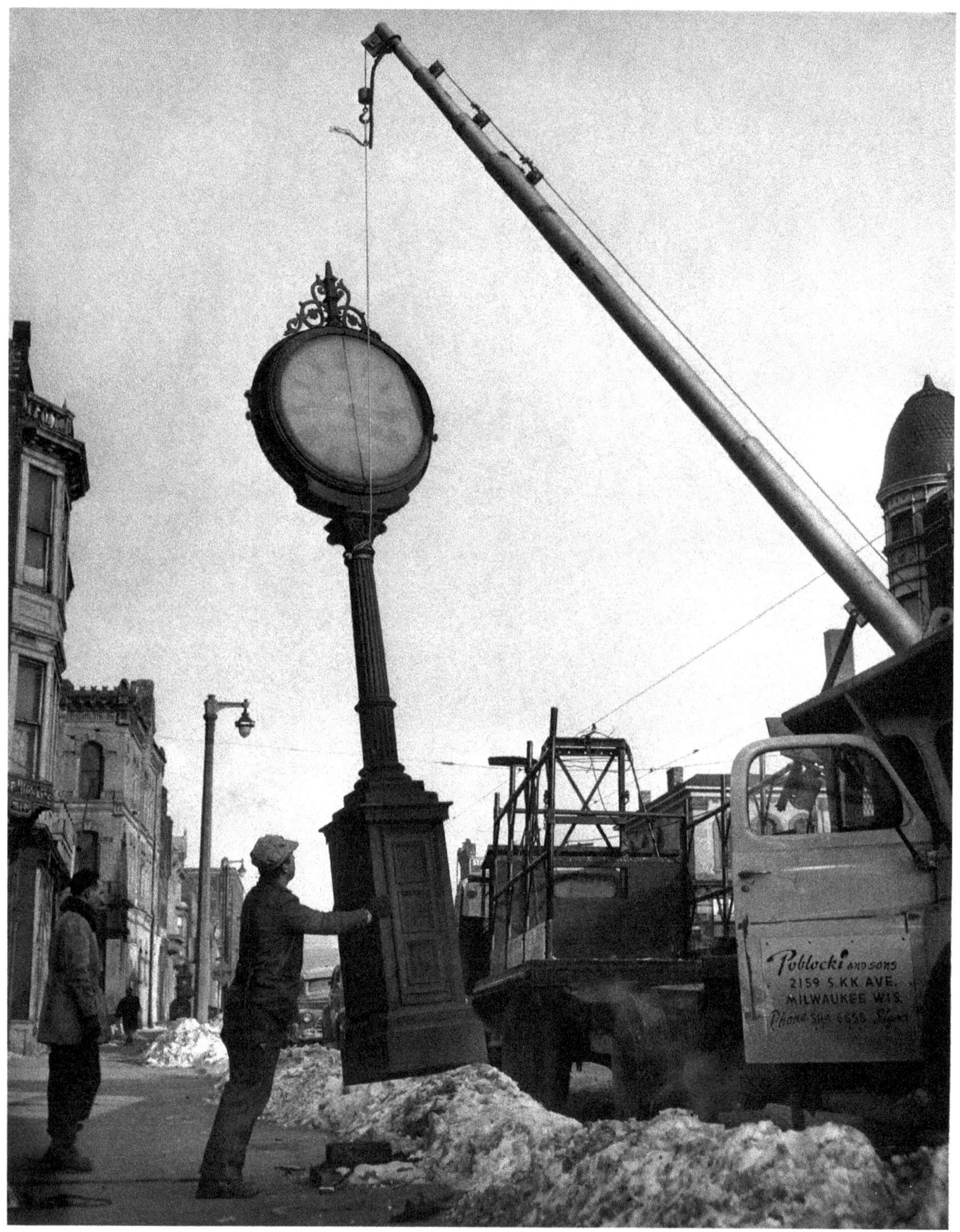

At one time fifty clocks of the kind pictured here existed around Milwaukee. They were removed, not once, but twice by two different city mayors. Today a few of these clocks have reappeared around downtown, most notably in front of the Milwaukee County Historical Society and the Milwaukee Public Museum.

On March 17, 1950, less than a month before the "official" opening of the Milwaukee Arena, quite a bit of work remains to be done. Now called the U.S. Cellular Arena, the venue has hosted countless basketball games, concerts, and special events.

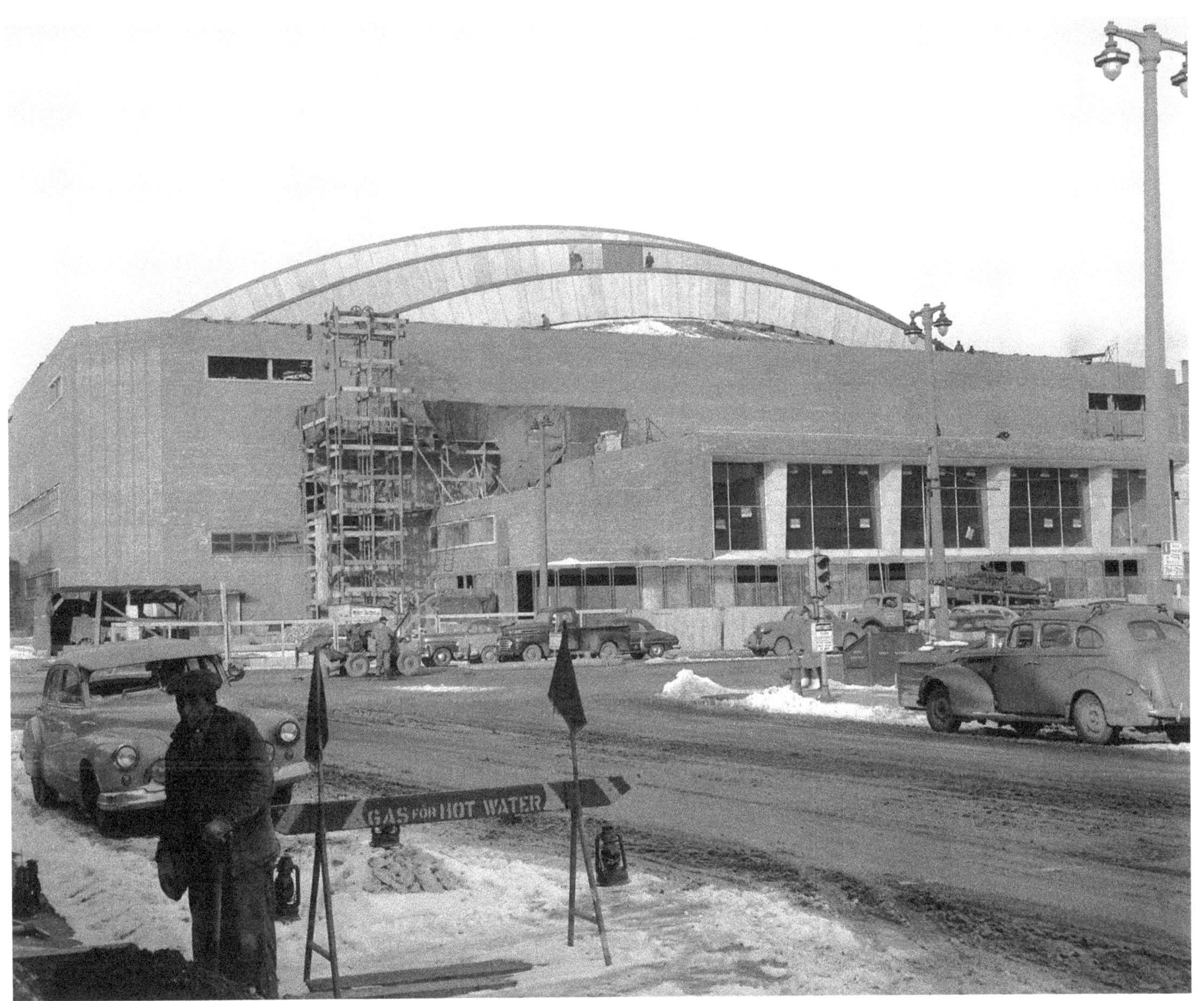

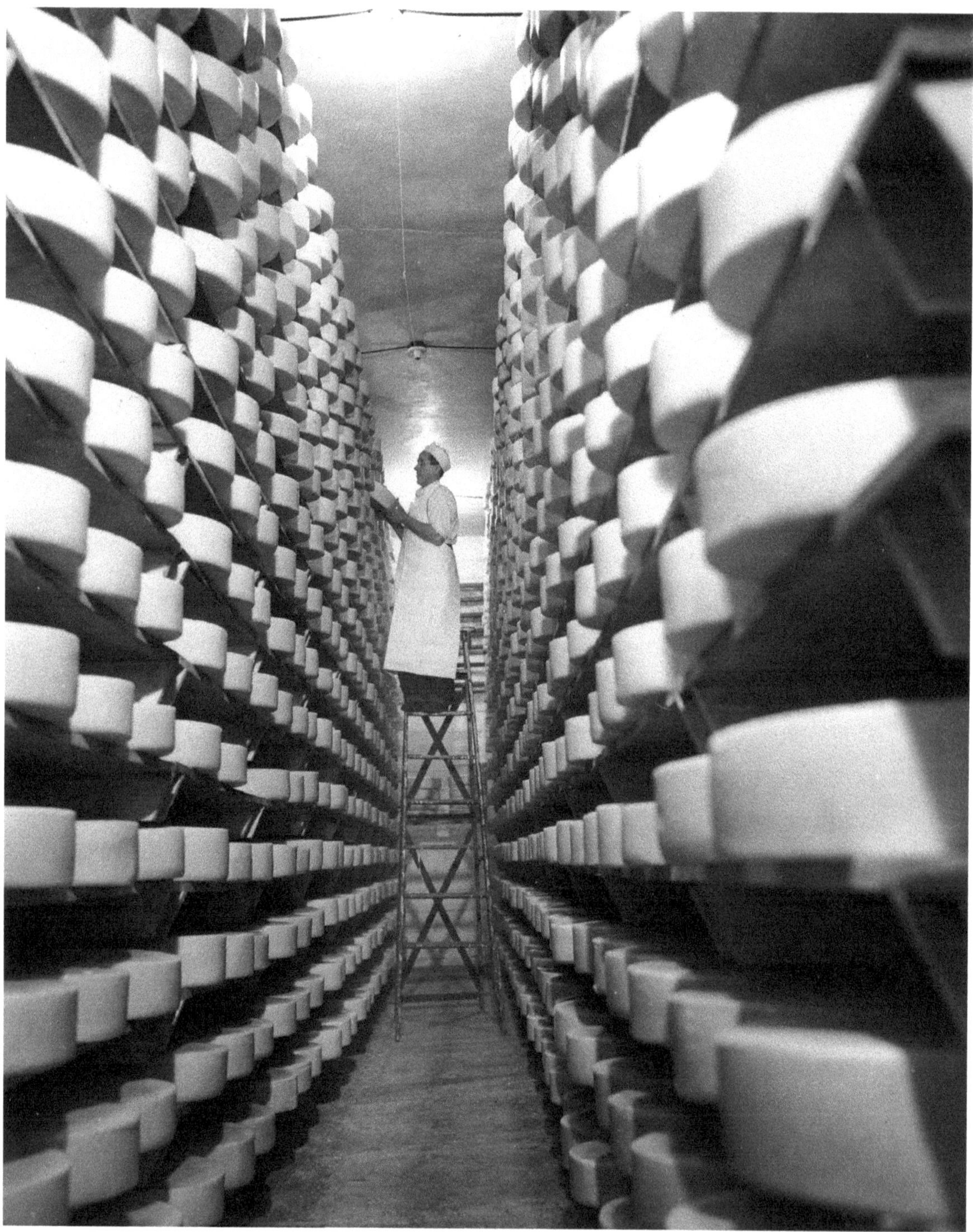

By the end of World War I, Wisconsin was the top dairy producer in the nation. In the 1940s "America's Dairyland" showed up on Wisconsin license plates. This 1952 photograph is one of many views of what storage for cheese looked like in those years.

Before the days of large supermarket chains, there came a transition from the neighborhood full-service grocer to the small self-service supermarket. This 1953 photo of the D. Kuhman market offers a view into that evolution.

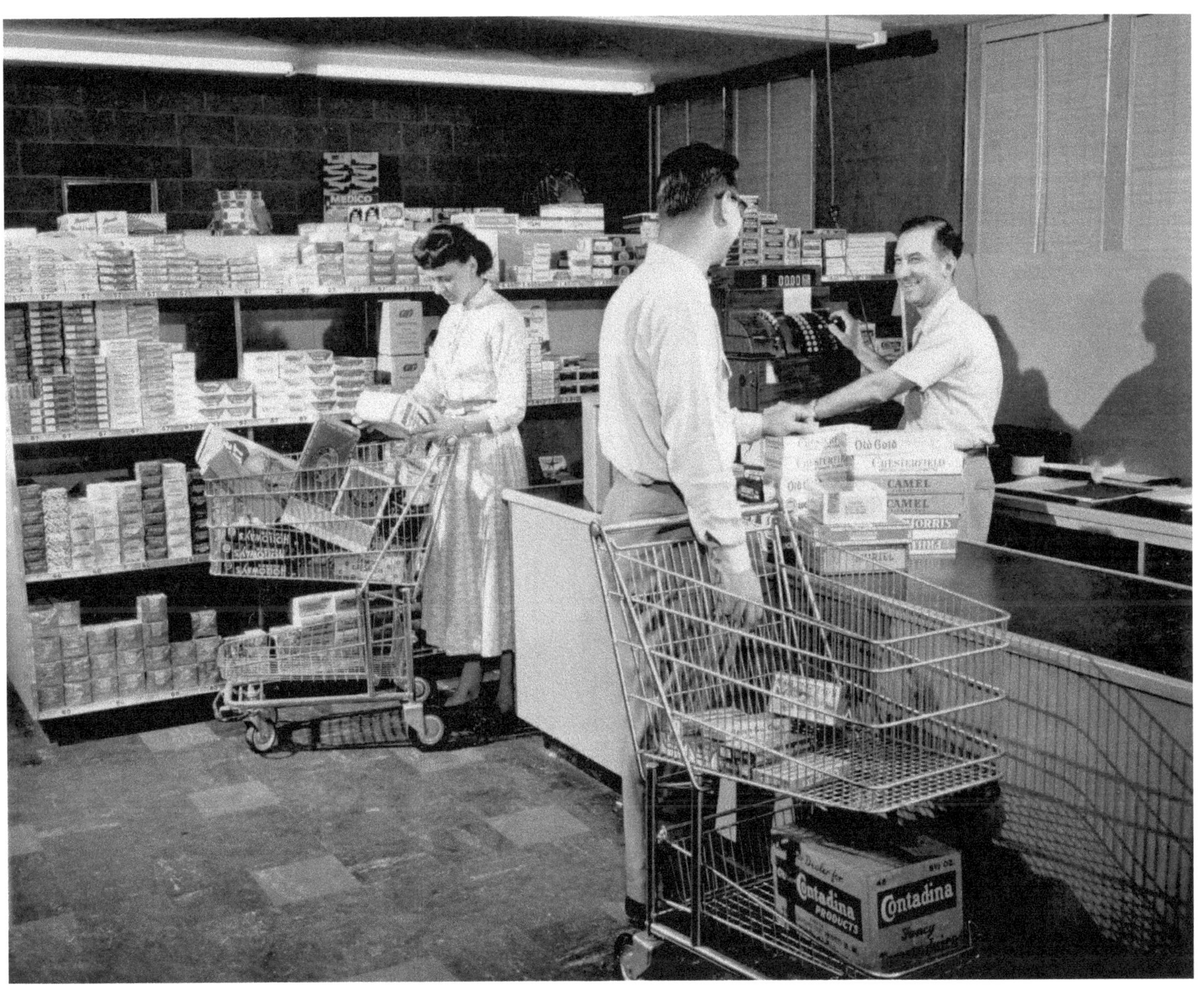

Following Spread: On September 20, 1953, past meets future, when streetcar #639 is replaced with a newer mode of transportation, the city bus. This change in public transportation was a goodbye to the days of "streetcar suburbs" and trolleys and a hello to the beginnings of today's system.

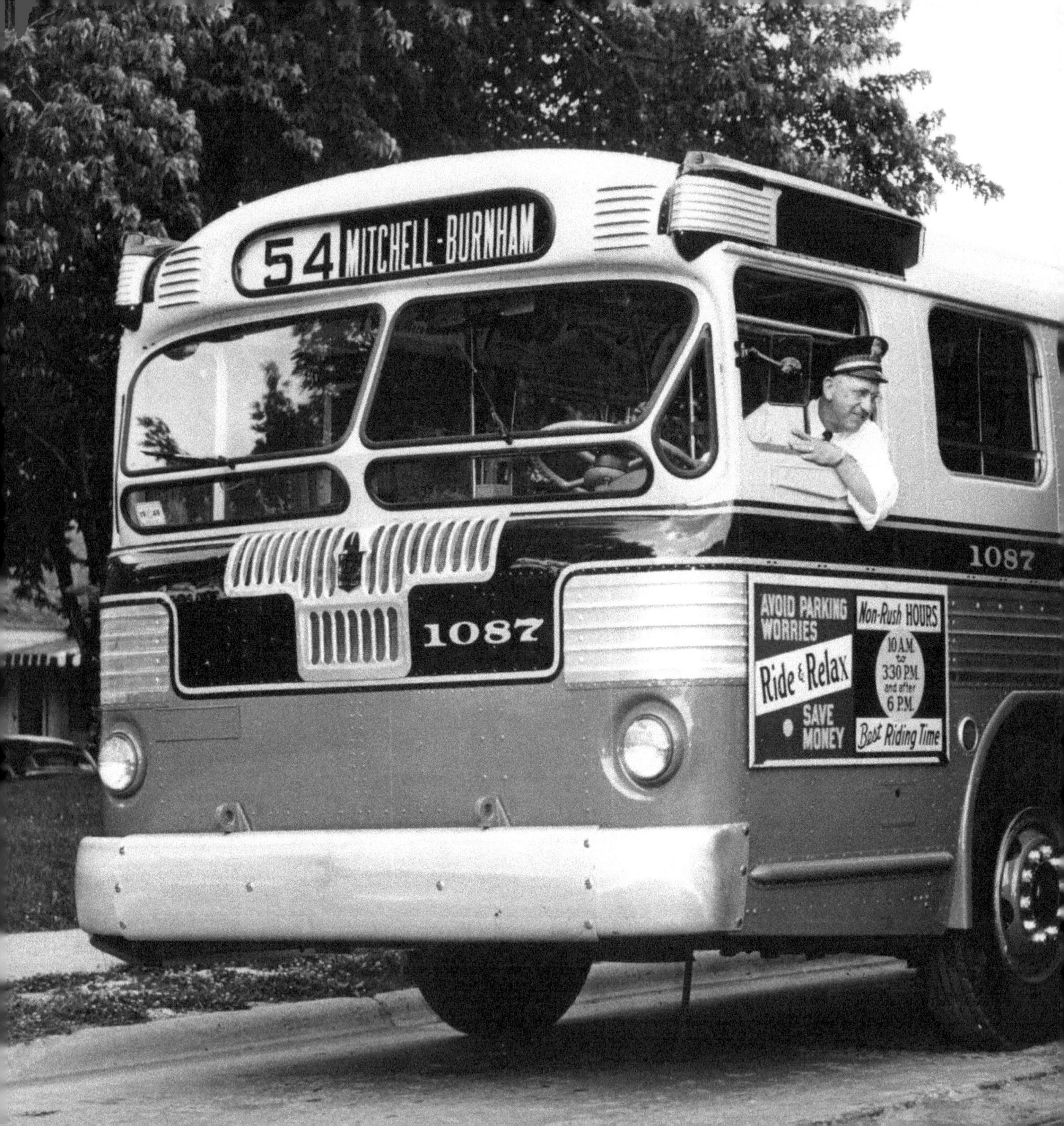
54 MITCHELL-BURNHAM
1087
1087
AVOID PARKING WORRIES
Ride & Relax
SAVE MONEY
Non-Rush HOURS
10 A.M. to 3:30 P.M. and after 6 P.M.
Best Riding Time

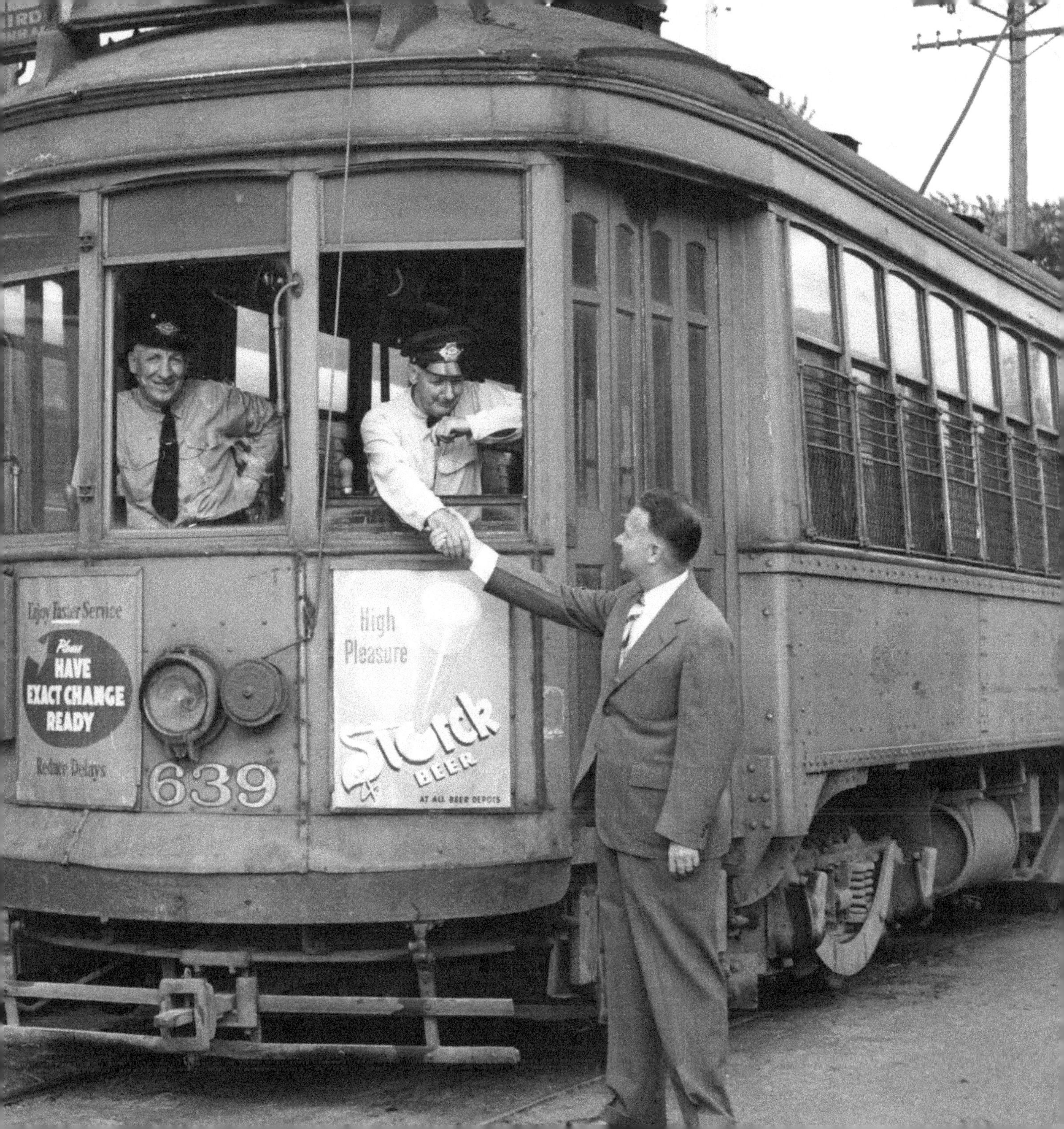
Enjoy Faster Service
Please
HAVE
EXACT CHANGE
READY
Reduce Delays
639
High
Pleasure
Storck
BEER
AT ALL BEER DEPOTS

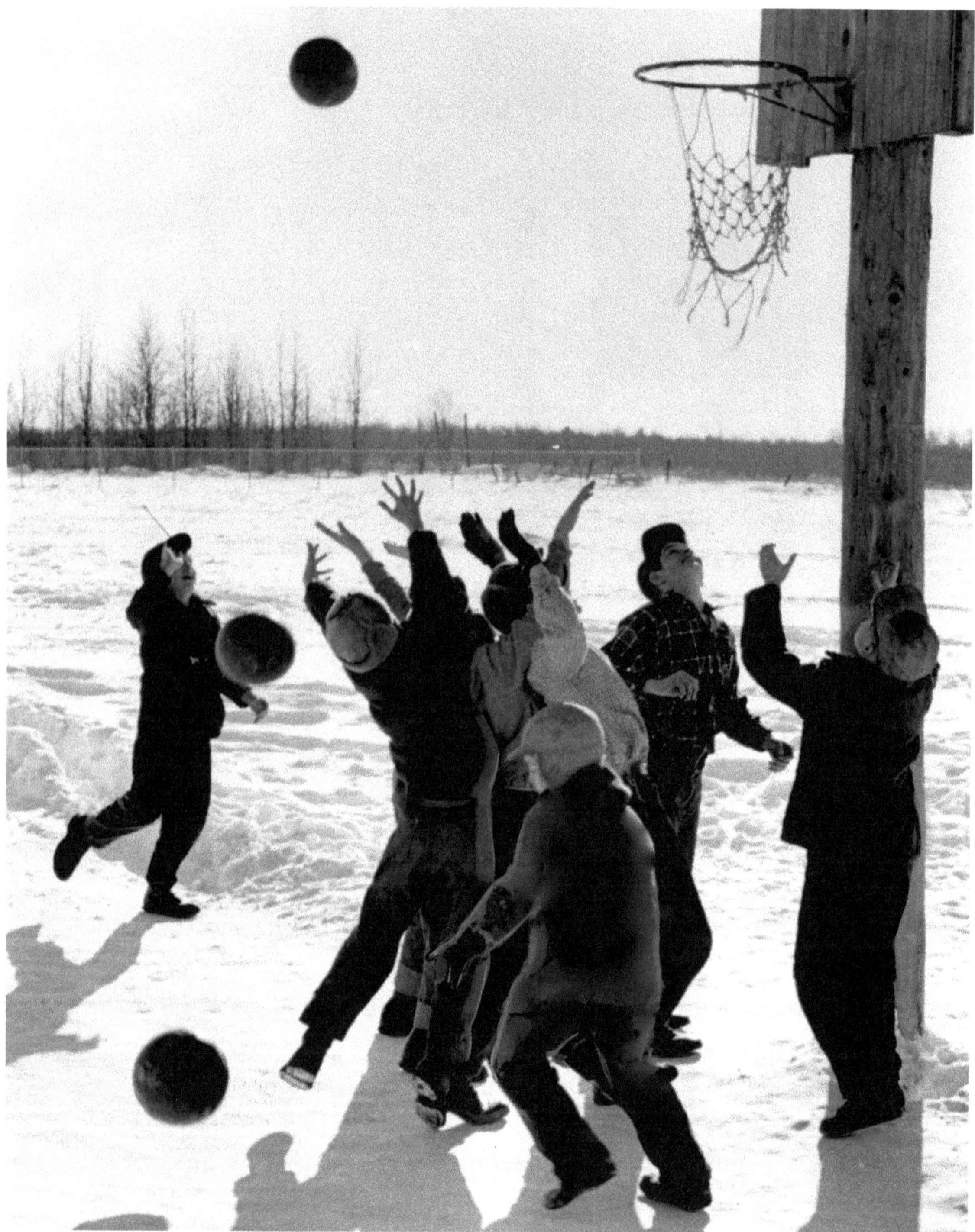

The winter of 1955 was bitter cold with temperatures falling below zero. These boys braved the chilly weather to enjoy some basketball in the snow.

Engineer Katherine Mather checks the composition of cement while working for the Waterways Experiment Station in 1956. The station was set up after a severe flooding of the Mississippi River in 1921.

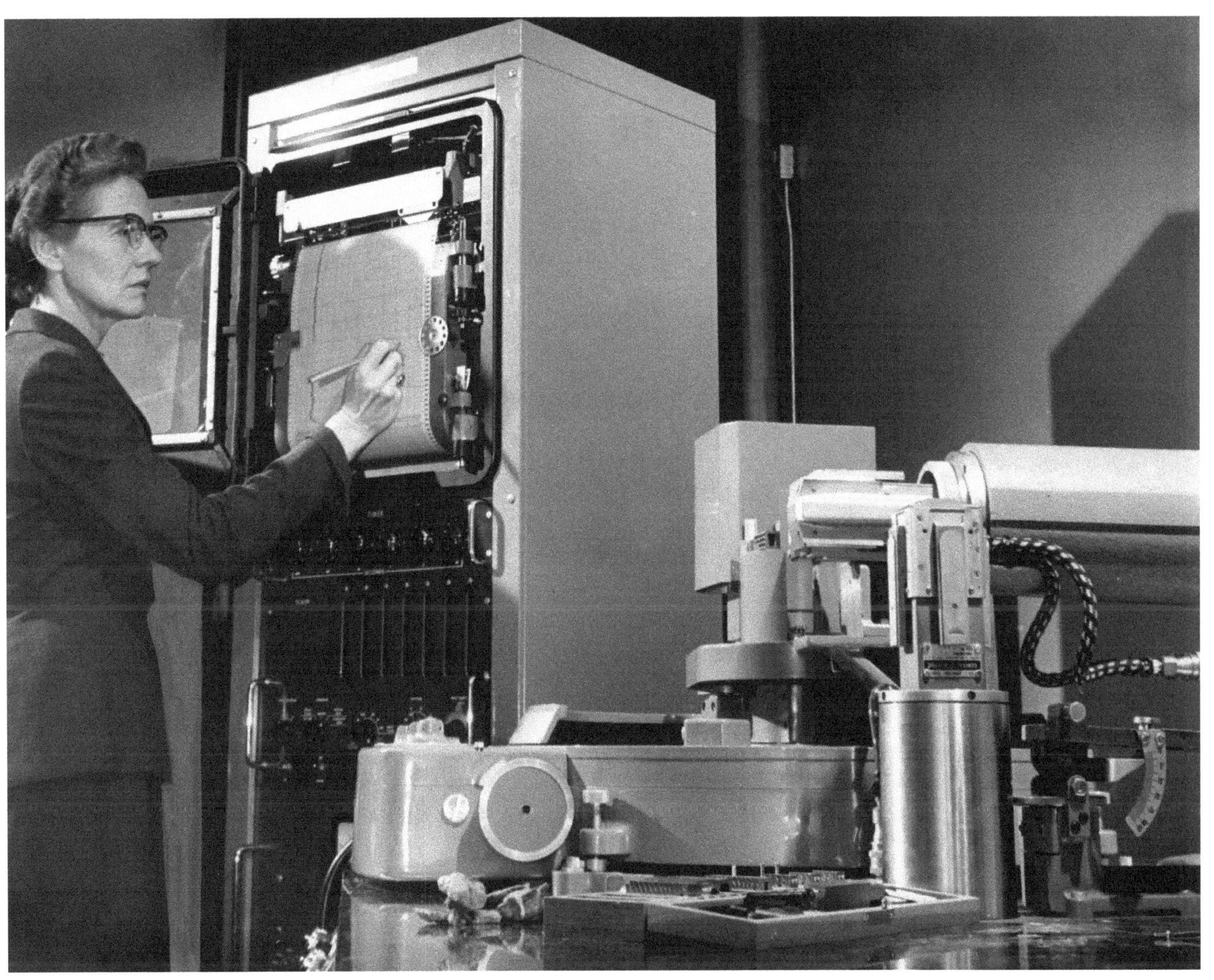

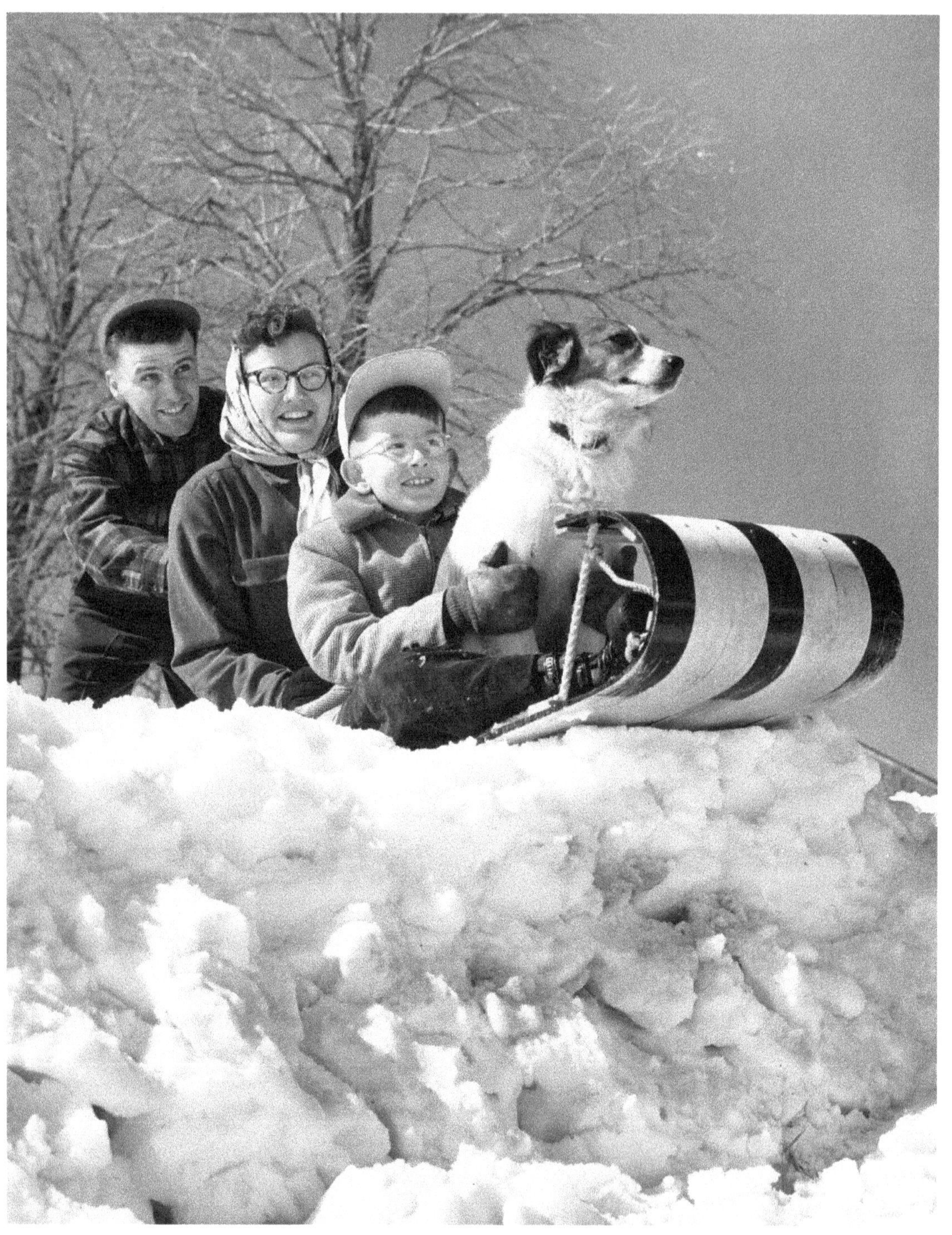

A Milwaukee family enjoys the winter weather in 1956. Milwaukee's parks offer the family excellent sledding as they prepare to race down the hill.

Two neighbors bet to see who would win the 1956 presidential election, Adlai Stevenson or Dwight D. Eisenhower. The loser is pulling the winner behind him in a show of defeat.

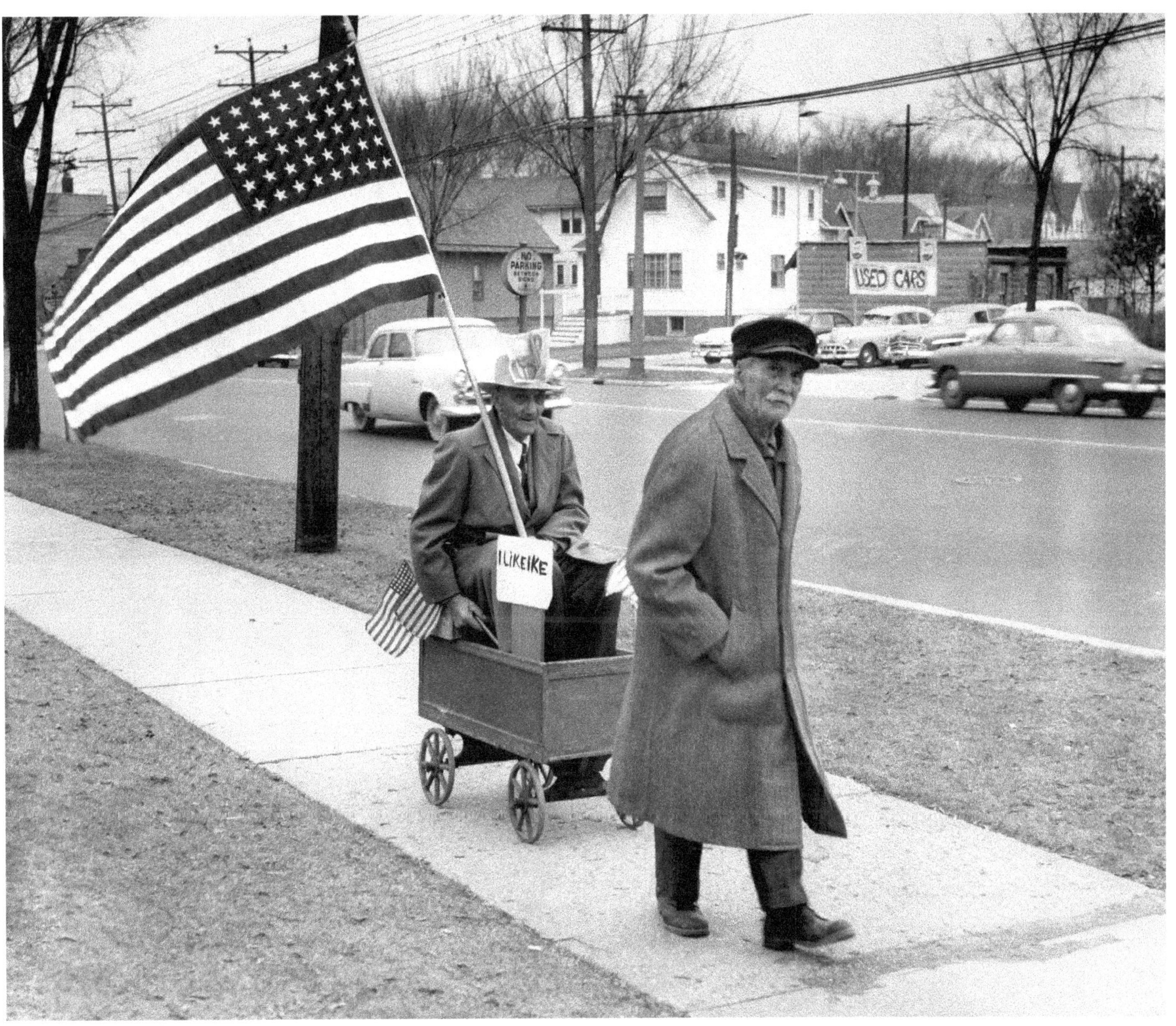

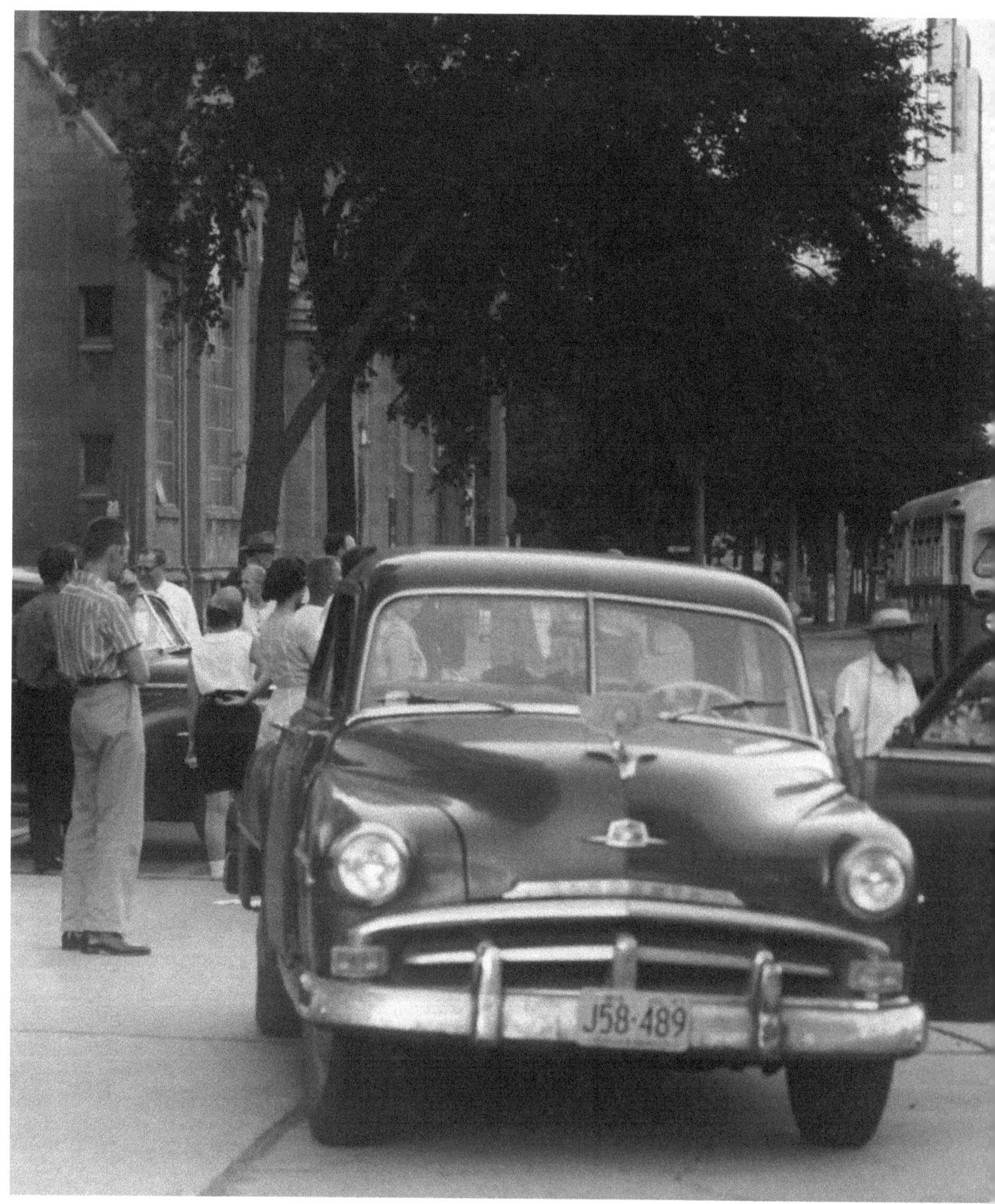
J58·489

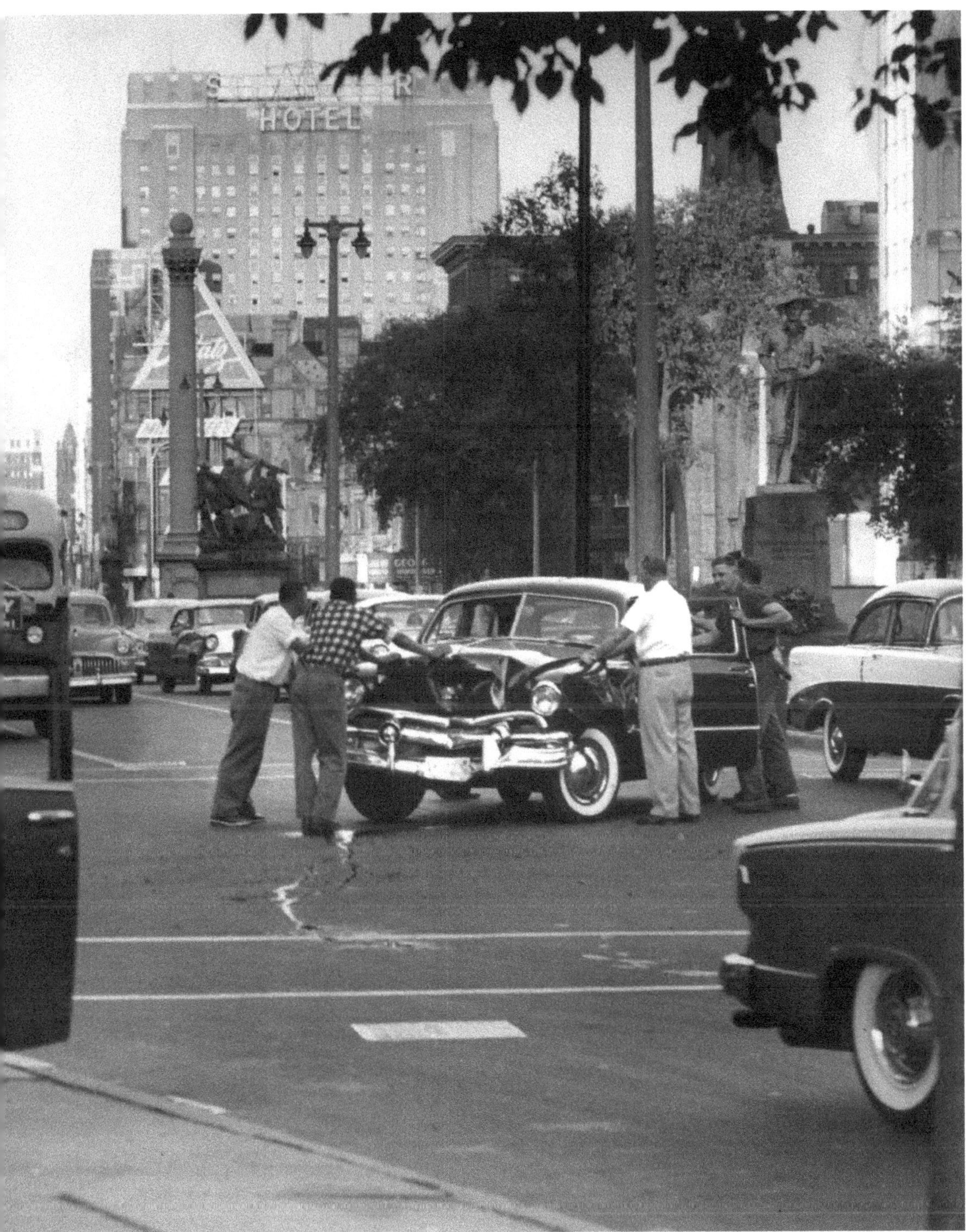

Along one of downtown Milwaukee's busiest streets, a car accident such as this one in the 1950s was not an uncommon sight. People gathered around to make sure that everyone was all right and to assist in moving the damaged vehicle out of the way.

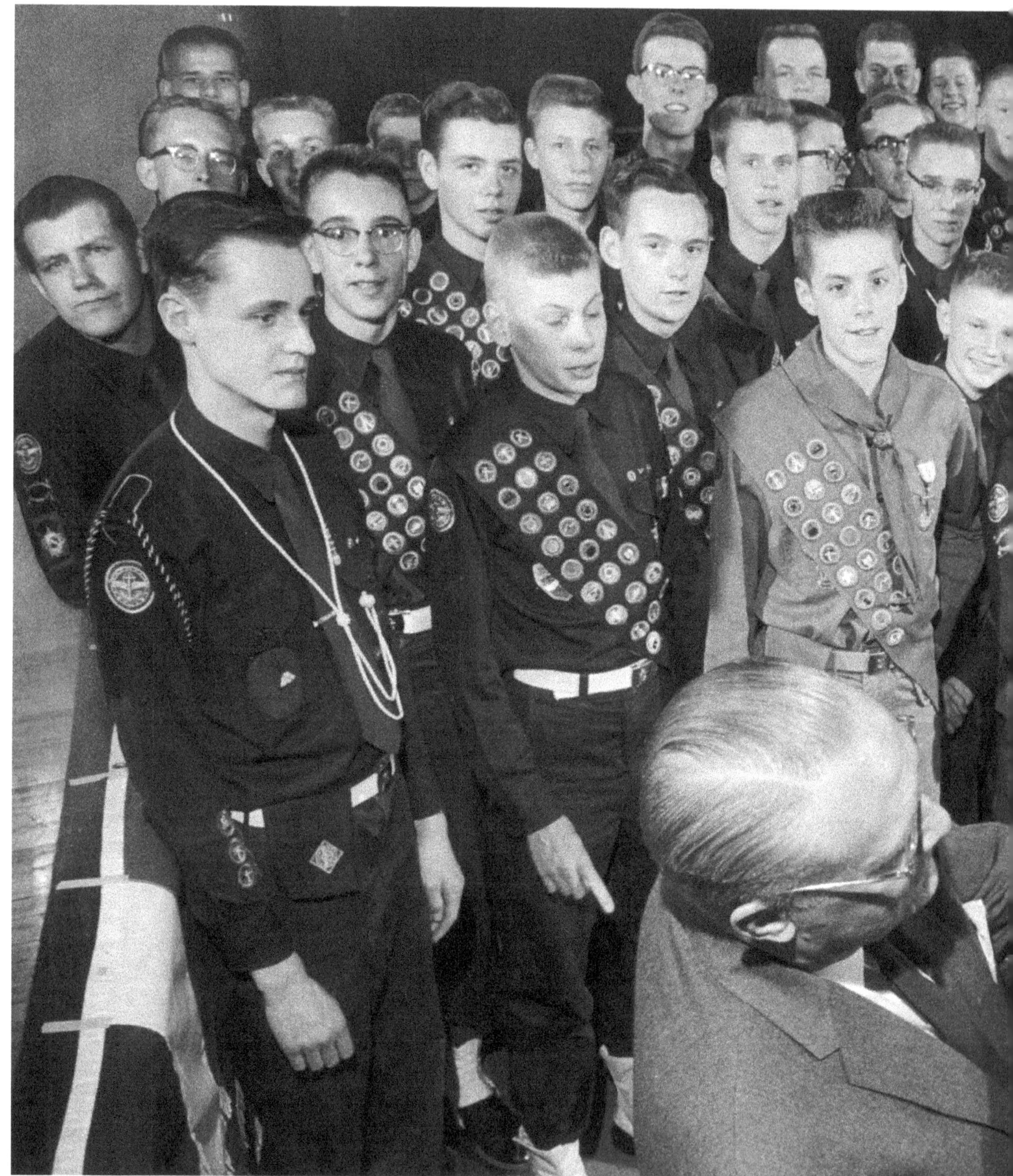

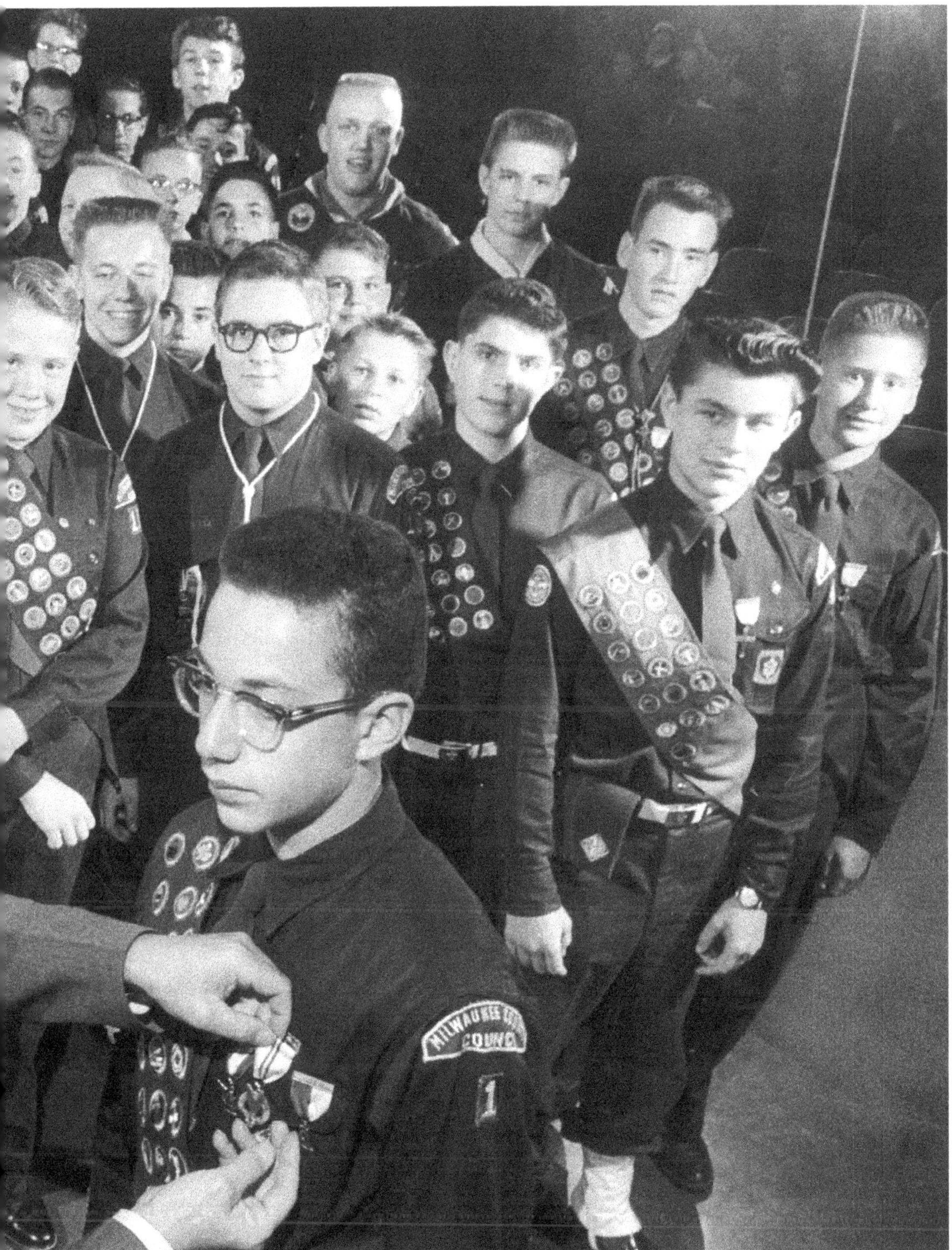

Boy Scouts and Explorer Scouts in this photograph receive the rank of Eagle Scout and the Explorer Silver Award in May 1957. Both awards are the highest awards offered.

A woman walks in the rain near the Civil War monument *The Victorious Charge.* The monument was built in 1898 and was restored to its original luster in 2003.

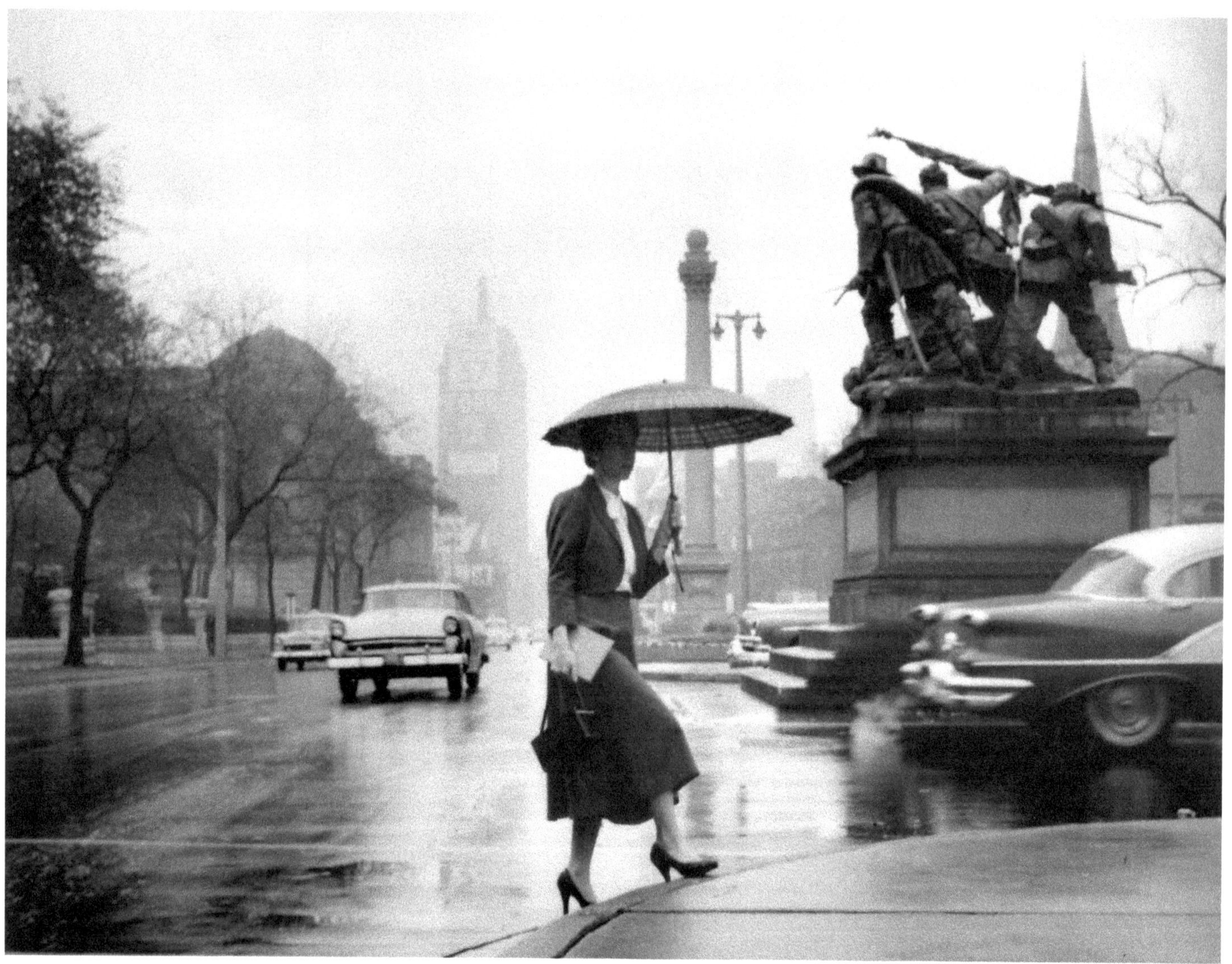

A Milwaukee drill team offers a firearms salute on Armistice Day in 1957. Nearby citizens stand observing the team with reverence.

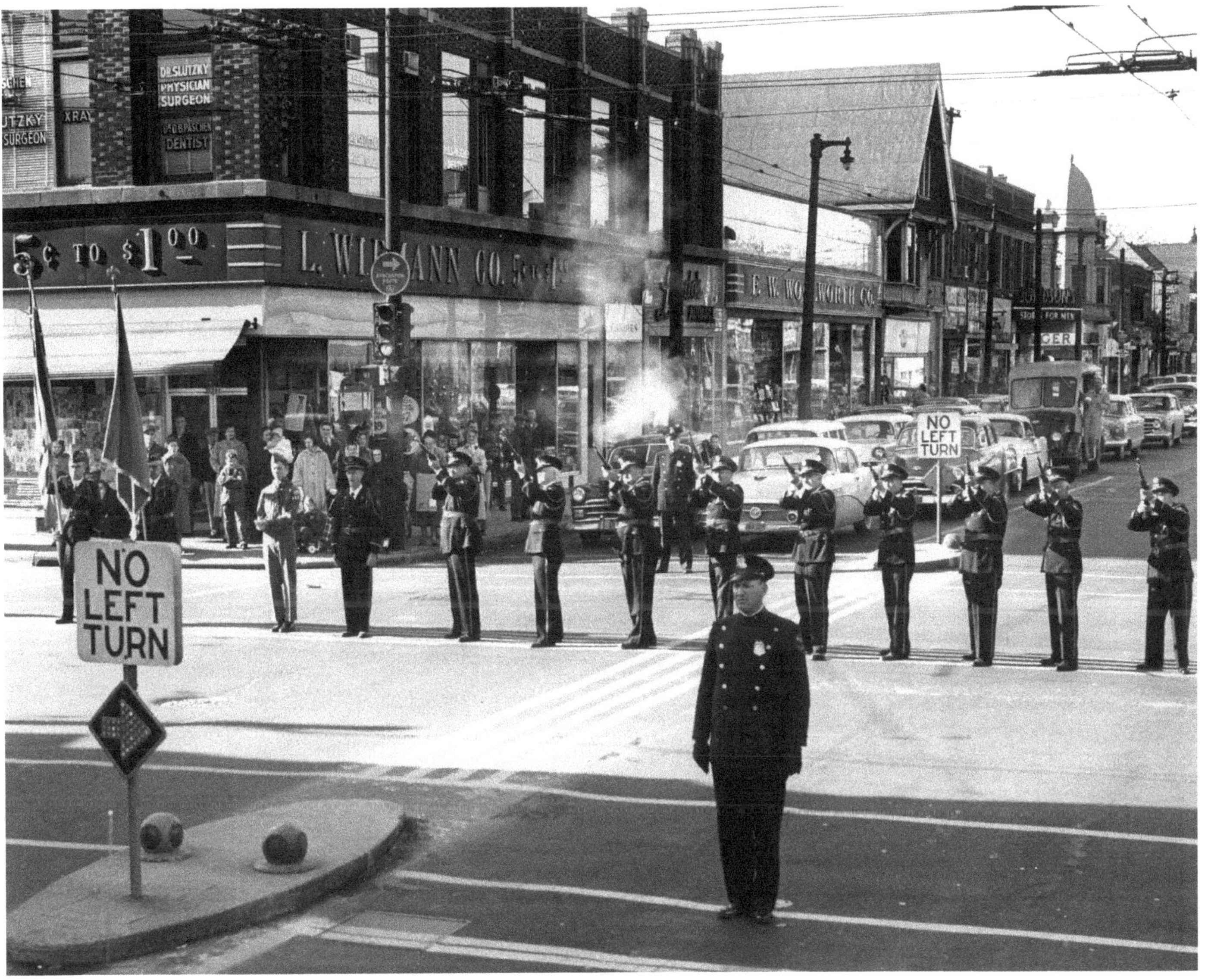

Milwaukee Braves manager, Fred Haney, and Casey Stengel, manager of the New York Yankees, pose for this photo in 1958 when the two teams met at the World Series. Eventually the Yankees defeated the Braves, perhaps vindication for the previous season when the Braves won the series.

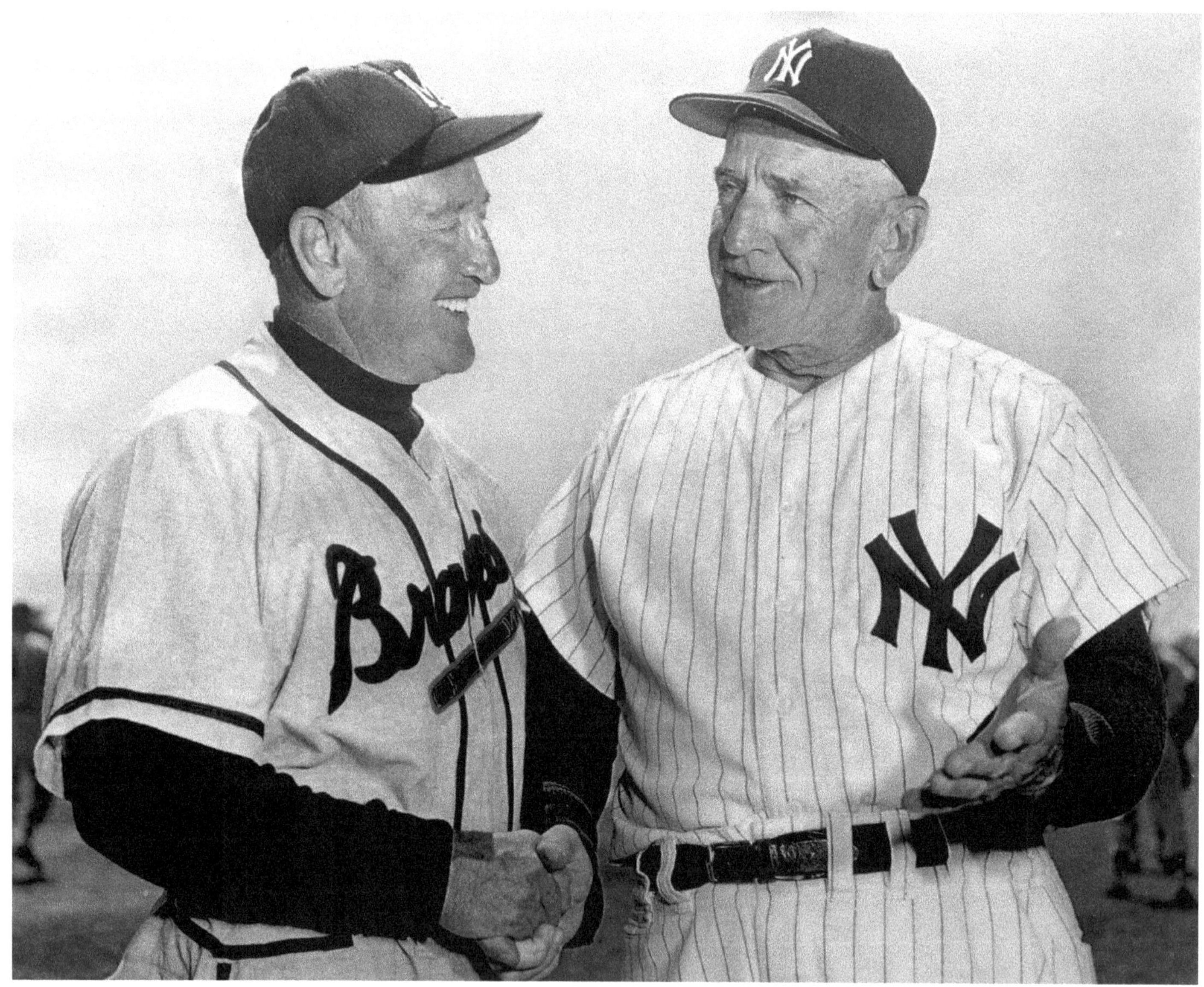

Two boys enjoy the warm Milwaukee weather in the summer of 1959, although the wind attempted to tip over their boat during their outing.

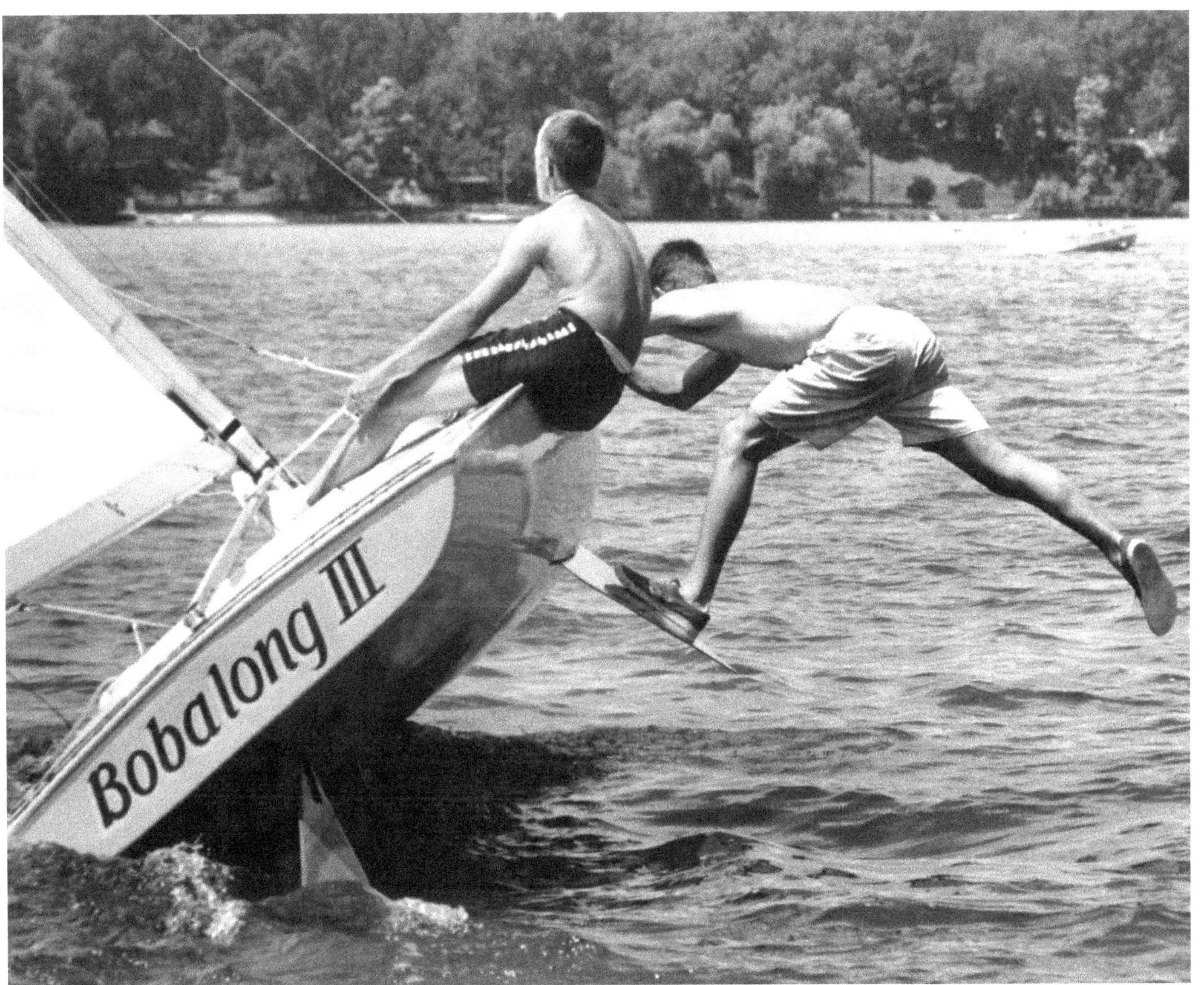

The Knights of Columbus held an annual "gay nineties" party, paying homage to the price of beer in the 1890s—5 cents. The Knights of Columbus have been active in the Milwaukee community and continue to support various charities around the city.

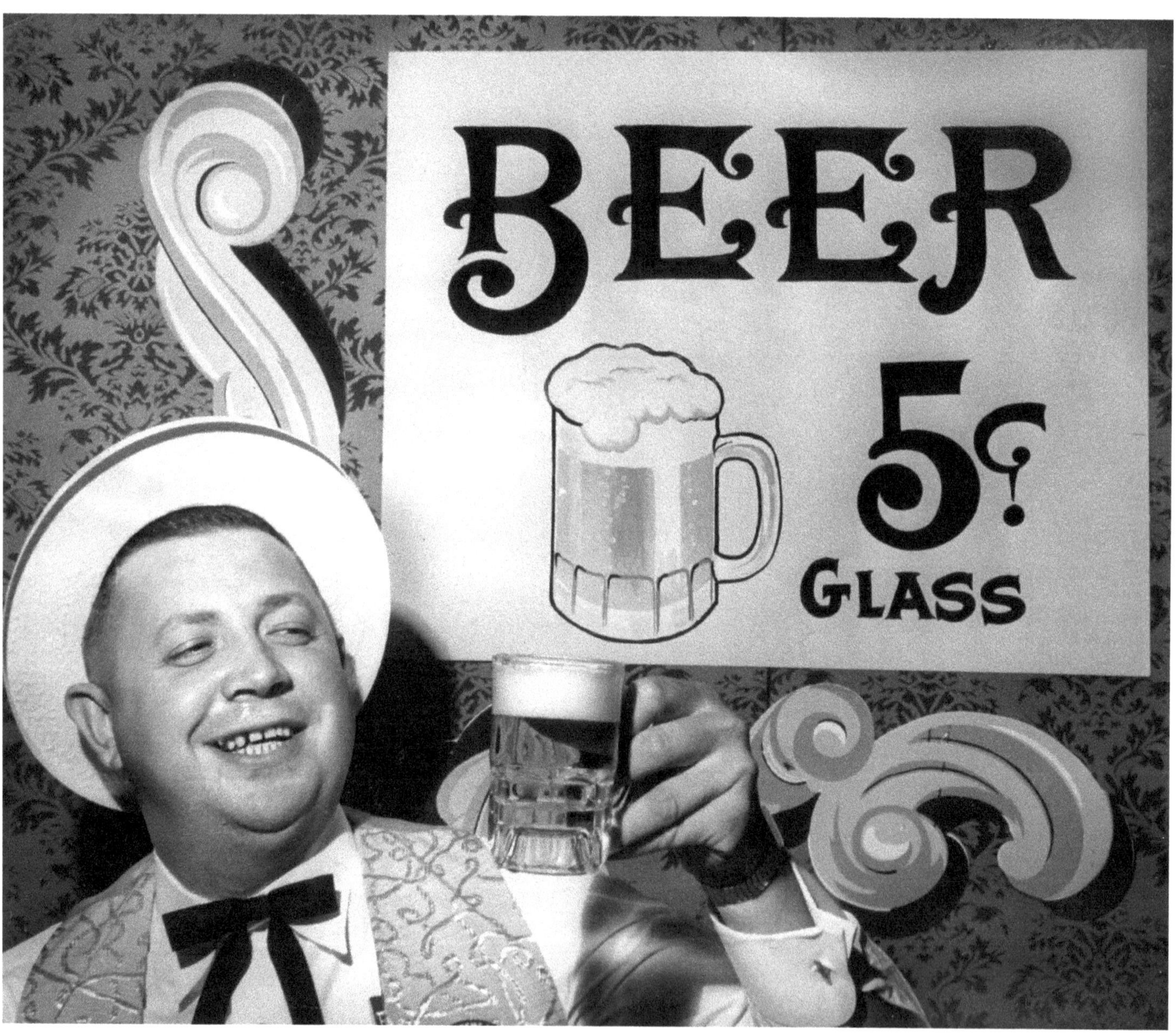

Students wish a fellow classmate farewell at General Mitchell Airport in Milwaukee. The airport is named for General William "Billy" Mitchell, a pioneer aviator of World War I. Mitchell was the grandson of Alexander Mitchell, of earlier Milwaukee fame.

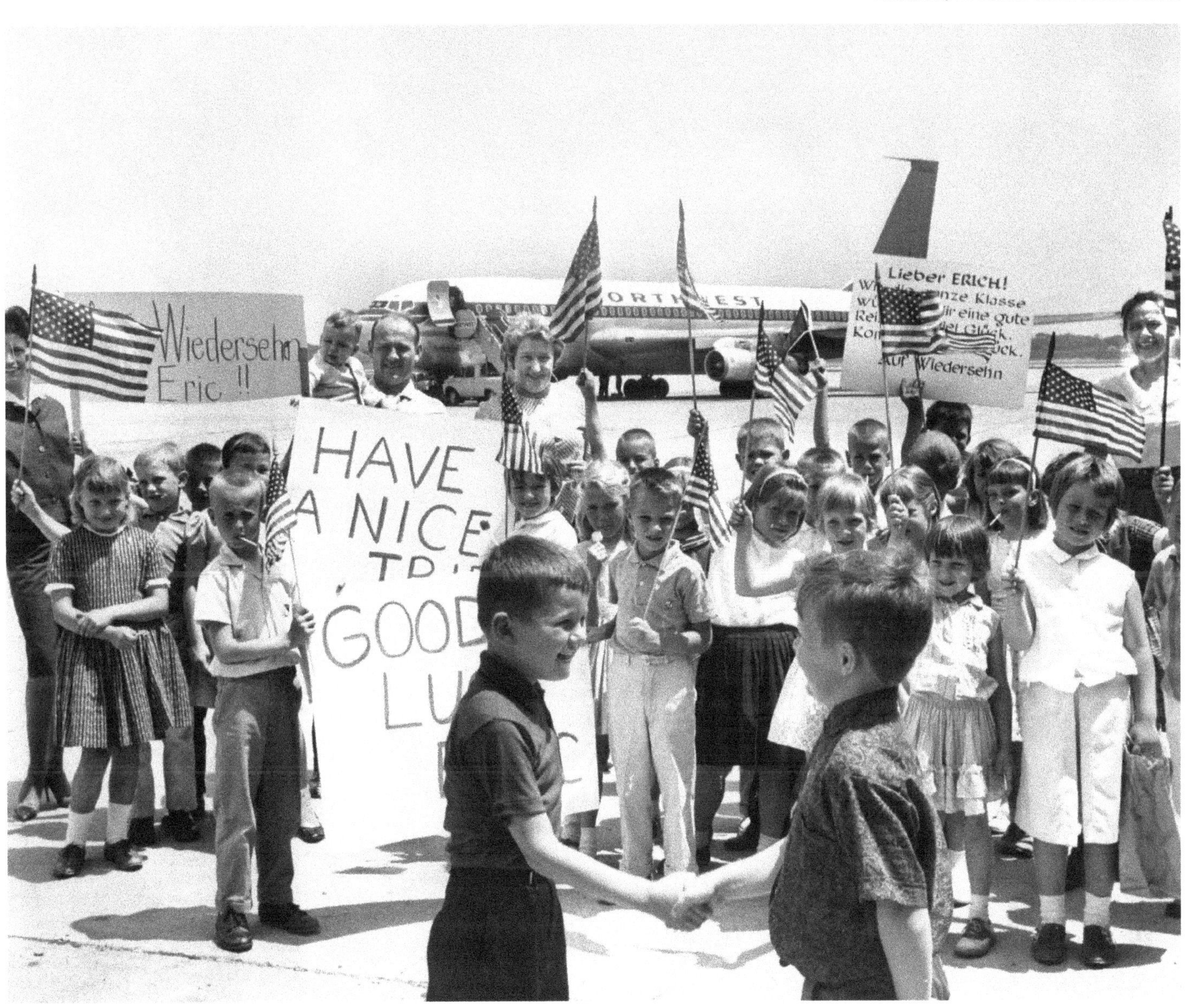

Employees of Milwaukee Astronautics calculate lunar trajectory paths in this 1963 photograph. Six years later, NASA's Apollo program would succeed in placing a man on the moon as Neil Armstrong and Buzz Aldrin touched down on the lunar surface in the lunar module *Eagle*.

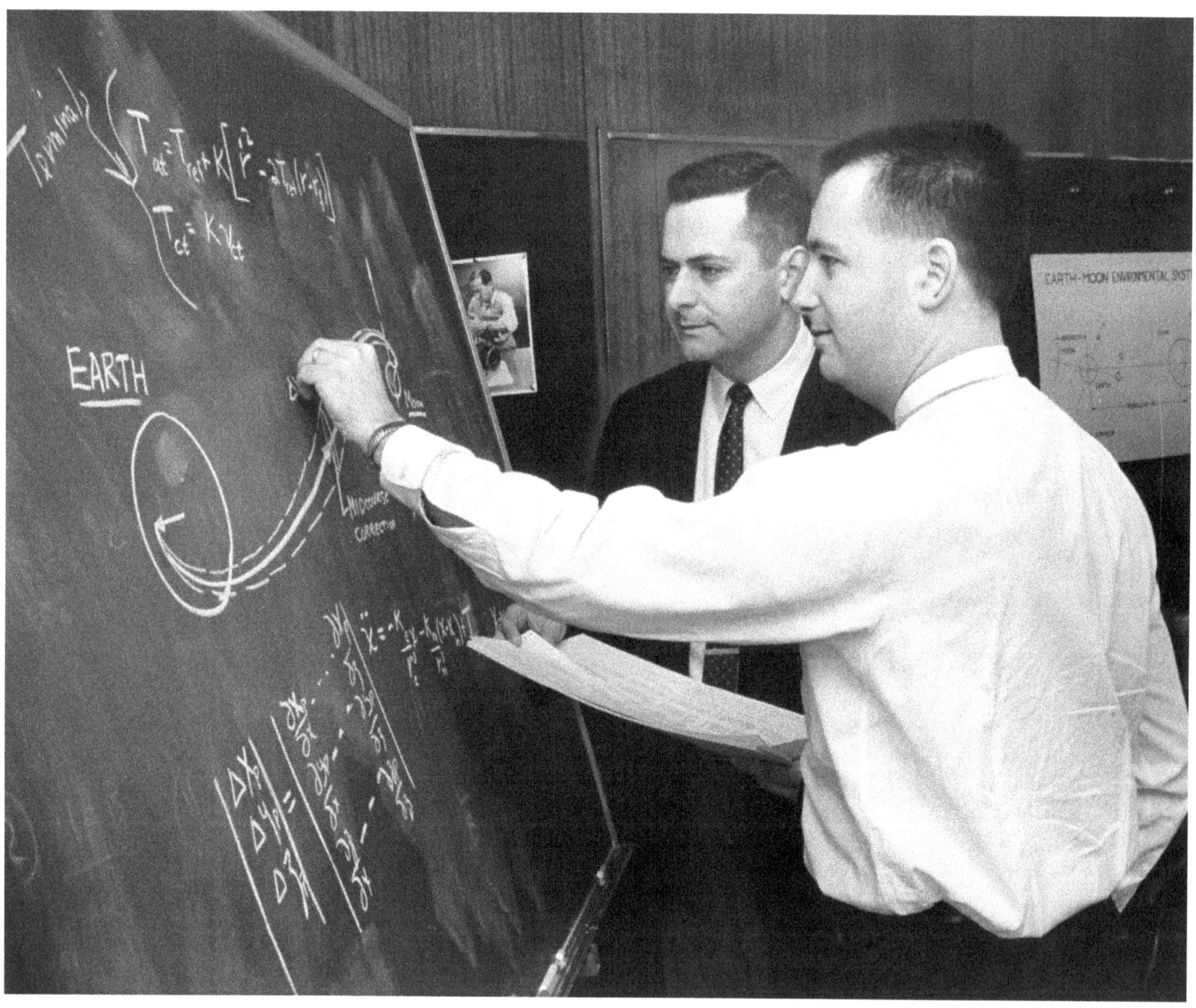

Badwater Bill and his burro register at the Schroeder Hotel in 1963. The Schroeder Hotel was completed in 1928 and, after many incarnations, is now the Milwaukee Hilton, located at 509 W. Wisconsin Avenue.

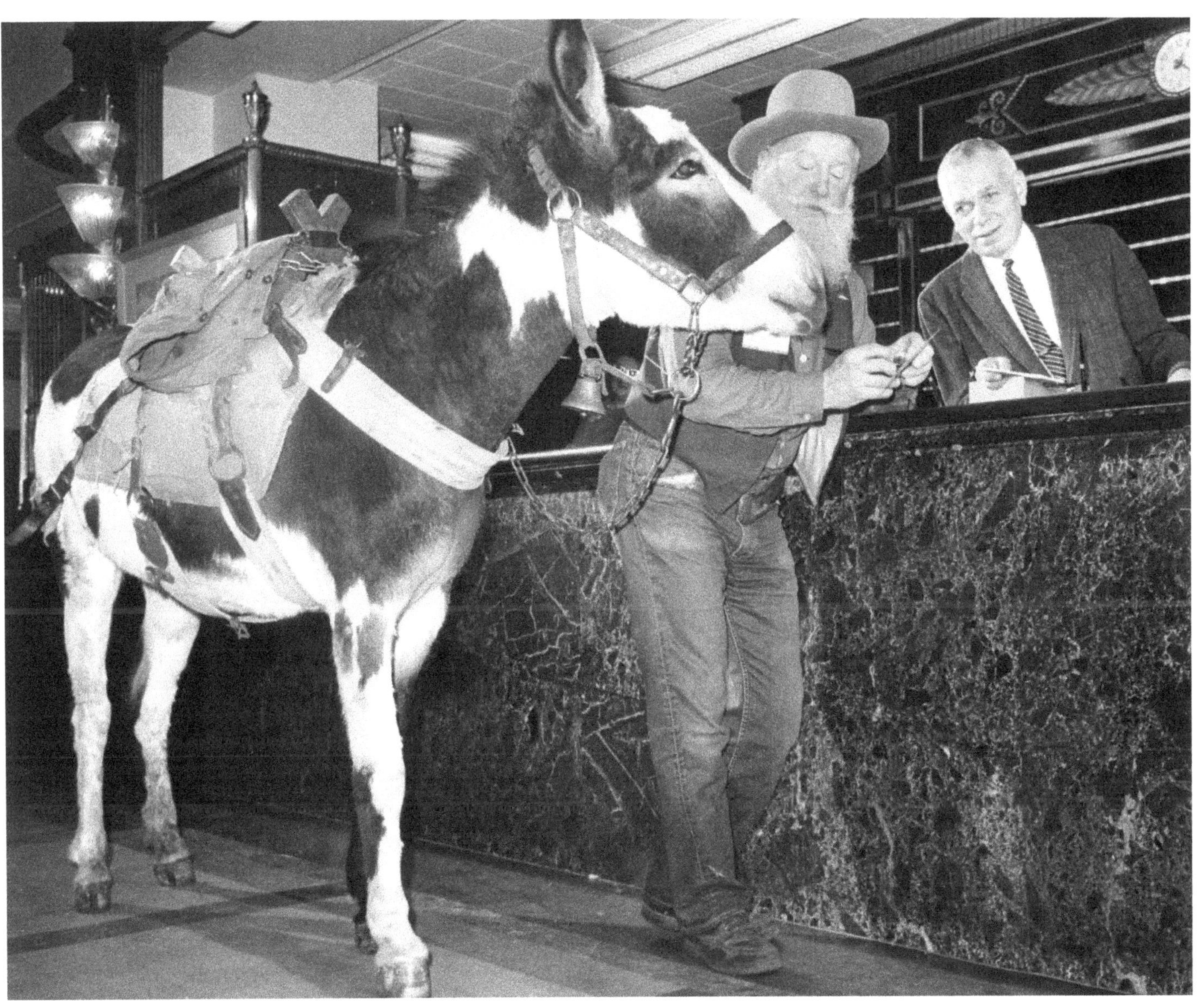

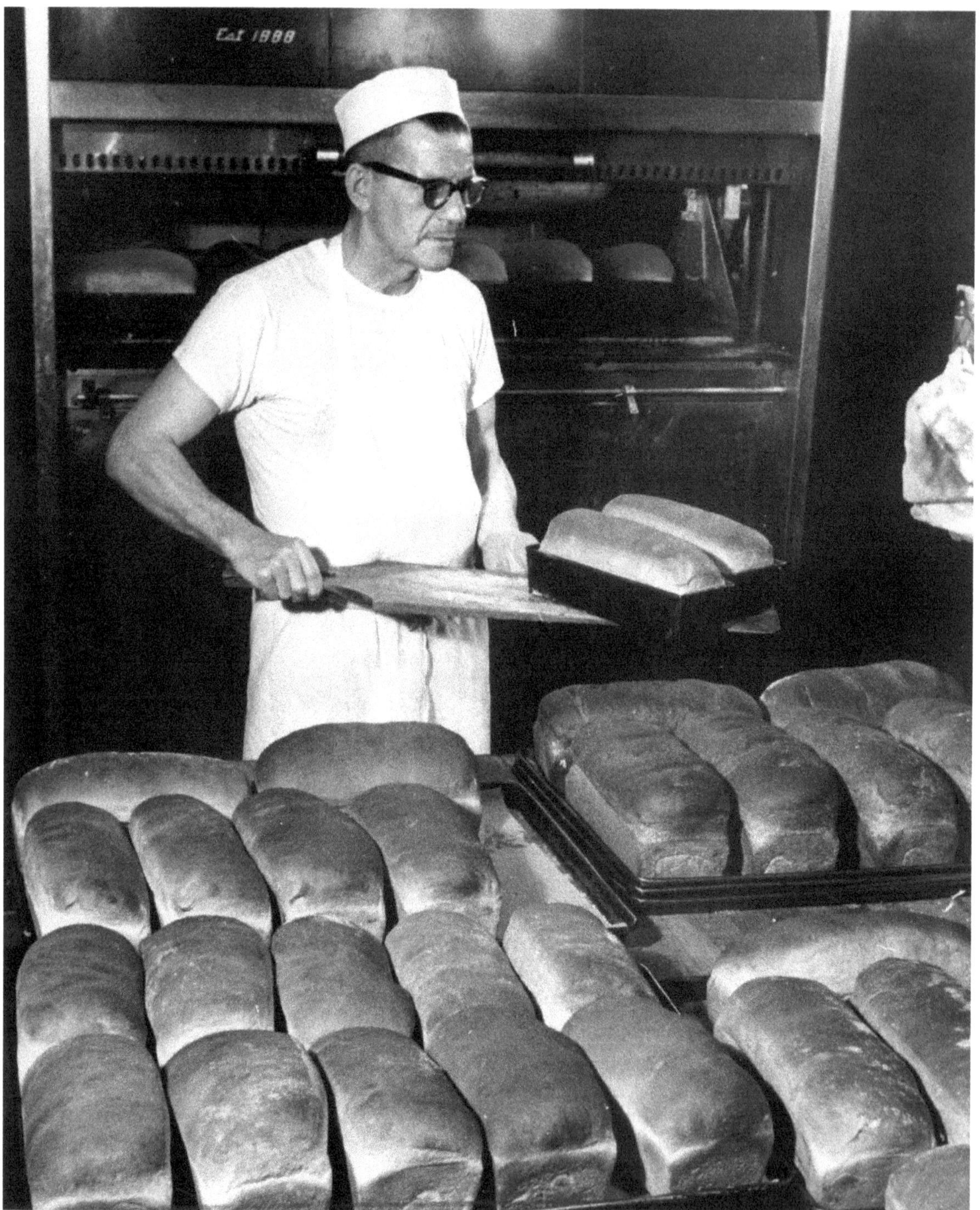

A baker removes bread from the oven in 1964. This bakery baked bread for both restaurants and the home.

Future drafters of Milwaukee sit at desks and work diligently with a compass and drafting machines in this photograph, taken in 1965. Many public high schools offered drafting classes like this one to teach students the trade.

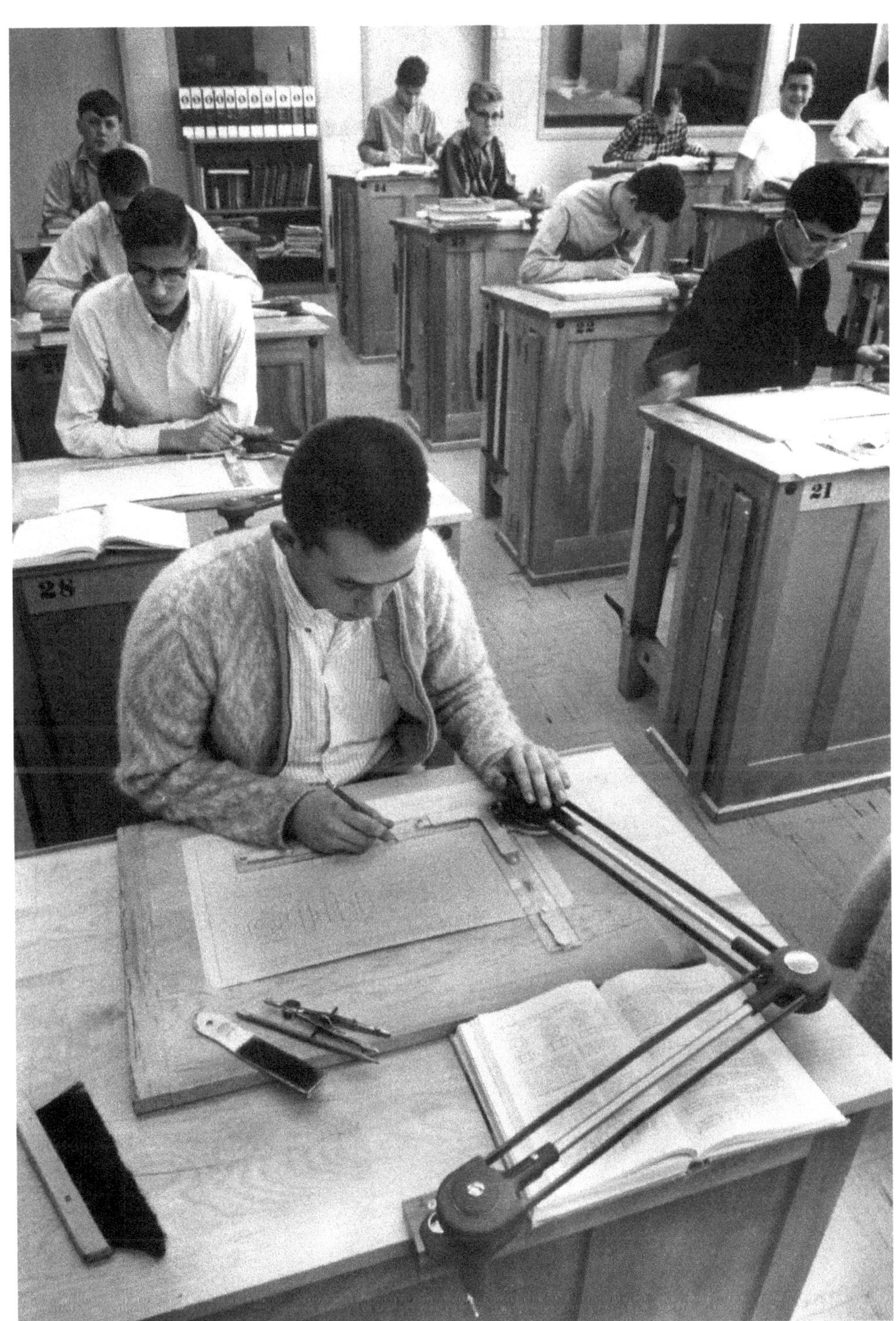

Members of Marquette University's naval ROTC line up for their annual review in 1967. Marquette University turns 150 years old in 2007.

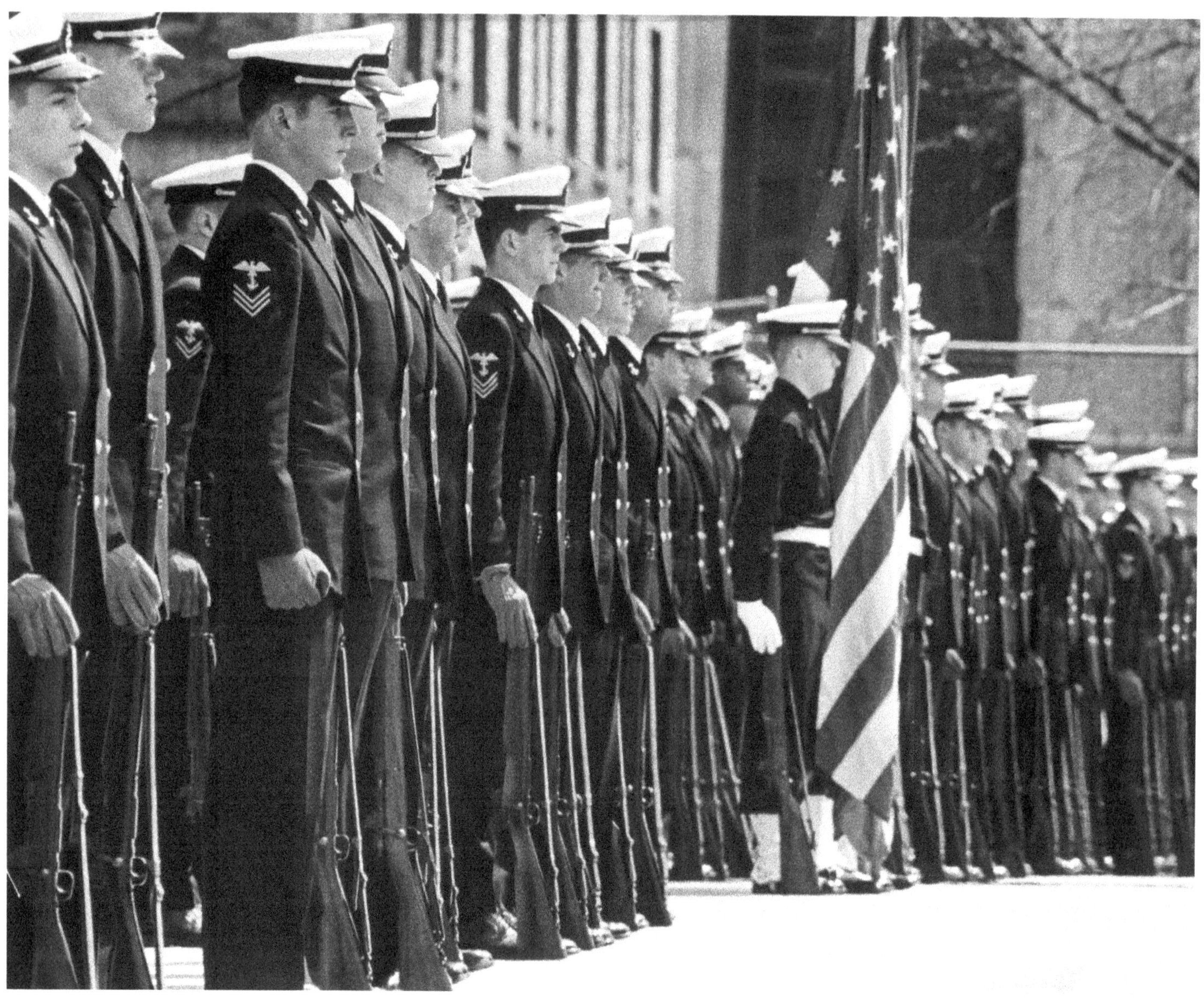

Cars move slowly along snowy streets on February 2, 1967. The snow hit Milwaukee just as the rush hour started, making commuters' rides home extra long. When the storm ended, only 4 inches of snow had accumulated.

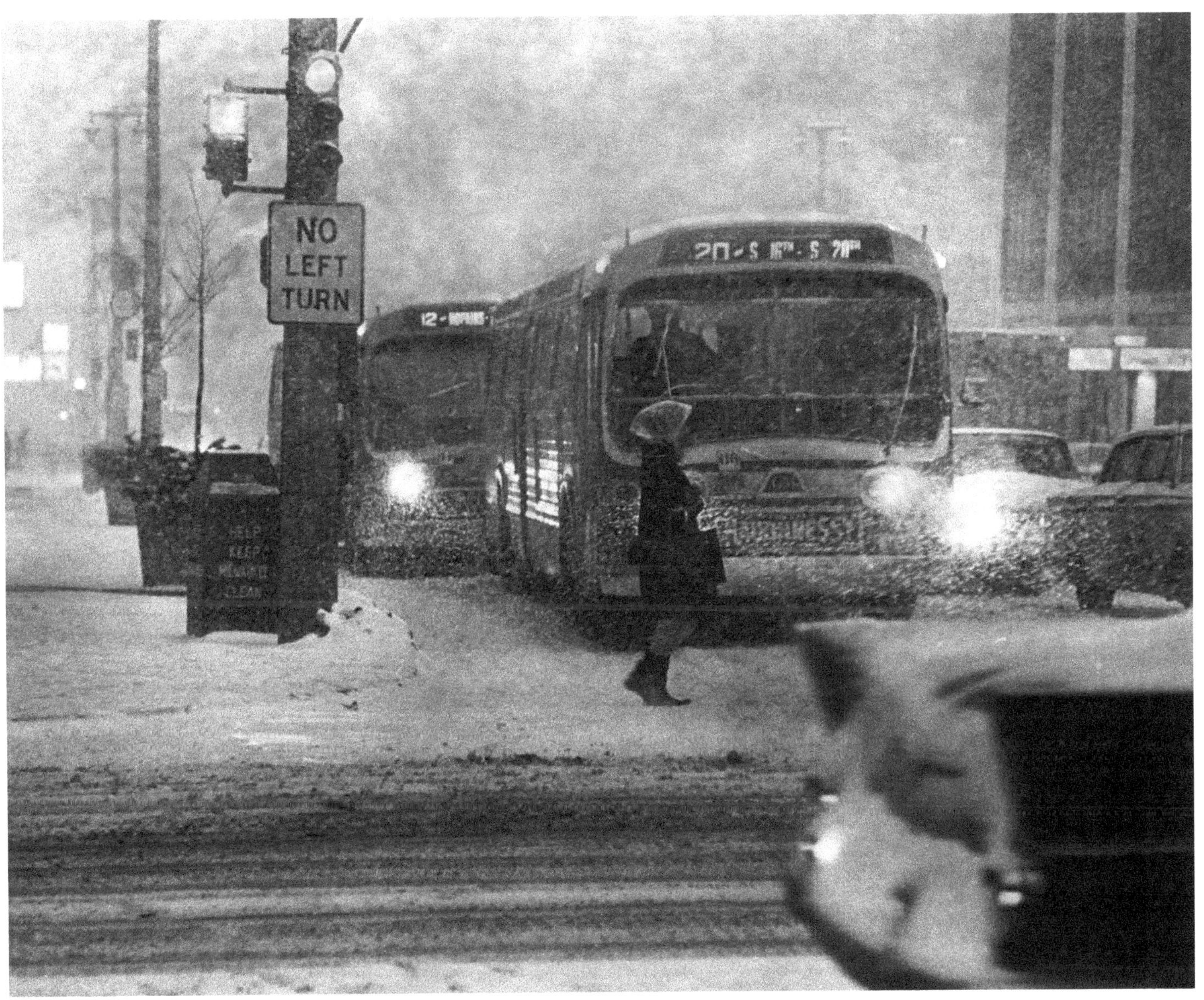

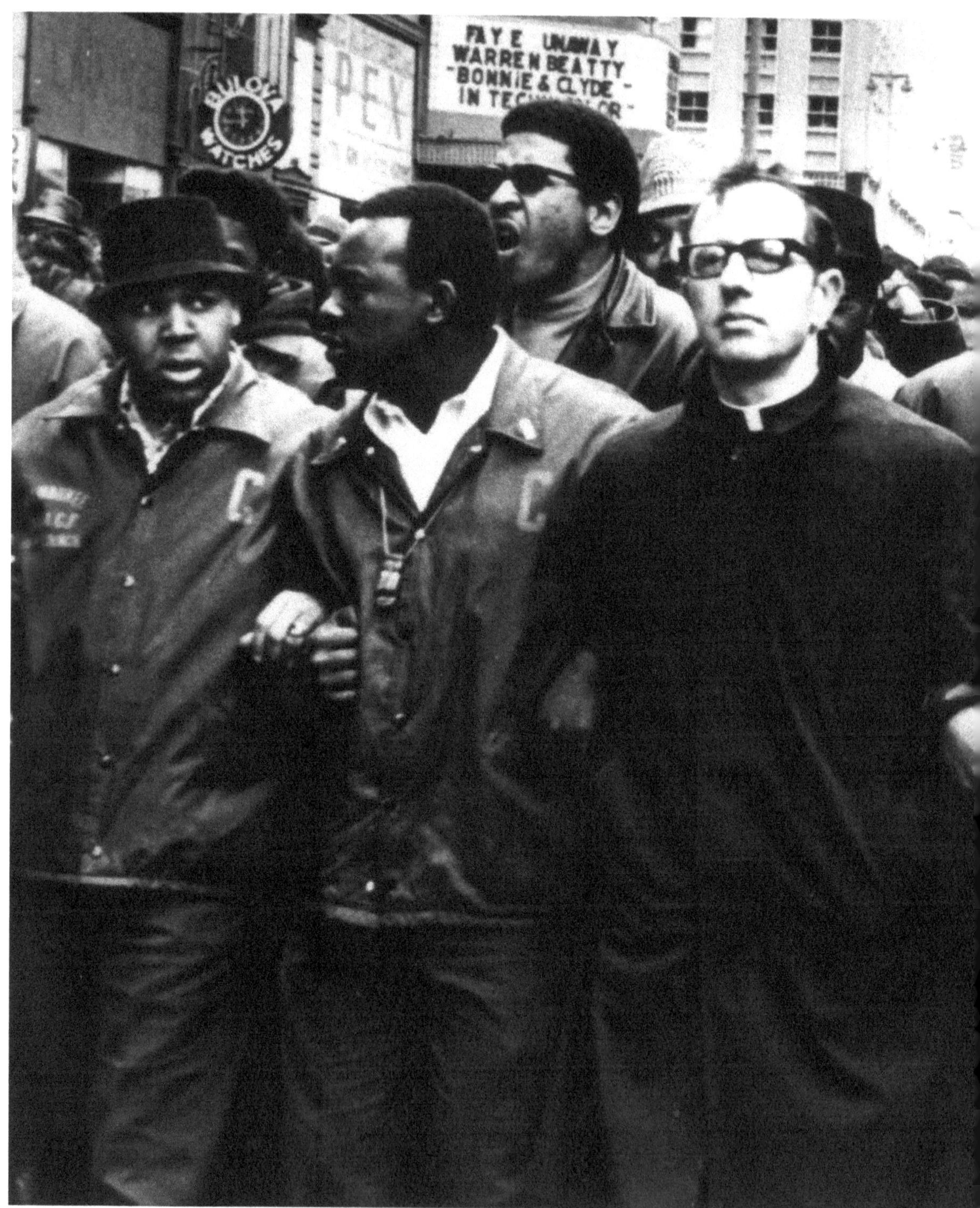
WARREN BEATTY
-BONNIE & CLYDE-
BULOVA
WATCHES

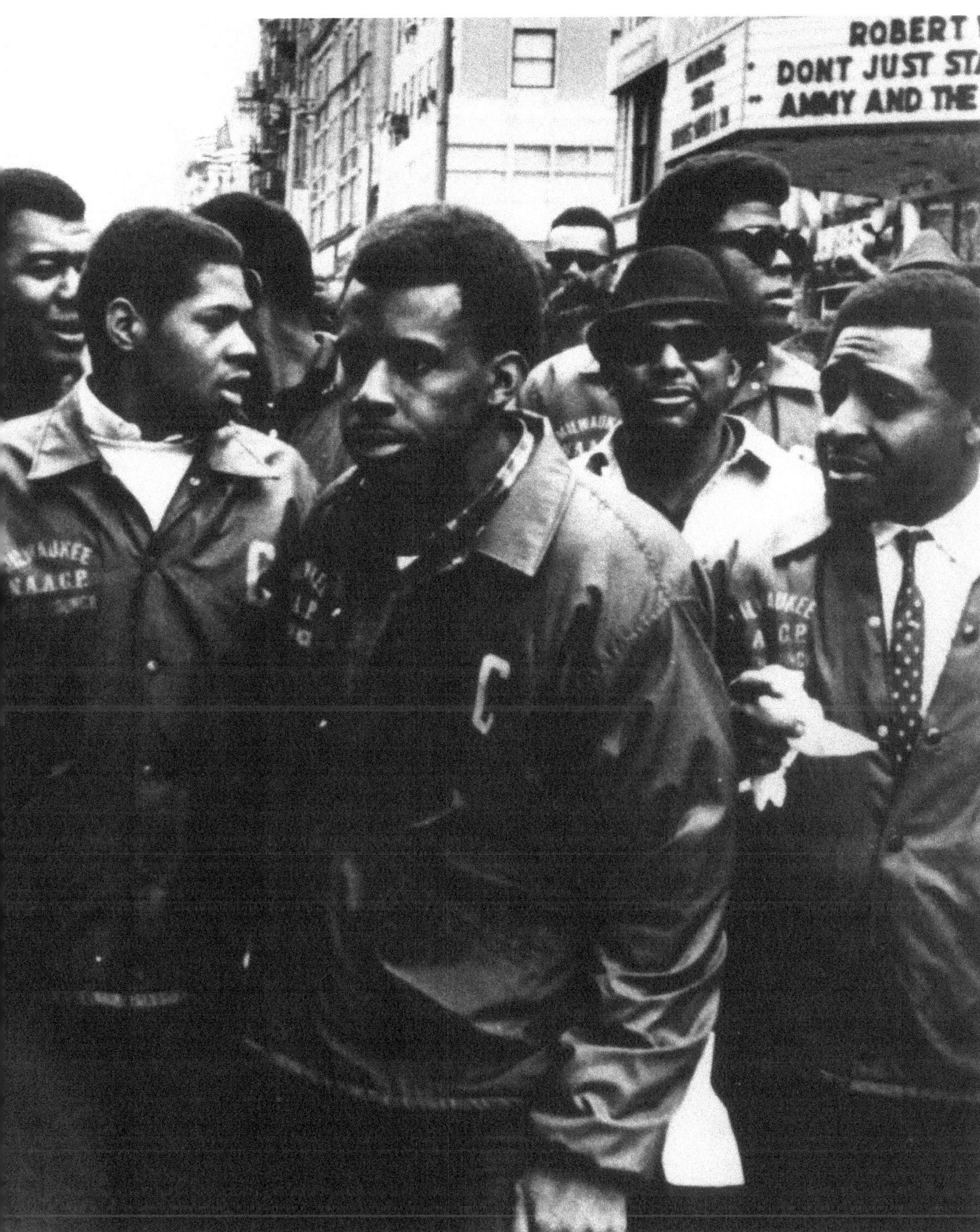

Father James Groppi was a priest and civil rights activist. He is seen in this photograph with members of the NAACP marching down Wisconsin Avenue in protest of the segregated Milwaukee schools. The former 16th Street viaduct was renamed the James E. Groppi Unity Bridge in his honor.

Businessmen from the Komatsu Manufacturing firm in Japan paid a visit to Bucyrus Erie manufacturing plant in South Milwaukee. Bucyrus Erie was originally started in 1880 and a plant was incorporated in Milwaukee in 1893. The company still functions today.

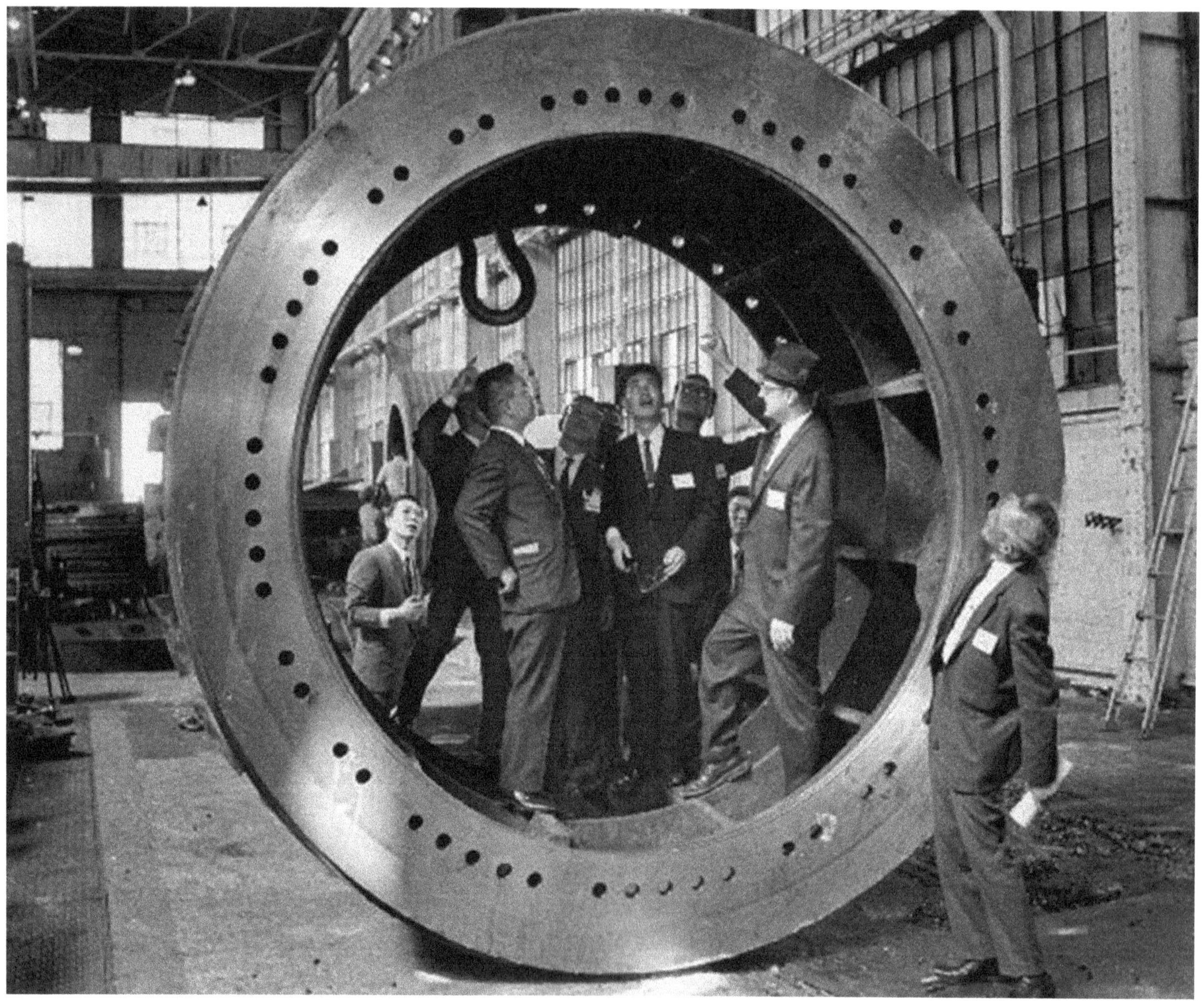

Notes on the Photographs

These notes, listed by page number, attempt to include all aspects known of the photographs. Each of the photographs is identified by the page number, photograph's title or description, photographer and collection, archive, and call or box number when applicable. Although every attempt was made to collect all available data, in some cases complete data was unavailable due to the age and condition of some of the photographs and records.

II Park Hill Avenue
Wisconsin Historical Society
WHi-24418

VI Apollo Honors
Wisconsin Historical Society
WHi-11361

X Water Tower
Milwaukee Public Library
RW 986

2 Union Depot
Milwaukee Public Library
RW 858

3 Chapman's
Milwaukee Public Library
RW 1280

4 The Iron Brigade
Wisconsin Historical Society
WHi-1993

5 Wisconsin Avenue
Wisconsin Historical Society
WHi-9482

6 Shore Bluffs
Wisconsin Historical Society
tWHi-6949

7 Chamber of Commerce
Wisconsin Historical Society
WHi-43409

8 Milwaukee River
Wisconsin Historical Society
WHi-24994

9 Swinging Bridge
Milwaukee Public Library
RW 864

10 Republican House
Milwaukee Public Library
RW 395

11 Division Street
Milwaukee Public Library
RW 636

12 Marquette's First Home
Milwaukee Public Library
RW 1255

13 Winery
Milwaukee Public Library
RW 651

14 Finney Residence
Milwaukee Public Library
RW 1278

15 Milwaukee Exchange
Wisconsin Historical Society
WHi-9215

16 Layton Hotel
Wisconsin Historical Society
WHi-9489

17 Caspar's Bookstore
Milwaukee Public Library
RW 1189

18 Panorama Artists
Wisconsin Historical Society
WHi-26071

20 Thermo Water
Wisconsin Historical Society
WHi-10617

21 Steam Fire Engine
Wisconsin Historical Society
WHi-9220

22 General Labor Strike
Wisconsin Historical Society
WHi-1990

23 Soldier's Home
Wisconsin Historical Society
WHi-7884

24 Soldier's Home
Wisconsin Historical Society
WHi-7403

25 Panorama Artists
Wisconsin Historical Society
WHi-26069

26 Railroad Office
Wisconsin Historical Society
WHi- 4506

27 German Market
Milwaukee Public Library
RW 943

28 Iron Brigade Reunion
Wisconsin Historical Society
WHi-10695

29 Broadway Theatre
Milwaukee Public Library
RW 940

30 Ellen and Rose Lemke
Wisconsin Historical Society
WHi-1400

31 Jones Island
Milwaukee Public Library
RW 1324; TAV. 9

32 **Haymarket Square**
Milwaukee Public Library
RW 490

33 **Reichardt and Devitt Co.**
Milwaukee Public Library
RW 1203

34 **Commission Row**
Milwaukee Public Library
RW 33

35 **Schlitz Park**
Milwaukee Public Library
RW 627

36 **Plankinton Mansion**
Wisconsin Historical Society
WHi-1023

37 **Circus Parade**
Milwaukee Public Library
RW 897

38 **Drugstore**
Wisconsin Historical Society
5487

39 **Grand Ave.**
Milwaukee Public Library
RW 289

40 **Stenographers**
Wisconsin Historical Society
WHi-6992

41 **Johnston Hospital**
Milwaukee Public Library
RW 432

42 **Waukesha Scoot**
Wisconsin Historical Society
WHi-24901

43 **McCormick Harvesting**
Wisconsin Historical Society
WHi-9708

44 **Making Cough Balsam**
Wisconsin Historical Society
WHi-2048

45 **Skating on the Milwaukee River**
Milwaukee Public Library
RW 748

46 **Laacke Sign Hanging**
Milwaukee Public Library
RW 1338

47 **Jahrmarkt**
Milwaukee Public Library
RW 420

48 **Fire Engine**
Wisconsin Historical Society
WHi-5029

50 **Nurses**
Wisconsin Historical Society
Whi-6942

51 **Muddy Street**
Wisconsin Historical Society
WHi-24426

52 **Gerber and Son**
Milwaukee Public Library
RW 895

53 **Fishing on Breakwater**
Wisconsin Historical Society
WHi-6941

54 **CM & STP Engine**
Wisconsin Historical Society
WHi-24902

56 **Girls Jumping Rope**
Wisconsin Historical Society
WHi-6943

57 **Otto Gahns Bakery**
Milwaukee Public Library
RW 1017

58 **City Hall**
Wisconsin Historical Society
WHi-3605

59 **Run on Bank**
Milwaukee Public Library
RW 1251

60 **HD Motorcycle, 1905**
Wisconsin Historical Society
WHi-2544

62 **Coal Wagon**
Wisconsin Historical Society
WHi-4697

63 **6th Street Bricked**
Milwaukee Public Library
RW 518

64 **Baseball Fans**
Milwaukee Public Library
RW 771

65 **School of Engineering**
Milwaukee Public Library
RW 1279

66 **Corliss Steam Engine**
Wisconsin Historical Society
WHi-7593

67 **Annual Scottish Games**
Wisconsin Historical Society
WHi-2080

68 **Substandard Housing**
Wisconsin Historical Society
WHi-4391

69 **Retzer Bros. Grocers**
Milwaukee Public Library
RW 731

70 **Classroom in 1909**
Wisconsin Historical Society
WHi-7469

71 **Ship in Harbor**
Wisconsin Historical Society
WHi-33062

72 **Suckling Pigs**
Milwaukee Public Library
RW 1229

73 **Rainy Day**
Wisconsin Historical Society
WHi-33070

74 **Ice Boat on Lake**
Wisconsin Historical Society
WHi-33138

75 **Loading Docks**
Wisconsin Historical Society
WHi-33087

76 **Milwaukee Streetcar**
Wisconsin Historical Society
WHi-24964

78 **TR in Milwaukee**
Wisconsin Historical Society
WHi-34909

80 **TR in Milwaukee**
Wisconsin Historical Society
WHi-2096

81 **Firemen Rescuing Victim**
Wisconsin Historical Society
WHi-3038

82 **George Malone**
Wisconsin Historical Society
WHi-32706

83 **Grain Exchange Room**
Wisconsin Historical Society
WHi-2051

84 **Gasoline Delivery Man**
Milwaukee Public Library
RW 1326

85 Bathing Beach
Wisconsin Historical Society
WHi-4691

86 State Fairgrounds
Wisconsin Historical Society
WHi-10089

87 Fish Flying
Wisconsin Historical Society
WHi-10211

88 Downtown Milwaukee
Wisconsin Historical Society
WHi-4690

90 W. S. Seaman Co.
Wisconsin Historical Society
WHi-36533

91 Tavern in 1914
Milwaukee Public Library
RW 1254

92 Packard Truck
Wisconsin Historical Society
WHI-36511

93 Bottling Beer
Milwaukee Public Library
RW 1388

94 Milwaukee Harvester
Wisconsin Historical Society
WHi-7605

96 Milwaukee Harvester
Wisconsin Historical Society
WHi-7629

97 Dancehall Wine Room
Wisconsin Historical Society
WHi-6510

98 Armour and Co.
Wisconsin Historical Society
WHi-36520

99 Continuation School
Wisconsin Historical Society
WHi-7477

100 Pathfinder Car
Wisconsin Historical Society
WHi-33058

101 Jens Confectionery
Milwaukee Public Library
RW 1410

102 Grand Ave.
Milwaukee Public Library
RW 1054

103 Troops Near Post Office
Milwaukee Public Library
RW 1286

104 Columbus Accident
Wisconsin Historical Society
WHi-33123

105 Women in Motor Corps
Wisconsin Historical Society
WHi-1952

106 Cream Separator
Wisconsin Historical Society
WHi-8156

108 Grocery Store
Milwaukee Public Library
RW 1302

109 Cracker Jacks Park
Milwaukee Public Library
RW 1227

110 Left-over Malt
Milwaukee Public Library
RW 1419

111 Americanization
Wisconsin Historical Society
WHi-5348

112 32nd Division
Wisconsin Historical Society
WHi-26240

113 Postal Worker Picket
Wisconsin Historical Society
WHi-22890

114 Allis Chalmers Co.
Wisconsin Historical Society
WHi-2045

115 Baseball Team
Wisconsin Historical Society
WHi-12117

116 Lawson Airplane Co.
Wisconsin Historical Society
WHi-10499

117 Highway Commission Truck
Wisconsin Historical Society
WHi-40300

118 6th and Wisconsin
Milwaukee Public Library
RW 141

119 WHA Radio Exhibit
Wisconsin Historical Society
WHi-23505

120 Oneida
Milwaukee Public Library
RW 1178

121 Ski Jump
Milwaukee Public Library
RW 389

122 Slovenian Tavern
Milwaukee Public Library
RW 1379

123 Milwaukee City Hall
Wisconsin Historical Society
WHi-5469

124 Turtles
Milwaukee Public Library
RW 893

126 Shoveling Snow
Wisconsin Historical Society
WHi-10005

128 Atlas Flour Mill Fire
Wisconsin Historical Society
WHi-4687

129 Elks Lodge Built
Milwaukee Public Library
RW 834

130 Milwaukee Post Office
Wisconsin Historical Society
WHi-43363

131 Bank Security
Milwaukee Public Library
RW 1340

132 Downtown Plans
Milwaukee Public Library
RW 1244

133 Tatera's Grocery Store
Milwaukee Public Library
RW 1316

134 Loening Amphibian
Wisconsin Historical Society
WHi-10689

135 Wisconsin Ave.
Wisconsin Historical Society
WHi-6946

136 Espenhain's
Milwaukee Public Library
RW 966

137 Swimming Park
Wisconsin Historical Society
WHi-24417

138 Wisconsin Ave.
Wisconsin Historical Society
WHi-6945

139 Curtiss Wright Field
Wisconsin Historical Society
10537

140 Toys on a Truck
Wisconsin Historical Society
WHi-18173

141 Schlitz Train
Wisconsin Historical Society
WHi-1929

142 Patrol Wagon
Milwaukee Public Library
RW 1393

143 Rail Yard Worker
Wisconsin Historical Society
WHi-9479

144 Delivering Ice
Wisconsin Historical Society
WHi-11133

145 Foundry Operation
Wisconsin Historical Society
WHi-7114

146 Delivering Milk
Wisconsin Historical Society
WHi-11002

147 Goodyear Blimp
Milwaukee Public Library
RW 1350

148 Delivering Candybars
Wisconsin Historical Society
WHi-6566

149 Speed Recorder
Wisconsin Historical Society
WHi-24893

150 Gas Stations
Milwaukee Public Library
RW 1057

151 Boarding School Bus
Wisconsin Historical Society
WHi-6583

152 Downtown Intersection
Milwaukee Public Library
RW 1103

153 Boy Scout Parade
Wisconsin Historical Society
WHi-33352

154 Railway Station
Wisconsin Historical Society
WHi-25022

156 Compounding Prescriptions
Wisconsin Historical Society
WHi-6016

157 FDR Tours Plant
Wisconsin Historical Society
WHi-2024

158 City Hall
Wisconsin Historical Society
WHi-23677

159 Officer Directing Traffic
Wisconsin Historical Society
WHi-41228

160 Farmer's Market
Wisconsin Historical Society
WHi-41230

161 Coffee and Gas Rationing
Milwaukee Public Library
RW 1249

162 Rainy Day Traffic
Wisconsin Historical Society
WHi-41030

163 Labor Day Parade
Wisconsin Historical Society
WHi-3214

164 Vocational School
Milwaukee Public Library
RW 1403

165 Falk Corp
Wisconsin Historical Society
11206

166 Anti-Franco Picketers
Wisconsin Historical Society
WHi-3202

167 Bronzeville Bombers
Wisconsin Historical Society
WHi-3049

168 Steelworkers
Wisconsin Historical Society
WHi-2954

169 Elsie the Cow
Wisconsin Historical Society
WHi-25601

170 Union Harvest Dance
Wisconsin Historical Society
WHi-41257

172 Tower Clocks
Milwaukee Public Library
RW 1237

173 Arena
Milwaukee Public Library
RW 1342

174 Cheese in Storage
Wisconsin Historical Society
WHi 2211

175 Supermarket
Wisconsin Historical Society
WHi-22998

176 Buses Replace Streetcars
Wisconsin Historical Society
WHi-25096

178 Winter Basketball
Wisconsin Historical Society
WHi-11617

179 Waterway Experiment
Wisconsin Historical Society
WHi-7019

180 Family Sledding
Wisconsin Historical Society
WHi-7857

181 I Like Ike
Wisconsin Historical Society
WHi-22947

182 Auto Accident
Wisconsin Historical Society
WHi-40931

184 Scout Awards
Wisconsin Historical Society
WHi-10843

186 Civil War Monument
Wisconsin Historical Society
WHi-24424

187 Armistice Day
Wisconsin Historical Society

188 Haney and Stengel
Wisconsin Historical Society
WHi-25507

189 Boys in Boat
Wisconsin Historical Society
WHi-2163

190 Beer Taps
Wisconsin Historical Society
WHi-23525

191 Mitchell Airport Farewell
Wisconsin Historical Society
WHi-8347

192 Astronautics
Wisconsin Historical Society
WHi-8314

193 Burrow Inn
Wisconsin Historical Society
WHi-23563

194 Baker Removing Bread
Wisconsin Historical Society
WHi-8309

195 Future Drafters
Wisconsin Historical Society
WHi-7486

196 Marquette ROTC
Wisconsin Historical Society
WHi-26242

197 Snowy Traffic Jam
Wisconsin Historical Society
WHi-41224

198 James Groppi at NAACP March
Wisconsin Historical Society
WHi-1912

200 Foreign Businessmen
Wisconsin Historical Society
WHi-7004

206 Vince Lombardi
Wisconsin Historical Society
WHi-1898

Green Bay Packers coach Vince Lombardi faces reporters during the Pro Football Writers Dinner in February 1969, one year after Lombardi announced his departure from Green Bay to Washington.

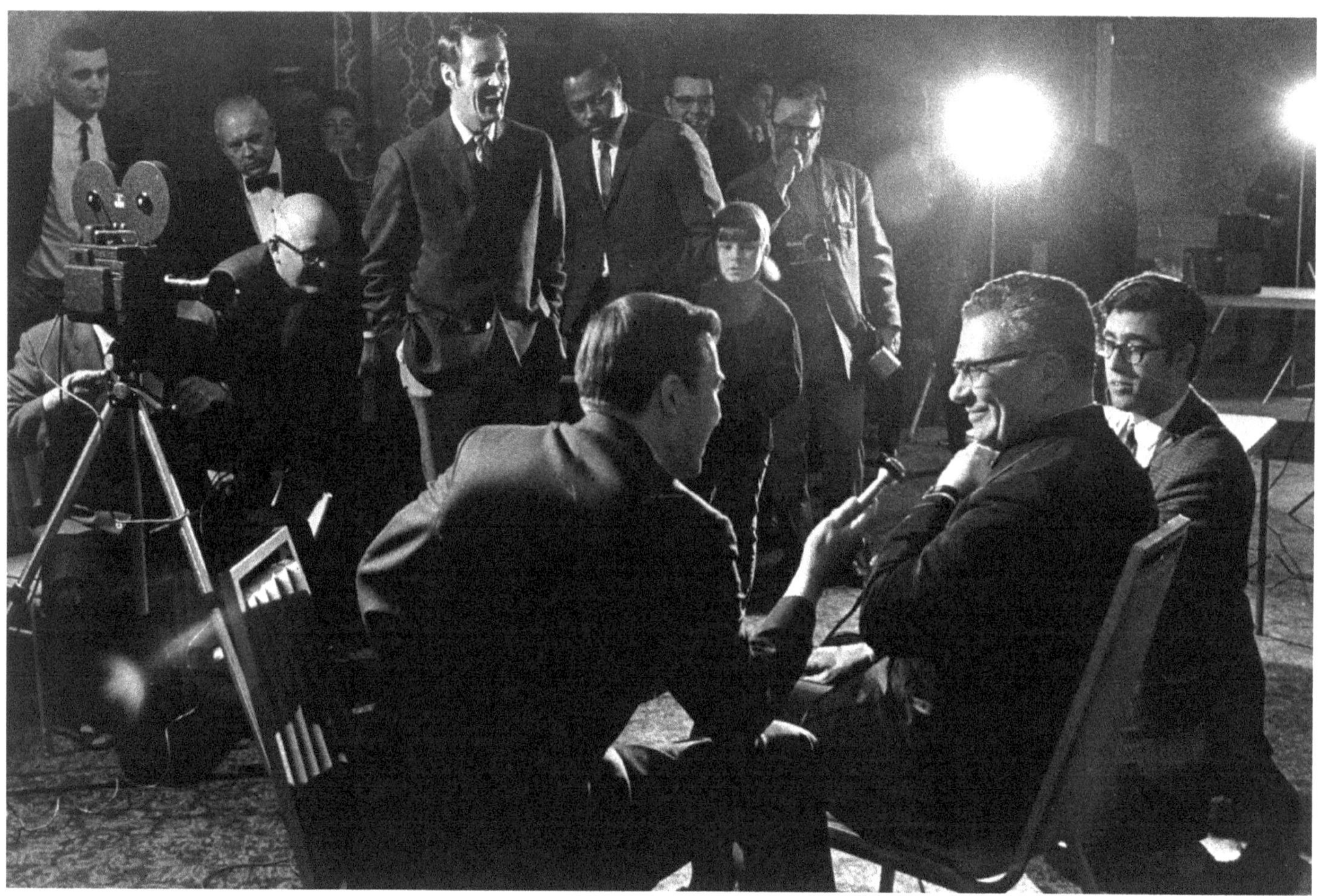

HISTORIC PHOTOS OF MILWAUKEE

Milwaukee is an American city quintessentially founded upon change. From its birth to the present, Milwaukee has consistently built and reshaped its appearance, ideals, and industry. Through changing fortunes, Milwaukee has continued to grow and prosper by overcoming adversity and maintaining the strong, independent culture of its citizens.

Historic Photos of Milwaukee captures this journey through still photography selected from the finest archives. From Milwaukee as the "breadbasket of the midwest" to its recovery through jobs created by the Works Progress Administration and other programs, *Historic Photos of Milwaukee* follows life, government, education, and events throughout the city's history.

This volume captures unique and rare scenes through the lens of hundreds of historic photographs. Published in striking black and white, these images communicate historic events and everyday life of two centuries of people building a unique and prosperous city.

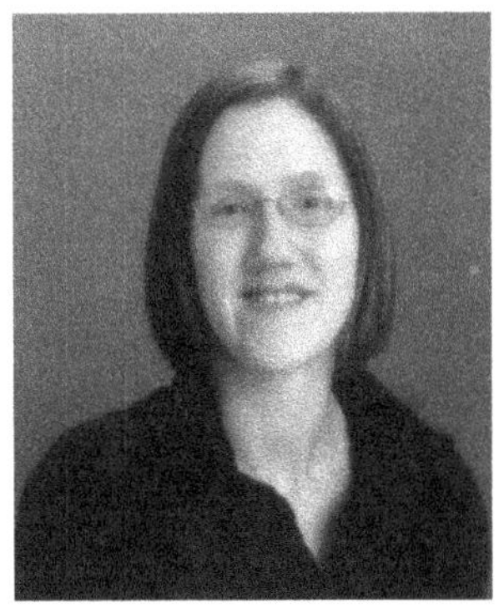

Elizabeth A. Chasco is a native of Milwaukee. She earned her bachelor of arts in English from Alverno College. She recently received her master of arts in history and her certification in museum studies from the University of Wisconsin Milwaukee. In the summer of 2005 she started researching the photograph collection at the Milwaukee Public Museum. Since then she has been able to reconnect many local photographs with their lost history through steadfast research.

WWW.TURNERPUBLISHING.COM

www.ingramcontent.com/pod-product-compliance
Lightning Source LLC
LaVergne TN
LVHW060610110826
845154LV00003B/68
* 9 7 8 1 6 8 3 3 6 9 5 1 6 *